CONFLICT AND WAR IN THE MIDDLE EAST, 1967–91

Also by Bassam Tibi

ARAB NATIONALISM: A Critical Enquiry

CRISIS OF MODERN ISLAM

HUMAN RIGHTS IN AFRICA: Cross-Cultural Perspectives (*co-author*)

ISLAM AND THE CULTURAL ACCOMMODATION OF SOCIAL CHANGE

THE STUDY OF THE MIDDLE EAST: International Perspectives (*co-author*)

TRIBES AND STATE FORMATION IN THE MIDDLE EAST (*co-author*)

Conflict and War in the Middle East, 1967–91

Regional Dynamic and the Superpowers

Bassam Tibi

*Professor of International Relations, University of Göttingen
and Research Associate, Harvard University*

Translated by Clare Krojzl

244006

in association with
THE CENTER FOR INTERNATIONAL AFFAIRS
HARVARD UNIVERSITY

First published as *Konfliktregion Naher Osten* by C. H. Beck-
Verlagsbuchhandlung in 1989

English translation first published 1993 by
THE MACMILLAN PRESS LTD
Houndmills, Basingstoke, Hampshire RG21 2XS
and London
Companies and representatives
throughout the world

ISBN 0–333–57009–X

A catalogue record for this book is available
from the British Library.

Printed in Hong Kong

Contents

Preface

This book is not simply a translation of my *Konfliktregion Naher Osten* as was originally planned. The crucial events of 1990–91 have changed the world to such an extent that they have necessitated new patterns of thought. Numerous parts of the book have therefore had to be rewritten, and new chapters added. In 1989, when the earlier and very different German edition was first published, the Middle East, conceptualised in this book as a regional subsystem, had a different configuration from that which it has now in the aftermath of the Gulf War. The pre-1989 international system also differed greatly from the one now beginning to shape the international environment of the Middle Eastern subsystem. In short, the regional and global changes of the 1989–91 period made the rewriting of this book imperative. A straightforward translation of the previous edition, completed in 1988, would have presented the Anglo–Saxon reader with a somewhat outdated study. This English edition is therefore to all intents and purposes a new book.

Work proceeded in the following manner: Clare Krojzl translated the three Parts of the German edition, omitting Chapter 7, and I then made a substantial revision of her translation. The present Introduction, Chapter 7 and the whole of Part Four are thus completely new texts, unlike the first updated and revised Parts. The new texts have been prepared bilingually – some in German and others in English. Having combined these in a new English draft, Clare Krojzl then returned them to me for further revision. Her work has thus been a mixture of translation and copy-editing of those parts, such as this Preface, written directly in English. As a result of this somewhat convoluted process of rewriting, editing and translating so as to accommodate the events of 1990–91, the present edition is a rather different kind of book – forming a sequel to the German edition. Rewriting has included a full updating of the Notes. Chapter 8 in Part Four is based on a current analysis of the much shorter Part Four that forms the conclusion of the German edition, while Chapters 9 and 10 are completely new. The earlier German edition predicted the recent Gulf War in the context of my analysis of the war epidemic that has spread across the whole of the Middle East – the most militarised regional subsystem in world politics.

Major recent changes addressed in the book are viewed from both regional and global aspects. On the international level the Cold War came to an end as a result of the new *perestroika* policy pursued under Gorbachev.

The end of the Cold War, an 'imaginary war' (Kaldor, 1990), has witnessed the replacement of many communist regimes in Eastern Europe by democratically elected governments. The breakdown of communism in Eastern Europe in turn led to the end of bipolarity, bringing about a cessation of superpower competition in Third World regional conflicts. During the Gulf crisis and war the two superpowers cooperated closely on both the superpower and UN levels. Subordination of Soviet policy to US demands, in the guise of the cooperative attitude of Soviet decision-makers, has given rise to a debate about the Soviet Union as an 'Incomplete Superpower' (Paul Dibb). Some commentators have suggested that the Soviet Union has ceased to be a major superpower even before it was dissolved in December 1991.

While these crucial global changes were taking place in the international system, a regional Third World power, Iraq, was staking a questionable claim to have emerged as victor from the 'longest war' since the Second World War, i.e. the Gulf War of 1980–88. On the strength of this dubious claim Iraq made a move towards territorial expansion. This had the parallel aims of relieving its ailing economy from the adverse effects of the 1980–88 war and enhancing its regional power base through access to the shores of the Gulf, thereby overcoming the disadvantage of being landlocked. These aims formed the background to the Iraqi invasion of Kuwait. In 1989–90, world attention focused on Europe, where the post-World War order was dissolving in the wake of German reunification, brought about by the breakdown of the communist regime in East Germany. Iraq seized on this opportunity as an auspicious moment to gobble up Kuwait in pursuit of its twin goals, mentioned above. Busy with other affairs on 2 August 1990 commentators, therefore, voiced scarcely more than verbal dismay at the Iraqi invasion. To the best of my knowledge, no commentator at that stage anticipated the internationalisation of the Gulf crisis in military terms. In its early days, it was perceived as little more than an Iraqi–Kuwaiti border dispute.

The Gulf War has provided further evidence to support the assessment put forward in the previous German edition of this book, that the geopolitical global importance of the Middle East is rated as second only to that of Europe. Ongoing changes in the international system are closely connected with the reordering of the Middle East itself in the aftermath of the Gulf War. Among the latter's repercussions, in addition to the surfacing of other conflicts in the region besides the Arab–Israeli one, is the fact that the Arabs are no longer able to divert attention from their own inter-Arab conflicts by focusing on Israel. The Palestinians are not the only people seeking their rights: there are also the Kurds and other ethnically suppressed non-Arab minorities (the Berbers in the Maghreb, the Dinka in Sudan, etc.). More than this, the Arabs themselves are in dire need of democratisation, and are sick and tired of the rhetorical exercises in distraction to which they are being subjected by their neo-sultanic oriental tyrants. Saddam Hussein is merely one of the more dauntless among these tyrants. The internal problems of the Middle East have thus surfaced and become global issues. The resolution of conflict in the region will not be forthcoming on global grounds alone, that is without addressing crucial specifically Middle Eastern conflicts, both internal and regional. Local–regional–global linkages lie at the heart of this book which stresses the regional dynamic of conflict, although not to the detriment of analysing the international environment of the Middle East. My critique of globalism was never aimed at replacing globalist outlooks with confined regional ones. It has always rather been motivated by a desire to establish patterns of combined, although not reductionist global–regional analysis. This has been the driving force behind the writing of this book, directing my efforts when I was at Princeton in 1986–87, and remaining unchanged while rewriting this book at the Harvard Center for International Affairs during the Spring Term of 1991.

I am deeply indebted to many institutions and individuals who helped facilitate my research through grants, affiliations, sponsorship and scholarly advice. In Princeton, the German Research Council (Deutsche Forschungsgemeinschaft) provided support for research carried out in 1986–87 for the previous German edition of this book. Professors Abraham Udovich, Carl Brown and John Waterbury of Princeton University were my close colleagues, and also supported my Princeton Fellowship. In the Middle East the al-Ahram Centre for Political and Strategic Studies in Cairo provided many affiliations in 1987–90, while numerous colleagues were generous with indispensable advice. Dan Tschirgi at the American University of Cairo was glad to incorporate my work into his Cairo Papers. At Khartoum University, I enjoyed being a visiting professor in 1987 before the disintegration of the Sudanese state. At Harvard, Professor Joseph Nye augmented the Volkswagen grant, which I am presently enjoying while on leave from Göttingen, with additional funds from his project on international institutions, to support my affiliation at his Harvard Center for International Affairs. I am also grateful to Joseph Nye for enriching my understanding of ongoing changes in the international system. Professors Samuel Huntington and Herbert Kelman have been close Harvard colleagues since 1982, when Samuel Huntington invited me to join the visiting faculty for my first Harvard term. Since that term Harvard has become almost my permanent scholarly home, and I feel a keen lack of such an inspiring International

Relations environment at German universities, which tend to suffer from provincialism. Reunification has exposed Germany to global challenges which this economically potent but politically insignificant country will be unable to meet if 'international studies' continue to be absent from the German academic scene as they are at present. Many Germans are reluctant to see their country playing a major role in world politics.

The President of my German Georg-August University, as well as my Göttingen colleagues from the Social Science Department, are happily not marked by the overall provincialism of the German academic scene lamented above. Thanks both to the President of the Georgia Augusta University, who provided funds, as well as to these colleagues, I have been able to establish a modest centre for international affairs in Göttingen without which the project for this book could not have been successfully completed. My research assistants Anke Houben and Kai Dierke have been unwavering in their assistance in rewriting this book and updating its materials, information and scope. My staff assistant Petra Geile carefully and patiently word-processed all new and rewritten drafts. As always she has shown commitment to our joint work and her assistance has been unfailing. Clare Krojzl has taken on the translation of a second book of mine into English. The demanding work involved in translating my earlier book, *Islam and the Cultural Accommodation of Social Change* (Boulder, Col., 1990), did not deter her from undertaking a further joint project. I am grateful to Keith Povey for copy-editing the manuscript and for the meticulous supervision of the production, to Denise Byrnes for proof-reading while checking and improving the language in the translation and to my research assistant Kai Dierke for compiling the bibliography and completing the index.

This time, my beloved wife Ulla was relieved from the ordeals arising from my writing, unlike earlier occasions when she was my editor and most critical reviewer. Her emotional support has nevertheless, as always, been an unfailing source of stability which, unlike some scholars, I avowedly need to keep me going through long and weekendless working weeks.

Center for International Affairs
Harvard University BASSAM TIBI

Introduction: Middle Eastern Wars from the World Historical and International Systemic Perspectives

This book is concerned with the broader context of major Middle Eastern wars since 1967. The study of international politics in the Middle East is the study of conflict and war. Students of International Relations deal for the most part with Middle Eastern conflicts as regional phenomena without giving prominence to the regional dynamic of conflict in that part of the world. During the first and second Cold Wars, which spanned the period from the Second World War until the breakdown of communism in Eastern Europe in the late 1980s, regional conflicts in general and in the Middle East in particular tended to be dealt with from the point of view of super-power competition. At that time, bipolarity was the prevailing structural component of the world order. Few authors recognised the Arab–Israeli conflict as having a dynamic of its own, so that most students failed to disentangle this conflict from the competition prevailing between the super-powers. The containment of communism, and of its penetration of the Middle East, was until recently the paramount issue.

Now the Cold War is over, and the once 'incomplete superpower', the Soviet Union, has virtually ceased to play any role worth mentioning in the Middle East, because it was until its dissolution in December 1991 absorbed in its own internal problems and disintegration. This change in superpower relations notwithstanding, conflict in the Middle East has not ceased. On the contrary, with the passing of bipolarity there is no longer a world order to act as a restraint on Middle Eastern states locked in their own violent conflicts. The recent Gulf War has made it clear that not even the Arab–Israeli conflict is the central issue triggering wars. Israel was kept out of this war. Recent developments have supported the view put forward in this book that conflicts in the Middle East have their own regional dynamic, while at the same time being incorporated into the global state system.

The first world order to emerge in history arose out of the Peace of Westphalia. All subsequent developments in this respect have been engendered by wars and their repercussions. From this point of view, conflicts and wars lie at the heart of this book, which is aimed simultaneously at dealing with the specifically regional dynamic of conflict in the Middle East and at placing Middle Eastern conflicts into a world historical and world systemic context.

Since the end of the Second World War, Europe has not been the theatre of war it once was between the first international system of states established in the aftermath of the Thirty Years War and the Second World War. The theatre of war has moved to the non-Western 'Third World', to which the Middle East belongs. The question that suggests itself is whether the West moved the theatre of war from its own centre, i.e. Europe, to the Third World.

As a political phenomenon, war is as old as humanity itself. Contrary to the claim of some left-wing-oriented peace researchers, war is not a phenomenon related to the rise of capitalism and to the capitalist state.[1] Defined in terms of modern war technology[2] and viewed from the vantage point of the 'industrialisation of war',[3] however, armed conflicts carried out by industrially organised and appropriately equipped armies may be regarded as a phenomenon of the modern age. Only in this sense can it be conceded that Europeans have exported the means of war to non-Western parts of the world.[4] Nevertheless, two destructive world wars[5] have significantly changed the attitudes of people in industrialised countries towards war. Kalevi Holsti argues that 'the general mood of vast publics in the industrial countries has been anti-war . . . populations in the Third World have quite different historical memories . . . the profound commitment to nationalist, ethnic and religious purposes . . . has thus made war in parts of the Third World a winning proposition'.[6] In terms of war statistics, the Middle East leads these various parts of the Third World. However, it is not merely 'changed attitudes expressed in the fear of war'[7] that underlies the absence of war in Europe. Significant though these fears have become, recent public responses to the Gulf War clearly show that the actuality of nuclear deterrence and self-deterrence have effectively nullified the Clausewitzian formula of war as an instrument of politics.[8] Some authors nevertheless continue to assert the appropriateness of the Clausewitzian conception of Western security, even in the nuclear age.[9] In other words, therefore, the decline of bellicose attitudes, combined with the deterrent destructive character of nuclear war technology, have made war most unlikely in industrial societies. This statement is supported by war statistics since 1945. In so arguing, I do not overlook the huge military expenditures of industrial societies in East and West alike. However, the purpose of armed forces in industrial parts of the world has altered substantially, in as much as the present task of armies is primarily to prevent rather than wage war.[10] Military force has become more of an instrument of deterrence than of war. This is not the case in the Third World, and certainly not in the bellicose Middle East.

Despite differing methodologies for the quantitative analysis of wars, the available expertise is unanimous in concluding that since 1945 wars have taken place primarily, if not exclusively, in the Third World. Dispute among scholars in this respect focuses essentially on the definition of 'armed conflicts' and on their respective qualifications for being termed wars. For example, the German peace researcher Klaus-Jürgen Gantzel and his associates[11] ascertain that 159 wars took place between 1944–45 and 1984, while in Holsti's work[12] we find the more conservative figure of 58 wars between 1945 and 1983. Since Holsti does not rank every shooting incident as a war, many insignificant wars – in international terms – are not listed in his cited table. Instead, he confines his analysis to a study of two types of conflict: inter-state wars and qualified armed intervention. For the purposes of this inquiry, however, these methodological differences are not as salient as the conclusion shared by all these scholars, pertaining to the observation that the occurrence of war has become a Third World phenomenon since 1945.

Many explanations can be put forward for the bellicosity of Third World states in general, and Middle Eastern states in particular. Best known among them is their lack, on the one hand, of an apocalyptic vision of war, related to memories of the two world wars, and, on the other, of a working system of mutual deterrence and security. A combination of bellicose state behaviour and highly favourable attitudes to war is therefore to be found among the populations of Third World countries, supporting the epidemic proportions the waging of war has reached in that part of the world.

Some authors have related Third World wars to superpower competition,[13] viewing them as a dimension of the East–West conflict.[14] However, even the earlier German edition of this book, published before the end of the Cold War, took a different stance and suggested an alternative point of view. Third World wars are related to regional conflicts with their own dynamic. They have affected superpower relations and been affected by them in equal measure, but they have never been caused by superpower competition alone. The end of the Cold War and the changed nature of American–Soviet relations[15] did not prevent the Kuwaiti–Iraqi regional conflict, or its escalation to a war.[16]

Most of the underlying causes of war in Third World countries are unequivocally endogenous. A variety of authors, including this one, have pointed to the weakness of the non-Western nation-states as a significant issue.[17] The very creation of states in the Third World was itself related to wars, since 52 per cent of armed conflicts were 'manifestations of state-creation enterprises'.[18] Holsti argues further: 'the structural problems of state weakness and ethnic/religious passions create high probabilities that wars of various kinds will continue to erupt there in the foreseeable future.'[19]

Anti-war attitudes have become predominant norms and values in industrial societies. In International Relations norms and values are also related to decisions.[20] The presumed existence of anti-war attitudes alluded to here 'has not yet taken on the character of universal legal or moral imperative. For the foreseeable future the Clausewitzian model of war remains regrettably valid.'[21] The simultaneity of a predominance of anti-war attitudes in the industrial world and the bellicosity of Third World states gives rise to a variety of substantive questions related to International Relations theory. I shall address here the question which touches on my contention in this book that the Middle East, though integrated into the international system, is a regional subsystem with its own dynamic of conflict. The Middle East is not only subsystemically different from the global system, but also normatively. The predominant public choices in that part of the world indicate that internationally prevailing norms and values are not honoured.

Unlike many International Relations scholars, for whom globalism is an unquestioned issue, the late Hedley Bull was acutely aware of growing trends towards 'a more regionalised world system',[22] and therefore questioned the vision of 'the shrinking of the globe'. Bull pinpoints this trend towards regionalisation by referring to the *simultaneity of structural globalisation and normative cultural–political fragmentation* in the international system.[23] The rise of fundamentalism[24] in various parts of the Third World as a 'Revolt against the West'[25] is one indication of this fragmentation. Holsti also takes fundamentalism into consideration, pointing out that 'religious fundamentalism may also shift views in favour of violence'.[26] During the Gulf War this prediction came true when Islamic fundamentalists subscribed to Saddam Hussein's repeated calls for a holy war 'of all Muslims against the entire West'. Our question concerning International Relations theory in this context is whether or not we can speak of a consistent international system in which the same rules, norms and values prevail. In Holsti's view, 'in the contemporary world, we really have two separate but overlapping international systems. The propensity to engage in warfare . . . is related to attitudes, and these attitudes have been significantly different in parts of the Third World to those that have prevailed in industrial countries since the Great War.'[27] A mutually honoured culture of negotiation to reach compromise over disputes, instead of resorting to violence, exists in the interaction among industrial states in East and West alike. An established statehood underlies this culture. In contrast to this, the bulk of young states in the Third World lack both this culture and an established statehood.

In short, for a better understanding of regional conflicts and of their dynamic, theoretical analysis in International Relations needs to move away from crude globalism and towards subtle regional differentiations. I refer to the argument of Kalevi Holsti directed against globalism, integrating it into my own approach which was developed prior to the publication of the recent work by Holsti, from which I am drawing. Holsti asserts: 'Despite all the rhetoric about global interdependence, the shrinking world, and the presumably unifying impact of technological innovations on social and economic life, a primordial sentiment seeks to assert autonomy, separateness, uniqueness, cultural survival, and ultimately sovereignty.' By way of a corollary in terms of conflict and war, Holsti continues: 'Since most of the states of the world are composed of multiple ethnic/language/religious groups, we could expect the future international agenda to be crowded with cases of civil wars, wars of secession, and the breakdown of multi-community states – all with the possibility of foreign intervention.'[28] Had Holsti been taking pan-Arabism into consideration and written this passage after 2 August 1990, he would have added 'annexation' to his list. In addition to the ethnic disintegration of states, some Third World states also look forward to a pan-national integration of states[29] (e.g. pan-Arabism), this being a major cause of armed conflicts in Third World countries. The Gulf War, which included foreign intervention to the extent of waging an international war, forms part of this Third World context, that is characterised by weak statehood in the belligerent states combined with a highly bellicose political culture of Islamic fundamentalism and expansive pan-Arabism.[30]

Going beyond Holsti, and further pursuing my efforts in the earlier German edition of this book, I suggest differentiating the Third World by subdividing it into regions, which I subject to scrutiny as *regional subsystems*. Given that most Third World wars, and the most serious among them, took place in the Middle East, I view the Middle East as the most important single subsystem in the Third World. For this reason, Part One of this book is devoted to the elaboration of this framework. Chapter 1 of Part One discusses the theory of the subsystem and develops it further. The application of this theory to the Middle East is pursued in Chapter 2.

The fact that since 1945 wars have occurred predominantly in the Third World does not in itself prove that the states located in this heterogenous geographical global expanse, spanning three continents, constitute a strictly delimited unit of analysis. This book, in which the geographical term *region* is linked with the International Relations concept of the *subsystem*, is intended as a contribution towards preparing the ground for a suitable unit of analysis, as part of an overall search for the necessary analytical framework. Obviously, this does not exclude inquiry into wars in the Third World on the comparative level. Apart from comparing one war with another, the regional context also suggests itself as a suitable unit of analysis for this purpose. Even from the purely statistical standpoint the Middle East is the most war-prone region[31] in the Third World, but this alone does not make it a suitable subject for case studies. The central argument here is that the Middle East constitutes a systemically delimited regional subsystem in its own right, and hence also a unit of analysis.

One of the advantages of using the 'regional subsystem' concept, drawn from the American discipline of International Relations, as a frame of reference for studying wars is that it permits a gradation of militarised conflicts. The three wars focused on in this book, the wars of 1967, 1973 and 1990–91, are thus from the statistical viewpoint only three among numerous armed conflicts in the same region. Today, they can be cited among other examples of well-known wars in the same region: between Libya and Chad,[32] Morocco and Polisario (West Sahara),[33] between the Sudanese state and the South Sudanese SPLA (Sudan People's Liberation Army), and not least what was only ostensibly the 'civil' war in Lebanon,[34] which Syria managed to conclude to its own advantage during the Gulf War. The Middle Eastern wars of 1967, 1973 and 1990–91 do, nevertheless, differ from the above-mentioned local armed conflicts in that these regional wars affected the entire Middle East region, understood here as a political entity in the subsystemic rather than merely the geographical sense (extending from Iran in the east to Morocco in the west, from Turkey in the north to the Sudan in the south). The first Gulf War of 1980–88, which began as a local border dispute between Iran and Iraq over the Shat al-Arab, was only partly regionalised as it proceeded (see note 31).

It should be noted here that the regional subsystem concept, which can assist in distinguishing between limited local wars, partially regional wars and wars affecting the entire region, is not merely a classification model permitting the classification of various conflicts. The concept can also contribute to an understanding of the regional dynamic of political developments in a region, and act as a check on the tendency to derive these from the international environment of a region.

Another of the driving forces behind this book, besides that of developing the concept of the regional subsystem as a partial unit in the modern world order – known in International Relations as the *international system* – will be to examine the interplay between a *subsystemic region* and its *international environment*. This will help us to avoid falling victim to one of two widespread extremes of thought in the study of wars in the Third

World. These wars can, for example, be interpreted as purely local or regional, along the lines of Africans fighting among themselves, or Arabs and Persians fighting for hegemony in the Gulf. Seen in this light, armed conflicts in the Middle East would appear to be distinctly and exclusively Middle Eastern in their character. The opposite extreme classifies belligerent parties in the Third World as proxies of great powers. Viewed in this manner, armed conflicts appear to be the result of competition between external powers. With regard to this latter extreme, it must be conceded that wars in the Third World always have an international dimension, in that they are usually waged with weapons systems produced in America, the Soviet Union or Europe, although some Third World countries have established domestic arms production facilities of their own. In this sense, the industrial countries are involved in all Third World wars. It is necessary to ask, however, whether the mere presence of military aid, arms supplies and military advisors from the former Soviet Union, the USA or Western Europe is enough to justify the thesis of the internationalisation of local wars. It should be stressed that when the international factor is raised to the level of an absolute in global analysis, local and regional conflict potential and the regional dynamic of conflicts tend to slip out of the field of vision. An examination of the interplay between the regional dynamic factor, conceptualised here as regional–subsystemic in character, and the respective interests of the superpowers in a region will therefore form one of the main objectives of this analysis of the Middle Eastern wars of 1967 and 1973, and of 1990–91. Although there was a major *involvement* of the two superpowers in the October War of 1973 – bringing them, as we shall be seeing, to the brink of a nuclear confrontation (see Part Three, Chapter 6) – it would be facile to speak here of an internationalised war. The expression *international dimension of regional wars* is more appropriate to the subject at issue. However, unlike the 1973 war, the second phase of the 1990–91 Gulf War (17 January to 28 February 1991) may be termed an international war.

The 'proxy wars' thesis, – the interpretation of regional conflicts as a southern dimension of the East–West conflict during the Cold War, or of the North–South conflict during the Gulf War ('conservative' and 'leftist' globalism respectively) – not only makes assertions that are out of step with the findings of war research, but in some cases can be completely overturned. The example of the 1973 October War will show how regional state actors (defined as *client states*) embroiled their indirect allies and arms suppliers, the great powers (here defined as *patron states*), so deeply in this war which had escalated out of a regional conflict, that the conduct of the patron states could no longer be reconciled with their imperial interests.

Both superpowers suffered a loss of influence as the war proceeded. Not only is the client state no mere proxy of the great power, but it can even make use of the patron state to serve its own interests.[35] One explanation for this was put forward by International Relations scholars in a symposium, led by Hedley Bull, on the contemporary meaning of 'intervention'. The findings are now available in published form:[36] with few exceptions, superpowers no longer intervene directly using their own troops. Nevertheless, regional allies cannot be controlled by the superpowers as readily as the latter's own troops. Both the USA[37] and the former Soviet Union[38] do, however, still intervene indirectly through arms supplies. Their own military potential further serves as a demonstrative bolster for international power articulated through diplomatic channels. The relevance of this for regional conflicts in which the superpowers do not intervene directly should not be overlooked. In the case of the Gulf War, direct intervention under the banner of the UN became necessary, on the one hand because the Gulf states are weak and unable to defend themselves, and on the other because the West could not countenance the build-up of an imperial–regional hegemony by Iraq. We shall be dealing with these issues in more detail in Part Four.

Having established the conceptual framework (the regional subsystem) and the question at issue (the interplay between regional dynamic and great power interests) in this study of the Middle Eastern wars of 1967, 1973 and 1990–91, we should now elucidate the focus of our inquiry. Neither efforts towards the theory of war nor analysis of the causes of the first two of these wars will be our concern here. Our central theme will be their repercussions. Wars have been waged since the dawn of mankind. As Quincy Wright points out, 'no general golden age of peace existed at any stage of human history'.[39] The Islamic Middle East, the cultural sphere to which this study relates, is indeed familiar with war as an essential element of its preponderantly Islamic culture. The fundamental Islamic concept of politics has the doctrinaire designation of the *Dar al-Harb* (the 'House of War') for all parts of the world lying outside Islam. Only the *Dar al-Islam* (the territory of Islam) is a 'House of Peace'.[40] Bearing this in mind and referring also to well-meaning, romantic Third Worldism,[41] which holds Europeans responsible for introducing war to the world outside Europe, we do not come into conflict with Quincy Wright's assertion of a four-stage historical definition of war. Before the colonial conquests, non-European peoples did wage traditional wars among themselves. It was Europeans, however, who developed modern warfare, based on the 'use of firearms to promote the policy of a group. The dispersion of many modern war techniques – weapons, formations, tactical movements, and strategic ideas – can be demonstrated from historical evidence. Doubtless, in this technological sense, war was invented in Europe only about five centuries ago and subsequently diffused throughout the world.'[42] The Middle East wars of 1967, 1973 and 1990–91 were all modern wars in the sense defined by Quincy Wright. It may strike some readers as carrying eurocentrism a stage too far by asserting that even the institutional context of these wars, namely the nation-state structure of the international order, has its roots in Europe. And yet these assertions are indisputably in accordance with the actual course of history. On the basis of major research carried out by an interdisciplinary group of scholars led by Charles Tilly, it is now known with exactitude that the Thirty Years War in Europe, followed by some years of negotiations leading to the Peace of Westphalia, concluded in Münster on 24 October 1648, resulted in a new European order – a state system that came to form the core of the present-day international system. According to the Peace of Westphalia, to quote Charles Tilly:

> all of Europe was to be divided into distinct and sovereign states whose boundaries were defined by international agreement. Over the next three hundred years the Europeans and their descendants managed to impose that state system on the entire world. The recent wave of decolonisation has almost completed the mapping of the globe into that system.[43]

Without wishing to exaggerate the historical importance of the Six Day War of June 1967 by placing it on a par with the Thirty Years War[44], it can nevertheless be advanced as an example of how the *consequences of a war* are often more important than the war itself or its causes. Like every European war, the war of June 1967 marked a watershed, in this case in the history of the Middle East. The Six Day War altered not only the map of the Middle East, but the entire structure of the region, shattering the legitimacy of its political systems and transforming its prevailing ideologies.[45] This reference to the Peace of Westphalia, therefore, is not merely intended to show how the order that emerged from this process formed the core of the present-day international system. It also aims to corroborate our concentration in this analysis on the *consequences* of the 1967, 1973 and 1990–91 wars under discussion. Readers will already be familiar with the central importance of the consequences of war in the European process of civilisation from the magnificent work by Norbert Elias.[46]

French involvement in the Thirty Years War, which had such far-reaching consequences, was led by Cardinal Richelieu. In terms of world history, this war, as has already been pointed out, led to the emergence of an international system that was initially confined to Europe. Seen from the European context, the war altered the structural fabric of the Continent, particularly since France built its position of European hegemony on the consequences of the war. Cardinal Mazarin derived foreign policy success from the Peace of Westphalia that Richelieu had initiated, thereby building on the achievement of his predecessor. Mazarin 'reaped the benefits of French gains from the Peace of Westphalia',[47] as Reinhard Bendix graphically expresses it, adding elsewhere that the war also had considerable local repercussions, that were not related to France alone. Serving first under Louis XIII, Mazarin continued in office under Louis XIV, who waged three major wars during his reign. The state of war and its consequences were decidedly among those factors which helped to cement the central state style of rule under Louis XIV, which was the 'extension of royal authority . . . administrative centralisation and reorganisation'.[48] The European absolutist state of the seventeenth century gave way after the French Revolution[49] to the modern nation-state,[50] which now forms the basic unit of the international system worldwide. The nowadays structurally weak nation-states of the Middle East are themselves the result of these developments,[51] which began in Europe and later came to encompass the entire globe.

The primary task of this Introduction is to place the Middle East wars of 1967, 1973 and 1990–91 in their wider world historical and international context. This book is an attempt to make a general contribution to the wider study of International Relations, rather than the narrower scope of an area study within Middle East studies.

The point of departure of this Introduction is the contention stated at the outset that since the Second World War armed conflicts do not as a rule occur among industrial states. What is known as the Third World is now the major theatre of war. This contention is supported by the data (notes 6 and 11) provided by Holsti and Gantzel quoted above. The 'environment' of these regional wars, however, is the international system, which encompasses the entire globe, but has its roots in Europe, as we have just seen. The European dynastic state system, established in the aftermath of the Peace of Westphalia, was the origin of the present system, the European states emerging out of a process of war to develop into nation-states. As Charles Tilly argues: 'war wove the European network of national states, and preparation for war created the internal structures within it'.[52] The European nation-states developed well-defined boundaries and enjoy mutual recognition. This original European state system 'has spread to virtually the entire world'.[53] Moreover, the process of globalisation was likewise supported by the global formation[54] of the world economy. The existence of an international system of states raises the questions, on the one hand, as to whether the globalisation of industrialised warfare is related to these processes, and, on the other, as to the interrelationship between the waging of war and the formation of states as we know it from European history – whether, in other words, this interrelationship also applies to the new non-Western states. Charles Tilly gives a positive answer to the former question, but doubts the analogy suggested in the latter: 'In the process, Europeans created a state system that dominated the entire world. We live within that system today. Yet the world outside Europe resembles Europe no more than superficially. *Something has changed in the extension of the European state system to the rest of the earth – including the relationship between military activity and state formation.*'[55] A recent example from the Middle East supports the findings of Tilly, based on cross-national data: Iraq. Prior to the Gulf War this state was the most militarised in the Third World in terms of expenditure on armaments. Yet this nominal nation-state now faces the threat of 'lebanisation', that is being dissolved, despite its efforts at coercion to impose a nation-state ideology. The reason for this is the lack in Iraq of those processes of institutionalisation that are needed to support the internal and external sovereignty of a state. The militarisation of Middle Eastern states does not, therefore, promote their civilianisation, as was the case with the European states. And yet Middle Eastern states remain members of the prevailing international system, despite being no more than nominal nation-states, and despite the lack of internal sovereignty that arises out of this.

According to the authoritative definition of Hedley Bull, a state system can only be described as an international system in the modern sense if it embraces a number of state actors with *internal* and *external* sovereignty in equal measure.[56] Most Third World states, however, are only nominal nation-states. Medieval European states had no internal sovereignty either, because they lacked central state executive power. In this respect, seventeenth-century France under Louis XIV was the pioneer. War 'made states' in Europe[57] and facilitated the underpinning of their internal sovereignty. Initially prior to the Peace of Westphalia, medieval states lacked even external sovereignty since they were under papal tutelage. While advanced non-European civilisations (the Islamic world, India, China, etc.) all had their own patterns of imperial and territorial states, before their contact with Europe they were unfamiliar either with the sovereignty of nations or with sovereignty under international law. These principles of national and international order only became universal when 'Europeanism conquered the world' (Helmuth Plessner).[58] To stress these facts is not to read European history into non-Western histories. In our age there is a 'world time'[59] that underpins world history. At present, the European nation-state prevails as a globalised pattern, although without the effects of civilianisation, that is real state formation as we know it from European history. Third World states are wagers of war. Nevertheless, there is no alternative to the nation-state in the present day. As Charles Tilly puts it: 'Destroy the state, and create Lebanon. Fortify it, and create Korea. Until other forms displace the national state, neither alternative will do. The only real answer is to turn the immense power of national states away from war toward the creation of justice, personal security and democracy.'[60]

An objection could be raised here in recalling the indisputable fact that the present-day international system has its historical roots in the consequences of the Thirty Years War, i.e. the historic provisions of the Peace of Westphalia. It would be appropriate at this point to examine that objection. With reference to Bull, Holsti and Tilly, who all take this historical fact as their starting point, we have just defined the international system as consisting of states that enjoy both internal and external sovereignty, or which at the very least formally accept one another's existence. It follows from this that the relationship between an empire and its vassal states is not part of the system of international relations as defined by Bull. The objection that could be raised here, therefore, is that the kingdom of France, with its central executive power, emerged from the Peace of Westphalia with a position of hegemony. A state system is based on interdependence not on suzerainty. Historically speaking, the result of the Thirty Years War was the emergence of a state system whose members wielded both internal and external sovereignty. And yet France was effectively a hegemonic power. In reality, however, France's position was considerably restricted by two, internal and external factors. Had this not been the case, it would only have been possible to speak of France and its vassals, not of a system of international relations. In fact a balance of power was arrived at within the state system. Edmund Burke, a classic author on political theory and a contemporary of the French Revolution, made a careful study of this specific historical situation as part of his overall political theory. According to Burke, no state should demand 'an unequal and inordinate superiority'[61] in a state system. This danger was a real one at the birth of the European state system, particularly in the reign of Louis XIV. In his excellent interpretation of Burke, Hans-Gerd Schumann describes how England was selected as 'the natural supervisor of French foreign policy and the balance of power in continental Europe'.[62] Russian entry into the European state system offered additional security. This *European state system, characterised by a balance of power*, survived into the twentieth century.

Wars constantly change the course of history, just as this European system itself arose as a consequence of war. It was again war, this time two world wars, that replaced this system with another. From the end of the Second World War until 1989, the end of the Cold War, the world was dominated by a *bipolar system* with the two superpowers, the USA and the former Soviet Union, at the two poles. Chapter 1 of this book will discuss in more detail the effects of this bipolarity on international politics, also showing how the European powers were relegated to middle-range powers. Our main concern here, however, is to elucidate the connection between the bipolarity prevailing in the international system during that period and the theme of this book, the Middle East wars of 1967 and 1973. These two wars offer two cases or examples, the analysis of which permits general statements about regional armed conflicts in the Third World. The Gulf War of 1990–91, to be dealt with in Part Four, took place under completely different circumstances in the international system.

The substance of the starting point taken by this book must rest on recourse to Charles Tilly's contention, already quoted above, that the European state system spread to the non-European world through violence, i.e. colonisation. It was out of the struggle against European colonial rule, i.e. *decolonisation*, that the modern states of Asia and Africa emerged. These states would have been inconceivable without the European system from which they originated. Nevertheless, it is the wish of these states to go their own way. Their problems cannot be explained solely in terms of their integration into the global system, influenced as they are by the international environment on all levels. Consequently, we can witness a simultaneity of the globalisation process side by side with trends towards regionalisation in international politics. The present-day situation has never been more aptly summed up than by the words of the late International Relations scholar Hedley Bull, who perceived 'a trend in contemporary world politics towards greater regionalism both in the organisation of peace and security and in the management of international economic affairs'.[63] Bull discerns two conflicting trends, represented by *integrationists* and *disintegrationists* respectively, both of which are however at work on the regional rather than the global level, hence giving rise to armed conflicts. Integrationists seek to go beyond existing national state boundaries through unification into states consisting of people of similar identity (e.g. Arab or African unity). The annexation of Kuwait by Iraq was such an act of integration. Disintegrationists, on the other hand, seek to break up the nation-state in the opposite direction: minorities living within the structure of the nation-state lay claim to their own nation-state (e.g. the Kurds, who want to form a state of Kurdistan). The fact remains that the world in which we live is still organised along nation-state lines, although experts now speak of 'anachronistic sovereignty'. Bull observes drily that integrationists and disintegrationists 'are alike intellectually imprisoned by the theory of the state system and are . . . as committed to it as the agents of sovereign states'.[64]

This reference to the trend towards regionalisation serves to underpin the idea that global analyses along East–West or North–South lines are an unhelpful framework for the study of regional wars, contributing little to the understanding of such armed conflicts. The recent end of the Cold War and superpower competition in the Third World should assist towards a departure from globalism as a frame of reference for the study of regional conflicts. Inquiry into these conflicts should be furthered in terms of their regional context, without neglecting the international environment.

Analysis needs to be based on the fact that rival state actors involved in a conflict are nation-states. For political, economic and geostrategic reasons the Middle East, which is composed of nominal nation-states, is one of the most crucial non-European regions. Both the superpowers and Western Europe have their own vital interests to pursue there. During the Cold War the two superpowers had their regional allies, described earlier in this Introduction as client states, with the important adjunct that a 'client' is not a 'proxy' that can be manipulated at will. During the Cold War and given the bipolar character of the world order at that time, the prospects for international security discussed in studies of Middle Eastern conflicts focused on avoiding a confrontation between the two superpowers. This perspective was a valid one for the Middle East wars of June 1967 and October 1973, but no longer held good for the most recent war in the region, when for the first time in their history the USA and the former Soviet Union cooperated closely to cope with the Gulf crisis and the international war that emerged from it.

Our theme here will be *war*,[65] and to be quite specific the regional conflict that becomes war through a process of escalation.[66] Scholarly interest will revolve around reflection on how it is that such wars remain contained within their regional context, and do not become internationalised, even though they always have an international dimension. It is impossible to speak of this theme and ignore the fact that we live in a nuclear age, in which war on a world scale would result in total destruction.[67] No scholar of conflict can afford to overlook this fact. If we start from this assumption, Robert Gilpin's contention dating from the bipolar era at first sounds comforting. Gilpin states that the superpowers, despite the discrepancies in their interests 'share a powerful interest in avoiding a nuclear war and stopping the proliferation of nuclear weapons'.[68] However, this would only be possible on the basis of the stability of the former bipolar world order, embodied by the two superpowers – a stability and ordering principle that passed with the end of the Cold War. The declaration of a 'New World Order' is an extremely vague formula, designated by Edward Mortimer as a 'World Disorder'.[69] As we have just seen, the international system now encompasses the entire globe and is no longer confined to Europe, America and the former Soviet Union. Although the Soviet Union was a European power, its southern republics belong to other cultural spheres, above all Islam. The fact that the contemporary international system remains regionalised in terms both of politics and civilisation,[70] even in the aftermath of bipolarity, applies to the former Soviet Union as much as its former republics in Central Asia. Unrest in the Islamic Middle East could have spillover effects in the Islamic Central Asian republics. Even during the bipolar era there were sources of destabilisation in the existing world order. One of these was the inability of the superpowers to control either regional conflicts or the many forms of instability manifested in the international system after the wave of decolonisation; this puts the system effectively out of their control.[71] Gilpin's work is concerned with world politics, not with regional conflicts, which are outside his field of interest. And yet he cannot avoid voicing concern over one region: 'The dependence of the West on Middle Eastern petroleum constitutes a worrisome factor in contemporary world politics. The maintenance of stable conditions in these areas over the long term is a formidable challenge.'[72]

This Introduction should not be concluded without dealing with the implications of the end of the Cold War and the bipolar world order, already mentioned above, that are associated with it. In discussing these implications we shall be touching on the future prospects for regional conflicts, particularly in the Middle East. In Part Four of this book we shall also give a more detailed account of the 1990–91 Gulf War (the invasion of Kuwait on 2 August was in fact the beginning of the war). The Gulf War was de facto the first war to occur in the new post-Cold War era. Some general thoughts need to be developed in this final section of the Introduction while also taking into account the changing world–historical and international–systemic context of Middle Eastern subsystemic conflicts as a variety of regional conflicts in the Third World. The Cold War linked with the East–West conflict has been described as an 'imaginary war' by Mary Kaldor, who maintains that 'the imaginary war replicated that Second World War experience and provided a mechanism for imposing or spreading the two systems to groups of nations'.[73] As was pointed out earlier, this Cold War and the superpower competition related to it never actually caused any regional conflict, despite the allegations of many Cold War political scientists. What it did do was affect conflicts by specifying blocs and giving meaning to the alliances attached to them.[74] In its way, the bipolar Cold War entailed an element of order in world politics. Viewed from the vantage point of the two leading superpowers, the dismantling of Cold War structures and the imaginary war 'permits progressive evolution of both systems'.[75] However, seen from the point of view of coping with regional conflicts in the Third World and restraining them from developing into armed conflicts, the end of bipolarity has entailed disorder in the international system. The United Nations[76] is not yet able to deal with the new situation in the confines of whatever 'New World Order'. It is probable that the Gulf War would not have broken out under bipolar conditions. This should not be misinterpreted as lamenting the passing of bipolarity, but rather as pointing out the lack of order in present world political conditions.

The international system is currently characterised by a simultaneity of different and at times mutually contradictory traits. Politically, it seems to be unipolar, with the United States as virtually the only acting superpower in world politics. This state of affairs gives rise to the crucial question of whether a politically united Europe could become the second superpower after the dissolution of the Soviet Union. Economically, the international system is a multipolar one, given the economic weight of Europe, in particular Germany, and of Japan. On the military level we are faced with the phenomenon for which Joseph Nye coined the term 'diffusion of power', also 'related to a strengthening of weak states'.[77] Iraq in the 1980s would seem to provide a clear example of this thesis. The implications of the strengthening of a small state like Iraq were a regional war in 1980–88 and an international one in 1990–91. The fact that the present international system is unipolar provides the United States with a position from which it could claim the role 'Bound to Lead'. However, this is unlikely to mean hegemony for the United States: The Soviet Union lost its superpower status even before its dissolution, 'in this sense the coming century may see continued American preponderance . . . US hegemony is not likely.'[78] The reason for this is that the international system is becoming more and more complex, while the two superpowers, particularly the former Soviet Union, are exerting less and less leverage over this complex system. The control of conflicts in the regional subsystems of the Third World will hence pose increasing challenges to the international system as a whole, as well as to its norms, rules and conflict-solving procedures.[79]

In the view of Robert Jervis, 'the erosion of both superpowers' strength has encouraged them to cooperate'.[80] The end of competition between the two superpowers in the Third World, the resulting limitation of their commitments in regional conflicts in Third World countries in terms of expenditure, etc., and finally the ensuing dissolution of the Soviet Union have helped to shape a new phenomenon in which 'political disputes within and between these countries . . . will break the surface, in all likelihood with major violence'.[81] As has been repeatedly argued above, regional conflicts in the Middle East and the rest of the Third World, despite having their regional dynamic, are linked to the structures of superpower competition. The latter once exerted a controlling, if not always decisive element in these conflicts. Now, however, these regional conflicts are being

> separated from the superpower rivalries by mutual disengagement often through the use of multilateral agencies such as the United Nations. For this to happen both superpowers must be willing to tolerate a wider range of outcomes in Third World disputes than they have been accustomed to . . . mutual disengagement . . . might not be better for the rest of the world.[82]

This prediction by Jervis is already reality. Where Third World countries once accused the superpowers of interfering in their affairs, they now accuse them of being absent from the scene. The disengagement of the superpowers in Black Africa, for example, has already brought the accusation of 'global apartheid' to the surface. However, disengagement of this kind may fail to occur in the Middle East on account of the crucial significance of this regional subsystem for both the international system and the world economy.

Aside from giving its consent to American moves on the UN level, the former Soviet Union was virtually offstage throughout the Gulf War. In reality, the leverage of the Soviet Union in the Middle East has been based almost exclusively on arms sales – Iraq being among the best clients in the region.[83] Under Gorbachev the Soviet Union did not only suffer an economic crisis, but was also busy dealing with its own internal affairs and ethnic turmoils.[84] There has not always been a pay-off for Soviet commitments in the Third World. It is 'because of this disenchanting experience that the USSR under Gorbachev's leadership began to take a more distanced view of the future development of the Third World states'.[85] The economic pressure to make cuts in Soviet weaponry and to reduce external involvements has been described as a 'diplomacy of decline'. Soviet Union expert Stephen White comments: 'The weakness of the Soviet position internationally reflected the weakness of the Soviet economy, which accounted for a small and diminishing share of world trade and provided no secure basis for the exercise of global influence.'[86] Even before it started undergoing these crises, which revealed its weakness as a superpower, experts refused to deal with the Soviet Union on an equal footing with the United States. Much earlier, Paul Dibb described the Soviet Union as an 'incomplete superpower'.[87] The willingness of the United States to honour the Soviet Union as a superpower and help it to cooperate and integrate itself in international institutions could not halt the decline of the former superpower and its ensuing dissolution. US efforts at finding a post-Gulf War order in the Middle East already indicated some recognition of a Soviet role in this process. The developments after the changes in the international system clearly show how difficult it is to maintain leverage over conflict potential in the Middle East. The easy military victory of the Gulf War was deceptive, in that it has gulled many into believing that peace will be as easy to achieve. Current events are revealing just how disordered the Middle East is. With world disorder exacerbating the situation in an already complex region, the Middle East is rife with unleashed conflict potential.[88]

Part One

The International System as a Configuration of Regional Subsystems: The Case of the Middle East

Introduction

The aim of this book is twofold: first, to contribute to an understanding of the development of conflict formation during the crucial conflict-ridden 1967–91 period in the Middle East – a region often referred to by journalists as a 'trouble spot'. The second aim is to make a theoretical contribution to the discipline of International Relations. In order to fulfil these two aims, we shall have to avoid the pitfalls both of press sensationalism (the taking of hostages, terrorism, oil sheiks, 'bloodthirsty' Islamic fundamentalists, etc.), and the kind of mathematical model-building used as an explanatory framework for deciphering international politics that so frequently strike even experts as questionable. Quantitative methods aim at accuracy supported by the quantitative processing of empirical data rather than interpreting the events themselves, on the basis of which general statements about events in international affairs are then formulated. The aim here will be to avoid both the above-mentioned extremes. The Middle East will not be dealt with in a sensationalist way, but practically and non-emotively as a topic in international relations. This approach implies making the region a *unit of analysis* and examining it in a scholarly way, without attempting to emulate, by means of complex models and quantitative methods, some quasi-natural science concept. It simply means that the Middle East is to be investigated as an object of scholarly inquiry within international politics, that is both at the specialist level and in such a way as to be accessible to the interested layman. The scholarly discipline of International Relations is at all events more concrete than that of quantum physics, because it is concerned with the scientific elucidation of issues that touch our everyday lives, and consequently concerns all of us, not only the specialist. The recent Gulf War is an illustration of this. Similarly, 'international politics' is a historical topic that is at best only open to interpretation. It cannot be unravelled with quantitative methods. Again, the Gulf crisis and the war it invoked clearly reveal that these aspects of international politics can only be dealt with adequately on an interpretative basis.

This first part of the book will be devoted to developing the frame of reference to be employed, giving reasons why such an approach is indispensable for the subject under issue (Chapter 1). This frame of reference will then be applied in an effort aimed at defining precisely what the 'Middle East' is and where its boundaries lie (Chapter 2). This conceptual part of the book will serve as a basis for analysing the 1967 and 1973 Middle East wars, as well as the recent Gulf crisis which triggered off an international war in the Middle East.

1 The Science of International Relations: Between Globalism and Regionalism

'International Relations' is a young social science discipline. It harks back to the end of the First World War, when, on 30 May 1919 at the instigation of the US President Woodrow Wilson, the American and British delegations at the Paris Peace Conference resolved to establish academic institutions in their respective countries with the aim of undertaking scholarly inquiry into international politics. This new discipline was to be devoted to studying the causes of war to pre-empt the widening of international conflicts into wars.[1] At that time, the international system still virtually mirrored the European states system, by then expanded to include the USA. This international system and its subsequent developments became the object of study of the new science.[2] This situation altered substantially after the Second World War. The emergence of this system and its globalisation has already been outlined in the Introduction. Whereas, prior to the Second World War, the European powers had been designated 'great powers', after the war the United States of America and the Soviet Union, who had emerged from the war as superior powers, were now ascribed the new designation of 'superpowers'. This historical context gave rise to a new configuration of the international system characterised by 'bipolarity' (Kaplan). The two superpowers became the central poles of a new international order, which itself seems to have come to an end through the breakdown of communism in Eastern Europe and the end of the Cold War.[3] The problem of defining the European states after the Second World War had to be broached under the conditions of bipolarity. As late as 1944 Fox,[4] who had coined the term 'superpower', still ranked Great Britain as one. In reality, however, the term only applied to the USA and the Soviet Union. Since that time, the European powers have ranked among the middle-range powers.

In the discipline of International Relations the concept of 'regionalism', which appears in the work of Haas, among others, was applied after the Second World War in the first instance to Europe, that is to European integration.[5] At that time, few Asian or African states were independent under international law. Since decolonisation, when former European colonies became independent states and hence able to participate actively in the international system, this new situation requires rethinking and thus a redefinition. According to experts who did not place the regionalism issue in this context as Haas did, Europe's position in this scenario was seen as lying within 'the Atlantic system', which was perceived as a 'partial' system, a concept which circumvents the superpower/middle-range power issue. Stanley Hoffmann, who formulated this interpretation, holds the view that the USA has more power and influence in Europe than vice versa. He thus stresses the idea of Atlantism as an alternative to the idea of European nationalism.[6]

However, since decolonisation this concept of regionalism has been largely transferred to the 'new states' and will be discussed further in the following section. There is, at all events, a continued need to make important distinctions within the then new bipolar structure of the international system, in order to classify in international political terms both 'middle range powers', such as the West European states and Japan, and the 'new states' of the Third World, taking into account the bipolarity between the USA and the Soviet Union. In the meantime, these new states, known as the developing countries, have become a central issue within the science of International Relations.[7] The end of the Cold War and the virtual retreat of the Soviet Union from international politics as a decisive superpower indicate a structural change in the international system that requires new thoughts and major revisions in the theory of International Relations. The dissolution of the Soviet Union changed the configuration of the international system.

OF 'SQUIRRELS' AND 'ELEPHANTS': THE NEW STATES IN THE INTERNATIONAL SYSTEM

In American English, the 'elephant–squirrel' word pair has the same conceptual content as the pair known in German and English as elephant–mouse. In one of the classics of International Relations literature, these terms are used to expound a theory that was to hold sway for over two decades. It was in 1944 that Fox published his classic work on the role of the world powers in international politics, and for at least twenty years his interpretation – that the international order cannot be comprehended in a scholarly way without taking into account the differences between elephants and squirrels in international politics – was predominant.[8]

According to this interpretation the 'elephants' of international politics are the superpowers. The perspective of a state of bipolarity between the

USA and the Soviet Union, and of a concomitant East–West conflict as a focus of international politics until 1989, was thus not a dominant factor merely during the Cold War years,[9] or even in the policies of the Western and Eastern industrial countries. Until the end of the Cold War the science of International Relations was regrettably negatively affected by this perspective. The globalism model inspired by the elephant–squirrel word pair was and remains the fruit of an outlook that perceives all international politics as determined by the two superpowers alone. In this light, the conduct of 'squirrels', that is of the foreign policies of the small states, can only be interpreted in terms of responses to steps taken by the 'elephants'. This conservative globalist outlook on international politics thus closely resembles that of Marxist theoreticians, who likewise speak of a global 'world market movement of capital',[10] deriving from it their interpretation of everything that happens in Asia, Africa and Latin America. After the end of the Cold War and the concomitant outbreak of the Gulf War a new perspective (North–South globalism) seems to be replacing East–West globalism. Both perspectives, however, prove to be futile for analysing the regional conflicts that lie at the centre of this book.

Since the dissolution of the colonial empires[11] in the 1950s and 1960s, the 'external conduct' of states outside the East–West conflict has come much more to the fore in International Relations inquiry. These states have their own needs and problems, and were not directly involved in this international conflict of the Cold War era. Since 1955, the year of the Afro-Asian Conference in Bandung, these countries have referred to themselves as the Non-aligned States.[12] In 1963, the American political scientist Leonard Binder coined the term 'uncommitted states' for these 'new states in the international system'.[13] This concept formed part of his attempt to achieve an adequate understanding of the policies of states outside the domain of the East–West conflict. His motivation stemmed from his critical position *vis-à-vis* Kaplan's quoted thesis of bipolarity (see note 3) and developed into a theory of a 'regional subsystem'. According to this, the world outside the superpower sphere is divided into geopolitical regions defined as 'subordinate subsystems'. Leonard Binder laid this foundation stone in a pioneering work published in 1958.[14] From then until the early 1980s leading scholars in the field continued to develop this theory.[15] The modern world consists of an international system sustained by sovereign national states: it has a nation-state based global order, but remains regionalist in character.[16]

These scholars thus advanced a new theoretical perspective as an alternative both to the globalist one described above and to the *limited* regionalist approach. The scholarly term 'regionalism' should not be misunderstood as inferring that the countries of a region should be studied in isolation, without regard to the wider global environment in which they are embedded. On the contrary, a regional subsystem must always be defined in the context of its supraregional environment, and delineated according to strict criteria in a methodologically appropriate manner. Obviously, the perspective of the subsystem approach does not seek to derive all events in the countries of a particular region from that global environment, specifically from the global structure of East–West relations. The central assertion of regional subsystem theory is that these partial regions of the international system have their own internal dynamic, although at the same time forming part of the overall systemic configuration of world politics. The dimensions of regional dynamic and of global politics ought to be handled as two mutually related intrinsic levels of analysis, without deriving the one from the other.

The new theory of international politics does not exaggerate the importance of the 'new states', being fully aware of their structurally generated weaknesses. One of the exponents of this new theory, Dominguez of Harvard University, describes these states in the title of his article 'Mice that Do Not Roar'.[17] He does nevertheless point out that false conclusions should not be drawn from this, since the peripheries of the global system, the world political regional subsystems, should be examined as 'actors in international politics, not merely as *objects* of policies'.[18] Dominguez's working hypothesis about 'mice' is that within regional subsystems 'the dominant traits of international politics in the peripheries arise from characteristics of subsystems in the peripheries. These traits are not mere extensions of politics in the center . . . the policies of countries in the peripheries are still strongly shaped by "local" or subsystemic factors.'[19] These specifics of the regional subsystem, defined in this book as 'regional dynamic', must always be explored in the context of the penetration of the periphery by the dominant system, or of how it fits into the global system. Regional dynamic is not autonomous, but neither is it a dependent variable, since neither penetration of the regional subsystems by the dominant system nor its integration in the global system is total. However, through the bipolar structure of the international system (system competition), the weak 'mice', or 'squirrels', can become sources of international conflicts, thus causing control to slip out of the hands of a former superpower. But even without this bipolarity the 'squirrels' retain their importance. A regional conflict, triggered by the respective regional dynamic, can thus have repercussions on the world political scene as a whole. Middle East conflicts, above all the recent Gulf crisis, attest to this theoretical concept pertaining to the interplay between regional and global factors in world politics.

Helping towards an understanding of these connections furthers the theory of regional subsystems. This theory marked a scientific step forward, and contributed to an improvement in real political decision-making processes. Politicians learned from their specialist advisers that world politics can be broken down into smaller units, that it takes place within regional subsystems that exist in their own right, despite being interconnected in terms of structure and interaction, and despite forming part of the global system. Globalist perspectives hamper the elaboration of deeper insights into the regional dynamic of conflict in subsystems such as the Middle East.

Science, and the science of International Relations more than most, is itself affected by the vagaries of politics: it is striking that the theory of regional subsystems was developed parallel – albeit not in the schematic sense – to the processes of détente taking place in East–West relations. After the end of the Cold War this theory is even more necessary than ever for a proper understanding of regional conflicts.

For some years now, the globalist outlook on world politics has also been returning to the scientific discipline of International Relations.[20] The first German edition of this book was completed in Princeton, partly on the basis of an international scholarly dialogue with colleagues in this field, specifically including those who first put forward the various components of regional subsystem theory. This revised English edition, completed at Harvard, represents an attempt to revive the regionally differentiated view of world political events, while focusing on one of the most crucial and conflict-ridden regions as an example.

Part One of this book is intended to introduce and develop a theoretical approach that interprets the world system as a configuration consisting of regional subsystems. In developing these ideas we should never lose sight of the fact that the science of International Relations deals with conflicts that threaten our very existence, and as such it is a discipline whose importance extends far beyond that of the purely academic sphere. This remark, however, should not be taken to mean that 'international politics' carries the same meaning that 'politics' has in everyday language. It remains a scholarly subject with its own strict professional standards, like all other scientific disciplines. International Relations is a social scientific discipline and not a variety of journalism on world politics.

Before advancing and elaborating the theory of regional subsystems, it is desirable first to explain the necessity for a theory with which to study and clarify the politics of the Middle East, the region that has been chosen as our focus and example, as well as an empirical basis for generalisation. In our discipline, 'theory' is a term frequently wielded in such a way that it has, on the one hand, almost become a subject in its own right – separate from the reality of world politics – while this has led, on the other hand, to a widespread and distorted notion of theory as being the opposite of reality. The word 'theory' awakens in many people the idea of models that are divorced from reality. I shall therefore discuss below the sense in which I understand the term 'theory' to support the view that I hold – that we need 'theory' in international politics for a better understanding of reality. International Relations is a social science, and like all disciplines of this kind is concerned with *people* and not with *nature*. The accuracy of the natural scientist is thus precluded here, and is not feasible in all disciplines even in the natural sciences. It follows, therefore, that the strictly experimental methods of the natural sciences are not applicable to our discipline either. Experiments can be repeated in labs, but not in social realities. Studying regularities in social structures is something different from studying regularities in nature. The efforts of many American social scientists to make their disciplines 'more scientific' by introducing quantitative methods are thus extremely dubious. The 'number-crunching' and purely abstract models associated with this do not render theoretical statements any more sound. A social scientist working with interpretative methods based on participant observation has no reason whatsoever to regard his social scientific knowledge as less scientific than the natural sciences, since his methods are of necessity different and developed to suit different subject matter.

Within the social and political spheres it is not possible to apply experimental methods to the extent that it is in nature, since a political event cannot be repeated or simulated in the laboratory. People and human entities must thus be differentiated from 'nature' as an object of study. The purpose of theory is to place facts into an appropriate order so as to be able to explain a particular phenomenon by means of an adequate interpretation. In as much as theory seeks to structure facts obtained from reality, it interprets them. How, for example, could the Africa policy of Qadhafi or the pan-Arab visions of Saddam Hussein possibly be explained using a mathematical model? On the other hand, a rejection of the possibility of an 'exact' computation of this policy should not lead to the highly dubious stance regrettably adopted, for example, by Theo Sommer in a leading article in the German weekly *Die Zeit*: 'In the Arab world, causes seldom produce the effects that Western logic would expect.'[21] To counteract Eurocentric arrogance of this kind it should be emphasised here that there is only one human logic. The internal differentiation of the global system into regional subsystems does not mean that each of the component parts has its own brand of logic. I subscribe to the view that every foreign policy, whether African or Arab, can be subjected to scholarly inquiry and analytical interpretation, although the kind of science that is concerned with people can be equated neither with the 'Western logic' imputed by Sommer nor with the natural sciences. Human knowledge is universal.

Having reached this point, we are now in a position to distinguish between common sense and scientific theory in the sphere of International Relations. In world politics, every phenomenon offers a wealth of facts, and any processing of those data, at whatever levels and using whatever method, entails some degree of selection and classification, and hence a certain interpretation. When speaking of world political events, one always needs a method in order to select facts in a certain way and classify them accordingly. The difference in the way one proceeds depends on whether mere 'opinion' is involved, as in the case of Theo Sommer, or a scientifically based theory. In one stimulating contribution, the International Relations scholar Michael Banks writes: 'It follows that it is wrong to think of "theory" as something that is opposed to "reality". The two cannot be separated. Every statement that is intended to describe or explain anything that happens in the world society is a theoretical statement.'[22]

The professional discipline of International Relations distinguishes between general theories, known as paradigms, and partial theories. The latter are concerned solely with the task of conceptualising – and thus help to explain – such component spheres of world politics as conflict, strategy, armament, or anthropological or psychological dimensions of the subject. Paradigms, on the other hand, are concerned, as in every discipline, with the particular scientific subject as a whole. The social sciences do not have a binding paradigm for every discipline, as is the case within the scientific commu-nities of the natural sciences, where the laws of nature are universal. Thomas Kuhn, who has attempted in a pioneering work to define the term paradigm, although referring to the social science disciplines as 'pre-paradigmatic', leaves open the question of whether some social science disciplines have yet acquired any such paradigms.[23] As a natural scientist, Kuhn has observed that among social scientists there can be more than one answer to the same question. He thus warns natural scientists of the danger of arrogance. He doubts 'that practitioners of the natural sciences possess firmer or more permanent answers to such questions than their colleagues in social science',[24] since the respective 'objects of study' are different, and the methods employed to investigate them therefore are also disparate. Kuhn's discussion of the paradigm concept led him to introduce the complementary concept of the 'disciplinary system', by which he means the 'common conceptual property of specialists within a certain discipline'.[25] In this sense, there are disciplinary systems within International Relations, but no unified paradigm shared by all scholars of our discipline which is characterised by scholarly pluralism.

No democrat would want to see a unified paradigm in the humanities such as is possible in the natural sciences, or as was asserted by social scientists in the Soviet Union, using Marxism-Leninism, before the *perestroika* reforms. Under democratic conditions there will always be a number of paradigms in the sense of 'disciplinary systems'. There is, nevertheless, a measure of agreement concerning both complexes of ideas that may claim the status of scientific theories and the minimum requirements that a frame of reference must meet in order to be accepted as scholarly knowledge, and thus as a paradigm.

The international system is a highly complex configuration displaying similarities and contrasts to an equal degree. Underdevelopment, for example, has taken on sufficiently disparate forms as an international phenomenon for us to be able to speak of contrasts. Scientific theory enables us to reduce this complexity so as better to describe and explain it. It is possible to reduce complexity without vulgarising reality or presenting distorted pictures of it. Concepts are used for this purpose, to break down the total phenomenon into its component parts and examine them individually before again relating them to one another as a totality. Regional subsystem theory is an example of this type of procedure: the international system is divided up into its constituent regions, which can then be analysed as regional subsystems. In the article quoted above, Michael Banks enumerates the chief concerns of the scholar of International Relations:[26] (i) the units that go to make up the international system; (ii) defining these individual units, or tools of analysis; (iii) the level of analysis on which research work is carried out; and finally (iv) the connections that emerge between these units of analysis. Banks adds that theories arrived at in this way cannot claim to be exact in the sense that they can in the natural sciences, because 'theories simultaneously express the political values of the theorist, and also help to shape the world which is being analysed.'[27] In terms of the theory of perception, this brings us to the Kantian idea of the *Ding an sich* ('the thing in itself') – the question as to how a phenomenon, in this case the international system, can exist in its own right, independently of the perceiving subject. Although many branches of science concerned with man and nature have become divorced from philosophy in the course of their development, the attainment of objective knowledge of reality remains the common *telos* of both philosophy and the modern sciences. The basic elements in philosophical epistemology have been integrated into the intellectually more sophisticated methodological schools of thought.

At the perceptional level, the question before us is how human perception, as a source of our concept of reality, can be reconciled with the 'thing in itself' as an objective entity. It is also incumbent on the science of

International Relations to seek truth in terms of the theory of knowledge, that is to attempt to bring our own concept of reality (*conceptus rei*) into line with reality itself (*essentia rei*). This book is related epistemologically to this Hegelian concept and not to an approach employing quantitative methods. It follows on from the line of thought of the Frankfurt School philosopher Karl-Heinz Haag (with whom this author studied philosophical thought as a young student in the mid-1960s):

> Thought seeks to adapt itself to an object in a way that is appropriate to it . . . The *essentia rei*, however, is in fact the Unknown. Perception, which would be the direct expression of the object, is hence impossible. Human subjectivity, with all its preconceptions, is just as much a part of perception as the object being perceived. The *conceptus rei*, being the result of perception, is an expression of the object after being processed by thought . . . Truth, as the *adaequatio intellectus et rei*, is the result of this process, which embraces both subject and object.[28]

This epistemological view, which may seem from the point of view of the quantitative school to be more philosophical than experimental, in the sense of being unscientific, will form the basis for the concept of regional subsystems as a *conceptus rei* to which we shall have recourse in this book. Our aim will be to study the interaction between regional dynamic and superpower penetration in the various regions of international politics, taking the Middle East as our case in point. The first step in this process will be to acquaint ourselves with the concept with which we shall be dealing in the following chapters.

THE ESSENTIAL ASPECTS OF REGIONAL SUBSYSTEM THEORY, ITS ORIGINS AND SIGNIFICANCE

As outlined in the Introduction, the European states system that emerged in the aftermath of the Westphalian Peace of 1648 heralded the modern system of international relations.[29] This system witnessed all types of political alliances except bipolarity, that is the domination of the system as a whole by two rival superpowers. The classical European balance of power was a flexible one of constantly shifting alliances. Reflection on this was incorporated into classical political theory, there being at that time no separate discipline of International Relations as such. The political theory of Edmund Burke (1729–97) revolves around notions of equilibrium in the state and the state system, as has already been shown in the Introduction.[30] Morton

Kaplan adopted this notion of the balance of power as the first of his six models of international politics, describing it as a system 'in which any combination of actors within alliances is possible so long as no alliance gains a marked preponderance in capabilities'.[31] It was only with the rise of the USA and the Soviet Union to superpower status, forming a 'marked preponderance in capabilities' in their 'blocs', that the European power equilibrium model dissolved. In the post-war era, the words of Alexis de Tocqueville (1805–59), written in the nineteenth century, must sound prophetic:

> The time will therefore come when one hundred and fifty millions of men will be living in North America, equal in condition . . . There are, at the present time, two great nations in the world, which seem to tend towards the same end, although they started from different points: I allude to the Russians and the Americans . . . Their starting-point is different, and their courses are not the same; yet each of them seems to be marked out by the will of Heaven to sway the destinies of half the globe.[32]

Tocqueville was far ahead of his time, prophesying with these words the unfolding of a global system concentrated into two world powers.

The decolonisation process gave rise to new states as nominal nation-states in Asia and Africa that were also to be taken into the international community, or to use International Relations terminology, were to become state actors in the international system which they have joined – to some extent as a destabilising factor. In 1955, the first few of these states gathered in the Indonesian city of Bandung to proclaim non-alignment as their foreign policy doctrine.[33] Historically speaking, the concept of non-alignment should be understood here to mean that during the Cold War these states were unwilling to be drawn into either the Western or the Eastern bloc. These states were and still are very weak, however: 'Mice cannot roar' (see note 17). Although their participation in international organisations has led to a voting majority, the fact is that this majority is not backed by corresponding political, military or economic capabilities. Yet the partici-pation of these new states in the international system has been accompanied by systemic change: the bipolar equilibrium has been undermined. Bipolar-ity was stable at the centre but not at the periphery, that is in the Third World. During the Cold War era the new states refused to join one or other of the world blocs, preferring instead to take part in world politics as a bloc of uncommitted nations in their own right while playing the super-powers off against each other and drawing advantages from bipolarity.[34]

The process of decolonisation formed the historical background to the theory of regional subsystems. New states that were uncommitted and non-aligned in relation to the global East–West conflict began to be taken into account on the one hand, while on the other the countries within this new group of states had to be both classified into regions and differentiated in terms of system. Notwithstanding ideological declarations of solidarity, the scholarly researcher can find no common homogeneous features ('Third World', 'Afro-Asian Movement', 'uncommitted nations') among the non-aligned nations. Like it or not, these new states have become integrated into the global international system since their decolonisation. Despite their overtly 'uncommitted' status they were until the dissolution of the Soviet Union politically, economically and/or militarily equally clamped, in terms of structure and interaction, in the bipolar structural vice of the dominant system. During the Cold War, there were thus 'uncommitted' nations like Cuba, that were closer to the former Soviet Union, as well as others, like Egypt under Sadat, that pursued a pro-Western policy. This leads us to the observation that even Kaplan's early definition of system theory allows for the existence of both loose bipolarity and tight systemic bipolarity. Even during the Cold War, the boundaries between the blocs were not hermetic, since the uncommitted nations had room to manoeuvre between them. The retreat of the Soviet Union from the Third World meant a loss of leverage for these nations. Viewed historically, bipolarity preceded decolonisation, crystallising just after the Second World War. Initially, at the height of the Cold War, it was rigid. The appearance on the scene of the new states led to a loosening-up of bipolarity.

In order to understand better the external conduct of the new states, it is helpful to divide the uncommitted nations, as well as other groups of state actors in world politics, into units of analysis that must be interconnected in terms both of structure and interaction. This applies even if they can only be linked together to different degrees, since region-specific interaction density or regional–structural interconnectedness helps to differentiate them from other groups of states. Regional subsystem theory explains the kind of loose bipolarity that in the first instance permits the oscillation of new states between the two superpowers, and thus points out the limitations of superpower politics. During the era of bipolarity, the superpowers were not even able to exert absolute influence on the small states, much less control them. This theory can also help to explain political developments within component regional international systems that are relatively independent of the bipolar structure of the global system. Regional conflicts can have important spillover effects on the global system itself, having consequences that went beyond regional boundaries into the global bipolar system during the

Cold War. The global effects of the Gulf War, which took place in an era of very close American–Soviet rapprochement, make clear the distinctly regional dynamic of a conflict in that region.

The theory of regional subsystems should not be confused here with that of multipolarity. The latter is based on the assumption that the international system consists of various blocs, centring around the middle range powers (Japan, Western Europe, China), whereas the theory of regional subsystems focuses its attention mainly on the new states in the so-called Third World.

Leonard Binder's above-mentioned skeleton of regional subsystem theory contains only a very broad, rough outline of the required frame of reference, since it was designed as a critique of Cold War globalism. It distinguishes between the global system and the dominant system of international relations, that is the bipolar system existing between the two superpowers. The 'new states' are subdivided into regional groups and conceptualised as subordinate regional subsystems. Although these state actors participate in the international arena as national states, that is as individual actors, their external conduct remains confined to the narrow regional context.

The basic assumption of this frame of reference is that every regional subsystem shows at the same time a *degree of autonomy* and a *degree of integration* in the global system. The limited degree of autonomy is linked with the regional singularities of the particular subsystem. It is also, however, a consequence of the inability of the superpowers, despite their dominance, to control and exert absolute influence on political processes beyond the centre of the international arena. The taking of hostages by Shiite fundamentalist militia men in the spring of 1987, in Lebanon, may be given as an illustration of this. Even the threat of the mighty US sixth fleet in the Mediterranean had little real effect on local and regional developments in the conflict potential that arose out of this action. Another example would be the operationally and tactically perfectly executed bombardment of Libyan towns by the US Air Force in April 1986, which nevertheless had relatively little impact on Qadhafi's policies. Compared to this, a regional defeat in the Chad War (March 1987) proved to be an immense blow for Libya,[35] contributing to a substantial weakening of Qadhafi's position, both locally and regionally. Afghanistan offers a clear example of a regional failure of the other superpower. These instances do not constitute an argument for exaggerating the regional factor, or for underestimating global influences. Pursuing the example of Qadhafi, international developments on the world crude oil market (a fall both in oil prices related to an oil glut and in the value of the dollar) also greatly weakened Libya. Hit by these external influences, Libya is no longer able to pursue its regional policies as it had before.

Binder's work[36] contributed to an improved concept of international politics in two respects. First, he combined empirical area studies[37] with International Relations theory, thereby pointing towards a way of overcoming the two extremes of simple description in the absence of theory in the field of area studies, and theorising in the absence of empirical studies in the general theory of International Relations. Secondly, his approach revealed the shortcomings of the global model: intraregional political developments have such a regional dynamic that the superpowers are not able to control them at will, despite the fact that these developments also form part of the international systemic context (internal–external linkage).[38] Tying the theory of international politics and social scientific studies of the Middle East together, Binder then arrives at an unequivocal conclusion: 'the existence of a bipolar system or the counter-balancing of the United States and the Soviet Union, cannot explain all post-World War II developments in the Middle East'.[39] In the first instance, the universal validity of the bipolar model as a frame of reference for explaining international politics, as first developed by Kaplan, is thereby thrown open to question. Secondly, the theory of regional subsystems, through its recognition of the *partial autonomy of these regional systems*, now stands out in contrast to the interpretation of the world system as a configuration whose complexity can only be dealt with adequately by the scholar on the global, regional, national and local levels by combining them in the analysis. To speak of regional subsystems does not mean that regional politics form an independent variable in world politics. It is rather a question of leaving methodological room for a regional level of world political analysis in its own right, without overlooking its external 'linkages'. The end of the Cold War has put an end to bipolarity, but not to the dynamic of regional conflicts. The Gulf crisis and the ensuing war have been a case in point in the light of this complex of questions.

Between the publication of the quoted article by Binder in 1958, a year after Kaplan's famous book (see note 3), and the beginning of the 1980s, an International Relations genre has emerged within scholarly literature whose authors specialise in investigating the component units of the international system.[40] These authors are unanimous in recognising internal differentiation within the international system as the background for the formation of partial systems. They do, however, differ in terms of method and terminology. I use here the term 'regional subsystem', since it seems to me appropriate, and I would regard it as unproductive to enter into the debate on the designation of terms. Purely for the reader's information, the definitions used in this literature are listed below:

1. subordinate international system (Binder);[41]
2. regional subsystem (Modelski, Thompson, Yalem, Young);[42]
3. subordinate state system (Brecher, Zartmann);[43]
4. partial international system (Stanley Hoffmann);[44]
5. international subsystem (Dominguez)[45], and
6. international region/subordinate system (Cantori and Spiegel).[46]

More important than the question of designating terms is that of determining the thematic substance of the subject: what exactly is a region or a regional subsystem? Which countries or national states constitute such a component unit in the international system, and how do they do so? What may be understood by the expression 'a regional subsystem with a regional dynamic'?

In the first of Binder's articles in the course of this debate, the subject of regionalism crops up in a rough form without providing satisfactory answers to these questions. Similarly, even in a later article Binder is content with the observation that component regional units of the international system, here termed regional subsystems, 'are primarily culture areas in which certain languages predominate'.[47] Resorting to culture as a basic criterion for defining acting units in the international system is inappropriate, even though culture is a substantive level in international politics. Nevertheless, the credit should go to Binder for his pioneering work, despite this shortcoming. Some articles following on from Binder's attempt to define the substance of the regional subsystem more closely and precisely. The remainder of this section will be concerned with a conceptual discussion of this subject, so that we can then proceed in Chapter 2 to discuss the specific subject of this book – to what extent the Middle East constitutes a regional subsystem and which state actors go to make up its national states, its component units. Apart from the obvious points that a regional subsystem is (i) a geographical unit (a group of countries that combine geographically to form a region) and (ii) that it is a component unit within the international system, there is no clear agreement among scholars on this. Thompson, who has done a study on the various definitions of regional subsystem in the specialist literature, has ascertained that various authors do not always mean the same thing when they speak of regional subsystems. He has assembled a list of twenty-one characteristic features that are given in this literature to define a region,[48] from which I select only a few here while developing my own approach.

Obviously, in order to form a subsystem the members of a group of states must lie in geographical contiguity. Since, however, the concept of a regional subsystem is not merely geographic, but relates also to the idea of a system, this criterion alone is not sufficient to delineate a region. The question is, what makes a group of states in a given geographical region a system? On the basis of my own research, I would regard the following as key criteria: (i) the structural interconnectedness between them (not only socio-economic, but also political, cultural and also ethnic), and (ii) the density of interaction, that is the degree of intensity of cooperation between the countries of a geographical region on all levels (political, economic, cultural and military). The notion of 'interaction' in this case equally covers cooperation and discord.

The definitions put forward in the literature raise various questions:

1. How many state actors can a regional subsystem have?
2. Do they have an image of themselves as a homogeneous entity and are they recognised as such by the outside world?
3. Does the group of states have its own regional organisation (Arab League, OAU)?

This brief list highlights a number of fundamental analytical problems in delineating a region. The existence of a regional organisation, for example, is not sufficient to define the group of states it embraces as a subsystem.

Africa, for example, has a regional organisation, the OAU, that embraces the entire continent.[49] At the beginning of the 1960s, West Africa was described by Hodgkin[50] as a subsystem. William Zartman, in a study that appeared several years later, designated the entire African continent as a subsystem; he distinguishes further subregions in Africa (West, East and Central). Contrary to this, modern research suggests viewing Africa as compounded of smaller subsystems which 'are still in the early stages of development and differentiation'.[51] This poses problems since, on the basis of present knowledge, Africa could be divided up into several regional subsystems rather than into subregions of the same subsystem. The fact that all African countries apart from South Africa are represented in the OAU does not suffice to make them a unified subsystem. In this book, a regional subsystem will be defined using the following central characteristic features, as outlined above: (i) geographical contiguity; (ii) regionally interconnecting structures; and (iii) a certain density of interaction, involving both political, as well as ethnic and cultural similarities, all of which give the region its specific character.

On this basis, a subsystem, in referring to Africa, must be understood on a much smaller scale. In the Middle East, on the other hand, the system is a more extended entity, since it does not lend itself, as in the case of Africa, to being reduced on the basis of a regional organisation (the OAU) as the central criterion. There, the relevant regional organisation is the Arab League. However, among the most important state actors in the region there are three states that are non-Arab, and therefore not represented in this regional organisation: Iran, Israel and Turkey. On the level of interaction, these three countries are principal state actors in the region and cannot be overlooked. In this connection, it becomes imperative to clarify, first, what is meant by interaction. Bruce Russett, who works with quantitative methods, reduces interaction to economic and political integration. In this sense he disputes the systemic character of state groups that have not yet achieved this kind of integration.[52] Many years after the publication of Russett's work, Robert Keohane arrived at a new viewpoint, in which interaction includes not only cooperation but also conflict and discord.[53] On the level of regional conflict, therefore, Israel, Turkey and Iran clearly all belong to the systemically defined region, despite the fact that as non-Arab states they cannot be members of the Arab League. The reality that these three states do belong to the Middle Eastern regional subsystem is abundantly clear in the aftermath of the Gulf War which revealed that no system of collective security can function if these three states are excluded. We shall be seeing in Chapter 2 just how little interaction takes place in this regional organisation, so that this criterion carries little explanatory weight here. The most significant patterns of interaction in this region are outside the regional organisation. The Gulf crisis shattered the Arab League to the extent of rendering it insignificant.

Of considerable significance, however, is the defining factor of the subsystem's systemic subordination. All regional subsystems are at the same time integrated both into the global system (the international system) and subordinate to the dominant world order. The conflict between the two dominant superpowers, here taking the form of the East–West conflict, thus constituted hitherto an important dimension for the analysis of external relations of a regional subsystem. The superpowers had competed for influence in the regional subsystems subordinate to them, thereby, without wishing to do so, creating a certain amount of room for manoeuvre for the 'new states' that were subordinated to them. Regional subsystems may be fragmented by local, ethnic, cultural, political or economically triggered conflicts. During the Cold War, the superpowers made the most of this fragmentation by forming alliances with some local state actors against others. In this way, a 'linkage' arises between the local, regional and international levels of a conflict. The presence of a superpower in a given region may manifest itself through a regional ally who, unlike a proxy, retains a degree of independence (sovereignty) from its patron.

In the Middle East regional system, therefore, before the end of the Cold War Syria was an ally of the Soviet Union and not a proxy, as argued by some authors. As a result of this 'linkage' (Rosenau)[54] between the local, regional and international levels, under the conditions of constantly increasing penetration of a region with the continued simultaneous existence of the region's own dynamic, the analysis of the intraregional, interregional and international relations of a regional system is fraught with complexity. In the face of such a complex structure, there can be no straightforward answers. The penchant towards extreme simplification, prevalent among some journalists writing on the Middle East, leads at the very best to inaccurate information, and at worst to a complete distortion of the existing realities. The aim here is to accommodate this complexity, and under no circumstances to succumb to the cliché of a gulf between scholars and journalists. These critical remarks are not intended as a sweeping generalisation. It is, for example, a pleasure to cite such first-rate German-speaking Swiss journalist authors as Erich Gysling and Arnold Hottinger, the German Wolfgang Günter Lerch,[55] British reporters such as Edward Mortimer and Tony Walker[56] and French ones such as Jean Lacouture and Eric Rouleau,[57] all of whom have contributed to an accommodation of this complexity in their news coverage. Unfortunately, this group forms a minority in international journalism.

The partial theory of 'patron–client' state relations[58] in a regional context can offer some preliminary help in reducing the kind of complexity described above. It should be reiterated here that regional national states are active actors in world politics and not simply objects of it. Superpowers adopt a 'patron' position as penetrators of a region, thereby developing a patron–client relationship with regional state actors either through economic aid (US economic aid to Egypt) or arms supplies (Soviet military aid). In this protective role, the involved superpower seeks to create a leverage, to use its regional allies, the clients, to act in its interests, but is unable to manipulate them entirely, because a patron-state cannot direct its client-states. The client, for example, can draw the patron into regional conflicts (as Syria did earlier with the Soviet Union, or Israel with the USA) which, in the event of escalation and a situation that spills over beyond the region's own dynamic (e.g. Middle East wars), can have grave international political consequences. On the basis of patron–client relationships that are not entirely under the control of the superpowers, regional conflicts can acquire a dimension that affects the global bipolar structure, in this case the East–West conflict. The Middle East, African and Southeast Asian regions have offered repeated examples of the global political dimensions of regional conflicts. The statement that these regional conflicts cannot be traced back to the bipolar structure takes other global viewpoints into account in its critique. A fixation on the North–South conflict, for example, offers no viable alternative to East–West globalism. The North–South scheme was revived and activated during the Gulf War after the East–West scheme had lost its validity. Clearly, however, the resort to this scheme provided no useful interpretations of the Gulf War. Regions must be appropriately researched as regional subsystems; each has its own regional dynamic of conflict, while at the same time being incorporated in the international order and its conflict potential. North–South centred analysis leads only to a repetition of the same old platitudes – as the recent Gulf conflict has shown – and can hardly be expected to contribute to a proper explanation of regional conflicts.

In International Relations theory, Johan Galtung, with his thesis of a 'feudal world order', put forward a misleading schematic viewpoint for the analysis of international patterns of interaction. By 'feudal system' Galtung understands an order based on 'a combination of rank concordance and an interaction pattern that is very largely dependent on pecking orders. By rank concordance, I mean the tendency for there to be two types of state actors in a given system; either state actors who take a high rank in all conceivable dimensions, or state actors who take a low rank in all conceivable dimensions.'[59] In as much as this thesis is concerned with a description of a hierarchical – or in Galtung's terminology 'asymmetrical' – order in the international system, it is a correct one.[60] However, the assertion that Galtung derives out of this seems to me, viewed from the conceptual framework that we have been developing here of a regionally differentiated world order, not only to pose problems, but to be quite simply false. Galtung likewise fails to present empirical proof to support his globalist argument: 'For good or ill, interaction is to some degree monopolised by those who take the highest rank in all spheres, with the result that among those who take the lowest rank in all spheres there remain virtually no direct links.'[61] Although, therefore, Galtung is normatively advocating justice in the world order, and does not share the conservative standpoint of globalism, what he is offering here is an ultra-globalist view of international politics. In the Federal Republic of Germany, the reception of Galtung's ideas had a seriously negative impact on left-wing oriented 'Third World Studies'. As a consequence of the adoption of this viewpoint, this research has been reduced to the mere schematic analysis of North–South relations,[62] which no less than the conservative globalist model, albeit with different emphases, likewise perceives Third World states as objects rather then as regionally differentiated state actors in the world political arena. In Galtung's view, in fact, there is hardly any regional interaction. North–

South globalists conspicuously lack the necessary empirical knowledge about the very Third World they care for on the normative level.

Departing from the speculative level of theory-building in the absence of empirical research, and turning instead to theoretical concepts that are based on empirical foundations, entirely different results are produced. An analysis of world regions located in the south of the international society (the developing countries) that conceptualises them as regional subsystems reveals that regional interaction, however weak it may be, is none the less of central importance. The regional pattern of interaction constitutes a central unit of analysis, both for understanding the particular region itself, and for analysing the 'linkages' that exist between it and the dominant system (the superpowers) in the context of the global system (the international society). One of the empirically oriented theoreticians concerned with the development of the concept of regional subsystems, William Thompson, in a favourable examination of the peace researcher Johan Galtung's normative thesis of a 'feudal world order', comes to the conclusion that the assertions made in this thesis cannot lay claim to 'universal validity'.[63]

In addition to the analysis of penetration of a regional subsystem by superpower interests in the form of patron–client relations, as they were designed during the Cold War, the analysis of a region's external and intraregional relations is also crucial.[64] Within a given region there are asymmetrical structures on all levels, just as there are in North–South relations. This necessitates stratification analysis for all regions, such as John Waterbury has carried out for the Middle East, showing the stratificatory regional structures (the social hierarchy in a region) among its member states.[65] A regional subsystem can also have a centre and a periphery. The regional centre may, although it need not, be equatable with a regional hegemonical power within a capability-centred hierarchy in a region. In the absence of a hegemonical centre, or in the event of a weakening of its former centre, a regional subsystem takes on diffuse polycentric forms which do not necessarily adversely affect the intensity of regional interaction. When, for example, the leading regional power in the Middle East, Egypt, was in a weakened position after the Six Day War (see Part Two, especially Chapter 4), the crucial interaction of this country with the rest of the region was not diminished. As a result of the effects of oil wealth in the years from 1973 to 1982, Egypt's interaction (e.g. labour migration) with the rich Arab states intensified despite the loss Egypt suffered in the aftermath of the Six Day War.

The external relations of regional subsystems are not restricted to interaction with superpowers. Their indisputable structural dependence on the superpowers notwithstanding, the way interaction proceeds does not always have to be focused around this dependence: processes of interaction can also arise between the regional subsystems themselves. On a global level, the movement of non-aligned states constitutes an example of South–South relations of this kind, although it is admittedly of limited importance. Votes at the UN and at non-aligned conferences, where vehement speeches are sometimes to be heard (e.g. the rhetoric of Castro in Havana, Qadhafi in Harare), carry little weight in international politics.[66] Votes and proclamations have little impact on the course of world politics, even at the regional level. When, however, South–South relations occur in a specific manner, in the form of interaction between regional subsystems in a non-rhetoric context, they can have considerable impact. An example of this would be Afro-Arab relations, led by the rich oil-producing countries with interregional political interests.[67] This is also an instance of how regional subsystems overlap. Arab countries of North Africa are thus at the same time members of the OAU and the Arab League.

Delineating a regional subsystem from the outside is not the only difficult task. Intraregional boundaries within a subsystem can also be of bewildering complexity. In the Middle East, the Arab, Islamic and Israeli spheres overlap one another. It is widely known that the Israeli state supplied the Islamic state of Iran with American weapons during its war with Iraq. During the first Gulf War Iran could fight the Arab state of Iraq, which was armed with Soviet weapons systems. Pro-American Egypt supplied Iraq with Soviet weapons and spare parts (from earlier arsenals), while Arab Syria, allied with the Soviet Union, supported non-Arab Iran against Arab Iraq. These confusing alliances are an indication not only of the diffuse systemic character of the region, but also of the high degree of complexity that characterises existing linkages. It is regrettable that some journalists, lacking a grasp of this complexity and the necessary knowledge about the region, simply assume that the events in this region are not comprehensible to 'Western logic'. By now it should be clear to the reader just how fraught analysis is from the very outset. This high degree of complexity must inevitably lead to more modest claims: it would be quite impossible to try to explain everything in a satisfactory manner. This book will, however, attempt to decipher regional–international ramifications and linkages (see note 38). I regard a regionally differentiated perspective as more helpful than a globalist model in terms of accommodating the complexity of conflict formations in the Middle Eastern regional subsystem, and for arriving at a proper understanding of the pattern of conflict and of its militarisation there. The recent Gulf War has abundantly proved the validity of the regionally differentiated perspective.

We are not concerned solely with analysis here. Scholarly perspectives are always imbued with value judgements. During the Cold War, globalists such as ex-President Reagan and numerous scholarly advisers who advocated his views in academic circles, saw the struggle against communism – unaffected by the disarmament agreements of the end of 1987 – as the central concern of world politics.[68] International Relations scholars with a regionally differentiated perspective, on the other hand, such as this author and many of his 'regionalist' colleagues, although never sympathetic to communism and always critical of it before it broke down, can see world political tasks of greater importance. How can one resolve the problems in regions of conflict by peaceful means? And how can such peace be ensured while at the same time satisfying the basic needs of the people living in those regions? The lessons of the recent Gulf War support this perspective of peaceful conflict resolution.

The Middle East is the principal trouble spot in world politics, whether seen from the superpower perspective (US and formerly Soviet foreign policy) or from the regional viewpoint. The list of Middle Eastern conflicts is quite long: the Arab–Israeli conflict and the wars related to it, the Palestine conflict, the Iran–Iraq Gulf War, the Lebanese War, the military conflicts in Libya/Chad, southern Sudan, the Polisario/Morocco conflict, and most recently the shattering Gulf War. This book does not aim to give a narrative description of these conflicts, but rather to examine the overall structural conditions of the development of the Middle Eastern subsystem since 1967. In keeping with the historical–structural perspective established in the Introduction, that in general the consequences of war can be crucial, the focus of analysis will be the consequences of the 1967 and 1973 wars. The present-day Middle East is a product of these developments: not a single political occurrence in the Middle East that can be adequately interpreted without recourse to the consequences of June 1967 and October 1973. In the Part Four, Chapter 8 the continuity between these Arab–Israeli wars and political developments during the 1980s will be shown. Chapter 9, devoted to the recent Gulf War, will present an analysis of the current gloomy shape of the Middle East. In the light of the Gulf War, Chapter 10 concludes this book with an analysis of the historical context of conflict and war in the troubled Middle East.

2 The Middle East: Its Location and Delimitation

Free of loaded value judgements, the word pairs East–West and Orient–Occident refer to the points of the compass where the sun rises and sets. In terms of cultural history, however, they express a centuries-old cultural tension between the Islamic Orient and the Christian Occident.[1] The term 'Middle East', however, is a modern political term, the often very loose geographical definition of a region that – as a geopolitical entity – came into being in the course of recent history, and that is hence expandable and contractible. The terms 'Middle East' or 'Near East' used in European languages are only meaningful from the European perspective. If one is travelling from India or China to Cairo or Damascus, one is moving westwards, and yet one speaks incorrectly in geographical terms of a journey to the Middle East. This term came about in the narrow context of the imperial interests of European colonial powers. The present-day superpowers, the USA and to a certain extent the former Soviet Union, have adopted it, despite the fact that it is inappropriate to their geographical location. When, during the Iran Contra scandal of 1986–87, Reagan was occupied with arms deals with Iran and Israel from Washington, or even from his ranch in Santa Barbara in California on the West Coast, the vexatious region in question was certainly not in the 'Middle' East in relation to him. No more does Damascus lie in the 'Middle East' in relation to Moscow. Even in the language of international organisations, above all the United Nations (since spring 1948), this region is known as the 'Middle East', even after the dissolution of the European colonial empires.[2]

Our primary concern here is to determine the extent to which this geographical region may be deemed a regional subsystem in the sense meant by political science. To clarify this problematique, however, it is necessary to explore the term 'Middle East', since the region clearly still bears traces of its history. In British imperial terminology the whole of Asia was known as 'The East', a region that embraced both the 'Far East', from the perspective of the British Empire, and the Ottoman Empire. To distinguish between the two, the terms 'Far East' and 'Near East' were introduced. The future of what was by the nineteenth century the crumbling Ottoman Empire, the 'Sick Man on the Bosphorus', lay in the hands of the European powers. In Chapter 1 we saw how relations between states in the

European states system at that time took the form of a balance of power between shifting alliances. The Europeans were not in agreement as to who should obtain which parts of the collapsing Ottoman Empire. These rivalries among the European powers were referred to as the substance of the term 'The Eastern Question'. A leading Middle East expert, L. Carl Brown at Princeton, retains the term 'Middle Eastern Question' as a frame of reference for the analysis of present-day politics in the Middle East.[3] This is because Brown likens the erstwhile conflict between regional and superpowers over the Ottoman Empire to the present-day situation, although the state actors and names have changed in the aftermath of the dissolution of the Ottoman Empire and the subsequent emergence of national states. It is for this reason that Brown puts forward the former territory of the Ottoman Empire as the geographical territory of a 'Middle East' region. According to Brown's definition,[4] this subsystem embraces all states within the geographical Middle East and North Africa with the exception of Iran and Morocco, which were not included in the former sphere of Ottoman hegemony. Technically, the contrast between the superpowers and the regional powers is equally valid for the present-day situation, and yet both the former and the latter have altered substantially. The USSR and the USA have taken over the former power role of the European powers, with the result that a bipolar system has emerged out of the former European balance of power. Many new states have arisen out of the Ottoman Empire, the former regional imperial power, which completely dissolved in the transition from empire to nation-state.[5] Nor is former Ottoman territory identical with or reducible to the present-day regional system. In other words, the location of the Middle East and the boundaries of this regional subsystem still need to be precisely defined. Without wishing to dispute the historical continuity stressed by Brown, it should be pointed out that the historical situation in the Middle East has undergone substantial changes since the two world wars. These changes require a revised delimitation of the 'Middle East' as the erstwhile focus of the 'Eastern Question'. The questions the student of the present-day Middle East has to grapple with are of a different order, and not a variety of the 'Eastern Question'.

The terms 'Near East' and 'Middle East' are often used interchangeably and with only the vaguest territorial delineation. In German the term *Naher Osten*, Near East, is more established.[6] In English, however, the same region is described as the Middle East. The history of the English usage of these two terms needs to be outlined here before describing the concept in terms of its scholarly meaning in the academic discipline of International Relations. The history of terms runs parallel with the political history of relations between the region and the former great powers.

Until the turn of this century, the East, viewed from Europe, was divided into the Near East and the Far East. It was in September 1902 that the outstanding American naval officer Alfred T. Mahan first introduced the term 'Middle East' in an article published in the British *National Review*. This new term was linked with the development of the strategic concept of a sea route from the Suez Canal to Singapore, so that Mahan's observations focused on Aden, India and the Gulf region. Part of this article was subsequently published in *The Times*, after which the *Times* correspondent Valentine Chirol took up the term, publishing from 14 October 1902 a series of articles on 'The Middle Eastern Question'. This led to the establishment of a new concept, the 'Middle East', whose centre was India. According to this definition, all strategic routes to India belonged to the region. This situation was to change after the First World War, however. The British Colonial Minister of that time, Winston Churchill, backed by the Royal Geographical Society, redefined the term in response to this change, modifying it to include the countries lying between the Bosphorus and the borders of India. The Eastern Mediterranean coast thus replaced India as the focus of the concept, although the Middle East, as defined in terms of the British colonies, still embraced India.

The Second World War necessitated a completely new definition. Great Britain was greatly weakened by this war, but it still had its colonial empire, and thus retained its great power status, since its interests were central for the formulation of dominant strategic concepts. Davison aptly sums up the situation after 1945: 'Like the Mahan–Chirol Middle East of forty years before, the Middle East of World War II was a strategic concept imposed from without by British interests. The center had shifted from India to Cairo, but the rationale was similar. As in Mahan's concept, so in the 1940s the fringe was fuzzy, the boundaries undelimitable.'[7] The borders of the region were not fuzzy because the concept was inconsistent: they had to be fuzzy to allow for new formulations in response to changing strategic situations. Since the 1950s, Great Britain can no longer be regarded as a major power: the Pax Americana has replaced the Pax Britannica in the Middle East,[8] so that the definition, formulated in terms of power politics, was now modified to suit American interests. Attlee, however, who succeeded Winston Churchill as British Prime Minister after the war, was the one who prepared the ground for this definition. Since that time, the 'Middle East' has consisted of the Arab countries and certain other countries bordering on them,[9] a definition that was to be adopted as the American definition of the Middle East from the Eisenhower administration onwards. Davison sums up the history of the term: 'For, as the term "Middle East" has developed in history to its present condition, the unifying principle has always been the political and strategic interest of outside powers.'[10] This assertion is correct in as much as it refers to the history of the term so far, as well as to the concomitant penetration of the region by the colonial powers, and nowadays by the superpowers.

The question arises, however, of whether in addition to this external definition and delineation of the region, analogous to superpower interests, there are not also internal criteria, specific to the region itself, for defining the Middle East as a subsystem. This question springs from the working hypothesis of this book, namely that world political regions, despite their integration in a global system (world order) dominated by the two superpowers (the USA and the former Soviet Union, who constituted until the end of the Cold War a dominant bipolar system), also have independent structures and a dynamic of their own. According to this hypothesis, the region is defined in terms of internal, substantial criteria that allow for the possibility of state actors within the subsystems act as independent subjects. The end of the Cold War has enhanced the latitude of action of regional powers (e.g. Iraq) and thus gives more prominence to the thesis of regional dynamic which is basic to this book.

The term 'Middle East' is retained here purely for the sake of simplicity: the reader should always bear in mind the Eurocentric conceptual history of the term that we have just elucidated. In the remarks that follow in the rest of this chapter, the 'Middle East' will be examined neither in terms of its geographical substance, nor simply in terms of its relevance for superpower interests. Instead, we shall be looking at it in the context of the regional subsystem, a concept that was developed early in Part One, and which we shall be developing further in the light of the characteristic features enumerated above: (a) geographical contiguity, (b) regional interaction, and (c) structural interconnectedness. The relevance of ethnocultural components in the formation of subsystems has already been touched on – without, however, accepting the criterion of the stateless 'nation' (e.g. the 'Arab nation') or of the alleged overall ethnic group (e.g. 'black African') as valid for the definition of a subsystem. In this book, 'subsystem' is viewed as a social scientific concept while ideological pronouncements are rejected.

The next question is whether the Middle East subsystemic region constitutes a multiethnic or multinational entity embracing all the nations contained in it, or whether it is primarily an exclusive Arab entity, as Arab authors argue. This second question touches on the boundaries of the region, which are very vague, encompassing no less than three continents: Africa, Asia and Europe (the European part of Turkey). Where then, exactly, is the Middle East?

The answer to both these questions depends on the frame of reference employed for defining a subsystem in the global society. One possible answer will be attempted below while also drawing on and discussing alternative answers.

INTERACTION AS INTEGRATION OR AS CONFLICT STRUCTURE? A MIDDLE EAST SUBSYSTEM OR AN ARAB REGIONAL ORDER?

During the foregoing remarks we quoted Bruce Russett (note 52, Chapter 1) who understands interaction to mean integration, therefore disputing the idea that two warring parties can belong to the same region. According to this view Iran and Iraq, or Israel and the Arab states, could not belong to the same region. Although not pan-Arab nationalist, limiting his scholarly interest to the use of quantitative methods, Russett none the less in this respect puts himself in the same boat as other scholarly authors who openly profess to pan-Arab convictions. In their now standard Arabic work *Al-Nizam al-Iqlimi al-'Arabi*, now in its third reprint, the two Egyptian social scientists Ali Eddin Hillal Dessouki and Jamil Matar, who are familiar with the body of Western specialist literature on the theory of regional subsystems, refute the validity of classifying the 'Arab nation' along with Israel, the imputed enemy of the Arabs, or with non-Arab Islamic peoples such as the Turks and Persians, within a single systemic unit.[11] This has been an influential work, as may be deduced from the rapid succession of reprints (1979, 1980 and 1983). However, the development of the idea of the 'Arab regional order' undertaken in this book became known internationally in English through a work published by the Egyptian social scientist Saad Eddin Ibrahim, which uses the term in its title.[12]

The central argument of Dessouki and Matar is that the term 'Middle East' is both Eurocentric and of colonial origin.[13] While this argument is irrefutable, it still leaves unanswered the question heading this chapter. Their definition – 'On the basis of geographical affiliation, as well as existing affinities in the linguistic, cultural, historical and social spheres, we may speak of an Arab system of states extending from Mauritania in the West to the Gulf region in the East'[14] – leaves a number of questions unanswered. Dessouki and Matar use the three criteria of geographical contiguity, cultural affinity and interaction, adding a fourth – Arab nationalism – as a binding factor: 'By this we mean Arab nationalism both as an intellectual current of thought and as a political movement. We thus define the Arab system of states not only in terms of regional geography, but also nationally as an Arab regional order.'[15] This definition does not relate to a notion of 'integration' in the sense meant by Russett. However, its reference to an idea of unified order or the consolidation of the whole solely according to similar shared characteristics as a criterion for the formation of a subsystem is also tantamount to integration. Those parts of the whole which cannot be integrated into a system on account of conflict or confrontation cannot, therefore, belong to it. With Dessouki and Matar, therefore, similarity and cooperation are the criteria of interaction.

Unlike Hillal Dessouki and Matar, or Egyptian colleagues of the al-Ahram Center for Political and Strategic Studies with whom I have discussed these questions, I apply objective rather than subjective criteria. The latter, as employed by Arab authors, use a cultural image of the self as a basis for defining a subsystem, and are thus not analytical. Similarly, I do not limit the substance of 'interaction' to cooperation, since it is in fact conflicts that bind states into a regional system. Thus processes of interaction include both cooperation and the proliferation of conflicts on all levels. In this sense, we adhere to Frederic Pearson's definition of regional systems as systems of interaction. Whereas the dominant system in international politics was bipolar until the end of the Cold War (the Soviet Union/USA), regional subsystems are unipolar, that is multifarious. Specifying his definition of interaction in more detail, and taking the Middle East as a concrete example, Pearson asserts that interaction embraces equally both conflict and cooperation, adding that in this discipline it can be summed up on both the regional and international levels using the following categories:[16]

1. Conflict (verbal and non-verbal): this category includes both articulations of conflict in speeches by heads of state and their spokesmen, and actual acts of conflict (these may be economic, e.g. a boycott, or military, i.e. troop movements and aggression).
2. Political considerations, in both the negative and positive senses: when Qadhafi, to take him once again as an example, includes the Arab countries in his pan-Arab concept, and Israel in his open war fantasies. These are both instances of political considerations. Pearson rightly maintains that this category 'does not consist of interactions as such, but it does provide a useful indicator of attention paid by governments, since leaders' statements are coded as to target and affect'.[17]
3. Participation: this category includes negotiations between governments, the conclusion of state treaties, as well as all forms of exchange (e.g. trade). Thompson, as well as Diskin and Mishal, has added to the above a further category of 'state visits'.[18]

4. Aid: this embraces all forms of aid, chiefly in the economic and military spheres. Prior to the return of Egypt to the Arab League, for example, Saudi Arabia provided Egypt with economic aid, while Egypt supplied Iraq with military equipment during its 1980–88 war with Iran.

This form of interaction characterised inter-Arab relations from 1979 to 1987, when the Arab states were formally boycotting Egypt (as a sanction against that country's separate peace with Israel), but were nevertheless maintaining their economic and military relations with Egypt. This understanding of the term 'interaction', used here to define the Middle East as an interactional subsystem, prevents us from accepting the biased interpretation of Hillal Dessouki and Matar. The regional subsystem under consideration here embraces non-Arab countries such as Iran and Israel, against which the Arab side has in fact waged wars, war being one of the forms that regional interaction can take. Turkey must likewise be taken into account in this analysis, since it also figures as a regional state actor in interaction with Syria, Iraq and Iran (the Kurdish question, and the running of the irrigation project based on the Euphrates, among other issues). These three non-Arab states were basic actors during the Gulf crisis and the ensuing war. The Middle East as a regional subsystem cannot be conceived of without referring to Iran, Israel and Turkey as major systemic–regional actors. According to Michael Hudson,[19] the Turkish invasion of Cyprus in July 1974 outlined not only the military importance of Turkey, but also the fact that Cyprus is part of the region. This is even more true now after the Gulf War than it was when he wrote it in 1976.

The population of Cyprus now includes Lebanese and Palestinians, who together make up some 6 to 8 per cent of its total. The importance of Cyprus is not merely a matter of statistics, because the island has a wider relevance than its role in Turkish military logistics. Cyprus became regionally significant during the Lebanese civil war for Lebanon and also for the Palestinians. This newly acquired geostrategic importance of the island has its counterpart in a new politico-economic role – its replacement of Lebanon as a centre of commerce – a matter to which we shall be returning later.

The question of whether a subsystemic definition of the Middle East should embrace only the Arab states or other state actors in addition was broached by Cantori and Spiegel at the very beginning of the debate. They deemed the Arab countries to be the core of the region, and the non-Arab states to be peripheral.[20] However, like the theory of the Arab regional order, this interpretation also poses some problems necessitating its rejection. The reason for this is that the terms 'core' and 'periphery' need to be defined in terms of their substance, and not geographically. According to Cantori and Spiegel's classification, for instance, Yemen and Sudan are part of the 'core', while Israel, Iran and even Turkey are on the periphery. Looking at these countries in terms of interaction, however, the exact opposite is the case. The recent Gulf War has strongly proved the central position of these non-Arab states in the Middle Eastern subsystem. On the level of conflict, Iran and Israel have always been at the hub of the region. While the definition of a regional dynamic embracing both conflict and cooperation can be used to delineate a regional subsystem unequivocally from the outside, that is in relation to its wider environment (system/environment), a system of this kind remains a crude analytical tool in need of internal differentiation. This latter task is even more complex than the first. With the aid of the process of interaction outlined above, we have so far defined the Middle East as an interactional subsystem. On the basis of this interpretation, we have identified non-Arab countries as equally important state actors in the regional subsystem, and indeed as major members of it. In Chapter 1, where conceptual terms were dealt with, other characteristic features of a region were acknowledged in addition to that of structural interconnectedness. These included secondary organisation (the existence of a regional organisation), as well as psychological criteria (the question of collective identity). This latter definition concerns the cultural self-perception of people in a region, that is their image of themselves in relation to their image of others.

On this basis it is necessary to make distinctions within the region. Arab and non-Arab members of the system need to be distinguished here in the first instance, and not even the Arab states themselves constitute a homogeneous block, as the ideological concept of a unitary 'Arab nation' would suggest. The Iraqi invasion of Kuwait clearly showed that inter-Arab conflicts are among the basic conflicts in the region. Nevertheless, we must concede with Cantori and Spiegel[21] that existing historical, ethnic, cultural, linguistic and socio-structural links between the members of a subsystem do form the background to the question of collective identity – i.e. the feeling of belonging to a region – and that these (the perceptions of the self and of others as the source of attitudes in regional and international conflicts) therefore have a rightful place in our subject matter. One of the lessons of the Gulf crisis, however, is that the question of collective cultural identity alone is not an adequate basis for defining a regional subsystem, or for dealing with it properly.

Before looking into structural interconnectedness within the Middle East, we should first clarify the problematique of identity in more detail, and then proceed to a discussion of the problematique of regional organisations. In view of the recent resurgence in universalist-oriented political

Islam, and the concomitant decline in identity-furthering ideologies of a secular and national character (pan-Arabism), the question arises whether it is not now obsolete to frame the problem of identifying the subsystem within overall Middle Eastern (i.e. Islamic) or only Arab boundaries. In the region itself, the term 'Middle East' (*al-sharq al-ausat*) is not quite accepted. The term 'Arab nation' (*al-umma al-'arabiyya*) is identified with Iraqi pan-Arab expansionism since the invasion of Kuwait. Political Islam now forms the hub around which a sense of collective identity is formed.[22] Ranged beneath this pre-eminent common feature of political Islam, particularisms may be encountered (Lebanese against Syrians, Libyans against Egyptians or Tunisians, Algerians against Moroccans, and most recently Iraq against Gulf Arabs). Another rung down, one finds religio-sectarian conflicts (Muslim against Christians in Lebanon and Egypt, Shiites against Sunnis in Lebanon, and Sunnis against Shiites in Saddam Hussein's Iraq), or ethnic divisions (the Kurdish question in Iraq and Turkey, etc., the black population of southern Sudan, the Berbers of Algeria, etc.)[23] – so much so that Fouad Ajami, for example, speaks of the 'end of pan-Arabism',[24] since 'Arabism' no longer seems to be a unifying factor in furthering identity in the region.

This observation has been abundantly confirmed during the course of the Gulf crisis. Can a vision of Islamism or Arabism really contribute to the identity of a region on the socio-psychological level, or is this an ideological fixation? I have already broached this question briefly in connection with the Iranian claim of an 'Islamic revolution for export' in a published paper originally given at a MESA congress in Chicago.[25] Among the conclusions based on these research findings is the assertion that the formation of identity is completed culturally on the basis of the *social production of cultural meaning*, taking place, in other words, in a local context. The two ideologies of an overall Islamism and irredentist Arabism are not, however, local but supralocal in character. Islam constitutes an unbounded universalism, compared to which pan-Arab nationalism has its visible bounds within the Arab-speaking population of the region.[26] On the levels of political cooperation and economic integration the Arab countries, with a population of more than 160 million, are a more manageable unit than the greatly diverse one billion Muslims of the world.[27] In terms of the question being addressed in this book, the part of the world inhabited by Arabs constitutes a core area of the regional subsystem. In contrast, there is no Islamic part of the world that could be said to form a political entity on the interactional and structural levels.

During the Gulf War Saddam Hussein's calls for '*Jihad*/Islamic holy war' were a desperate attempt at an overall mobilisation of 'all Muslims against the West' in Saddam's unholy war. The idea of a 'world of Islam' is an ideological invention of European Orientalists[28] with no correlative in real life. The 'Organisation of the Islamic Conference', Saudi-controlled and financed by petro-dollars, is a fabrication of propaganda, but is no unit of analysis for the proper subject matter of International Relations. Political Islam is both a phenomenon of the times and an expression of crisis.[29] Its manifestations are culturally, politically and socially very diverse; they may seem to consumers of the sensationalist media to be the expression of a 'Muslim revolution', but to the informed, discerning observer they appear in a different light. Islamism could hardly form the basis for the identity of a regional subsystem, however much Muslims may seem to constitute a unity in the face of non-Muslims – albeit primarily on the religious level. Without wishing to dispute Islamic solidarity, I would like here to emphasise the thesis stated in my MESA paper (see note 25), that Islam can only provide the socio-psychological basis for the formation of identity on the local level – not supraregionally.

The second question, concerning the existence of a regional organisation, can be swiftly dealt with. It is true that regional organisations are put forward in the specialist literature as a criterion, albeit only a secondary one, for the delineation of a region. However, as we have already demonstrated in Chapter 1, taking the Organisation for African Unity (OAU) as our example (see Chapter 1, note 49), such an organisation cannot be equated with a subsystem. Algeria and Kenya, for example, are both members of the OAU, but nevertheless belong to two different regional subsystems and are diverse on all levels and by all means. In the Middle East region, Iran, Israel and Turkey are not Arab League members,[30] but they still number among the most central state actors of the region. Somalia and Djibouti, on the other hand, are members of the Arab League, but they can not even be counted as part of the periphery of the subsystem. The Gulf crisis shattered the Arab League and split it up. During this crisis the regional non-Arab states had a greater significance than many members of the Arab League.

SUBSYSTEMIC STATE ACTORS, THEIR STRUCTURALLY DETERMINED RANKING AND THEIR RELATIONSHIPS TO THE EXTRA-REGIONAL ENVIRONMENT

The existence of a structural link in the economic sphere between two state actors in a world political region presumes the existence of political co-operation. Moreover, in contrast with interactional links, it precludes certain types of conflict. To put forward the thesis that economic integration is part and parcel of the structural interconnectedness in a region is by no means to contradict our critique of Russett's reduction of interaction to integration. Economic integration cannot occur without political cooperation.[31] All failed attempts at economic integration in the Third World are constrained politically; as in the case of the Middle East, they can be traced back to inter-Arab political rather than to economic causes.

On this level we must, like Dessouki and Matar,[32] concede that the Arab countries constitute a regional entity in their own right within the Middle East subsystem. A sense among Arabs of belonging together (pan-Arabism, see notes 24 and 26) could constitute a factor furthering political cooperation in the pursuit of economic integration. Over and above this political consciousness, further structural similarities can also be discerned among the Arab countries that would make such an economic integration feasible. The 1962 agreement on Arab economic unity achieved in 1964, albeit in a not particularly effective form, the Arab Common Market (ACM).[33] However, political rivalries have prevented Arab integration from becoming a reality. It was only during the 1970s that oil wealth, by virtue of the massive boost it gave to inter-Arab economic relations, contributed indirectly to the cementing of existing structural links.[34] Hillal Dessouki and Matar themselves point out that inter-Arab rivalries have had the most persistent detrimental effects on hopes for Arab economic integration.[35] This confirms Andrew Axline's thesis in *International Organization* (February 1977) that economic integration is impossible without corresponding political cooperation. Cultural–ethnic closeness ('Arabness') may promote political cooperation, but it could never be a crucial basis for a precondition for economic integration.

We must nevertheless distinguish here between economic integration as a form of action pertaining to structural interconnectedness, and purely formal economic relations that are interactions and nothing more. In terms of its rate of expansion in trade relations, non-Arab Turkey leads the region as a whole:[36] in 1972, the value of Turkey's exports to the Arab countries amounted to only US$71 million; by 1975 this had increased to $168 million – an eighth of Turkey's total exports. Cyprus should also be mentioned here: the value of Cypriot exports to the Arab countries increased by 270 per cent between 1973 and 1975 alone. Since the Lebanese civil war broke out in 1975, Cyprus has to a large extent taken Lebanon's place as a centre of commerce. These factors, on the one hand, justify the inclusion of Turkey and Cyprus in the Middle East subsystem, while, on the other, serving to highlight the distinction between economic interconnectedness (through commerce, for example) and economic integration. The latter is restricted to Arab countries alone,[37] being inseparable from the political integration being aimed for.

In this chapter we shall be pointing out first evidence of structural interconnectedness, chiefly in the economic sphere of the subsystem, and secondly, attempt on the strength of this to ascertain whether there is a ranking among the state actors in the region. Bearing in mind that the region is by no means homogeneous, one may speak of subregional component parts that resemble one another more than they do other parts of the subsystem.

A closer examination of common structural and psychological features shared by state actors in the subsystem compels us to make this differentiation: a bald distinction between Arab and non-Arab state actors would be too crude. Michael Brecher has applied the centre-periphery scheme to the region.[38] According to his interpretation, Israel is rightly assigned to the core – in contrast with the Cantori–Spiegel scheme – but the whole of the Maghreb is placed on the periphery. In Spiegel–Cantori, on the other hand, the Maghreb (Morocco, Algeria, Tunisia) constitutes a regional subsystem in its own right.[39] Michael Hudson has rightly discerned that 'it is simplistic to envisage the region in terms of a single core and periphery. There are a number of distinct but not entirely autonomous subsystems – patterns of conflict and cooperation each involving one or more major and several minor state actors.'[40] In addition, therefore, to distinguish between Arab and non-Arab state actors, Hudson suggests subdividing the Arab part of the subsystem into subregional component parts: (i) The Near East (in Arabic the Mashrek, i.e. the East); (ii) North Africa (in Arabic the Maghreb, i.e. the Arab West); and (iii) The Gulf region (Saudi Arabia and the Gulf sheikdoms as GCC members). Hudson's justification for this subdivision of the Arab region into three subregions is the four respective criteria of geographical contiguity, a minimum of social communication, recent shared history that can be drawn upon, and the prevailing standard of modernisation.[41] The comparison of existing structural features as a basis for this differentiation is not invoked by scholars alone. Taking into account another methodological criterion, the self-perception of inhabitants of a region, it will be seen that the Arabs distinguish themselves to a large extent according to whether they belong to the Mashrek, the Maghreb, or the Gulf (in Arabic, *khalij*). To this criterion must then be added regional differentiation on the level of regional organisations, since although the regional institution of the Arab League (see note 30) unites the states of all these subregions, the Gulf states have their own political security organisation, the Gulf Cooperation Council,[42] since the regional problems of the Gulf have different priorities.[43] Similarly, in the sphere of economic integration, the states of the Arab West, designated by the term Maghreb, also form a separate, although still Arab entity in their own right,[44] and are formally united in the Union du Maghreb Arabe.

Core and peripheral state actors may be discerned in each of these component regions of the Middle East subsystem, although there is a degree of overlapping, especially since all three belong to the same subsystem, whose state actors may make their presence felt on any or all levels.[45] Saudi Arabia, for example, may be counted as a core state actor in both the Gulf region and the Mashrek alike; by providing Morocco with economic support in the war it once waged against Polisario, it may also be counted as a state actor in the Maghreb. Among the most recent evidence of Saudi influence is its major role in the Gulf War[46] and the return of the Arab League to Cairo in September 1990 prior to the Gulf crisis and the ensuing war. Petrodollar-cheque diplomacy was the tool used to exert this influence, which made possible the all-Arab summit of 8 November 1987 in Amman, before which appropriate payments were made to Syria. This diplomacy did not work during the Gulf crisis.

In order to understand the ability of specific state actors to influence political decisions, it is necessary to be informed about the foreign policy tools at the disposal of those participants. In foreign policy theory, we use the term 'leverage' to denote the political, economic or military tools at the disposal of a state for furthering its foreign policy aims – which form the structural basis of all foreign policy. Analysis of these tools provides the scholar with information about the foreign policy potential of specific state actors. To restrict ourselves for the time being to Arab members of the subsystem, and referring to the work of John Waterbury and Saad Eddin Ibrahim, we might make the following two attempts at a regional stratification of the Middle East.

According to Waterbury, the Arab countries form a unified complex, although their interactions need to be subregionally differentiated. These countries can be subdivided on the basis of stratification into five groups:[47]

1. the group of countries that export crude oil and other raw materials (phosphate), which are relatively developed, but which are nevertheless in full need of their hard currency income (e.g. Iraq, Algeria, Morocco);

2. the group of countries that are rich in crude oil, have low populations and which are at the same time extremely underdeveloped, although they have large hard currency reserves (Saudi Arabia, the Gulf states and Libya);

3. the group of countries that are poor in resources but structurally developed compared to the other Arab countries (e.g. Egypt, Tunisia);
4. the group of countries that are both poor and also structurally extremely underdeveloped (both Yemeni states, Mauritania, Sudan).
5. Lebanon and Jordan, which do not fit into any of the above categories, being special cases.

The second attempt at stratification was devised by Saad Eddin Ibrahim,[48] who, like Waterbury, employs the concept of social stratification to describe the internal arrangement of strata in the Arab region, using the term 'new social order' for this structural arrangement, a term adopted from Matar/Hillal Dessouki. In Ibrahim's view, this social order rests on the following stratification:

1. The five rich Arab countries (Saudi Arabia, Kuwait, the United Arab Emirates, Libya and Qatar), whose population amounts to no more than 6 per cent of all Arabs, but whose gross social product in 1977 reached US$56 billion. The corresponding figure for all Arab countries together, including these five, amounted to US$142 billion;
2. The group of 'well-to-do' Arab states, which includes Oman, Bahrain, Iraq and Algeria respectively before the Gulf Wars and the economic crisis of 1988–92;
3. The group of the 'struggling middle', who just manage to balance their expenditure with their existing resources, and who have no population problems (Tunisia, Syria, Morocco);
4. Finally, the group of poor Arab states, which are characterised by a disproportion between their poverty in terms of resources and their high populations. Egypt heads this group, in addition to the two Yemens, Sudan and Mauritania.

To make his treatment of this classification more than a purely formal one, Ibrahim attempts to discern incongruities within the Arab 'new social order'. These pertain to the educational sector, military facilities, and not least to labour reserves.[49] Egypt, for example, which occupies the lowest position in the stratification model outlined above, none the less occupies the highest position with regard to its education system, military potential and labour reserves. The petro-dollar nations, on the other hand, rank lowest according to these criteria: Saudi Arabia not only has the least developed education system, and hence the highest illiteracy rate, it is fully incapable of manning the modern defence systems at its disposal. The Gulf War clearly showed the vulnerability of the kingdom. A major proportion of the local population, moreover, remains outside the labour reserve, since the bedouin despise manual labour, while women are still not allowed to appear in public outside the domestic sphere. The appearance of female US troops deployed in Saudi Arabia caused trouble. The exclusion of the female population effectively reduces the potential workforce by more than half.

However, the stratification evident in the core region of the subsystem, the Arab part of the Middle East, still only throws light on the structural basis of conflict potential among the Arab states themselves. Among the lessons of the Gulf War is the insight it provides into inter-Arab relations,[50] which are so complex in themselves that anyone ought to be able to see the sense in departing from a globalist view and making regional subsystems the level of analysis in world politics. When other types of conflict potential in the region are added to that of inter-Arab discord, the picture becomes even more complicated. Regional conflicts in the Middle East can be seen to be of worldwide political importance – not in the globalist sense, however – when one bears in mind that both the USA and the former Soviet Union had crucial regional interests there. These interests, or the perception of them,[51] together with the linkage (see Chapter 1, note 38) between regional developments and global world politics, and with the inability of the outside powers to exert full control over their regional allies,[52] combine to make the Middle East the single most crucial regional subsystem in world politics today. Here, the regional engagement of a superpower can indeed have repercussions in global politics. The internationalisation of the Gulf crisis and its development into an international war make this statement clear.

On the analytical level, we may distinguish three main areas of conflict in the Middle East as a regional subsystem with its own regional dynamic of conflict:

1. The Arab–Israeli state conflict,[53] together with the Jewish–Palestinian conflict:
2. Inter-Arab conflicts, which take many different forms, and which could become militarised as in the case of the Gulf War. Syria and Iraq, both ruled by the Ba'th Party, although characterised by factions of different religio-sectarian persuasions, represent two exemplary poles of such a conflict.[54] The pivotal inter-Arab conflict, however, is concerned with the issue of regional leadership. The height this conflict reached around the time of the 'Arab Cold War' under Nasser[55] has been surpassed by the Gulf War, when Arab troops fought against Iraqi forces. Even on the periphery of the subsystem, in the Western Sahara, the struggle between the local 'liberation organisation', Polisario, and Morocco,

once assumed an inter-Arab form – sometimes between Morocco and Algeria, at other times between Morocco and Libya, Algeria and Libya having at various times and under various conditions each supported Polisario against Morocco.[56] The formation of the Union du Maghreb Arabe in February 1990 did not end these tensions fully.

3. Inter-superpower conflicts carried over into the region. During the Cold War, the USA and the former Soviet Union acted out these conflicts with their various regional allies under constantly changing conditions. Prior to the Gulf crisis, the Middle East policy of the USA[57] was explicitly conceived with reference to that of the Soviet Union, and vice versa.[58] The end of the Cold War and the dissolution of the Soviet Union seem to have ended this part of the history of conflict in the Middle East.

Five geographical conflict zones may be cited in which regional conflicts have already escalated to military form, that is where parties to a conflict have waged war on each other.

1. The Arab–Israeli conflict itself, in the context of which the wars of 1948, 1956, 1967 and 1973 were fought out (see note 53). The Israeli invasion of Lebanon in June 1982 may be added to this,[59] although Lebanon is in fact also a regional trouble spot in its own right.

2. Arab–Iranian tensions in the Gulf were evident long before Khomeini's seizure of power, being based on Iran's claim to regional leadership in the Gulf and on account of the Shat-al-Arab border conflict. The eight-year Iran–Iraq War should be seen in this context.[60] The Gulf conflict zone shifted from Arab–Iranian tensions to Arab–Arab tensions after the Iraqi invasion of Kuwait. The Gulf War of 1990–91 proved to be the most shattering event in Arab politics since 1967 (see note 46).

3. The Lebanese War:[61] experts are unanimous in their definition of the Lebanese conflict region as *le monde arabe en miniature*. In Lebanon, all the various forms of linkage within the Middle East conflict structure are discernible: superpowers, regional state actors from all levels (Palestinian, inter-Arab, Israel and even the Arab–Iran conflict, since non-Arab Iran has both a military presence in Lebanon with the Iranian Revolutionary Guard, and religio-politically through Shiite preachers). Syria used the Gulf War to lay a tacit grip on Lebanon and to disarm rival militias.

4. The Red Sea zone:[62] although at present somewhat in the shadow of the three trouble spots named above, it is none the less of central impor-

tance, since it joins the Middle East subsystem with that of East Africa. Ethiopia's[63] involvement in Red Sea politics and in the two Yemens before their unification in May 1990 indicate the interregional link between Middle Eastern and African politics.

5. The Western Sahara conflict:[64] on the formal level, this conflict on the periphery of the subsystem is a simple struggle between Morocco, which has made territorial claims to the former Spanish Western Sahara, and Polisario, which is seeking national independence. From the Arab standpoint, however, Algeria and Libya have at various times been involved in the conflict, through their supply of arms to Polisario, while Saudi Arabia's involvement has taken the form of economic aid to Morocco. The conflict itself has also caused Afro-Arab divisions within the OAU. The formation of the Union du Maghreb Arabe by the five North African Arab states helped to calm this conflict.

The Chad dispute cannot be viewed as a conflict zone of the Middle East for methodological reasons, since the dissension is primarily a Central African concern, or the attempt of an Arab country, Libya, to penetrate this region. The Chad conflict, which came to an end after December 1990, is thus a subject for inter- rather than intraregional relations (Middle East/ Central Africa).[65]

CONCLUSION

By way of summing up, after a systemic delineation of the Middle East based on more than political geography,[66] as well as an internal differentiation of three subregions and five conflict zones, we are now equipped to answer the question: where is the Middle East? The Middle East subsystem includes all the countries of the Mashrek (Near East), the Maghreb (North Africa) and the Gulf region. Iran, Israel, Turkey and Cyprus are non-Arab state actors within this subsystem. The two East African states of Somalia and Djibouti do not belong to it, however, although they are members of the Arab League, and although they play a subordinate role in the Red Sea conflict zone. Besides Ethiopia, Somalia will only be mentioned in the scheme as a peripheral state actor in the Red Sea conflict zone. In listing subsystem members together with further data, such as their subdivision into subregions and conflict zones, obviously, some overlapping does occur. It will be clear, for example, from the identification of state actors within conflict zones that a single state actor may be involved in several such zones. However, a state actor can only be assigned one place in any one definition of a subsystem. The latter is an entity based on political events: it is never determined by geographical factors alone, but always remains a changeable political phenomenon. For this reason its boundaries, structure and membership are in need of constant revision and fresh definition.

In accordance with the understanding reached in the Introduction that the consequences of war often prove to be historical turning points, the following chapters will be devoted to an examination of the wars of June 1967 and October 1973 in the Middle East, as well as to the study of the Middle Eastern subsystem in the 1980s, that is the impact of these two wars on the subsystem. The Iraqi invasion of Kuwait occurred as a result of these regional developments and also of the change in the international system after the end of the Cold War. The third Arab–Israeli war introduced a new phase in the continuing epoch of crisis, and although the fourth such war of October 1973 did not end this ongoing discord, it nevertheless laid the foundations for the separate Israeli–Egyptian Camp David peace agreement. Without Egypt's military might, an Arab–Israeli war cannot widen into a total regional conflict within the subsystem as a whole. The Israeli invasion of Lebanon in 1982 is proof of this: the war in Lebanon was no longer an Arab–Israeli war involving the entire region. From the 1980s until the present day, the region's chief concern is a quite different theatre of war – the Gulf. The truce between Iraq and Iran of August 1988 did not amount to peace, nor did the ending of hostilities in the recent war, on 28 February 1991. Peaceful solutions to the central conflicts of the subsystem, such as security in the Gulf, the Arab–Israeli and Palestine controversies and intra-Arab rivalries, remain to be found. The uprising in the Israeli-occupied territories (the *intifada* in Gaza and the West Bank) that has been taking place since December 1987 became peripheral during the most recent Gulf crisis and war. The consequences of the wars of 1967 and 1973 led to the Gulf War, and continue to make themselves felt. Their analysis therefore remain a topical subject. By unravelling these problems, we are helping to shed light on the prospects for the future of the region. The recent Gulf War (see Part Four) has rendered these prospects gloomy and has contributed to a further complication of the conflicts with which this region has been burdened.

Part Two

From Arab Renaissance (*Nahda*) to the Six Day War of 1967: The New Historical Epoch after June 1967

Introduction

Modern Arab history since the late nineteenth century falls into a number of distinct periods, according to Abdallah Laroui, the internationally renowned historian and philosopher. The most recent of these was heralded by the Six Day War, the beginning of a new epoch in the history of the region. We shall be looking into Laroui's period categories in some detail later in Part Two. If we leave aside the Maghreb, where colonisation began in 1830, as peripheral to the heartland of the Arab cultural domain – which even Laroui, himself a Maghrebin, is prepared to do – then the Arabs may be seen to have experienced a *nahda*, or renaissance, in terms of their confrontation with the by now superordinate European culture. This *nahda* began around 1850, that is well before their colonisation by the European powers after the First World War. Geographically, this process focused primarily around Greater Syria, the Levant and Egypt. Laroui puts this forward as the first basic epoch in modern Arab history. In his scheme, the Six Day War represents the fourth such epoch, persisting to the present day, and forms the subject of this part. In Part Four, we shall have to reconsider Laroui's periodisation, adding the time since 2 August 1990 as the most decisive turn of events in modern Arab history.

The Six Day War was more than a turning point in the history of the Middle East, however. It entailed major structural changes in concepts and terminology within the discipline of International Relations. Without wishing to advance Eurocentric arguments, it may be noted that the June 1967 War in the Middle East had repercussions as far reaching for the region as comparable wars have had in Europe (see Introduction). The Arab state system has been in existence since the founding of the Arab League in 1945. However, prior to this date, there existed a degree of limited inter-state interaction between state actors who had achieved independence as sovereign states in terms of international law. Chief among these were Iraq under King Faisal (from 1930, *de jure* from 1932), and Egypt (1923) under King Fuad, or after 1936 under his son Faruq. The newly founded Saudi monarchy (1932), whose territory had never been a colony, was to join this nucleus Arab state system. During those years, as well as after 1945, inter-Arab conflicts were royal and focused around the Hashemites and the Saudis, since the latter had effectively driven the Hashemites (Sharif Hussein of Mecca) out of the Arabian peninsula. With British support, two sons of Hussein, former Emir of Mecca, became monarchs of Iraq (Faisal) and of Transjordan (Abdallah).

In other words, inter-Arab politics in the 1930s and 1940s was the privilege of kings in the shadow of dynastic disputes in Arabia, Iraq/Jordan and Egypt. The Egyptian King Fuad cherished a wish to become Caliph of the Arabs. After the collapse of the Ottoman Empire and the abolition of the Islamic caliphate, another ruler, Sharif Hussein, Emir of Mecca, fulfilled this dream for a few brief days. In March 1924, he was proclaimed Caliph by his son Abdallah, but was forced to abdicate in the same year under pressure from the Saudis, who drove him out of the Hijaz. Since his British allies failed to support him, this marked the end of attempts to establish a new caliphate among the Arabs.

The *coup d'état* known as the 23 July Revolution, carried out by the 'Free Officers' under Nasser in 1952, marked the end of this royal phase in recent Arab history. Pan-Arabism of the kings and pan-Islamism were now replaced by military revolutionary populism as a new pattern of pan-Arabism. After the departure of Faruq from Egypt, royal heads rolled one after the other in the region: the Hashemites in Iraq (1958), the Zaidite Imams in Yemen (1962), and the Idrises in Libya (1969). Nasserism as populism, therefore, was the historical alternative to royalism. It raised high hopes, but proved to be an illusion. As Nasser himself emphasised in his *Philosophy of Revolution*, the fall of the monarchy was one of the effects of the first Arab–Israeli war in 1948. The birth of Nasserism was a consequence of war, as was its demise – victim to the consequences of the 1967 War. Indeed, one of the results of the recent Gulf War will be the shattering of Ba'thism, the other variety of pan-Arab populism.

The Six Day War was more than a military event, however. In the few days between Monday 5 and Saturday 10 June 1967, the entire structure of the Middle East regional system was transformed. It will be the task of the following chapters to examine this event and its consequences in more detail. Chapter 3 will investigate the war itself, although primarily from a geopolitical rather than a military standpoint. Chapter 4 will then analyse its regional and international repercussions.

3 The Six Day War of 1967: The Background and Multifaceted Character of an Escalated Regional Conflict

After the Cuban crisis of October 1962, a direct hotline, the 'red phone', was set up between Washington and Moscow. It was used for the first time in June 1967 during the Six Day War[1] – a fact which serves to highlight the crucial importance of the Middle East as a central international region, both then and now. This hotline contact is also illustrative of the central thesis of this book: Kosygin did not succeed in taming Nasser, his regional ally, thus bringing the escalation of the regional conflict under control. He informed the American President that the Soviet Union would not intervene in the event of an outbreak of war if the United States also refrained from military intervention. The USA was equally unable to exert any influence on Israel's conduct during the crisis. Since the Suez War the two super-powers had been building up their spheres of influence in the region, but without thereby gaining control of its distinctly regional dynamic. Regional developments in the Middle East subsystem, as well as changes in their political significance, are however related to corresponding changes in the world order since the Second World War and are thus not isolated regional events.

As we saw in Part One, the Second World War had transformed the world order by giving it a bipolar structure in the form of two superpowers: the USA and the Soviet Union. The European powers emerged weakened from the war, thus forfeiting their great power status.

The historical consequences of the Second World War did not manifest themselves immediately after 1945. In both geographical and temporal terms they developed gradually rather than materialising all at once. Although the new bipolar structure crystallised rapidly after the end of the war in Europe, it did not at first globalise into a worldwide phenomenon. At this stage, the European powers still had their respective former domains, largely in the former colonial regions. The Middle East countries had been incorporated into the European colonial empires during the nineteenth century, or after the First World War at the latest.[2] After the Second World War they remained largely under either British or French influence, apart from Iran, the Arabian peninsula excluding the Gulf sheikdoms, North Yemen and Turkey. France, for example, had retained a significant proportion of its colonial empire in North Africa. Great Britain had kept its power in the Arab East, even in the newly independent countries (e.g. Egypt 1923, Iraq 1932). In the Gulf subregion, however, the Pax Britannica was already waning in favour of a Pax Americana.[3]

The year 1945 marked a turning point in the world order. Changes taking place in Europe had repercussions all over the world, although there were time lags. The former great powers were not to lose their influence in the Middle East, for example, until 1956. It was as a result of the Suez crisis in that year that the region was fully incorporated into the bipolar field of the USA and the USSR. The Suez War involved wider issues than that of the Arab–Israeli conflict: the former colonial powers of Great Britain and France were also among its state actors.[4] Together with Israel, they defeated Egypt in military terms, but lost the war politically. It is important to note here that the ability of Nasser to transform his military defeat into a political victory in Suez 1956 served as a model for Saddam Hussein during the 1990–91 Gulf War. Despite his rhetoric of '*um al-ma'arik*' ('the mother of all battles'), he was aware of his military weakness but hoped to win the war through political steadfastness. Saddam failed to see that the situation in the Suez War was completely different from that of the Gulf War. In 1956, there were two superpowers, the USA and the Soviet Union, who disapproved of the Anglo-French Suez adventure, and forced the two former great powers to defer to them. There was nothing like this in 1990–91.

The years between the Suez War of 1956 and the war of June 1967 brought major changes in their wake. The two superpowers penetrated the Middle East, ousting Great Britain and France. The war in Algeria had been one of France's chief motives for becoming involved in the Suez War, being concerned to prevent Nasser's Egypt from providing the Algerian liberation movement, the FLN, with further military support.[5] The war in Algeria also came to an end, and the country gained its independence in 1962. France then abandoned its idea of Algeria as a *département d'outre mer* – an overseas province.[6] Great Britain in turn withdrew from its former sphere of influence, the Persian Gulf, completing the process in 1971. In economic terms, the USA had effectively replaced Britain long before that.[7]

As we saw in Part One in connection with Leonard Binder's work, the Middle East is a 'subordinate international system', that is a partial system integrated into a global order, and penetrated by great or superpowers.[8] This does not mean that the region is merely a chessboard for major state actors. It has demands of its own in terms of emancipation, and its own ideas about its future development. Nasserism,[9] both as an ideology and as an experiment in development, was an expression of expectations nurtured by the peoples of the region for their own future, as well as a model for them. Although, as noted previously, the Suez War was a military defeat for Egypt, that defeat was neutralised politically by the intervention of the two superpowers, the USA and the Soviet Union, against the former great powers France and Great Britain and their regional allies. Military defeat was thus turned into political victory, and hence into another source of legitimacy for Nasser's Egypt. It enabled him more than ever before to claim a leading role for Egypt in the region on all levels.

From 1956 to 1967, Nasser's Egypt was regarded as the centre of the Arab Revolution (*al-Thauɪa al-'Arabiyya*) and as the embodiment of the pan-Arab aspirations connected with it. Egypt was providing both political and military support to the Algerian FLN and other Arab underground and liberation organisations. The unification of Egypt and Syria to form the United Arab Republic (UAR) in February 1958 was only one link in this chain.[10] The coup by Syrian officers in September 1961 was to shatter Nasser's experiment, leading to the secession of Syria from the UAR. However, this only led to a more radical stance by the Egyptian development model. When Nasserist officers in North Yemen abolished the monarchy and declared a republic, the Saudi monarchy felt threatened and sided with the deposed imam-king against the Republicans. In response, Nasser did not content himself with the usual propaganda, deploying to Yemen Egyptian troops who for a time numbered as many as 90 000.[11] The Yemen War that broke out in 1962 symbolised one dimension of Arab intraregional struggles. On the one hand, radical republics were in conflict with monarchic social orders,[12] while, on the other, radical elements in the Arab world were in a state of mutual enmity. Nasserism and the pan-Arab Ba'th Party,[13] for example, never enjoyed harmonious relations – at best only tenuous passing alliances. Unlike Nasserism, Ba'thism seemed to survive the 1967 war. The recent Gulf War, however, has marked the decisive end of this variety of pan-Arabism as a legitimacy device.

Prior to the war of June 1967 the Middle East subsystem was split by intraregional conflicts of various kinds, while at the same time rapidly becoming an object of competitive struggle between the globally competing superpowers. The way regional fighting forces were armed may serve to illustrate this. At that time, Israel was still predominantly armed with French combat aircraft and some British arms, chiefly Centurion tanks, and only just beginning to change over to American weapons systems.

Egypt, Syria and Iraq in contrast were then armed almost exclusively with Soviet weaponry. After the Suez War, Egypt was still open in terms of foreign policy. In the event, it was the intransigence of the Eisenhower administration in the USA,[14] and particularly of Secretary of State Dulles, for whom 'positive neutralism' and non-alignment were synonymous with communism, that drove Egypt into the arms of the Soviet Union.

From 1957 onwards, therefore, Egyptian fighting forces were supplied with Soviet arms, so that by 1967 they were fully 'Sovietised' in terms both of armament and military training. Israel, on the other hand, turned increasingly to the USA after 1956, so that the anti-American de Gaulle began to distance himself more and more from Israel. In 1967, Israel still had an air force primarily equipped by France and financed by reparation payments from Federal Germany.[15] However, incipient close links between Israel and the USA were not de Gaulle's only reason for putting a stop to French aid, and even openly condemning Israel for aggression in June 1967. France was not merely cultivating friendships but in the first instance looking after her own interests, which then as now were the decisive factor in the shaping of French foreign policy in the Middle East.

Briefly then, before the outbreak of the Six Day War, in June 1967, the Middle East had already been completely penetrated on the international level, and integrated into the existing bipolar world order. It could safely be described as an internationally subordinate regional subsystem. By then, each superpower had its regional allies, but this does not mean that the superpowers had limitless potential to control events. They were able neither to prevent the outbreak of war nor to influence its course. The core conflict at the root of the entire subsystem and its central regional rivalries – the Arab–Israeli conflict – was concealed behind the regional configuration of superpower rivalry. The Arab core states, Egypt, Syria and Iraq, were allied with the Soviet Union, while Israel was the US ally in the region. This does not imply that the Arab camp was either united or unequivocally on the Soviet side. Inter-Arab rivalries between camps designating themselves as 'traditional' or 'progressive', as well as the split between Ba'thism and Nasserism, have already been pointed out above. In a masterly book, Malcolm Kerr describes these inter-Arab rivalries as the 'Arab Cold War'.[16]

THE SIX DAY WAR: THE COURSE OF THE MILITARY CONFLICT

Taken as a military event, the third Arab–Israeli war lasted six days. It broke out on Monday 5 June 1967 and ended with a truce on 10 June. The decisive military phase of this Six Day War, however, lasted no more than a few hours. This is not to refute the reality of the use of force of which war undoubtedly consists, but rather to point out that the outcome was already basically clear by midday, or to be precise around 10.35 on the morning of the day that had begun at 7.45 with a sortie by the Israeli air force. By that time in fact, the Egyptian air force had been almost entirely put out of action, destroyed on the ground. This compelled Egyptian ground troops to operate without protection from the air, although this should not be taken as an inference that the failure of Egyptian ground troops in Sinai is attributable solely to their having to fight without air force back-up. Despite the fact that the Egyptian army and navy had to act without air protection and conduct their operations under bombardment from the Israeli air force, Egyptian ground troops could still have prevented, or at least held off, a total Israeli victory on the strength of their concentration in Sinai, the size of the peninsula, and the limited capacity of the Israeli air force, which by then had only a few heavy bombers at its disposal. In the event, however, Egyptian ground troops were not adapted for mobile warfare, and failed just as the Egyptian air force – destroyed on the ground – had done. Later Arab accounts nevertheless exaggerate the importance of the air strike, which was indeed a brilliant tactical manoeuvre, attributing the failure of Egyptian ground troops entirely to the lack of air protection. Although the Israelis had won the air strike, Egyptian ground troops could at least have reduced, if not prevented, the securing or long-term consolidation of that air strike, if they had had good coordination and communication systems, and been more mobile.

Even more significant than the fact that neither the Egyptian army in the Sinai desert nor Syria, Iraq and Jordan, Egypt's allies, were informed of the destruction of the Egyptian air force, is that even Nasser himself did not learn of it until hours later. He later confided to an ambassador in Cairo: 'It was nearly four in the afternoon before someone came to me and said: We have no more planes.'[17] Edgar O'Ballance, the military expert, even states that it was evening before Nasser was fully briefed about events.[18] While the Egyptian air force was being bombed on the morning of 5 June, the Commander-in-Chief of the Egyptian armed forces, 'Field Marshal' Abdulhakim 'Amer, was on a flight with his commanding officers making a tour of inspection over the Sinai desert in an Ilyushin 14 plane. In order to ensure his safety, Egyptian air defence had been given orders that day not to shoot over Sinai. The Ilyushin 14 was neither able to land there during the fighting nor to circle the area and fly back to Cairo. It was late morning before the 'Field Marshal', who is alleged later to have committed suicide during the period of Nasser's house arrest, was able to return to

Cairo. By this time, the decisive military action of the Israelis, undertaken to achieve complete air control, was virtually complete. Another consequence of the dilettantish military strategy of the Egyptian Field Marshal was that Egyptian air force bases, the target of the Israeli air force, had no orders, since their commanding officers were not at headquarters, but in the company of Field Marshal 'Amer flying over the Sinai desert. Many officers were also missing from their headquarters for other reasons. General Sadiq Mahmud, for example, had been celebrating into the late hours at a party with belly dancing the night before.[19] In June 1967, the command-issuing structures of the Egyptian armed forces were both rigid and markedly personalised. Without 'Amer and the commanders, the rest of the military were helpless. The Israelis exploited this and deliberately avoided shooting 'Amer's plane down to prevent the swift appointment of a successor.

A rich language can form part of the cultural wealth of a people by enabling its members to express themselves creatively. The self-same linguistic resources, however, can also produce the opposite effect, that is a radical rhetoric that impedes recognition of reality. Such was and still remains the tragedy of the Arabs, the third Arab–Israeli war being a vivid example of this. Lamenting the relationship of the Arabs to their language, the Egyptian diplomat Azzam describes how for them 'this language is still not simply a means of communication, but an aesthetic art capable of intoxicating people and the masses, and of rousing them to a state of euphoria'.[20] Although Nasser furthered the escalation of war militarily with an appropriate concentration of troops on the Israeli border, his use of language was far more forceful than that of arms. Today, more than two decades after the war itself, we know that Nasser was engaged in a political manoeuvre, not war as such. He hoped to score a political victory over Israel along the lines of the Suez conflict without the necessity for war, in contrast with 1956. He hoped, in other words, to bluff his way through.[21] This is difficult for outsiders, unfamiliar with the relationship of the Arabs to their language, to understand. The world witnessed a similar situation with regard to rhetoric and verbal radicalism when Saddam Hussein issued a challenge to the entire world in 1990–91. Another aspect of the problem is that language can also intoxicate the person who uses it, so that the man putting on the show begins himself to believe in what he is dissimulating. It does not appear to have occurred to Nasser (or to Saddam) for one moment that his political manoeuvre might escalate to the extent that war, and thus military defeat, would become inevitable. In the end, Nasser's powers of reasoning were paralysed by his own rhetoric, as was recently also the case with Saddam Hussein.

The mother tongue of this author is Arabic and the radio broadcasts of that time can still be recalled. At the verbal level, Arabs were led to believe in victory even as Arab soldiers were running around helplessly in the Sinai desert. My friend, the Damascene philosopher al-'Azm, a Yale graduate, remarked in an account written shortly after the defeat that 'Arab thinking has been deeply influenced by a concept of war whose origins hark back to the days of chivalry and sword duels, of personal valour and direct confrontation. We may recall the many poems that were heard from all radio stations, and read in all the press – poems about the clash of swords, the galloping from behind enemy lines and other manifestations of individual valour.'[22] While Arab radio stations were lauding the destruction of the Israeli air force in forceful language, Arab ground troops were already sharing the same pitiful fate as that of their air force. For their part, the Israelis allowed the world to go on thinking that the Arabs were still a threat to them, suppressing reports of their military successes. This was not out of modesty, however. In the absence of propaganda, and taking extreme logistical risks, they pressed forward with their blitzkrieg operations until their troops had reached the east bank of the Suez Canal in the south-west, the Jordan in the east and the Syrian Golan Heights in the north. The Israeli leadership feared that the UN Security Council, if it were to learn that the Arab threat had been successfully dealt with, might call for a ceasefire too soon. With their bare-faced lies and totally fabricated reports of victory, therefore, Arab politicians and their radio stations played straight into the hands of the Israelis, enabling the latter both to delay the ceasefire resolution of the UN Security Council and to press forward with their blitzkrieg operation.

The Israelis themselves were surprised at their own success, the extent of which exceeded their expectations. Thus, they did not have any overall strategic plan, but were working with detailed tactical plans of action devised on the spot by their commanding officers. This extremely flexible command doctrine in fact enabled Israeli troops to march forward without encountering substantial resistance.

Before looking in detail at how the war proceeded from the military viewpoint, it is important to outline the military potential on the two respective sides.[23] The Arab side went into the field with a certain complacency, assuming their superiority in numbers over the Israelis to be a clear military advantage. This corresponded to a widely held view among the public. Edgar O'Ballance, however, says that the Arab states at that time were able to mobilise approximately 300–400 000 soldiers, and the Israelis, despite their minority status in terms of numbers, some 270 000. On the battlefield, it is not only the number of soldiers that counts but above all the efficiency of the armed force in question, in particular the ability to handle modern technology properly. The military potential and equipment of the two parties to the war are worth looking at. Since the decisive phase took place in the air and lasted only half a day, our first remarks should focus on this aspect, followed by a brief description of the ground combat. The heavy stress laid here on the air battle does not imply the false notion that Egyptian ground troops failed solely on account of the absence of air protection.

The Israeli air force was equipped largely with French planes, although it also had some British and American equipment – helicopter surplus from the Korean War. Most of their planes were of the Mystère, Super Mystère and Mirage type. At that time, Israel was spending 50 per cent of its military budget on maintenance of its air force, then manned by a personnel of 8000, although this could be made up to 20 000 with additional mobilisation. The most significant data, however, concerns the number of pilots and fighter planes: Israel had 1200 pilots and 470 combat-ready planes. The most important military advantage of the Israelis was, and probably still is, the efficiency of its supplies and its combat-readiness.

In contrast, the Egyptian air force had as many professional personnel at its disposal as Israel had in times of mobilisation – 20 000, and virtually the same number of planes – 450. The latter, though, were for the most part Soviet MiGs (15s, 17s and 19s, TU-16s, IL 28s, SU7s, as well as the most modern MiG 21s). Taking into account that training for these planes was not very far advanced, Egypt in fact only had as many fully trained pilots as it had planes, while Israel had 1200 pilots for 470 planes. Another detrimental factor for the Egyptians was the low standard of supplies to the Egyptian air force. Since the Israelis were able to keep their air force at a level of 90 per cent combat-readiness at any time, having an average of three pilots to every plane, as well as a high standard of supplies to their weapons systems, they were in a position to make full use of their air force capacity. After refuelling or technical maintenance, for example, they could fly a plane with another pilot. There is little to be said about the Syrian, Jordanian and Iraqi air forces, since these were hardly employed at all in the case of Iraq, easily destroyed in the case of Jordan, or put out of action in the case of Syria. The Iraqi air force had mixed equipment, including British Hawker Hunters and then recent Soviet technological advances such as MiGs, totalling 220 planes. Syria had 120 MiGs, and Jordan only 22 planes of the Hawker Hunter type.

Actions carried out by Palestinian irregulars against Israeli settlements formed the background to the war. They came for the most part from Jordan and to a lesser extent from the Gaza Strip, at that time under Egyptian control. In February 1966, a radical faction of the Ba'th Party (Generals

Astassi, Jadid and Assad) came to power as a result of a coup. As usual, the rhetoric of the Palestinian question had been used as a central political platform to establish their legitimacy. The new Syrian leadership backed Palestinian actions, but from Jordanian rather than Syrian territory. This led to an intensive massing of Israeli troops on the Syrian border in May 1967. Meanwhile, the Ba'th and Nasser were competing for pan-Arab leadership. Seeking to reinforce his position, Nasser called on Rikhye, the Indian General in command of the UN peace-keeping force stationed on the Israeli–Egyptian border since 1956 with the consent of the two super-powers, to withdraw the blue-helmeted UN troops. He had clearly not thought through the possible consequences of such an action. Since Rikhye did not have authority to carry out such an order, the decision was passed to the UN Secretary-General, U Thant, who at first was not prepared to agree to Nasser's request. Instead, he asked the Israelis for permission to station a UN peace-keeping force on their territory. The Israelis refused.[24] On 17 May, the day before U Thant called for the withdrawal of the UN blue-helmeted troops, Egyptian troops replaced Indian and Yugoslav soldiers (50 per cent of the blue helmets) with the consent of Yugoslavia and India. Israelis and Egyptians were now positioned on the border with no peace-keeping force to act as a buffer between them. Nasser took the next step: he declared the Madiq Tiran – the straits in the Gulf of Aqaba – to be Egyptian territorial waters, closing the waterway to Israeli sea traffic. This effectively blocked the strategically crucial Israeli port of Elat. Egyptian troops then marched into Sinai. Syria and Egypt, previously enemies, entered into a military alliance, while even King Hussein of Jordan, also formerly an enemy of Egypt, was prepared for his troops to be under Egyptian command. Iraq declared its military solidarity and announced military operations, which in fact never took place – false reports were broadcast by Radio Baghdad.

All this set the perfect atmosphere for war. No one could have guessed that war was not Nasser's intention, or that he would go so far only for the sake of a bluff, but this is what he did. We now know, both from the way Egyptian troops were stationed, as well as from their state of readiness, that Nasser's primary aim was to make a political demonstration of his military potential so as to strengthen his pan-Arab legitimacy by means of a political victory (by obtaining sovereignty over the Madiq Tiran).[25] Michael Hudson regards the Palestinian question as the core issue for obtaining such legitimacy.[26] We know today (among other things from John Waterbury's seven-year fieldwork in Egypt[27]) that the Egyptian model was in a state of structural crisis even before the June war, although this was not yet apparent. Nasser's Egypt was furthermore undergoing a crisis of legitimacy.

Nasser calculated that Israel would accept the blocking of the Gulf of Aqaba as a *fait accompli*. If this proved not to be the case, he thought that the Israelis would make an attack on Sharm-al-Sheikh in the form of a tactically limited operation. He therefore stationed élite troops there under the command of General Shadhli. The Israelis for their part encouraged Nasser in this misconception by making regular and frequent reconnaissance flights over the Red Sea, as well as by feigning amphibious operations. Egypt was relying on its radar shield equipment in the event of an air attack. Nevertheless, it did have 150 Soviet SAM-2 surface-to-air missiles stationed on eighteen launchers (although under Soviet control). Nasser assured the then Secretary-General of the UN, U Thant, and Kosygin, the Soviet premier, that Egypt would not attack or start a war. Nasser was convinced that the Israelis could not fight on several fronts at the same time, thus ruling out the possibility of their making a first strike. The Egyptian–Syrian–Jordanian encirclement of Israel seemed perfect – sufficient deterrent for Israel not to venture an attack. Nasser read the military situation, therefore, as leading to an acceptance by Israel of a *fait accompli*, and at the very worst to a limited conflict that could be safely brought to an end by the UN Security Council with the support of the two superpowers (see note 25).

The concept of perception adopted from psychology by the discipline of International Relations, and which appears in the pioneering research of Robert Jervis,[28] is of crucial importance to a proper comprehension of the question at issue. It contributes towards an understanding of the tension between real political situations and the perception of them by the respective decision-makers. This framework helps to explain the consequences of misperception in a conflict situation such as the one here.

While the Israelis gambled just as much as Nasser did, they had the advantage of a more efficient army than the Egyptians, with a social structure that was more conducive to efficiency. Even under the radical Nasser, relations between officers and men in the Egyptian army resembled those between feudal overlords and their peasants. The Israeli army, on the other hand, has a democratic social organisation with none of the immense social gulf that hampered the Egyptian army in June 1967. This contrast was also to have repercussions on fighting morale among the troops. In addition, the Israeli armed forces had more modern arms than the Egyptians, and their personnel was better trained and more skilled in the use of modern technology. In the Israeli army, decisions are made on a rational, technical basis with specific functional goals in mind, not by political authorities. Thus although the Arab armies were modern in terms of military equipment, their organisation was incompetent. This fact was exacerbated by a high degree of politicisation, a process that advanced in the Arab armies at the expense of improving professional standards. The Syrian army may be mentioned here as exemplifying the lack of professionalism. Since coming into existence in the post-colonial era, it has made a name for itself as a *coup d'état* army.[29] Any government that comes to power through a coup is obliged to station its best and most loyal military personnel in the capital in order to protect itself against a counter-coup. In June 1967, a full third of the Syrian army was stationed in and around Damascus, and only a third on the Israeli border. The Egyptian army was, furthermore, completely devoid of intermilitary functional communication channels: the *rais* or President – Nasser himself with his closest associates – had to be laboriously informed of every single military action.[30] Nevertheless, he was not informed about the destruction of his air force. The entire structure of command was equally rigid and personalised, leaving no room at all for individual initiative or independent action. Fear of a coup lay at the root of all military maxims. When, therefore, on the morning of 5 June Nasser's closest associates were flying over Sinai with their 'Field Marshal' 'Amer, there was neither a single officer to issue orders, except for General Chief of Staff Fauzi, nor was there anyone to inform the *rais*, Nasser, of what had happened at the air force bases. In the third major country in the region, Jordan, there was not even a Ministry of Defence. In his book, *My War with Israel*, King Hussein informs us that he was completely and directly in charge of military action.[31] In Jordan, the military have not managed to transform the monarchy into a republic.[32] This personnel control is in fact the secret of King Hussein's political survival. To date he has survived all political crises in the region since coming to the throne in 1952.

In terms of both military strategy and operations the Israelis had their tactics well thought out. Although they were also taking an enormous risk, it cannot be compared with the risk Nasser was taking in expelling a UN peace-keeping force and closing the Gulf of Aqaba on the one hand, and being on the other hand inadequately prepared for military engagement (there were some 50 000 Egyptian troops still in Yemen) that he naively believed would never take place. There are reasons for comparing this behaviour with that of Saddam Hussein before 17 January 1991.

Contrary to the expectations of the Egyptian military, the Israelis left all Egyptian radar installations completely undisturbed.[33] During the first air attacks on 5 June, Israeli planes flew so low that they did not even appear on the Egyptian radar screens. At 7.45 am, Israeli radio reported that Egyptian troops had crossed their border and initiated hostilities. At that time, in fact, very low-flying Mystère planes that could not be picked up on radar, in a total of ten staggered groups of four, were taking off from a number of air force bases in Israel and flying in a westerly direction over the Mediterranean before veering off towards Egypt. Forty high-flying Mirages provided a fighter escort. The low-flying aircraft gained height shortly before reaching their targets, with only a few minutes available in which to circle them three times before flying back to base. As the Israeli planes gained height shortly before their destination, thus appearing on Egyptian radar screens, Egyptian pilots who were present and ready for action just had time to hurry to their planes. The Israelis gave them just enough time to do this before destroying them with their crews. Two out of the three approach runs were used to shoot down Egyptian planes with their pilots, and the third to bomb the runway. The forty Mystères flew back to base after ten minutes and were immediately replaced by a further forty Israeli planes.

In this way, during the eighty minutes between 7.45 and 9.05 am, forty Israeli Mystère planes at a time made a total of eight air attacks on seventeen Egyptian air bases to the west and south of Cairo, in the Delta and on the Suez Canal, dealing a crushing blow to the Egyptian air force. The success of the operation exceeded even Israeli expectations. They interrupted the operation for only ten minutes, on the assumption that the Egyptians would deploy their bombers stationed to the south of Cairo and outside the range of the Israeli air force. At that time, Egypt had twenty-five air bases, of which only seventeen were close enough to be put out of action by the Israelis. The bomber attack that they expected did not materialise, however, because 'Field Marshal' 'Amer and his commanders were at that very moment flying over Sinai in their Ilyushin 14. The Israelis resumed their air attacks after 9.15 am, once again with forty Mystères for each ten-minute attack, to be replaced by a second echelon, again shielded by a high-flying Mirage fighter escort. By 10.35, the seventeen accessible Egyptian air force bases out of the total of twenty-five had been put out of action: 300 Egyptian planes had been destroyed either on the ground or in aerial combat, and 100 pilots killed. The Israelis reported ten planes as missing, but had in fact lost nineteen Mystères, which was still a low number compared with Egyptian losses.

It became clear during combat itself that few of the fully trained Egyptian pilots were on the alert, and that the ability of the air force as a whole to react to an alert was very limited indeed. Military experts were astonished to learn that the Egyptians had their planes lined up close together, 'ready for inspection', which made it very easy for the Israelis to destroy them on the ground. Although the Egyptians used their SAM missiles, the

Israelis flew too low and fast to be hit by them. They flew a total of 240 sorties from 7.45 am to 10.35, including those of their Mirage flying escorts. Not even Nasser was informed of the results of this first lightning attack until four in the afternoon or later (reports vary: see notes 17 and 19). The Arab estimation of the overall situation was based on the assumption that Israel could not fight on several fronts at once. The Israelis, on the other hand, assumed that the Arabs would not attack in a single coordinated action. Nevertheless, they did not leave anything to chance. Their secret service, electronic deception and the broadcasting of false reports all contributed to their victory. Little is known about the electronic deception involved, since neither the Israelis nor the Arabs have published any details about it. It is known, however, that the Israelis faked a message from 'Field Marshal' 'Amer to King Hussein, whose armed forces were under the command of the Egyptian General Riad, asking the king to refrain from an immediate attack. During the decisive air battle from 7.45 to 10.35 am, therefore, all was quiet on the Israeli–Jordanian border.

The Israelis duped the Arabs with false reports, even irritating the military with the deployment of electronically controlled equipment. The fact remains, however, that the Arabs also duped themselves. Although the Egyptian air force had already been effectively put out of action by 10.35 on the morning of the first day of the war, the Egyptians reported that they had shot down 160 hostile Israeli planes. The Iraqis even went so far as to assert that their air force had bombarded Tel Aviv, when in fact not one of their 220 planes had engaged in combat up to that point. False reports of Egyptian success in turn encouraged King Hussein to launch an attack on Israel. By now he suspected that the message he had received from 'Amer via the Israeli secret service was a false one. The Jordanian air force had only sixteen trained pilots for their twenty-two Hawker Hunter planes. During the course of the morning, they were all put into action against Israeli targets, returning unharmed from their first mission at 11.30. After 10.35, the Israeli air force flew further attack missions against Egypt. Around midday, however, the Israeli Mirages were deployed to attack the two Jordanian air force bases in Amman and Mafraq. All twenty-two of the Jordanian planes were destroyed while being refuelled or during maintenance work. King Hussein had initially wanted to engage his air force in a combined Syrian–Jordanian action. However, the Syrians were not willing to cooperate in a coordinated action with their enemy Hussein. Whenever they were asked by the king – as he himself tells us[34] – they requested a thirty-minute delay, as their planes were apparently not in combat-readiness. The king decided to act unilaterally, only to lose his air force in a single Israeli retaliation – the Jordanian planes were completely destroyed in a bombardment lasting twenty minutes. The Israelis were able to attack Mafraq and Amman for such a long stretch because the flight time is shorter than to Egypt, thus lengthening the span between refuellings. It was 11.45 before the Syrians attacked Israel with twelve MiG 21s in a completely uncoordinated action that sent the Haifa oil refinery up in flames. The Israeli air force retaliated with an attack at 12.45, bombing the two air force bases at Damascus and Marg-Rial, south of the Syrian capital, again destroying a major part of the Syrian air force on the ground. On the first day of the conflict, therefore, the Israelis managed either to cripple or put completely out of action the Egyptian, Syrian and Jordanian air forces. A single Iraqi TU 16 bomber bombed Nathanya on the second day of the conflict, and was shot down by the Israelis on its return flight. This was the only active Iraqi involvement in the war: thereafter the Iraqis did not engage in any more air combat, thus preserving their air force. The Israelis were unable to attack Iraqi air force bases, which at that time were outside their range.

The ground war during the remaining five days of the war was a military catastrophe. Having separated Egyptian troops in the Sinai using electronic deception, the Israelis bombarded them with napalm. General Murtagi, Egyptian commander of the Sinai troops, assumed from the unabated air attack on his troops that the Egyptian air force was out of action. Seeing that his ground forces were outflanked and about to be encircled, he decided to put all the means remaining at his disposal into a concerted effort to escape encirclement. He lost contact with his troops on the second day. The Egyptian army had in fact effectively lost its strategic coherence on the first day after the capture of al-Arish. On the third day, the communications system of the entire Egyptian ground forces broke down. Presumably the Israelis contributed to this through technical manipulation. Many Egyptian soldiers, abandoning their tanks and weapons arsenals to escape napalm bombing, and scattering randomly in the desert, lost their lives. Two-thirds of all wounded Egyptian soldiers were suffering from napalm burns.[35]

The Egyptian troops had no option but to capitulate or try to break out. Choosing the latter, they attempted to retrieve part of their weapons arsenal. This move resulted in one of the greatest tank battles in history, involving a thousand tanks on each side. The Egyptians tried to move their tanks across the Suez Canal to the West Bank, while the Israelis tried, not entirely successfully, to prevent them: the Egyptians managed to run a hundred tanks across the canal. O'Ballance, who reserves most of his praise for the Israelis, cannot help admiring the Egyptians for managing to put up such a fight in this tank battle, in the absence of both communications systems and coordinated command authority. On the fourth day, by which time the

Israelis had reached the canal zone, they agreed to the ceasefire call by the UN Security Council which had already been accepted by Egypt.

Following the bombing of Jordanian air force bases the Israelis went on to capture the Old Quarter of Jerusalem, as well as the entire West Bank, where they established full control by the third day of the war. The Iraqis deployed a battalion to Jordan, but it was shot out of the air and put out of action on the first day. Aside from propaganda broadcasts, the Iraqi contribution to the war was restricted to this battalion and the TU-16 bomber incident mentioned above.

After Israeli air attacks on Syrian air force bases the Syrian border remained quiet at first. On the third day of the war, however, Syria sent an infantry brigade to Jordan that penetrated about five miles into the Jordanian interior. However, the Syrians refused to put this brigade under the command of the Egyptian General Riad, who was also in command of the Jordanian army. The infantry brigade therefore returned to Syria on the fourth day of the war without having engaged in the fighting. On the sixth day – by which time Israel had captured the Gaza Strip, the Sinai desert as far as Sharm al-Sheikh in the south-west, and the West Bank including Jerusalem in the east – the Israelis made an air-supported attack on Syrian positions that had hitherto remained quiet. The remnant of the Syrian air force was not engaged, so that Israeli soldiers were able to advance unhindered on the Syrian army while their air force dropped napalm on Syrian positions. As a result of its positions and its concentration on domestic political disputes, the Syrian army had not been fit for combat with Israel for a long time. While the Israeli secret service had been collecting intelligence on Arab armies and developing methods for duping them, the primary task of the Syrian secret service had been to monitor domestic opposition and spy on Syria's own army with a view to rooting out possible subversives. The Syrians paid a heavy price for this with their military defeat in the Six Day War, whose repercussions went far beyond the military sphere, as we shall be seeing in Chapter 4.

4 The Regional and International Repercussions of the Six Day War: The End of Nasserism and the Beginning of a New Historical Epoch

Like other major wars in world history (see Introduction), the Six Day War was more than a military event: it changed the Middle East irrevocably, even shifting its boundaries. Israel expanded, triggering another wave of refugees like that of 1948.[1] Not only the geography, but also the demography of the region took on new dimensions. Although some 200 000 people fled from the Israeli occupied territories, a sizeable Arab population remained and has proved more difficult for Israel to control than the military success of the blitzkrieg was to achieve. Egypt, on the other hand, the political centre of the Middle East regional subsystem, was in a state of collapse, not only militarily but also economically, thereby losing its claim to Arab leadership. Its political system, regarded as exemplary for pan-Arab superiority during the 1950s and 1960s, forfeited its legitimacy in the aftermath of the Six Day War. The Arab sheiks of the rich oil states in the Gulf, who had felt threatened by Egypt even before the Yemeni War, now after the Israeli blitzkrieg, stepped courageously out of their palaces and acted the part of magnanimous benefactors to the defeated. Obviously they did not do this without expecting something in return. The defeat of June 1967 not only changed the map of the Middle East, but also upset the established structures of the subsystem. It must be conceded, however, that the recent Gulf War, which has been the most crucial event in the Middle East since the First World War, will induce greater changes from its repercussions than the 1967 June War ever did.

Not even the standing of the superpowers in the Middle East remained untouched by the outcome of the 1967 war. First, the Soviet Union saw to it that Egypt was rearmed. Egyptian tanks of Soviet origin, intended not for desert combat, but for potential conflicts in Central Europe, had failed

80

in the Middle East war, and not only on account of the obvious multifarious incompetence of the Egyptian military. Confidence in the Soviet Union was shaken, and the USA saw an opportunity to make its presence more actively felt in the region. Israel had proved to be the more capable ally, and since then has been viewed as a strategic asset for the USA in the area.[2] The Six Day War thus heralded a decline in Soviet influence in the region that went hand in hand with an expansion of the American presence – a process that was to continue with the repercussions of the October War in 1973 and reach its zenith in the recent Gulf War. Let us now take a closer look at the regional and international aftermath of the 1967 war, the traces of which continue to shape both the Middle East subsystem itself and its potential for conflict. The Gulf War of 1991 cannot be understood properly without bearing in mind the regional changes induced by the 1967 war.

THE MIDDLE EAST SINCE 1967: DEFEAT AND ARAB SELF-CRITICISM, THE DECLINE OF NASSERISM AND THE RISE OF 'POLITICAL PETROLISM'

As we have seen, the Moroccan historian Abdallah Laroui[3] attributes such enormous importance to historical developments since the Six Day War that they in his view constitute one of the four main phases of Arab history since 1850. His period categories begin in 1850 with the rise of the European colonial challenge to the structurally backward Middle East – the historical phase of renaissance (*nahda*) lasting until the turn of this century – in which the Arabs tried to combine their own traditional culture with adoptions from Europe, primarily modern European science. The second historical epoch began after the First World War, taking the form of an Arab struggle for independence (the period of decolonisation). By the 1950s, the majority of Arab states had achieved national sovereignty, although the newly established nation-states were still contained within colonially drawn boundaries.[4] It was for this reason that pan-Arabism – as a response to this colonial legacy – formed the characteristic feature of the third historical phase, which in Laroui's view came to an end with the crushing defeat of the Six Day War. He describes the fourth epoch since June 1967 as a crisis that has persisted to the present day. This crisis forms, in my view, the structural and historical background to the Gulf events of 1990–91.

The discord arose out of disappointed hopes and shattered illusions, finding full expression in self-criticism. In my own writings in Arabic and German I have described this phase using the expression 'From Self-glorification to Self-criticism'.[5] By then, even uneducated Arabs grasped that they had been deceived and drawn into this situation by the propaganda lies of their political leaders. For educated Arabs, the printed word provided a means of coming to terms intellectually with the situation in which they found themselves. Among the many books and articles that appeared at that time, the repeatedly reprinted work of the Damascene philosopher Sadiq Jalal al-'Azm, *Self-criticism After the Defeat*, remains outstanding.[6] Al-'Azm calls on his Arab readers to realise that politics is different from Arab poetry, in which one finds only the two extremes of disparagement (*dham*) or praise (*madih*), a bedouin practice that dominates the Arab culture. Even Nasser, who saw himself as a modernist, took on a bedouin way of thinking in his statements after the defeat: Egyptian soldiers had not had the chance to show their valour, because the Israelis had not confronted them face to face as courageous men do, but attacked them from the air.[7]

Nasser had clearly not grasped that the days of chivalrous duels between knights were over, as al-'Azm rightly comments. He also calls on Arabs to take responsibility for themselves in critical situations, instead of laying the blame for their failures at other people's doors.[8] As in previous cases, so too the 1967 defeat was attributed to conspiring 'external forces', this time using the erroneous argument that the Americans and British had supported the Israelis during the air battles. This conspiracy approach helped to divert attention from the Arabs' own shortcomings. Nasser issued a public statement after the defeat: 'We were expecting them to come from the south-east (i.e. from Sharm al-Sheikh), but they came from the north.' Alert, quick-thinking journalists were not alone in being astounded by this. Even though most Arabs subscribe to the conspiracy approach, Nasser's credibility had now gone for ever. After June 1967 he was no longer the hero who personified their hopes. Under different circumstances, a new hero, Saddam Hussein, a man of much lower calibre, had to go through a similar experience on an international scale.

Nasserism was the principal victim[9] of the Six Day War that heralded a new epoch in Arab history. In his internationally acclaimed book, Fouad Ajami calls this new phase the 'Arab predicament'. He writes:

Yesterday's radicals – the Ba'th Party and President Nasser – were the principal victims of the defeat: whereas they once had stood for revolt against an older, more traditional, more compromised leadership, they themselves were now on trial. A younger generation was to see, in the full light of the defeat, the shortcomings of that brand of radical nationalism that had held sway from the early 1950s up to 1967.[10]

Whether Saddam's defeat in the recent Gulf War may pave the way for the emergence of a self-critical younger generation remains to be seen, although it is highly doubtful.

In my own quarter century of work studying Arab writings from the *nahda* era onwards, I have not encountered a single historical period in which so much literature was written, published in Arabic and discussed as in the few years from 1967 to 1970. Many of those actively involved in this process, the author included,[11] were convinced that this phase of 'self-criticism after the defeat', this transformation from self-glorification to self-criticism, would bring disillusionment in its wake. Some Arab officers did write works at that time dealing in the same old jargon with the military dimension of pan-Arabism and the 'Zionist conspiracy' against the Arab nation. These included, for example, Ammash, an Iraqi, and Kaylani, a Syrian.[12] By then, however, the time for this kind of old rhetoric seemed to have passed. Ajami rightly points out that the Arab mania for rhetoric in literature and politics was one of the central objects for criticism and self-criticism in the post-June 1967 period.[13] Regrettably, this productive manner of self-criticism did not take root. The re-emergence of Arab rhetoric during the Gulf crisis and war was not reassuring in this respect.

So far, our remarks have been confined to the intellectual and cultural atmosphere created by the June 1967 defeat. Let us turn now to look more closely at the political changes involved. Arab political systems, designated after the war as *anzimat al-hazima* ('regimes of defeat'), were initially shaken and thus insecure, taking refuge in self-justification in the time-honoured manner, and seeking to lay blame at the door both of domestic traitors (officers) and above all conspiring enemies of the Arabs abroad (imperialism and Zionism).[14] The oil-producing Arab states were not affected by this: they were beyond the vagaries of the 'third battle' and had lost none of their zest for taking the initiative. In the same year as the defeat, an Arab summit conference was held in Khartoum (August–September 1967), resulting in a degree of rapprochement between the 'radical' and 'conservative' Arab nation-states. Saudi Arabia, the Gulf sheikdoms and Libya, at that time still a kingdom, offered Egypt petro-dollars in return for political concessions. The first of these was the withdrawal of Egyptian troops from Yemen, and hence an end to the war there between royalists and republicans. Since that time, Saudi Arabia has emerged as a hegemonic power.[15]

This general political transformation also touched the Cairo-based Arab League, which had been active both in the Yemeni war from 1962 to 1967 and in many other inter-Arab conflicts. Prior to June 1967, the Arab League had also been a major instrument in Nasser's pan-Arab policy.[16] Founded in

1945,[17] this regional organisation continued to exist in Cairo after June 1967, and Egyptian authors writing for the influential journal *al-Siyasa al-Duwaliyya* ('World Politics') still insist that the 'Arab League constitutes the appropriate framework for all joint Arab action'.[18] In reality, however, since the fourth Arab summit of Khartoum the Arab League has been superseded by the semi-formal institution of the Arab summit. Butrus Ghali, by then Professor of International Politics and until his appointment as UN General Secretary Minister in the Egyptian Ministry of Foreign Affairs, recognised as early as 1970 that subregional units within the Arab League – namely, Iraq and former Greater Syria; Egypt, Sudan and Libya; the Arabian peninsula; and the Maghreb states – offer far more secure structures for the formation of alliances.[19] Two years after Nasser's death, the Arab League was no longer an important forum for major pan-Arab announcements.

The day-to-day work of the League was by now concerned with specific, functional subunits of a non-political nature, for example, postal services, transport, health, etc.[20] Major issues were now discussed at Arab summit conferences,[21] which, in view of the formation of sub-bloks and the fragmentation of the Middle East subsystem, could be obstructed at will by the deliberate absence of certain heads of state. The moving of Arab League headquarters from Cairo to Tunis in 1979, more than a decade after the Six Day War, marked the definitive loss of its political pre-eminence. The return of the League to Cairo in September 1990 did not change this situation. The Arab League has split into rival factions; the last Arab summit at Cairo, held in August 1990, not only revealed the great fragmentation of the Arab states system but also proved to be a fiasco.

The Arab part of the Middle Eastern international regional subsystem has consequently been without a political centre since 1967. Until the emergence of Saddam's Iraq, none of the other Arab states seemed to be structurally strong enough to bear the burden of being a regional power. The dominance of Nasser's Egypt in the Arab region was not merely a claim, nor was it based solely on the pan-Arab ideology. Structurally, Egypt is the strongest and most developed country in the region, with the largest Arab population and, relatively speaking, the most developed structures in the spheres of education, communications, transport and the military.[22] Lastly, Egypt is the cultural centre of the Arab Orient: Ajami calls it the mirror of the whole region.[23] Nasser's claim to leadership had had structural underpinning. When in September 1969 one of Nasser's followers, Qadhafi, toppled the monarchy in Libya, attempting quixotically after Nasser's death to take over his role in the Middle East, he was bound to fail. This was not only because Qadhafi[24] lacked Nasser's charisma, but above all because

Libya lacked the overall capabilities as structural prerequisites for such an assertion to superiority.

Although Nasser never officially relinquished his claim to leadership between 1967 and his death in 1970, in real terms he no longer wielded the necessary authority. The propaganda radio station *Saut al-'Arab* ('Voice of the Arabs') was shut down; Egyptian troops were withdrawn from Yemen, and all infiltration activities in royalist Arab countries were halted. In place of Nasser's Egypt as the centre of pan-Arabism, Arab multilateralism now came to the fore, displaying a number of pragmatic variants of local nationalism. Tareq Ismael, who in his work also has recourse to the theory of the regional subsystem in the conceptualisation of political events in the Middle East since 1967, speaks of a 'fragmentation of the . . . system'. According to this view, the region has become more vulnerable to penetration by foreign powers, notably the superpowers, since the loss of its subsystem centre.[25] We shall be looking at this fragmentation in more detail in the final chapter, in the context of the Iraqi claim to assume Arab leadership.

For the time being the important thing to note is how this fragmentation came about. Robert Springborg has an apt way of expressing the process: 'The new pragmatism, realism, conservatism, or whatever label one chooses to apply to recent trends of thought and action in the Arab World, is a result in part of the Arabs' newly discovered wealth.'[26] Springborg has in mind the power of Arab petro-dollars, since the pan-Arab social revolutionary vision was effectively dead and buried after the Arab summit conference of Khartoum in the year of the defeat. Its place was taken by the pragmatism of the Arab petro-dollar sheiks, that are the bedouins of the Arabian desert who became rich through their oil revenues. Hassan Abu-Talib describes this process many years later: 'New centres of power and political leadership developed in the Arab region. Oil wealth offered an alternative to the idea of pan-Arabism . . . The conservative state . . . prevailed, now dominant on the Arab scene . . . This tendency has become clear since the Khartoum summit of 1967.'[27] These new centres proved too weak, however, to reverse the process of fragmentation at work within the subsystem. The efforts of the Iraqi dictator Saddam Hussein to overcome this by establishing Iraqi leadership had the opposite effect: it contributed to a degree of fragmentation never witnessed before in Arab politics.

The question now arises as to whether Bahgat Korany's term 'political petrolism'[28] was the fruit of Arab 'self-criticism after the defeat'. At the very least this was not the intention of enlightened and well-informed Arab intellectuals in their books and articles in the period from 1967 to 1970. For all Nasser's faults, one can scarcely ignore the fact that the replacement of the political leadership of Egypt – a highly developed centre both culturally and structurally (at least by the standards of the region) – by that of Arab desert bedouins can only spell political decline. Some years ago, I raised the question of whether there had been a transition in the region 'from centre of revolution to petro-dollar centre'.[29] The answer to this is not so simple, but may be examined here in the light of more advanced research than was possible in 1984. In a 1980 issue of the journal *al-Siyasa al-Duwaliyya* devoted to this theme (published by the al-Ahram Centre for Political and Strategic Studies), El-Sayed Yassin, by then director of this institute, makes the distinction that in spite of a manifest shift of power in the region one cannot speak of a transition from an 'Egyptian to a Saudi epoch'. Although Saudi Arabia has played a central role (since June 1967) 'one cannot therefore assume that Egypt has lost its importance in relation to Saudi Arabia'.[30] Yassin's argument is that Saudi Arabia is unable to constitute a regional centre on account of its poorly developed capacities. Cheque-book diplomacy is in fact the only instrument at the disposal of Saudi Arabian foreign policy. It is unable to wield either military or economic power effectively enough to achieve its ends. Turner and Bedore have called the Saudi strategy a 'policy of purse-strings'.[31]

The dominance of the 'petro-purse' in the Middle Eastern regional system dates from post-June 1967 developments, and was given another major boost with the 1973 October War (see Chapter 7), when crude oil prices rose so dramatically that Saudi cheque-book diplomacy reached an all-time high. Since 1967, Egypt had been dependent on Saudi and Kuwaiti contributions. Prior to June 1967, from the stance of his pan-Arab premises, Nasser had regarded oil wealth as common Arab property and had ensued the consequences. The tables were to turn on him in his own lifetime, however. After the defeat, the rich Arab nations were being asked to invest in the poor Arab countries, including Egypt, and not only in Europe and America.[32] In the 1980s Saddam Hussein used his country's oil wealth to support his leadership. The recourse to the formula 'poor Arabs against rich sheiks' during the Gulf War served only as an ideological tool. Iraq was a rich Arab nation, not a poor one.

To be carried out successfully, any policy needs both an economic base and a competent political leadership equipped with legitimacy. In international relations, military might is another major factor without which no state can carry any weight outside its own borders. After the June defeat, Egypt was powerless to meet any of these preconditions.

Besides resistance to the dominance of the oppressive intelligence services under Nasser (the oppressor Sarraj was Minister of the Interior), Egyptian nationalisation policy of July 1961 was another major cause of Syria's secession from the United Arab Republic (UAR) in September

1961. Nasser's riposte to this was to pursue an even more radical policy, since in his view 'Arab political reactionaries' had been at the root of that particular 'conspiracy' against the UAR. Specifically, he pressed forward with even more intensive nationalisation, resulting in an integration of Egyptian industry and agriculture in a state sector run by Egyptian officer-managers in civilian guise.[33] This 'public sector' was in deep crisis by the time of the Six Day War. In Waterbury's view, far from bringing about a rise in productivity, it contributed to a massive decline. The effects of this hit hard in a country like Egypt, whose population increases by an average of 3 per cent annually, since only a discernible increase in production can cope with this yearly population growth of over a million. In his now standard work on the subject, already quoted above, Waterbury describes the crisis in the public sector as follows:

> The crisis that overtook Egypt in 1965–66 was first felt in 1964 and was exacerbated, but not caused, by Egypt's military defeat in 1967. It was also not caused by MNCs pumping Egypt's foreign exchange reserves dry through remitted profits, nor by deteriorating terms of international trade, nor by the unchecked consumption of luxury imports for the middle classes, nor, finally by the international capitalist banking community. It was caused by the gross inefficiencies of a public sector called upon to do too many things: sell products at cost or at a loss, take on labor unrelated to production needs, earn foreign exchange, and satisfy local demand. It was also caused by the neglect of the traditional agricultural sector which, while taxed, was not reformed so as to become an engine of growth in its own right.[34]

It was against the background of a lamentable economic situation that Egypt escalated its conflict with Israel, apparently oblivious of the fact that a war could really break out for which it was totally unprepared. The training of its officers lagged behind the technological standard of their equipment, while the combat-readiness of its armed forces was minimal. As if this were not enough, 50 000 Egyptian soldiers were still deployed in Yemen. It was this economically weakened Egypt which then had to face the further setback of the (80 per cent) loss of its military arsenal and the best-trained members of its armed forces – the pilots killed in the conflict. After June 1967, Egypt even lost its income from the Suez Canal, which was closed on Nasser's orders as a result of the sinking of ships during the war. Nasser wanted to ensure that the Israelis would not be able to use the canal for their own shipping in the aftermath of the war.

Against this backdrop, Nasser departed for Khartoum to negotiate with other Arab heads of state, above all the Saudis. The Saudi King Faisal and President Nasser were long-standing enemies. It was therefore a severe humiliation to the latter to have to offer the Saudi king the withdrawal of his troops from Yemen in return for petro-dollars, but he had no choice. Faisal met Nasser halfway, although without relinquishing his sceptical view of him.[35] Egypt stopped broadcasting radio propaganda against Saudi Arabia and withdrew its troops from Yemen. This did not result in amiable cooperation between Egypt and Saudi Arabia, however. It was not until after Nasser's death, under President Sadat, that a Saudi–Egyptian axis came about that was to persist from 1973 until Sadat's visit to Jerusalem in 1977.

Since 1965, a monthly periodical, the *al-Tali'a* ('The Avant-garde'), had been appearing in Cairo. It was the mouthpiece of the leftist Nasserist wing of the then state party, the Arab Socialist Union, the ASU,[36] and a protégé of Nasser's. Under President Sadat, its publication was stopped in 1974, and the ASU itself was later disbanded.[37]

Since President Mubarak's pursuit of a more liberal policy, *al-Tali'a* has been published again since May 1984. One of the first of these more recent issues focused on the theme of 'The Saudi Monarchy, a Financial Power'.[38] The editorial itself points out that Egypt and Saudi Arabia have always constituted 'two mutually exclusive models for the other Arab states to follow'.[39] The relevant articles in this thematic issue draw attention to the tension between these two rival models of development, which were both already in existence in the last century. In the first half of the nineteenth century, starting in 1805, Egypt under Muhammad Ali introduced a programme of modernisation from above – that is by the state – similar to the one being introduced in Prussia. Its aim was to bring the country in line with Europe. The Arabian peninsula, not yet Saudi, was at that time the home of the Wahhabi movement, which was pursuing diametrically opposed goals. Muhammad Abdul Wahhab preached that all modernisation was the work of the devil, being *bid'a*, 'innovation', i.e. deviation from Islam. The Ottomans were unable to bring the Wahhabis under control, as they were allied with the Saudi prince of the Nejd through marriage. It was only with the aid of the reformed modern Egyptian troops of Muhammad Ali that they were able after a lengthy war (1811–18) to put down the Saudi–Wahhabi 'fighters of God'.[40]

The mutually exclusive models of archaic Wahhabism and the state modernism of Muhammad Ali are seen in the *al-Tali'a* articles as analogous with the tension between Nasserism and the political Islam of the Saudis. Nasser's ideology was one of Arab solidarity, *al-tadamun al-'arabi*, while Saudi monarchists call Arabs to religious solidarity, *al-tadamun al-Islami*. While Nasser linked pan-Arabism with modernisation and emancipation, the Saudis offered the alternative of an archaic, politicised Islam and alliance with the West. The rise of the Saudis in the Middle East, in the period since June 1967, has been linked with efforts to fill the vacuum left by 'the end of pan-Arabism' (Ajami) with political Islam. Ajami calls June 1967 the 'Waterloo of pan-Arabism'.[41] The question remains, however, why pan-Arab rhetoric was not replaced by the hoped-for enlightened visions of the future. This, after all, had been what 'self-criticism after the defeat' had aimed for. Informed Arab political writers such as Sadiq Jalal al-'Azm did not criticise Nasser in a spirit of enmity. Nasser's model of a modern, secular pan-Arab society free from the influence of external powers and underdevelopment remained undisputed, and it had been in this sense that Nasserism had embodied all aspirations in the region before June 1967.

Criticism of Nasser was not directed at his model as such, but at his unfulfilled promises. Lacouture, Middle East correspondent of *Le Monde*, correctly explains the link between the two when he writes that Nasserism was not only a hope but also an illusion: 'the role of illusion was great because the means did not really fit the ends . . . It was an era of eloquence . . . It can perhaps be summed up as a time of poetry, and it must be said that poetry and politics do always have very close relations, and poetry can lead to political difficulties and disappointments.'[42] But who has taken Nasser's place now as political poet in Arab politics? Certainly not clever statesmen who could steer the region on to a better course. Lacouture expresses the transition fluently and cogently: '·the orator has given way to the manager, the banker . . . Egypt is outclassed by massive oil producers . . . the time of the Canal is past and the day of the Gulf has dawned.'[43] Recently, an Arab orator attempted, to no avail, to establish a Gulf variety of Nasserism. Indeed, Saddamism has proved to be a farce of Nasserism, the latter having been a tragedy.

To sum up the regional repercussions of the Six Day War: the former regional centre of Egypt was weakened on all levels and pushed into the background in favour of the Arab oil-producing states, including Iraq. The latter are none the less too backward to be able to take on the role of geostrategic and political leadership, let alone offer a model for development. During the 1980s, several Arab states laid claim to replace Egypt's leadership. Chief among these were Syria, Algeria, Iraq and Libya. Saudi Arabia has never voiced a claim to leadership, although it is *de facto* the principal state actor in the region since June 1967. The central issue for Saudi Arabia has always been to ensure its own security. Its foreign policy, therefore, does not aim at leadership, but rather at the pursuit of a 'policy of crisis containment in the region'.[44] Contrary to this is the politics of Iraq: The effort pursued by Iraq to annex Kuwait and thereby build up an economic basis for an Iraqi-led region led to the Gulf War and to the disaster connected with it.

Aside from the overthrow of the monarchy in Libya, and other coups in Syria, Iraq and Sudan, the rise of the Palestinians to become an independent political force marks one of the most important changes in the region since June 1967. The Palestinians, whose refugee numbers rose by more than 200 000 after the Israeli occupation of the Gaza Strip and the West Bank, felt betrayed by the other Arab nations, and claimed the right to represent themselves, whereas up to that point Arab states had acted as their custodians on both regional and international levels. Palestinian writers, including 'Allush, Hawatima and Shafiq,[45] all belonging to different wings of the Palestinian nationalist movement,[46] now wrote proclaiming the right of the Palestinians to speak for themselves. Naji 'Allush, whose book gives voice to all the various positions within the Palestinian resistance movement,[47] makes it plain that the discrete existence of a Palestinian nation separate from the other Arab states is the common denominator in the goals of all these factions. Writing about Palestinian guerrillas, the Norwegian researcher Daniel Heradstveit explains in his monograph: 'The June War forged new paths for the Palestinian Arabs in the struggle against Israel. It was now clear to them that they would have to conduct this struggle themselves, and that the Arab governments could not be relied upon.'[48] It was more out of fear of them than love for them that the oil-producing Arab states made sure to purchase peace from the leading Palestinian organisations within the PLO. It should be remembered that there are substantial Palestinian minorities in all the oil-producing Arab states – all potentially capable of being engaged in terrorist action against oil installations. After 1967, therefore, the PLO rose to become both a significant economic and political factor in the politics of the region, despite the modesty of its military strength – as was to become all too apparent during the Israeli invasion of Lebanon. First, the PLO built up a base in Jordan. However, in a horrendous civil war,[49] King Hussein forced the Palestinians in September 1970 to re-establish their bases outside that country. Lebanon was to become the next Palestinian diaspora for the PLO, but in 1982 they were also deprived of this base. They had to leave it after the Israeli invasion. In 1990–91, they suffered a regression from the autonomy they had won through hard work. Their submission to another self-acclaimed Arab hero, Saddam Hussein, has amounted to a major setback for their cause.

After June 1967, the Soviet Union had directly re-armed Egypt, while the USA was providing Israel with massive arms supplies. By 1971 Egypt had 450 MiG planes, 100 warships, 1350 tanks and an unknown number of SAM missiles stationed on many launchers. This process of rearmament had been accompanied and supervised by 20 000 Soviet military instructors. Since pilots cannot be trained overnight, the Soviet Union had also placed some 200 Soviet pilots at the disposal of the Egyptian air force,[50] although they were not involved in the 'War of Attrition'. This war was both highly costly and incurred heavy losses, since after every gun battle on the border the Israelis undertook retaliations through bombing raids. After a turbulent year (Nasser's acceptance of the US Rogers Plan, and Palestinian rejection of it), including the civil war in Jordan (Black September), Nasser died of a heart attack on 28 September 1970.

The scholarly journal *Asian Affairs* asked a number of Middle East experts to write a page each about Nasser, all of which were published under the title 'Nasser and After'. The most telling comment was to come from Geoffrey Furlonge, who suspected that Nasser would 'be denied the title of greatness on account of his failures . . . but it will nevertheless be recognised that he changed the Middle East more than anyone since Muhammad Ali'.[51] Reviled between 1967 and 1970, Nasser none the less took his place in Arab mythology after his death, as can be seen from the thirty articles contained in a special issue of the *Qadaya 'Arabiyya* journal (Beirut) edited by the great Arab historian Anis Sayigh.[52] This special issue bore the title *Abdul Nasser: wa ma ba'd* – the Arabic equivalent of 'Nasser and After'. But the mystification of the dead cannot obscure the fact that his death marked the definitive end of a historical epoch. The efforts of a low quality pan-Arab leader, Saddam Hussein, to emulate Nasser by reviving pan-Arab dreams in the guise of military expansion ended in disaster. Saddam ignored the historical facts pointing to the irreversible end of a historical epoch.

THE FORMER GREAT POWERS AND THE NEW SUPERPOWERS IN THE REGION: THE INTERNATIONAL REPERCUSSIONS OF THE JUNE WAR

Among the repeated themes raised in Nasser's speeches and statements was his emphasis on the central goal of his 'revolution': to minimise and oppose foreign influences in Egypt and all non-aligned countries. He reiterated this foreign policy orientation in a UN address on 27 September 1960.[53] Clearly, it was not Nasser's intention to provoke through his own policy exactly what he expressly claimed to be combating. However, the Suez War did result in increased penetration of the Middle East subsystem, a trend stepped up to an even greater extent in the aftermath of the Six Day War. Nasser hoped in June 1967 to emerge as political and diplomatic victor without having to wage a war, as he had succeeded in doing after Suez in 1956. The recent Gulf War provides a comparable experience. Saddam wanted to invade Kuwait to enhance the economic basis for a regional leadership under Iraqi hegemony. As a result he recast the region into an international theatre of war. Chapter 3, in a reference to the research of Robert Jervis, pointed out the tension between perception and reality, which often diverge substantially. Political decisions made under such tension can lead to serious conflicts. The former great powers, for example, misread the nature of the changed world situation both before and after the Suez crisis. The gulf between perception and reality is a psychological problematique that may also be applied to international politics.[54]

In the Introduction and in Part One we examined the development of the former European system of equilibrium into a bipolar system in the context of the structural history of international society, as well as the erosion of bipolarity after the end of the Cold War. Looking at the various regions within world politics (the Middle East, African or south Asian subsystems, etc.), bipolarity had, on the one hand, not yet become the predominant structure, while, on the other hand, the former great powers had failed to perceive adequately the shift that had taken place. The political leaders of Great Britain and France, for example, continued to lay claim to great power status, pursuing both in Europe and in their former spheres of influence a policy based on that perception. The Suez crisis[55] represents a superb example of this. The objective of Ben-Gurion, Eden and Mollet, the three major decision-makers of Israel, Great Britain and France, the state actors involved, was to topple the stronghold of pan-Arabism in Egypt using the same means, war, but for different motives. Israel feared for its own existence, France for its influence in the Mediterranean in general and the Maghreb in particular, and Britain for its possessions in the Gulf, above all the oil fields. Before the Suez War broke out, foreign powers were in the process either of attempting to defend existing spheres of influence (France and Great Britain), or of penetrating these territories (the USA and the Soviet Union) and contending over them. The two by then existing superpowers, the USA and the USSR, for example, were both courting Egypt with equal vigour. The Western arms monopoly in the region was first broken by the Soviet Union in September 1955 when Soviet arms were supplied to Egypt by the then CSSR. The USA, meanwhile, provided Nasser with development aid to the value of US$40 million, which Nasser used in May 1953 to establish the *Saut al-'Arab* propaganda radio station, which broadcast to the Gulf region.[56] The Americans also agreed to finance construction of the Aswan Dam. This decision was later revoked by the Eisenhower administration following Nasser's public rejection of the pro-West policy Eisenhower had anticipated.[57] The Soviet Union promptly stepped into the breach, promising what the Americans had refused.

In fact, aside from the military pact of Baghdad (1955) the rivalry between foreign powers on the eve of the Suez Crisis did not essentially relate to the East–West conflict at all. It was still primarily a matter between the former Western great powers and the new US superpower. While the British Premier Eden made decisions more on the basis of his Nasserphobia than on expert knowledge of the by now total shift in world politics, Moscow and Washington rather than London and Paris had become the most important political nerve centres in the new configuration of the international system. American economic penetration of the Middle East had also progressed in leaps and bounds. Before the Second World War, the US share in Middle East oil revenues had been 15 per cent that of Great Britain 70 per cent. Already by the early 1950s, this ratio had been reversed to 60 per cent for the USA and 30 per cent for Great Britain.[58] Britain, of course, still had her zones of influence, while the Baghdad Pact (Turkey, Iraq, Iran, Pakistan) was a British brainchild. British hostility towards Nasser began with the latter's refusal to enter into the pact. He later succeeded in building up a pan-Arab front against it. The pact fell victim to the Suez adventure, and the weight Great Britain had once carried in the Middle East went with it: after the Suez War, Great Britain was more or less out of the running for good. Donald MacLean speaks wryly of the 'Collapse of the British Caliphate' in the Middle East: 'Until the winter of 1956, despite a major contraction of British power during the first post-war decade, the Middle East was still recognisably a British sphere of influence. Today London's ability to determine the course of events is very limited . . . a (former) leading actor, found itself in the wings.'[59]

It can scarcely be overlooked that after the Anglo-French attack on Egypt, on 31 October 1956, the USA did not seek to support Nasser so much as to suppress the influence of the British in the Middle East: 'The United States was in a position to use and did use Britain's financial difficulties and shortage of oil to force an unconditional withdrawal from Egyptian territory.'[60] Another author, Anthony Verrier, points to the influence at that time of the American oil lobby on the Eisenhower administration, as well as on Secretary of State Dulles, who 'was determined to remove Britain from the Middle East'.[61] Eden, the British Prime Minister, was faced with a choice: either to give in to American demands for an unconditional withdrawal and obtain needed oil supplies and support for the devalued pound sterling, or to stand firm, but take the risk that sterling could 'go down that drain and take Britain with it'.[62] With the Suez War over, Britain resigned herself to the USA's superpower status and lost its importance as an independent state actor in the Middle East.

France, the other erstwhile great power, had a healthier economy and could make its presence felt more confidently on the international scene. Whereas the British presence in the Middle East sank into obscurity under Eden, under Mollet two years later (1958) the *grandeur* of France survived, although the Fourth Republic declined after the Algerian uprising. During the Six Day War era, France, led by Charles de Gaulle, was still a country committed to *grandeur* as a framework for the conduct of foreign policy. Mollet's France was fighting against Egypt in its stance as a regional actor supporting the liberation struggle in Algeria, the most important French colony (see Chapter 3, notes 5 and 6). By June 1967 Algeria was a sovereign state on whose goodwill France was dependent: Algerian oil was supplied to France, and the former great power retained a substantial economic influence in the Maghreb region as a whole. We have already noted in the military account of the Six Day War that de Gaulle's critical approach towards Israel was not born of a concern to cultivate friendships, but was contingent upon French interests.

France was thus seeking to adapt its needs to its reoriented interests. Hartmut Elsenhans, an expert on Algeria and oil matters, explains French Middle East policy as follows: 'France's attempt . . . to define the French claim to great power status with worldwide responsibility on the basis of privileged relations with the Third World resulted in oil policy being incorporated into a new type of global strategy in relation to the Third World.'[63] Algeria occupied first place in this hierarchy, followed by the other Arab oil producers. This explains French Middle East policy during the Six Day War, and most especially the way it turned away from Israel and towards the Arab countries. Understandably, the Arab Maghreb states were on the side of Egypt in the June War; this manifested itself, for example, in symbolic deployment of Algerian troops to Egypt. The strategic considerations of France's new regional alliances were adjusted accordingly. France wanted to remain a great power and to be recognised as such by the superpowers. It also wanted to retain the western Mediterranean as a French sphere of influence. In the light of all this, it is not surprising that France condemned the Israeli aggression and called for the immediate withdrawal of Israeli troops from the occupied territories.[64]

On 22 November 1967, the UN Security Council passed Resolution 242 calling for an end to hostilities between Israel and its Arab neighbours, likewise envisaging both an Israeli withdrawal from the occupied territories and Arab recognition of the state of Israel.[65] France turned this resolution into a platform calling for a Middle East peace solution under the tutelage of the four great powers – the USA, the USSR, France and Great Britain. It was none the less clear, as Edward Kolodziej phrases it, that 'the French diplomacy in the region after the Six-Day war aimed more at minimising the adverse effects of Middle East conflicts on France than at easing or mediating them'.[66] Within the same strategic option, France backed the Soviet claim to a right of consultation in the Middle East, since this would be a counterbalance to the USA and hence in the French interest.

During the Six Day War, the Johnson administration paid little heed to France, while President Nixon later made it expressly clear that the former great powers had little say in such matters. The Rogers peace plan[67] devised by the American Secretary of State accorded a role in the solution to the conflict exclusively to the USA and the USSR. In vague terms, the Rogers Plan, like Resolution 242, also foresaw a withdrawal of Israeli troops from the occupied territories, but solely under the auspices of the two super-powers, and involving direct negotiations among the regional state actors. This was a broad hint to de Gaulle and his claim to *grandeur* for France in world politics. Kolodziej, who has made a substantial study of French foreign policy under de Gaulle, sums up the situation then as follows: 'Since the Six-Day war deepened superpower penetration of the Mediterranean, expansion of France's role and influence in the region after 1967 depended increasingly on its capacity to affect superpower relations in the region.'[68]

The former European great powers nowadays wield little authority either in the Middle East or in other parts of the world, although French political leaders often seem to have rather a distorted perception of the real situation. In March 1966, France under de Gaulle called on NATO, dominated by the USA, to move its headquarters from Paris to another, non-French city within a year. Since that time, France has pursued an independent defence policy while still remaining a member of NATO.[69]

This is not merely a matter of different perceptions but also of divergent interests. Many years ago the well-known Marxist author Ernest Mandel expressed the incongruity of these interests in a form which, although ideologically biased, none the less resembles that of de Gaulle in a number of respects (the Europe–America dichotomy), while at the same time drawing attention to a real factor.[70] In their energy policy in particular, Europeans have quite different interests from the Americans, which is one reason why they also pursue a separate policy towards the Middle East. Attempts to hold a Euro-Arab dialogue need to be seen in this light. Although generally labelled 'cultural exchange',[71] this is really a question of ensuring future oil supplies to Europe.[72] This Euro-Arab dialogue was understandably only introduced in response to the oil embargo during the 1973 October War (see Chapter 7). It proved fruitless. In the first place, the Europeans did not articulate their energy-related interests sufficiently unequivocally and confidently, resulting in woolly foreign policy. Secondly, the dialogue ignored the fact that there were by then only two superpowers in the existing world order and that the European states are unable to act in this terrain without the USA. The American energy expert Robert J. Lieber expresses this arrogantly but aptly when he writes that the means for coping with the European energy situation are 'beyond the reach of the European Community. It was the United States alone which possessed the continental size, the domestic energy resources, the economic strength and even the military power which [would] . . . enable the West to address [the] uncertain consequences of the crisis.'[73] The other major European state actors, chiefly Great Britain and the Federal Republic of Germany, resigned themselves to this state of affairs. In contrast, French political leaders had a perception that made them unable to come to terms with such a characterisation. Before the emergence of the bipolar international order, the former European great powers had been able to ensure that their interests prevailed over those of their opponents purely by means of military intervention.

The Suez War was one of the last major examples of intervention by former great powers. However, in a bipolar system in which both superpowers are armed with nuclear weapons, and where a war between them would result not in victor and defeated but in mutual destruction, the importance of military intervention as an instrument in world politics has declined.[74] This does not mean, of course, that superpowers do not interpose at all – Vietnam and Afghanistan are examples of such action by the USA and the Soviet Union. Under the conditions of bipolarity, military intervention no longer seemed to be a political instrument of the superpowers but more that of small and middle-range states. Now, after the end of the Cold War, the Cuban crisis of 1962 seems like distant history, when the superpowers sought to avoid any confrontation that could lead to an escalation along the old lines (the scheme: 1. conflict potential, 2. escalation, 3. crisis, 4. war). During the Gulf crisis military intervention as a political instrument for implementing the UN Security Council resolutions has been revived. However, this took place with the consent of both superpowers after their Cold War rivalries had ended. The dissolution of the Soviet Union in December 1991 creates a new situation in world politics.

The way the superpowers have exerted influence also differs in a number of respects from that of the former great powers, who have adapted to this change in procedure. International political theory uses the term 'leverage' to describe the new instrument of foreign policy. A dominant state actor can exert its hegemony by using non-military means, although symbolic threats with military means form part of the procedure. Recently, in the case of Iraq, the threat to use force did not work and force had to be used to convince Saddam. This is an exceptional case, however.

In international politics, no state actor can achieve leadership standing without having at its disposal the prerequisite military capabilities. This is one of the reasons why, among the former European great powers, France nowadays occupies the most respected position in the international ranking order. Instruments for the indirect exertion of influence, that is those which no longer occur through intervention, are thus also related to military considerations. Besides economic measures, arms supplies and military training are major features for exerting influence. They ensure that the dependence of one state actor from another is maintained. Arms lose their value, however, when the availability of spare parts falters.[75] This statement applies to all Third World states seeking after military might.

The disadvantage of indirect superpower military intervention in a conflict via a regional state actor (USA intervention in Grenada or Soviet intervention in Afghanistan being exceptions) is that the superpowers are unable to exert full control over the course of events, and hence do not always achieve their desired goals. Hedley Bull asserts: 'Indirect intervention has the disadvantage, compared with direct intervention, that the intervener does not control his local proxy states . . . in the way he controls his own armed forces.'[76] The matter broached in this quotation also touches on the central problematique of this book: the reciprocal relationship between regional and international factors. This in turn raises the point as to how superpowers can become involved in regional conflicts, bearing in mind their inability to direct these in the desired direction. The Gulf War has been a unique case because the entire international community was united – and in full assent – against the aggressor state, Iraq.

Prior to the Gulf War, with few exceptions, the superpowers carried out intervention in the Middle East in an indirect way after the Suez crisis, mainly through alliances with a regional state actor. This brings us back to the pattern mentioned in Part One of patron–client relations. The most important move in such an alliance is the equipping of the regional state actor with weapons systems, the training of its troops and the supply of technical know-how. This does not mean, however, that the Soviet Union was the patron of the Arabs and the USA the protector of Israel, although the pro-Israeli stance of the USA, on account of the influence of the Israel lobby in the American Congress,[77] cannot be overlooked. The fact remains that the USA also has Arab alliance partners in addition to Israel, chief among which are Saudi Arabia and Egypt, which are also supplied with American arms. During the Gulf War the Arab–American alliance against Arab Iraq was a clear case. The Middle East as a whole has been the largest arms outlet in the Third World.[78] The Gulf War has made this assessment clearer than ever.

The penetration of the Middle East by the superpowers since the Six Day War has indeed been most apparent in the military sector. A number of the former great powers, notably France, have managed to retain some potential for influence in the region in this way, notably as arms suppliers. Introducing an analysis of military expenditure in the Middle East, Fred Gottheil states: 'In the Middle East, the military sectors are the most rapidly expanding, the most technically advanced, and enjoy the highest national priority. It has become hardly an exaggeration to describe their civilian sectors as decreasing residuals.'[79] Gottheil is able to support this statement with a quantity of statistical data and five tables showing how military expenditures are 'no ordinary expenditures', representing 'levels of critical importance'. Table 4.1 is a simplified version showing the rise in military expenditures since June 1967:

Table 4.1   Military expenditures of central state actors as a percentage of GNP before and after the Six Day War

Year	Israel	Egypt	Iraq	Jordan	Syria
1961	8.2	7.0	8.1	14.7	8.8
1967	13.8	12.7	10.3	12.0	11.9
1969	25.1	13.3	10.0	18.0	14.4

Source: Fred Gottheil, *Journal of Conflict Resolution*, vol. 3, 1974, p. 503.

Comparing the expenditures of the Middle East's central state actors with those of the industrial states in both East and West, one arrives at the conclusion that in the case of the former, military expenditure as a percentage of GNP is several times greater than that of the latter. Gottheil rightly concludes: 'It is difficult to envisage real economic development in the Middle East under these conditions.'[80] The military expenditures of Israel and the Arab states as conflict partners serve to finance arms purchases among the superpowers and the European countries. Development aid in the form of loans provided by the USA and the former Soviet Union was also largely used to obtain arms and to finance military training. This makes the military sphere one of the central domains of regional penetration by the superpowers – a process that does not seem to have ended either with the passing of the Cold War or the defeating of Iraqi aggression in the Gulf War.

Contrary to the propaganda of local state actors, the two superpowers were not directly involved in the escalation of the conflict during May 1967 or in the outbreak of war on 5 June. Indeed, both were greatly concerned, although less out of a love of peace than the fear of the consequences of a direct confrontation. Eugene Rostow was articulating this concern in the name of US President Johnson when he said that the Middle East was 'a more dangerous crisis than Vietnam, because it can involve a confrontation with the Russians, not the Chinese'.[81] The superpowers had lost control of the regional dynamic of the conflict, as is now known from hotline contacts between President Johnson and Premier Kosygin. An outbreak of war might have been prevented, however, if the UN had had a more competent General-Secretary than U Thant. It is now clear that the withdrawal of the United Nations Emergency Force (UNEF) from the border could have been postponed until tension had eased.[82]

After the Six Day War, all the state actors had a breathing space in which to take stock of the consequences of the hostilities. Data on the rearmament of Egypt by the Soviet Union has already been given above. Although the Israelis had won the war militarily with French Mirage and Mystère planes, they had lost France as their arms supplier since de Gaulle was no longer willing to supply them. Even before the June War, the USA had begun to arm Israel, providing Hawk air defence missiles in 1962 and Patton tanks in 1965. In 1966, there had been an agreement on the supply of forty-eight Skyhawk fighter planes. These were not delivered, however, until after the war in 1967.[83] When the Six Day War broke out the USA was fully occupied in Vietnam, yet despite this President Johnson concentrated almost exclusively on the Middle East throughout the week of the war. The State Department issued an official statement to the effect that the United States was 'neutral in thought, word, and deed',[84] so as to stress their 'non-involvement' in the war. It is known from Steven Spiegel that President Johnson was furious about this statement. While stressing the non-involvement of the USA in the war itself, he emphasised that American sympathies were firmly on the Israeli side.[85]

Despite substantial American interest in oil deposits from the Middle East, until the Six Day War the region was secondary in US priorities. In other words, the Vietnam War alone cannot be used as an explanation for the USA's lack of a foreign policy concept with regard to the region. Nasser's radical policy was perceived as a threat to American interests, but in the first instance it was the rivalry between Egypt and Saudi Arabia that formed the basis for American distinctions between pro-Western and anti-Western regimes.[86] The incompatibility between Israel as a US ally and the Arab countries aligned as a bloc against Israel was not systematically thought through in terms of American foreign policy until after the Six Day War. US preoccupation with Vietnam, however, left no scope for the development of an American Middle East concept. The dichotomy in

American foreign policy between a virtually limitless alliance with Israel and the parallel pursuit of US interests with its Arab allies, above all in the Gulf,[87] remains to this day – even after the Gulf War – one of the great unresolved questions in American foreign relations.[88]

After the Six Day War an American arms embargo was imposed on the whole of the Middle East (i.e. Israel, Jordan and Saudi Arabia). The Johnson administration nevertheless announced in the same year that the Skyhawk fighter planes promised to Israel would be delivered after all, as in fact they were. In 1968, the following year, the US Israel lobby successfully pushed through the supply of fifty modern Phantom fighter planes to Israel. For the Pentagon, Israeli experiences gained in the Middle East were of military significance for the American war in Vietnam. Israel's willingness to place Soviet war material captured in Sinai at the disposal of the Pentagon was also rewarded. This material was examined to ascertain its military effectiveness, especially since similar arms were being used in combat in Vietnam.[89] At first, the USA tried to use the supply of Phantom fighter planes to secure rights over the deployment and supervision of military installations. The Israelis refused to make any concessions on this score, however, and the planes were finally supplied unconditionally.

Since that time, the Middle East conflict has occupied a more important place in overall US foreign policy, although a strategic concept has still failed to materialise. Middle East policy under President Johnson had no foundation other than Resolution 242 of the UN Security Council and a vague Five Point Plan of the White House:[90]

1. The right of all states in the Middle East to exist;
2. Fair treatment for refugees;
3. Unimpeded sea traffic for all nations;
4. Limits to be set on the arms race;
5. Respect for the territorial integrity of all states.[91]

This plan left open the question of if, when and how Israel would relinquish the occupied territories.

The upgrading of the Middle East in US foreign policy was accompanied by the assignment to Israel of a role as 'strategic asset'. The American political scientist Cheryl Rubenberg, an American Jewess, disputes the thesis that Israel's interests are identical with those of the USA. She describes the emergence of this foreign policy doctrine in the light of the consequences of the Six Day War for the US superpower:

> Israel's spectacular military performance validated the thesis that Israel could function as a strategic asset to the United States in the Middle East.

Thereafter, within a remarkably short period of time, that idea became enshrined as an absolute tenet of orthodoxy in American politics. The belief about Israel's strategic utility was expressed in U.S. policy through the provision of virtually unlimited quantities of economic assistance and military equipment.[92]

Conflict linkages in the Middle East comprise the reciprocal effects of local, regional and international factors. Egypt's standing in the region was not all that was affected by the June defeat; the legitimacy of its claim to leadership also suffered a crisis. It was in an attempt to rescue this legitimacy by making a demonstration of activity against Israeli occupation that Nasser conducted the War of Attrition against Israel in the canal zone from March 1969 until August 1970. The Israelis responded by deploying their Phantom jets, newly acquired from the USA, which unlike the former French Mirage and Mystère planes were able to fly deep into the Egyptian interior to make bomb attacks.[93] The Soviet Union reacted by stepping up its arms supplies to Egypt. By then, both the superpowers were indirectly involved. This provides an example of indirect intervention by superpowers in a regional conflict involving combat, but without Egypt or Israel acting as the proxies of the respective superpowers. The example of the War of Attrition also demonstrates the thesis of the reciprocal relationship between superpower involvement and regional dynamic in a conflict.

In contrast with the economically more powerful USA, the Soviet potential for economic penetration of the Middle East was limited. In the case of the USA, however, economic penetration preceded the military aspect, in the first instance by breaking the economic monopoly of the former great powers, notably in the oil sector. This was followed by military penetration of the region through its ally Israel. A Soviet breakthrough in the region first occurred in 1955 through arms deals with Nasser's Egypt, mediated by the CSSR. The largely military character of Soviet penetration persisted until the end of the Cold War.

There is little point in going into any detail here about Soviet Marxist theory, according to which the USA, unlike the Soviet Union, is pursuing an imperialist policy in the Middle East, this being the reason for its economic interests there. Arms pertain just as much to the economic as to the military sector and, although Marxist authors know this, they deliberately focus the link between armaments and economic growth on Western capitalism alone, choosing to ignore that the same holds equally good for the Soviet Union.[94] Indeed, the Soviet armaments industry lied at the very core of its economy: next to the USA it was the biggest arms exporter in the world.[95] 'Soviet arms trade today is on a scale that can no longer be concealed',[96] writes Klaus von Beyme, who also points out that some 10 per cent of Soviet hard currency revenue came from the arms trade. After 1945, Europe was the central focus of Soviet strategy, just as it was for the USA. The fact that the bipolar structure which emerged after the Second World War did not become a worldwide phenomenon until the 1950s has already been pointed out. The Soviet Union under Stalin had only a peripheral interest in the Middle East, revolving around two issues: (i) their own Muslim population and its religio-political ties, and (ii) Turkey on the southern flank of the Soviet Union. In its stark and uncompromising 'friend or foe' orientation, Stalin's doctrine of two camps is akin to the foreign policy orientation of Secretary of State Dulles in the Eisenhower administration. However, the new states forming in Asia and Africa wanted to go their own way and not be directly tied to one of these two camps.

It was not until 1953 under Khrushchev that the Middle East, South-East Asia and Africa fell within the Soviet field of vision. The major breakthrough in Soviet arms deals with Egypt via the CSSR (arms in return for cotton) came in the Khrushchev period.[97] The Baghdad Pact, which united the pro-Western states in the Middle East on the southern flank of the Soviet Union, was perceived as a threat. It was hoped that mobilisation of Nasser's pan-Arab camp against this regional military pact would kill two birds with one stone: both thwart encirclement of the Soviet Union and at the same time win over an influential ally in the Middle East. Even at that stage, however, the Soviet problem with such objectives was the lack of influence over local élites educated along Soviet lines – Egypt is a case in point[98] – whereas Western countries can by contrast often count on Western-trained élites. Added to this are the ideological tensions between communism, Islam and Arab nationalism. These have resulted in the well-known dichotomy in Soviet foreign policy: the fact that it has regional allies who ban communist parties in their own countries, or who even persecute communists. The Soviet Union had often abandoned local communists in a region in order to pursue foreign policy interests. The Middle East was a classic example of how the Soviet Union backed countries in which communists are persecuted.[99]

In the 1950s the Soviet Union had not yet developed a foreign policy concept for dealing with the new states, although the doctrine of peaceful coexistence propounded under Khrushchev after the abandonment of Stalin's two-camp doctrine did offer considerable room for manoeuvre.

At the beginning of the 1960s the concept of a 'non-capitalist road to development towards national democratic revolution' was evolved, being elucidated in a systematic way in a three-volume Soviet ideological work entitled *Class and Class Struggle in the Developing Countries*.[100] This innovative foreign policy doctrine was so elastic that it could be applied at will to any situation[101] – Egypt under Nasser was presented as the leading model for a country on the non-capitalist road to development towards a national democratic revolution. Among the most important criteria as to whether a country is on this road or not was its links with the Soviet Union. Klaus von Beyme rightly characterises this policy as 'predominantly opportunistic and reactive'.[102] Like Soviet Marxism in general,[103] the policy was primarily an ideological legitimation for the Soviet Union's by then pragmatic approach, in which its own national state interests were paramount. During the Cold War such a pragmatic policy allowed ample room for the sacrifice of local communists to the 'great goals of the world revolution'. Prior to its dissolution, the Soviet Union detached itself from the bulk of communist activities in the Third World.

After the Suez War, Egypt was the first country in the Middle East in which the Soviet Union was able to gain a foothold. Following the fall of the monarchy in Iraq, the Lebanon crisis of 1958 and the fusion of Syria and Egypt into the United Arab Republic in February of the same year, it began to look as if the Soviet Union was pushing the West out of the Middle East. Once again, however, instabilities, domestic crises and interstate conflicts (including rivalries between the Ba'th Party and Nasser) placed limits on the potential for Soviet penetration. The Soviet Union could not handle its Middle East partners, which were non-communist regimes, in the same way as its East European allies,[104] who were controllable both institutionally and militarily.

Khrushchev's demise in 1964, one year after the Cuban crisis ended, heralded the joint leadership of Kosygin and Brezhnev, for whom the Middle East had become top regional priority next to Western Europe. Egypt and Syria, and for a time Iraq, were then the regional clients of the Soviet patron, just as Israel was and remains the client of its counterpart. Robin Edmonds graphically describes the significance of the Middle East for the Soviet Union:

> If the Cuban aid programme was in financial terms the most costly legacy of Krushchev's policy towards the Third World, in political and strategic terms by far the most important was the Soviet commitment to the Middle East . . . A glance at the map is enough to know that strategically the Middle East is for Russia – whether Tsarist or Soviet – what the Caribbean is for the United States.[105]

The Soviet Union was hence unable to abandon Nasser after his defeat in June 1967, and proceeded to rearm his armed forces.

When in March 1969 Nasser forced the Israelis to become involved in a war of attrition on the east bank of the Suez Canal, using superior artillery obtained from the Soviet Union, the Israelis avenged themselves by making Phantom fighter plane bomb attacks deep into the Egyptian interior. Despite American aid to Israel and Soviet aid to Egypt, neither of the superpower patrons was willing to be precipitated by its regional client into a supraregional confrontation. During the War of Attrition (March 1969 to August 1970) and after Nasser's visit to Moscow on 22 January, Egypt was so well equipped with radar and surface-to-air missiles, among other things, that it became increasingly difficult for the Israeli air force to reach its bombing targets in Egypt unscathed. Many of the new Soviet installations were also manned by Soviet personnel, so that the Soviet Union was able somewhat to tame its regional ally in its War of Attrition. Meanwhile, the USA had refused to supply more Phantoms to Israel as long as the latter contributed to an escalation of the conflict with their bomb attacks. The conduct of the two superpowers during the War of Attrition[106] between Egypt and Israel reveals their double-tracked strategy: to support the regional ally while trying to ensure that the conflict did not reach such a degree of escalation that it threatened to spill over into a supraregional conflict between the superpowers themselves.

Nasser's death in September 1970 triggered a domestic crisis that was to have repercussions on Soviet foreign policy. A power struggle between a 'leftist' faction centred around Sabri and a 'rightist' faction around Sadat resulted in victory for Sadat.[107] In 1971, the Soviet President Podgorny signed a fifteen-year friendship treaty with Egypt, its various clauses providing for very close links. Meanwhile, the Soviet Union continued to supply arms, of which the Arab countries became the main recipients. Friendship turned out to be short-lived, however. In July 1972, Sadat expelled his Soviet military advisers.[108] No one guessed then that this step, tantamount to an estrangement from the vigilant 'big brother', was the prelude to a fresh passage of arms in October 1973. The Soviet Union would never have allowed it. The fourth Arab–Israeli war continued the historical process that had begun in June 1967 by further weakening the radical forces in the region and strengthening the petro-dollar sheiks. A political draw for Egypt in the October War against Israel was not only to clear the way for a severance of Egypt from the Soviet Union, but much more than this, to prepare the ground for a separate Egyptian-Israeli peace, which made virtually any overall Arab–Israeli war unthinkable. The most recent Arab–Israeli war in 1982 had to be restricted to a war in Lebanon.[109] By launching the Scud missiles on Israel during the Gulf War Saddam Hussein was taking a gamble on an overall Arab–Israeli war. He failed, however.[110]

Part Three

The 1973 October War: The Regional Dynamic of the Middle East Conflict and the Superpowers. Arms, Oil and Shifts in Regional and International Alliances

Introduction

In June 1967, the Israelis achieved a military triumph that no strategist could fail to acknowledge. Drunk on victory, they returned to their barracks and mentally suppressed the distinction between politics and war. The defeated Arabs had been brought to their knees not only by the self-delusion of their demagogical leaders, but also by the sheer incompetence of their armed forces. Peace is not possible between two parties respectively drunk on victory and mortified by humiliation, if peace is understood to be more than a mere laying down of arms. The Israelis were still thinking of conflict in military rather than political terms by presuming the right to dictate peace terms on the strength of their victory on the battlefield, and they were in no mood for compromise. Unhappily, the Arabs compensated for this crushing defeat with another retreat into the kind of rhetoric assumed to have been rendered obsolete by the 'self-criticism after defeat'. The internal Egyptian struggle for Nasser's successor is itself a clear indication of the new President's conviction from the very outset that there was no future for an alliance with the Soviet Union. Sadat realised that the Egyptian economy was in need of the petro-dollars of the oil-producing Arab states, and that his country required financially strong economic aid of a kind that could only come from the USA, not from the Soviet Union.

In a comprehensive and conceptually oriented monograph on Egypt, Peter Pawelka shows how the Egyptian political system underwent a 'restructuring' after the June defeat. This system was 'shifting away from development oriented towards internal markets and seeking instead links with the globally dominant structures within the world economic system'.[1] This systemic transformation, incipient under his predecessor, became even more marked under Sadat. The October War merely accelerated and stepped up the process. Internal systemic transformation was accompanied by corresponding shifts in external political alliances. Although Egypt could clearly never have conducted the October War without Soviet arms support, a move away from the Soviet Union had been apparent since 1970. It came as no surprise to alert, well-informed experts, therefore, that the October War brought in its wake a shift in Egypt's alliance politics.

Victory made Israel arrogant. Although the territories it had captured – the West Bank, Gaza Strip and Golan Heights – are a political pawn, the fact that Israel now has to control territories with Arab populations is a burden in terms of security policy. This is particularly true of the West

Bank, as the *intifada*, the political uprising of the Palestinians, has shown.[2] One of the lessons of the recent Gulf War for Israel must have been the fact that the occupied territories are more of a liability than an asset. Saddam Hussein sought to underpin his occupation of Kuwait through linkage to the occupied territories. The solution of this problem may free Israel from such linkages directed against its own security. Conspicuously, however, Israeli decision-makers are not yet ready to learn this lesson. The fact remains that the spectacularly victorious passage of arms of June 1967 diminished the readiness of Israeli political decision-makers to make any concessions. This has not proved a good basis for peaceful conflict resolution. John Bulloch rightly argues that a new war would never have come about had it not been for Israeli intransigence: 'A unilateral withdrawal by Israel to the line of the Sinai passes – only a little further than its eventual withdrawal from Sinai negotiated at such a cost in blood and damage in 1973 – would almost certainly have prevented any new conflict.'[3] With regard to the present it must be noted that the Palestinian backing of the Iraqi dictator Saddam Hussein during the Gulf War was an indication of their desperation as a result of the intransigence of Israeli policy, even though this explanation should never serve as an excuse for the self-damaging attitudes of the Palestinians during the crisis and the war. They thereby destroyed the confidence-building measures achieved earlier through hard work between Israelis and Palestinians.

Whereas the 1967 war had been the result of the unchecked escalation of a conflict, the war of October 1973 was a planned strategic act on the part of Egypt, with the participation of Syria. Towards the end of the war, Henry Kissinger managed to grasp the nature of the situation, going on to seize full control over events with his shuttle diplomacy. The USA was the real victor in the 1973 October War.[4]

5 The Yom Kippur, Ramadan or October War? Historical Continuity from the Six Day War to the Nineteen Day War

When the fourth Arab–Israeli passage of arms was launched with air attacks at 14.00 hours on Saturday 6 October 1973 – a blitzkrieg planned and initiated this time by the Arabs – both sides were celebrating religious feasts. The Arabs were in Ramadan, the Muslim month of fasting, while the Israelis were celebrating Yom Kippur. The Arabs therefore refer to this passage of arms as the *harb Ramadan*, the Ramadan War, which also forms the title of a comprehensive account of the war in Arabic written by three Egyptian generals.[5] The Israelis describe the same war as the Yom Kippur War, after the name of their feast. The less value-laden term 'October War' has been chosen for use in this book to indicate the non-partisan scholarly position taken.

In the period from 1967 to 1973 weapons system technology had advanced considerably. As the Vietnam War had come to an end, and military strategists had no more battlefields on which to test out new death-dealing technologies, the Middle East seemed to offer a welcome opportunity. By October 1973 the region had been completely penetrated by the two superpowers. The Soviets had their clients in Syria and Egypt, the USA in Israel. In contrast with June 1967, when the superpowers had both taken pains to avoid being forced by their clients into direct involvement, they both stepped into the military arena in the October War, although stopping short of sending their own soldiers into combat. In June 1967, the Israeli secret service had tapped a telephone conversation between King Hussein and President Nasser, in which Nasser suggested to the king that the mass media of their two countries broadcast a report attributing defeat to American and British participation on the Israeli side,[6] which was not the case on that occasion. In October 1973, the USA launched an intensive airlift operation between their home military bases and Israel; it was used to supply everything from tanks to planes, which could be deployed in combat only hours after delivery.[7] The Soviet Union also provided Egypt and Syria with arms supplies by air and sea. The American military correspondent Frank Aker, who has given a military science account of the October War, states frankly that 'each side was continually probing and testing the weapon capabilities of the other.'[8] As we saw in the previous chapter, Nasser's policy was intended to lessen the influence of foreign powers in the region, but in fact achieved the exact opposite, opening one door after another to superpower intervention. As the German–Israeli political scientist Dan Diner states, Israel, unlike Egypt, had been to a greater extent dependent on the support of external powers from the very outset.[9]

If one had to sum up this war (6–22/24 October) in only a few words, it would suffice to say that the Arabs (not only their leaders, but the Arabs in general), who had emerged from the June 1967 war not only militarily defeated but humiliated in every possible way, managed in this later blitz attack to prove, above all to themselves, that they were serious adversaries capable of putting up stiff opposition in combat. Mutual respect is a major factor when negotiating lasting peace. There can be domination and humiliation between perceived super- and subhumans, but not peace. The American military expert Aker, avowedly on the side of the Israelis, still concedes in a matter of fact vein: 'The attacking forces of the Yom Kippur War had been found to be better trained, more skilful, and far more courageous than the panic-stricken victims that had fled before the Israelis in 1967.'[10] The decisive historical function of the October War for those involved – whatever course the war took – was that it altered their perception both of themselves and of the enemy. The self-respect of the Arabs was restored and the Israelis had to learn to take the Egyptians seriously. In terms of regional impact, the epochal significance of the Six Day War was far from matched by the October War, but the latter nevertheless proved to be of greater military and international significance.

Both from the military standpoint and in terms of the thesis central to this book of linkages between regional conflicts and potential supraregional ramifications, the international political significance of the October War was considerable. In military terms this nineteen-day passage of arms offered a 'military paradigm'[11] by enabling the capabilities of American and Soviet weapons systems to be tested on a high technological level for the first time since the Second World War, in a way that had not even been possible in the Vietnam War. The October War brought with it the risk of a nuclear confrontation between the USA and the Soviet Union. In the event of the US government failing to check Israel, the Soviet leadership threatened on 24–25 October to intervene on Egypt's behalf. On 22 October, the UN Security Council adopted a ceasefire resolution, to which Israel agreed but then failed to abide by. The US government reacted to the Soviet threat by deciding to place its strategic fighting forces on alarm level 3.

First, however, let us take a brief look at the military dimension of the October War. In the military science literature the scholar is faced with conflicting accounts of the war. The analysis of the Israeli scholar Galia Golan,[12] for example, contradicts that of the Egyptian generals Badri, Majdub and Zahdi (as quoted above, see note 5), who wrote the standard Arabic work on the 'Ramadan War' – in terms of the account itself and in its evaluation of the war. An accurate depiction both of the military conflict and the interconnectedness of regional and international factors involved in it are essential to any account. Reference throughout to works by non-Arab and non-Israeli military scientists will enable us to verify partisan accounts of the war.

The first difference that emerges in the literature concerns the duration of the war. The Egyptian generals speak of twenty-three days (6–28 October), others of nineteen days (6–24 October, i.e. up to the second ceasefire resolution of the UN Security Council). The Egyptian account seeks to draw a veil over the switch from victory to semi-defeat that occurred in the second and third weeks of the war, while the Israeli version is at pains to play down the consummate tactics of the Egyptian crossing of the Suez Canal. None the less, one cannot fail to notice how a general such as Sharon, second to none when it comes to overestimating himself and underestimating the Arabs, frankly concedes honour to Egyptian soldiers: 'I have been fighting for 25 years . . . and all the rest were just battles. This was a real war.'[13] Whereas Israeli military personnel were later candid about their shortcomings in the October War, the above-quoted Egyptian generals insist that the Egyptian army achieved only victories, clearly distorting their account of the third phase of the war to this end. This phase consisted of successful mobile warfare on the part of the Israelis, seizing the initiative from the Egyptians, who failed to capture sufficient territory. The turnabout was made possible in the first instance by the technologically sophisticated American airlift of supplies from the USA via the Azores to Israel, although subsequently halted by the USA so as deliberately to forestall an imminent Egyptian defeat. The military deadlock that ensued opened the way for Henry Kissinger to direct the superpower intervention, which in turn prepared the ground for a brilliant volte-face in Egyptian foreign policy, as we shall be discussing in more detail below.

On the Egyptian side, there were two major preconditions without which it would have been impossible to fight the October War. The first was the experience they had gained from the War of Attrition (March 1969 to August 1970). This border 'skirmish' in fact cost Israel more men and military equipment than the entire Six Day War.[14] Egyptian losses, of course, were even greater, although not as great as in June 1967 (80 per cent of all their military equipment). They were still not enough to cancel out the effects of Israeli air attacks on the Egyptian rear with American Phantom fighter planes. During the War of Attrition, which would not have been feasible without Soviet armament,[15] Egypt was able to train its fighting forces in the use of newly acquired Soviet weapons systems. Chief among these was the SAM missile system that was to make Israeli air attacks on Egypt very risky, since their planes could no longer attack without exposing themselves to possible hits by mobile SAM 6 missiles.

The second precondition for an outbreak of war was the expulsion of Soviet military advisers[16] by Sadat in July 1972. This enabled Egypt, now in possession of Soviet arms, to deploy its fighting forces as it liked. The October War would never have taken place if Soviet military advisers had remained in Egypt. It still needs to be borne in mind, however, that neither Israel nor Egypt and Syria could have conducted the October War without direct support from the two superpowers, that is both the supply of arms during the war and satellite reconnaissance. This marks a significant difference between the June War of 1967 and the October War of 1973.

Hostilities began at 14.00 hours on Saturday 6 October 1973 on the Syrian and Egyptian borders with Israel.[17] At that time, Israel had a 90-mile border with Egypt along the banks of the Suez Canal, from Port Said to the Gulf of Suez. In the north the border with Syria was, and still is, only 40 miles long, whereas the border with Jordan is some 225 miles long. Apart from trenches there was no buffer zone on the Syrian–Israeli border, a fact which enabled 700 Syrian tanks to cross the armistice line and press forward unhindered, accompanied by bulldozers and flails. By nightfall on the first day of their attack the entire Golan Heights, occupied by Israel in the Six Day War, had been recaptured.

Along the Egyptian border the situation was much more complex, since the now inactive Suez Canal separated the two warring parties. Between its opening and the June War of 1967, some 110 years, the waterway had had to be regularly dredged to keep it navigable, the dredged sand being dumped on the east bank of the canal, since the West Bank was inhabited and not a desert. Using this sand, the Israelis had built a defensive wall, naming it after General Bar-Lev. In places this sand was up to 20 metres high; the sand and stone bunkers built up in this way enabled the Israelis to observe all movements on the opposite bank. Flame-throwers had been installed in the sand, to be fired over the canal should an attacker attempt to cross. Behind the wall, there were twenty-five fortified installations armed with infantry mortars and anti-tank weapons, as well as Israeli tanks and artillery.

Even in international political conflicts, symbols have their part to play, and for the Arabs, the Bar-Lev Line symbolised invincible Israeli superiority. By crossing the Suez Canal and destroying the Bar-Lev Line, the Egyptians reversed the meaning of that symbol. The capture of this line gave them back their self-respect. After this momentous event, the great and well-known writer Taufiq al-Hakim wrote in the Cairo newspaper *al-Ahram*: 'By crossing over to Sinai, we have crossed over from defeat . . . Egypt will always recall this moment in its history with pride and gratitude.'[18] The Egyptian generals Badri, Majdub and Zahdi write in quasi-ritual language: 'In less than six hours, our fighting forces had annihilated the Bar-Lev Line . . . thereby washing themselves clean of the shame of the Six Day War.'[19] We know from these generals that the operational and technical details of the action were worked out over a number of months; the credit for its success goes to Egyptian engineers.[20] Timing was likewise planned to the minute. Egyptian strategists counted on the Israelis not anticipating an attack by Muslims during Ramadan, the Islamic month of fasting. They further calculated that the Israelis would be unprepared for an attack if they themselves were celebrating Yom Kippur on 6 October. The twelve-hour long nights of October, as well as the weather, were also conducive to their plans. Another tactical advantage was the sun: as it set in the afternoon, it would dazzle the Israeli soldiers, thus impeding their defence of the Bar-Lev Line against Egyptians crossing the canal.

First, 8000 Egyptian commandos in the dinghies crossed the canal, covered by heavy artillery and from the air. The Egyptians were armed with easy-to-use Soviet Sagger anti-tank missiles, carried with them in cases, with which the Israelis were unfamiliar. Light ladders were to aid them in scaling the top of the sand wall. The Sagger anti-tank missiles were deployed against Israeli tanks to great effect. Some 200 Egyptian MiG or Sukhoi planes and TU-16 bombers had attacked and neutralised some of the major Israeli air bases in Sinai. Egyptian engineers had developed a high pressure water system with water pumps to produce a water-jet from the canal aimed at the other bank in order to bore a hole in it and cause it to cave in. Prior to this, the Egyptians had successfully misled the Israelis by launching decoy attacks and managing troop amassments in the north. The Israelis thus concentrated their troops on that side of the canal strip, while the Egyptians to the south were using their highly developed Soviet PMP vehicles to construct pontoon bridges and cross the Canal (ten for tanks and ten light bridges for the men). Additional dummy bridges were also built to dupe the Israeli air force. Egyptian helicopters brought commando troops behind the Bar-Lev Line; these were then able to launch missile attacks on the stronghold garrisons from behind. Troops on the line itself were thus encircled, cutting them off from military reinforcements. Peter Allen, giving an account of the October War, writes: 'No one had really foreseen a situation in which the Egyptians . . . without a punitive Israeli response . . . would cross the Canal with such speed. The first day's fighting had placed the Israelis on the defensive for the first time since 1948.'[21] The military scientist Frank Aker confirms this: 'The Egyptians were able to mount a blitzkrieg-like attack'.[22] Neither the Israeli air force, the flame-throwers on the Bar-Lev Line, the Israeli artillery, nor the tank brigades stationed there were in a position to fend off the Egyptian attack on that first day.

Well into the middle of the following week, the Arab side, despite heavy losses on the Syrian north front, was able to press forward with tactically limited successes. These were none the less tainted by the fact that they were no longer seeking to hold on to the initiative: the attacking Arabs allowed the prerogative of acting first to slip out of their hands. In Glassman's view, the Arab side proved unable to transform its tactical victories into strategic positions.[23] The military science literature[24] refers to two factors to account for this. The first was the principle of deploying the Egyptian air force only with extreme caution and economy – an Egyptian command practice of recalcitrance that was to result in the loss of valuable time. The price they paid for this was that neither the Israeli artillery nor their supply routes fell to the Egyptians. The June 1967 catastrophe of the Egyptian air force had not yet been forgotten. The Egyptian command did not want to put its air force at risk: since then, Egyptian MiG planes had been kept in concrete-reinforced hangars designed to withstand air attack.

The second factor was the absence of 'deep strategic penetration' on the Arab side. Syrian soldiers on the north front failed to realise that they could have continued to press forward with no difficulty, encountering only minimal resistance, after recapturing the Golan Heights.[25] On the Egyptian front, the commander-in-chief was unwilling to take risks, similarly failing to send his troops outside the range of air protection from SAM missiles.

The chief strength of Israeli fighting forces, their combination of fast regular troops with a tactical air force, was disposed of on the very first day by the first ever deployment of mobile SAM-6 missiles in an Arab–Israeli war. This effectively neutralised the Israeli air force: the fixed SAM-2 and SAM-3 missiles with which the Israelis were familiar had been technologically surpassed by the Americans in the Vietnam War, the know-how then being passed on to the Israelis, but SAM-6 missiles were an innovation.

On the first day of fighting, the Israeli air force lost thirty Skyhawks and ten Phantom fighter jets – all shot down by SAM-6 missiles.[26] On the southern front, SAM-6 missiles transformed Egyptian air space into a *cordon sanitaire* against the Israeli air force. They could be put to better use here than on the Golan Heights, giving the correlation between radar capability and the features of that terrain.

After the brief pause that followed the successful Arab blitz attack, the Israelis concentrated on a strategic concept designed in the first instance 'to get Syria out of the war'.[27] The Syrians also had SAM-6 missiles, which had offered air protection to their tank offensive, numbering at first 700, later increased to 1000. Initially, therefore, the Syrians were safe from attack by the Israeli air force. However, the SAM-6 missiles could not be deployed to optimal effect on the Golan Heights. Added to this was the fact that Syrian military personnel were not so technically skilled in the use of this missile system as were the Egyptians. This enabled the Israelis to find weak spots in the Syrian air defence system after their initial massive aircraft losses on the first day. Using a detour flight path over Jordan and the Golan Heights, and armed with American Maverick and Shrike air-to-surface missiles, they were able to decipher the frequency technology of the SAM-6 system. When on 7 October Syrian forces then went over, for the first time in the Middle East, to deploying Soviet FROG-7 surface-to-surface missiles (with a 37-mile range), firing a total of sixteen into Israeli territory, the Israelis responded with a shift of tactics: deep penetration into the enemy rear through strategic bombings of the Syrian interior. On 7 October, they bombed the Syrian Ministry of Defence, as well as other civilian buildings in Damascus, including the Soviet Cultural Centre. This deep strategic bombing led the Syrian military command to make the fatal error of redeploying their mobile SAM-6 missile ramps to the vicinity of Damascus. An opening was thus left in the air defence system over the Golan Heights, allowing the Israeli air force to take rapid advantage and attack Syrian tank brigades in operation there. Then the Israelis pursued the goal of destroying the Syrian economy. This was their answer to the offensive tank units. The oil refinery in Homs and the oil-loading port of Banias were set alight from the air. Even the Damascene electric power station was bombed, leaving Damascus without electricity for a while. These bombings proved to be highly effective in terms of war psychology.

The Syrian ports of Latakia, Tartus and Banias were so massively attacked by the Israelis that the Syrian leadership feared an amphibious landing. Two tank brigades were withdrawn from the Golan Heights and redeployed in the coastal region. Of course, the Israelis had no intention of launching such a suicidal coastal landing. However, the withdrawal of both the mobile SAM-6 missiles and the two tank brigades considerably weakened the northern front in the Arab war against Israel. When on Monday 8 October Iraq deployed a squadron of twelve MiGs to assist on the Syrian front, Syrian SAM-6 missiles shot down half of them by mistake, while the Israelis destroyed the other half by engaging them in aerial combat.[28]

Although using the same Soviet weapons systems, the Egyptian fighting forces were more successful, disciplined and better trained than the Syrian. A possible explanation for the professionally superior Egyptian military command undoubtedly lies in the sectarian non-professional officer recruitment from among minorities that was prevalent in the Syrian army after 1970, combined with its high degree of politicisation.[29] By November 1970, it was more akin to a political association of Alawite minority clients than an efficient military force.[30]

From 10 to 12 October Egyptian forces completed their crossing operation, achieving full control of both banks of the Suez Canal. Meanwhile, Syrian troops were being forced back on to the defensive. The military impact of the SAM-6 missiles had by this time already been neutralised, enabling the Israeli air force to regain its former air superiority. From 8 to 10 October the Golan Heights were recaptured, and by Wednesday 10 October Israeli troops had reached the road linking Kuneitra and Damascus. The Syrian leadership called on Egypt for relief, which could only be provided at the cost of heavy losses, since their bridgehead on the east bank of the canal was not sufficiently deep into their territory, and hence incapable of supporting a flexible defence against Israeli advances. The Egyptian position could have been 'hacked to pieces'. Despite this, however, the Egyptians did launch an offensive on 13 October, intending to force the Israelis to withdraw their troops from the north front to the south.[31]

Israeli military commanders were on the whole no keener to embark on military adventures than their Egyptian counterparts. However, entirely on his own authority and without military coordination, the Israeli General Sharon, together with a small troop of 200 soldiers, crossed the canal in the night of 15–16 October.[32] Given a situation in which Egyptian military commanders were on the move in the enemy hinterland, Sharon and his men sought out the SAM-6 missiles stationed there and destroyed some of them, thus creating a gap in Egyptian air defence. This seriously impaired the Egyptian surface-to-air defence belt, altering the subsequent course of the war in favour of the Israelis. Two things had made Sharon's action possible: (i) a day before he crossed over, on 14 October, there had been an all-day tank battle, one of the most important in history, on the east bank of the canal, involving a total of over 2000 tanks on the Egyptian and

Israeli sides. On 15 October, therefore, the Second and Third Egyptian armies were busy regrouping and reorganising. Sharon was able to take advantage of this, and (ii) profit from the fact that the Second and Third Egyptian armies were equally responsible for controlling the Bitter Lake at the Suez Canal, without precisely demarcating the lines between themselves. It had not occurred to the Egyptians that the Bitter Lake, lying behind their troops on the east bank, could be regarded as an objective for attack by the Israelis. This was their Achilles' heel.

Provided with defence from the air, the Israelis managed to build bridges, enabling Israeli tanks to cross the canal. Further tank battles ensued on 16 and 17 October. Egyptian troops were now no longer fighting as before protected by a secure air space, and therefore needed backing from their air force. As a result, the Egyptian air force was not actually deployed until 17 October, apart from the first day of their attack. Up to that point air confrontation had been between SAM-6 surface-to-air missiles and Israeli planes. There were numerous air battles with heavy losses on both sides. Beginning on 17 October, Israeli forces embarked on mobile warfare. On 19 October, they managed to encircle the Third Egyptian army, stationed between the Bitter Lake and the Gulf of Suez. On that day, the Soviet premier, Kosygin, left Cairo on his way to Damascus for talks with the other Soviet client state, Syria, on conditions for a ceasefire. The Soviet Union called on the USA to send Secretary of State Kissinger to Moscow for superpower talks on a ceasefire – later to be adopted as a UN Security Council resolution. On 20 October, Kissinger flew to Moscow and had six hours of talks with Brezhnev. On 22 October, the UN Security Council adopted Resolution 338 calling on the two warring parties to observe a ceasefire commencing at the latest twelve hours after the passing of the resolution in New York. Resolution 338 comprised three points: in addition to the ceasefire call, it also required the implementation of Resolution 242 of 1967, and peace negotiations under international auspices.[33] However, the Israelis did not cease hostilities and a further resolution was passed on 23 October.

The military offensive of the nineteen-day war launched by Egypt and Syria on Saturday 6 October was described by the Arabs as the *Ma'rakat Badr* (the Badr Battle), a designation illustrating the degree of fusion of religion and politics in the Middle East. In the seventh century, on 19 March 624, the Prophet Muhammad had fought and won the original Battle of Badr.[34] Referral to this thirteen centuries later in October 1973 served a purely legitimating function. Such historical recourse to the glorious past also highlights the tendency of political decision-makers in the regionally acting states to ignore the reality that nowadays it is the superpowers who determine the outcome of regional wars, even if they are not able actually to steer the course of them. Neither Islam nor Judaism was of any significance in the October War, despite the fact that both religions were invoked in the events by the two warring parties. The salient factors in that conflict were military technology, the ability of regional actors to handle that technology, and the willingness of the superpowers to permit their clients access to the capabilities at their disposal.

The 'love' that existed between patron and client ceased during the era of superpower competition at the point where the regional involvement of the superpowers threatened to spill over into a global confrontation – which both superpowers were at pains to avoid. This brings us to the central question raised in this book throughout the years of superpower competition during the Cold War. Were the superpowers capable of harnessing the regional dynamic of a subsystem (which although subordinate to them was not subject to their complete control) to the extent that regional conflicts would exert no effect on their own superpower relations? The answer to this question was negative in 1973. The fact that the superpowers ended their Cold War and were in agreement in 1990 did not prevent the Gulf crisis, nor its development into an international war in 1991. In the same year of that Gulf War the Soviet Union was dissolved and transformed into a Commonwealth of Independent States (CIS), which is no longer is a superpower. No *New World Order* has emerged, thus resulting in a kind of disorder detrimental to keeping regional conflicts in check.

6 The Superpowers and the October War

Faced with the threat of a direct confrontation between the superpowers, Israel and Egypt were at first compelled by their respective patrons, the USA and the Soviet Union, to acquiesce to paragraph 1 of UN Security Council Resolution 338, and comply with the ceasefire agreement. Israel, however, continued hostilities: on 23 October, Israeli troops succeeded in completely encircling the Third Egyptian Army. Although it had already been encircled on 19 October, it had retained access to the road link to Cairo, which was its supply route. On October 23, the UN Security Council met again and adopted a further resolution, no. 339, reiterating the cease-fire call expressed in Resolution 338. Israel continued fighting, however, thereby precipitating its patron into an international political crisis. The Soviet Union could not now abandon its client without jeopardising its credibility as a superpower.

During the Cold War years the existence of a bipolar international system made it impossible for regional wars to be decided on the battlefield alone.[1] From Jon Glassman's[2] list of the war material deployed in the October War, it is known that the weaponry used was at least comparable with that deployed in major Second World War battles, if not more. Tank losses, for example, were double those during the crucial El-Alamein battle.[3] However, the outcome of the October War was not decided on the battlefield. 'A shallow treatment of the Yom Kippur War might deal only with the combatants,' writes Aker. He adds that 'this conflict . . . was neither won nor lost on the sands of the Sinai and the lava hills of Golan'.[4] Had Egypt and Syria not been armed by the Soviet Union, or Israel by the USA, the October War could not have taken place at all in the form it did. Even with the huge arms arsenals at their disposal the two belligerent parties could not have fought for more than a week, and yet they lasted out for nineteen days. The Soviet Union supplied its client both from the port of Odessa and by air. The Syrian army was in fact even rearmed during the war itself, to make up for its heavy losses.

The USA acted similarly on behalf of its Israeli client. The American Sixth Fleet formed the logistical base for an airlift from the USA to Israel. The USS *Franklin Roosevelt* and the USS *Independence* aircraft carriers provided the necessary platform for transport planes, which were fuelled first in the Azores and then either directly in flight or on the aircraft-carrier the USS *Kennedy*. Fearing an oil embargo, European states refused their Western ally access to their airports. European NATO arsenals could be deployed, however. This enabled the two superpowers to test out on each other not only their respective weapons systems, but also their logistics. The October War was to go down in history as the greatest battle of material ever to take place within the bipolar structure of the international system.

ON THE VERGE OF A MILITARY CONFRONTATION BETWEEN THE SUPERPOWERS

A study of the October War is of crucial importance to the question being addressed in this book – not from the military science perspective, but rather in terms of the complex interrelationship between regional conflicts and their international environment. Reference to the military events of this war, therefore, is made purely and simply with this in mind. At its height, the October War brought the whole world to the brink of a nuclear confrontation between the two then rival superpowers. When Israeli forces failed to comply with the ceasefire resolution adopted by the UN Security Council on 22 October, continuing to pursue their strategic goal of encircling the Egyptian Third Army and cutting it off from its supply routes, the Soviet Union stepped up its warnings to Israel and its patron the USA by making corresponding demonstrations of military force.[5] *The Red Star*, for example, published an official declaration stating that 'most serious consequences would result' if Israel continued to ignore the ceasefire.[6] On 24 October, seven divisions of Soviet airborne troops were on the alert ready to take the offensive. There were some 90–100 Soviet warships in operation in the Mediterranean, of which at least half were combat-ready. The USA had a comparable military presence in the region. Central Europe was affected by the situation inasmuch as the two superpowers would have to draw on their arms arsenals in Eastern and Western Europe to reinforce their potential in the Middle East. For NATO in particular, this produced dangerous breaches in the West European security system as a consequence of a withdrawal of American conventional arms in Europe and their redeployment in the Middle East.[7] It is worth noting here in passing that the October War of 1973 precipitated one of the most serious crises in the history of NATO.[8]

On 24 October, the US Security Council under President Nixon decided to put all conventional and nuclear military units on the alert. [9] Prior to this, Brezhnev had suggested in a message to him that both superpowers make a joint military intervention to ensure implementation of the ceasefire resolution adopted by the UN Security Council on 22 October. This message also expressed the intention of the Soviets to undertake a unilateral military intervention if the USA failed to meet this condition.[10] Nixon's response was an emphatic no, expressed together with the US view that a unilateral Soviet intervention would constitute a violation of Article 2 of an agreement made on 22 July 1972 between the two superpowers, whereby each undertook to seek to prevent nuclear war.[11] Nixon writes in his memoirs that this was 'the most serious threat to US–Soviet relations since the Cuban missile crisis'.[12]

The Soviet military press stressed the validity of UN Security Council Resolution 338, threatening Soviet intervention should the USA fail to convince its client to comply.[13] On 25 October, a Soviet freighter coming from the Black Sea passed through the Dardanelles into the Mediterranean, heading for Egypt. US radar observations picked up nuclear weapons on board, possibly intended as nuclear warheads for Soviet SCUD missiles deployed in Egypt, of which several had already been fired on 22 October.[14]

The situation might be summed up as follows: first a regional war broke out between several core members of the Middle East subsystem, the two superpowers functioning as patrons of the respective belligerent regional state actors, who were their clients but not their proxies. Israel was not the 'lackey' of the USA, any more than Egypt or Syria were 'lackeys' of the Soviet Union. The clients were pursuing their own distinct interests, which differed from those of their patrons. This regional war precipitated an international crisis when the two superpowers, on the one hand, failed to control their clients and to affect their conduct in the conflict, but on the other were unable to leave them in the lurch. A defeat for a client in a militarised conflict is a defeat for the patron superpower itself. The Arab defeat in the Six Day War had had repercussions for the Soviet Union. A superpower confrontation comes into being when a war between regional clients shifts from the client to the patron level. The paradox of such a state of affairs as that of the 1973 October War, which may be regarded as typical for the escalation of a regional conflict within the then bipolar conditions of the international system, is that the two superpowers were obliged to demonstrate their readiness for war in order to maintain their superpower status. At the same time, they were also endeavouring to de-escalate the conflict and bring it back to the regional, client level it had started on. The terrifying aspect of this situation is the very real danger of a world war breaking out in such a tense uncontrolled political set-up. Using the example of the October War, and evaluating the events on 24–25 October, Shoemaker and Spanier correctly assess the situation in their discussion of the patron–client relationship: 'In such an environment, the political intentions of Moscow and Washington [i.e. for a world war not to break out] were of marginal importance; war could begin at the hands of a nervous pilot or naval gunner.'[15]

The superpowers were careful, therefore, not to keep up their threatening postures for too long. They managed to de-escalate the conflict by shifting it back on to the regional level. In order to achieve this end they pursued diplomatic efforts as an alternative method for containing the conflict within regional bounds. Given that client states are neither proxies nor vassals, a conflict situation of this kind presents both superpowers with the risk of either winning or losing regional allies. This possibility did not apply, however, in the singular case of Israel, which is substantially dependent on the USA and lacks the option of exchanging an American alliance for a Soviet one.[16] Unlike the USA, the Soviet Union was faced with the real prospect of losing its regional ally. The October War enabled the USA to take the political initiative and gain momentum in the region through Kissinger's shuttle diplomacy, aimed among other things at detaching Egypt from its Soviet ally.

The successful crisis management of the October War shows that the superpowers were capable of regulating their interaction on the basis of rules of the game recognised by both sides, so that the escalation of a regional conflict from the client to the superpower level remained at least to some extent predictable and under control. The client level of a conflict, however, remains unpredictable – given the absence of any recognised rules of the game among the belligerent states as actors. This aspect of the regional dynamic of subsystemic conflicts is what is so difficult to grasp from the international bipolar perspective, although such conflicts are equally difficult to explain in purely regional terms. In other words, the global bipolar structure of the international system on the one hand, and the distinct regional dynamic typical of the subsystem on the other, need to be analysed in terms of their mutual interplay.

To express in more specific terms these middle-range conceptual remarks on the patron–client relationship with reference to the October War, it may be pointed out in the first instance that the USA and the Soviet Union were equally taken aback by the outbreak of war. Since decision-makers make decisions on the strength of their perception of experience up to that point, the USA and the Soviet Union, recalling the Six Day War, considered a victory of the Arab states over Israel to be beyond imagination. At the very beginning of hostilities, they both urged their clients to accept a ceasefire. The USA was in no doubt that the Israelis would emerge the victors, and the Soviet Union likewise considered their Syrian and Egyptian clients to be at a military disadvantage to Israel. Still at the stage of trying to convince their clients to agree to a ceasefire, they continued to reassure each other on a lower level – that is not involving the hotline between Moscow and Washington – of their intention not to become involved and of containing the conflict on the regional level. It is clear from Sadat's strikingly egocentric account of the war ('I crossed the Canal') that the Soviet Union was being uncooperative, the Soviet Ambassador in Cairo, Vinagradov, having in mind only one topic of conversation during the war: 'ceasefire'. For his part, Sadat was seeking military supplies and arms from the Soviet Union.[17] The same applies to Israel which, instead of acquiescing to American calls for a ceasefire, demanded more arms as Sadat did,[18] so as to compensate for its heavy losses, particularly on the first day of fighting.

For the Arabs, the situation on 8 October, two days after the outbreak of war, would have been the ideal time for a ceasefire. The Syrians on the northern front had recaptured the Golan Heights, while on the southern front Egyptian troops had gained full control of both banks of the Suez Canal, although they had not ventured to storm the Sinai passes. Repeated calls on the part of the Soviet Ambassador in Cairo for a truce before the Israelis retaliated went unheeded, since Sadat's condition for a truce was a return to pre-1967 territorial boundaries, which were not acceptable to Israel.

October 9 was a turning point for both superpowers. Despite a fractional improvement in Israel's position on the northern front, it was clear that Israel had suffered severe losses on the first two days of the war and that war could not continue without external backing. This situation necessitated a revision by the Americans of their understanding with the Soviet Union that they would exercise restraint. The Soviets were likewise obliged to throw their policy of restraint aside when they saw that Egypt had achieved unexpected successes on the one hand, while the Syrians on the other were beginning to suffer heavy losses. A patron cannot simply abandon a client to its fate. The first Soviet deliveries of supplies reached Syria on 10 October, and Egypt on 11 October.[19] Similarly, Israel received its first supplies from the United States on 10 October, the supply scale being stepped up sharply from 13 October.[20] The reluctant entanglement of the two superpowers in the October War, although initially at least kept within manageable proportions, was escalated from the regional to the international arena by the conduct of the clients, not their patrons. Control of their clients had slipped through the patrons' fingers. Unexpected developments on the battlefield accelerated this escalation from the regional to the international level. One indication of this are the airlifts used to supply war material: the daily tonnage of the US airlift to Israel was double that of supplies going daily to Egypt and Syria together.[21]

This loss of control over their own clients, together with the decision by the patrons not to lose their allies to the war, drove the two superpowers to the verge of a nuclear confrontation. Tension first began to mount on 22 October when SCUD missiles were fired from Egypt on to Israeli troops on the West Bank of the canal (a range of 150 miles); the height of tension being reached, as has already been mentioned, on 25 October. In his book on American foreign policy, Stanley Hoffmann draws the real lesson to be learned from the October War: 'The events of 1973 revealed that in that part of the world peace was inseparable from our welfare.'[22] Recently, the Gulf War has reinforced this already very true statement.

Of all regional subsystems in the international order, the conflict-ridden Middle East poses the greatest threat to international security. The reason for this is not merely its huge geostrategic and economic importance for both the superpowers and Europe. Its regional dynamic deserves more serious attention than it has so far been given. While the other subsystems in Asia, Africa and Latin America each have their own regional dynamic, the Middle East still stands out among them as being of extraordinary international political importance. This is equally true of the relevance of its resources and of the extreme complexity of its regional–international linkages. Conflicts in the Middle East are one of the main sources of international conflict, and have already formed the focus of three out of the four major crises that have so far erupted between Europe and the USA within the North Atlantic alliance (1956, 1966 and 1973). The end of the Cold War and of superpower competition in the Middle East have by no means contributed to an alleviation of conflicts there, which have their own regional dynamic.

Despite the fact that the October War occurred during a period of international détente, this did not prevent the two superpowers from being drawn into the war by their regional clients, bringing them to the brink of a nuclear confrontation. Indeed, this war heralded the end of the détente phase. Gabriel Sheffer speaks here of a 'tyranny of the weak': despite their dependence on their superpower patrons, regional actors were capable of tyrannising their protectors. Sheffer presents the October War as a classic example of the 'independence in dependence of regional powers'.[23] Although the superpowers displayed a certain symmetry in their behaviour during this war, 'their reactions were nevertheless determined to a large extent by the regional powers' behaviour'.[24] To document his thesis, Sheffer offers the example of Israeli–US and Egyptian–Soviet relations during the war.

Whereas the USA gained terrain through the October War, the Soviet Union had to learn two hard lessons. The first was that neither military aid nor a military presence could regulate the conduct of a regional client. The second was that a willingness to engage in military intervention, and hence risk confrontation with the other superpower, was implicit in any super-power's regional policy in the Middle East. Paul Jabber and Roman Kolkowicz, pointing this out, feared that the loss of Egypt as a regional client state would furthermore compel the Soviet Union to make its presence felt even more decisively than in 1967 and 1973.[25] The fact that after the Middle East war of 1973 – and until 1989 – Syria was the only Soviet client left in the core region may help to explain why the Soviet superpower prior to its decline showed such a commitment to it, persisting until the end of the Cold War. According to the 1983 SIPRI Yearbook, Syria accounted for 9.4 per cent of total Third World arms imports (valued at US$47 710 million for the entire Third World), thus – despite its modest size – occupying first place among the twenty Third World states importing arms from the industrial states.[26] However, this high degree of commitment to Syria still did not enable the Soviet Union to dictate or even steer policy in that country during the years of alliance, any more than the USA is able to impose options for the resolution of conflicts on its client Israel.

This increasingly marked autonomy of regional dynamic *vis-à-vis* exter-nal powers, which persists despite the dependence of regional state actors on their superpower patrons, highlights both the complexity with which the search for a peace concept in the region is fraught, and the likelihood of such a concept only being found in some dim distant future. The end of the Cold War and of the concomitant superpower rivalry in the Middle East render this set-up more complicated. On the one hand, regional dynamic persists, as the Gulf crisis has clearly shown. On the other hand, the end of bipolarity and the ensuing dissolution of the Soviet Union are proving to be a destabilising factor in the Middle East. Bipolarity once provided the international system with a balance of power that has now been lost.

FROM BATTLEFIELD TO DIPLOMACY: KISSINGER'S 'STEP-BY-STEP' STRATEGY AS A PRELUDE TO THE TURNABOUT IN EGYPT

The date 25 October 1973 marked both the peak and the end of the threat of a superpower confrontation. The USA could not allow the Egyptian Third Army, encircled and cut off by the Israelis, to be destroyed with American arms supplied to Israel during the war. A long-term disadvantage for the USA in the region arising out of this situation was to be feared. This in turn removed any reason for Soviet intervention. On the very same day, the two superpowers succeeded in having a third ceasefire resolution adopted by the UN Security Council – one that envisaged the deployment of a United Nations Emergency Force (UNEF) in which neither American nor Soviet units should be included. An hour before the resolution was adopted, Kissinger announced at a press conference 'that . . . the conditions that produced this war were clearly intolerable to the Arab nations, and that in the process of negotiations, it will be necessary for all sides to make substantial concessions'.[27] This announcement ushered in an active US role in the regional conflict that Kissinger had already initiated with his 'shuttle diplomacy'. At first, the Soviet Union sought to de-escalate the conflict together with the USA, only to find itself increasingly pushed into the background during the course of negotiations and later to be driven out of the region altogether. Three years later, in 1976, the Soviet Union found that even its Egyptian client had been wrestled from it by the USA. After the end of the Cold War the Soviet Union stopped supplies to its remaining ally, Syria, and virtually gave up its superpower position in the region before it dissolved.

Both structural and personal circumstances alike were to have a bearing on developments after the 1973 October War. Kissinger should therefore not be regarded as the lynch-pin of events, notwithstanding a generally held view that he was the dominant political figure and architect of the post-war regional order in the crucial eight months after October 1973, in both the regional and international spheres.[28] Among the structural factors working in Kissinger's favour, and one that continued to hold good until Soviet retreat from the Middle East, was the Soviet Union's lack of either strategic or economic leverage in the region. The supply of arms was the crux of Soviet foreign policy, but even before the October War Egypt had been caught up in an economic crisis that arms supplies could not resolve. It is amply clear in retrospect that Sadat was pursuing political aims in his war. The October War served to improve his political stakes. Fully realising that arms obtained from the Soviet Union would only support a limited war, his decision to go to war aimed at effecting a turnabout in Egypt's overall policy, on the basis of a stronger strategic position for political negoti-ations.[29] This explains why Kissinger found in Sadat virtually his only unreservedly cooperative partner for the shuttle diplomacy he initiated in November, and which was to last with interruptions until the summer of 1974. Quandt rightly observes: 'Only the talks with Sadat were devoid of difficulty.'[30] Kissinger himself writes of Sadat in the warmest terms in his memoirs.[31] Edward Sheehan, who has written a novel-style bestseller about Kissinger's Middle East shuttle diplomacy, writes of the great liking of the two politicians for each other, although they were 'a pair of foxes . . . each of them intent on manipulating the other for his own purpose'.[32] Sadat made it plain that the October War – despite all the odds – was to remain a victory for Egypt. He expected the USA to rescue the Egyptian Third Army by exerting pressure on Israel, promising in return to shift to a pro-Western policy and to agree to talks with Israel with a view to demilitarising the conflict.[33]

Kissinger, however, had his own agenda, which he sums up as the pursuit of the following aims: to thwart Soviet arms supplies to the region and to prevent a humiliation of the Arabs by the Israelis, leading to bilateral talks between Israel and its opponents. This process unfolded in the form of Kissinger's strategy of 'step-by-step' diplomacy, aiming 'to cement ties with Egypt, which was courageously willing to show the way'.[34] De-escalation of the international crisis arising out of the regional war in the Middle East was achieved through cooperation between the two super-powers. The USA guaranteed that the Egyptian Third Army would not be crushed, and ensured that 125 trucks loaded with food and medications reached encircled army units.[35] Talks between Israeli and Egyptian military commanders took place at a point 101 kilometres along the road from Suez to Cairo. This point became the site of the Egyptian–Israeli ceasefire and disengagement talks. These merely served as a preliminary to the Geneva peace conference they were working towards and at which the regional state actors were to negotiate under the auspices of the superpowers.

The International Middle East Conference took place on 21 December, Kissinger stressing that peace was the main concern of the acting states,[36] but adding that it could only be achieved step by step. The first step was to arrive at an agreement on troop disengagement. Kissinger had already prepared the ground for this on his first Middle East trip on 5 November, although he had his work cut out for him. Egypt was calling for an Israeli troop withdrawal to behind the 22 October lines (in accordance with the ceasefire resolution of the UN Security Council), whereas Israel was calling for an Egyptian withdrawal to behind the lines prior to the outbreak of war on 6 October – that is Egyptian withdrawal from the east bank of the Suez Canal. This posed Kissinger with the problem of finding a way of reconciling these conflicting expectations, while at the same time outmanoeuvring the Soviet Union. When the Geneva peace conference began on 21 December 1973 only representatives of Egypt, Jordan and Israel were present beside the two superpowers; Syria refused to participate. The conference was therefore postponed after its first meeting. It was only after the Gulf War of 1991 that another International Middle East Conference could be held in Madrid October/November, 1991 and then continued in Washington and Moscow 1992, even though without results. In 1974, Kissinger then managed to bring talks back to the bilateral level, thereby keeping them under American control. In fact, Geneva had been 'a bitter disappointment' for the Soviet Union.[37] When Kissinger met Brezhnev in Moscow on 26 March 1974, a meeting he describes as the 'toughest and most unpleasant' he had ever had, he was accused of ignoring the Soviet Union as a superpower, and was put under pressure to resume negotiations in Geneva.[38] He had nevertheless made some headway before this altercation.

On 18 January 1974, the first Egyptian–Israeli agreement to disengage troops had been signed. Describing the situation at that time, Sadat emphasised that this new development marked 'the beginning of a relationship of mutual understanding with the USA . . . This beginning was interpreted by the Soviet Union as the end of our relations.'[39] Sadat was thereby sending out appropriate signals to Israel – that he was the first Arab politician publicly to proclaim his discernment of the 'mistakenness of the generally held view that Israel represented American interests in our region . . . Israel pays no heed whatsoever to anything except its own interests.'[40] These words contain an implicit call for direct talks with Israel. To date, many Arab political decision-makers still hold the view that Israel is a 'bastion of the USA' in the Middle East, therefore being convinced that only pressure from the USA can force Israel to make concessions. This is one of the reasons for their refusal to enter into bilateral negotiations with Israel and one of the great obstacles to peace in the Middle East. Israeli politicians responded to Sadat's signals in time, as their conciliatory gestures prove, particularly since they could not have been the result of US pressure alone,[41] although Kissinger was not inactive at the time.

In his book on the October War, the Israeli Brigadier-General, Chaim Herzog, who was elected President of Israel ten years after the end of the war, criticises how 'Israeli commanders [in the wake of the Six Day War] had emerged from it feeling that it was possible to accomplish everything with a tank and a plane'.[42] Hence their 'error', in Herzog's correct view, of underestimating the Arabs.[43] This has been the Israeli obstacle to peace. Even before the Egyptian–Israeli peace process, Herzog (1975) expressed the hope 'that in the initial successes of the Yom Kippur War the Arabs regained their national honour, and this may ultimately facilitate the development of a dialogue and negotiations between the two sides'.[44] In the eight months after October 1973, Kissinger's shuttle diplomacy[45] prepared the ground for such a dialogue, which – years later – was finally able to come to fruition under American mediation. There is still hope that an Egyptian–Israeli dialogue could be enhanced to the level of an overall Arab–Israeli dialogue. The meetings of the recent International Middle East Conference 1991/92, however, did not smooth the way for this needed dialogue.

The first agreement on troop disengagement made on 18 January 1974 envisaged a withdrawal of Israeli troops from the west bank of the canal, also leaving a strip thirteen miles wide along the east bank. In return, the Egyptians were to pull their artillery back from both canal banks, leaving only a small force of 7000 men on the east bank of the canal as a symbol of their sovereignty.[46] A buffer zone was set up between the two warring parties on the east bank, patrolled by a UN Disengagement Observer Force (UNDOF). In March 1974, Egypt and the USA resumed diplomatic relations, the American flag being raised in Cairo at the US embassy on 1 March on the occasion of the opening of the embassy building. While Kissinger was attending this ceremony, the Soviet foreign minister Gromyko was arriving in Cairo,[47] failing to bring with him the anticipated economic and military advisers requested by Egypt. Cognisant of a turnabout in events, albeit initially at least a smooth one, the Soviet Union had called a halt to arms supplies and all other forms of aid to Egypt. Kissinger was in Cairo with his 'flying state department',[48] a Boeing 707 equipped with the communications technology of a mobile state department, symbolising not only Kissinger's role as a key actor in that conflict situation, but also the new presence of the USA.

His mission in the Middle East went on until May 1974; he himself states that the 'Syrian shuttle' posed the severest problems,[49] as Syria was still a client of the Soviet Union and in receipt of Soviet arms supplies even when aid to Egypt had been stopped.[50] Once in Damascus, Kissinger had to allow for the presence of Soviet politicians expecting to have a say in matters. However, despite its by then client – albeit not proxy – status *vis-à-vis* the Soviet Union, Syria did pursue its own interests and sign an agreement on troop disengagement,[51] which understandably contains far fewer concessions to Syria than to Egypt on the part of Israel. The Israelis returned, with minor adjustments, to their boundaries prior to the outbreak of the 1973 war, retaining the strategically important Golan Heights and the occupied Palestinian territories they have kept under their military rule since the 1967 War.

Subsequent evaluation of this shuttle diplomacy has contained some criticism, for example from the prominent Harvard Professor Stanley Hoffmann, that Kissinger was more of a tactician than a far-sighted strategist.[52] Kissinger's activities in the Middle East were taking place parallel with the Watergate Affair[53] in Washington, which kept President Nixon fully occupied until his resignation. This left Kissinger a completely free hand and a delegated authority in handling the Middle East. Quandt never-theless rightly acknowledges that a politician can only act within the range of available options, and that in these terms Kissinger did in fact accom-plish a great deal.[54] His success in achieving troop disengagement on both the Syrian–Israeli and Egyptian–Israeli borders effectively eliminated the war on both fronts. This was to have far-reaching consequences, as subsequent developments were to show. The transformation of an im-minent Egyptian military defeat into a quasi-victory through Israeli withdrawal from both banks of the Suez Canal, and the reopening of the canal on 5 June 1975, strengthened the US position in the Middle East subsystem at the expense of its counterpart, the Soviet Union.

During those months, however, the Soviet Union was not the only state that found itself out of the running as a result of US foreign policy, now largely steered by Kissinger, with the indefinite postponement of the failed peace conference in Geneva, in December 1973. The West European allies were likewise not consulted,[55] despite the crucial importance of the Middle East for their energy supplies.

In the final weeks of the October War, the Arab states imposed an oil embargo on the Western states that were supporting Israel, thus precipitat-ing the first major international energy crisis. Although the Western allies had denied the USA access to their airport facilities for its airlift transpor-tation of arms to Israel, the USA none the less went over the allies' heads in deploying allied NATO weapons arsenals for these purposes[56] – a factor that exacerbated international tension. The earlier existing bipolar and nuclear character of the international system highlights the limitations of Western Europe, without underestimating European potential. When a con-flict in a non-European region, for example the Middle East, escalates into a crisis, taking the form of war in its most extreme stages, the chief concern is that the crisis might not be successfully contained within its regional context. This concern persists even after superpower competition has ceased. In such a situation, internationalisation always entails an escalation from the regional to the international level. This leaves the West European states either as mere mute actors, or playing ancillary roles as subordinate Amer-ican allies – aside from cases such as France, where a country succumbs to an overestimation of its own importance and lays claim to superpower status.[57]

However, this subordination of Western Europe either to the bipolar structure of the international system during the Cold War, or to the US since the end of bipolarity, by no means implies that European interests are identical with those of the Americans. Indeed, the energy crisis of 1973, an epiphenomenon arising out of the October War, illustrates just how wide the gulf between these two sets of interests can be, energy policy being a case in point. None the less, the fact remains that Western Europe does not constitute a united coherent force within the international system, nor does it possess the military and economic power needed to replace the bipolarity of that system into multipolarity. The US is 'Bound to Lead', as Joseph Nye argues.[58] It is deplorable that Western Europe is divided in pursuing its own interests in the Middle East autonomously. The subordination of the European role to the US during the 1990–91 Gulf War supports this assessment.

Turning to the repercussions and lessons of the October War, we can see that Kissinger's shuttle diplomacy led to a shift, within the by then existing bipolar power constellations of the Middle East. Egypt ended its association with the Soviet Union, turning instead to the USA. The dangers of that regional war were nevertheless felt directly in Europe, since an international crisis arose out of this militarised conflict as a result of the involvement of the two superpowers on 24–25 October 1973. Mercifully, this emergency lasted for only one day, in terms of the fighting forces of the superpowers being on the military alert. It came to an end on 25 October with the acceptance by the two superpowers of UN Security Council Resolution 340, leading to de-escalation on 26 October and cancellation of the nuclear alert.[59]

To draw this chapter to a conclusion, we might define a crisis, along with Snyder and Diesing, as a sequence of conflict-laden interactions between two or more states which can lead to war.[60] The Middle East war of June 1967 arose out of a short open crisis, the October War of 1973 out of a latent crisis that had been going on for several years.[61] Nixon and Brezhnev, leaders of the two superpowers which had been pursuing a policy of bipolar détente since the Cuban crisis of 1962, decided in 1972 to place this détente policy on a more secure footing. In the 1967 June War militarised conflict had successfully been contained within the region, whereas in the October War escalation had led to an international crisis that could no longer preclude nuclear confrontation. Snyder and Diesing have pointed to the circular phenomenon whereby détente policy on the one hand helps to keep international crises under control, while on the other hand international crises themselves serve as the desirable catalysts facilitating the management of détente policy.[62] These two authors cite the crisis that emerged from the 1973 Middle East war on 24–25 October as a classic example of this phenomenon. This might sound like an argument for playing with fire to show that one can play with it, betraying a tautological line of thought. The fact is that détente policy was the outcome of lessons learned from an international crisis, the Cuban crisis of 1962–63, and that it was greatly shaken by another international crisis, the 1973 October War.

Our analysis of the conceptual framework of the October War leads to the conclusion that the regional war, in the context of the bipolar international system that prevailed until 1989, contained the seeds of a nuclear confrontation between the superpowers through the process of its internationalisation. We should bear in mind here the crucial distinction to be made, as has already been mentioned above, between the 'international dimension' of a regional war and the 'internationalisation' of that war. Regional wars, particularly those involving the most important regional subsystems, merit the concerned interest of a far wider public than a narrow circle of experts. Of all the militarised conflicts that have erupted[63] since the Second World War, the 1973 October War and the 1990–91 Gulf War provide the best example of the impact of regional conflicts on world politics. As regional conflicts, both had repercussions on worldwide developments and their associated ramifications within the international system, while in turn being affected by global developments, and yet without any discernible loss of regional dynamic.

7 October 1973: The War with Arms and the War with Oil: Petro-dollar Power and the 1973–77 Saudi–Egyptian Axis; its Revival during the Iran–Iraq War and its Aftermath

The June War of 1967 first and foremost brought epoch-making repercussions in its wake. In terms of effects it was superseded only by the 1990–91 Gulf War. It ushered in a new historical era in the region which together with Laroui we have termed an 'epoch of crisis' (see Chapter 4). From this standpoint the October War appears by comparison no more than a link in a chain of historical events – simply the continuation of a phase of historical developments that had already been set in motion. Viewed in military and geopolitical terms, however, the October War offers even today a topical and inexhaustible object of study, particularly with regard to 'linkages', that is the interconnectedness of the local, regional and international levels of the international system. The preceding analysis of the course of events during the October War and its effects on relations between the superpowers support this assertion.

This concluding chapter of Part Three will be concerned with shedding light on one of the concomitant processes accompanying this war, namely *employment of the oil weapon as a policy instrument*. This employment is often referred to as the 'oil war', a term that presupposes the simultaneous waging of two parallel wars by the Arab states against Israel and its allies. G.M. Brown regards this employment of the oil weapon as the decisive factor: 'The Arab oil cuts, embargoes and price increases imposed during and since Yom Kippur represent the most spectacular, effective and possibly the most far-reaching use of resource diplomacy since the American actions against Japan in the early forties.'[1] The sharp drop in oil prices[2] as a result of the flooding of oil markets since 1982, a phenomenon known among oil experts as the 'oil glut', detracts nothing from the basic perspective of this statement. Oil remains a major resource in the international economy, in both political and economic terms;[3] it is through oil that the Middle East retains its significance as the most crucial international subsystem, second only to Europe – two-thirds of all known oil reserves are located in this region. Without wishing to assert that the 1990–91 Gulf War was an oil war, we can nevertheless safely draw the conclusion that this recent war has once again confirmed the importance of the Middle East both for the world economy and for the international system of states. For the time being, however, the October War will be the central focus of consideration in this chapter.

Closely linked to the 'oil war' of 1973, which occurred parallel with the real military combat of the October War, was the unfolding of an alliance between Egypt and Saudi Arabia. However, the Saudi–Egyptian axis proved unable to withstand the conclusion of the separate peace agreement between Egypt and Israel on 26 March 1979, resulting out of what was perceived at the time as Sadat's spectacular surprise visit to Jerusalem[4] in November 1977. The 'Iranian Revolution' of 1979 which was subsequently, especially during the Khomeini era, to bring political Islam to bear on a massive scale against 'US imperialism and Zionism', as well as according a central position to its conception of Islam as a political system (*nizam islami*), represented above all a challenge to Gulf Arabs.[5] It compelled the Saudis, who likewise legitimate themselves through Islam, to dissolve the axis with Egypt. At Camp David,[6] Egypt had done more than conclude a separate peace agreement with Israel. It had also made itself the most important Arab ally of the USA in the whole region. The consequence of this was isolation for Egypt in its Arab environment.[7] In this chapter we shall be examining the problems of the Saudi–Egyptian axis in the years from 1973 to 1977, after analysing the employment of the oil weapon. Paradoxically, Iran was at one and the same time a major factor working for the isolation of Egypt in the Middle East and for the return of Egypt into the Arab state system. Saudi fear of the Islamic claim of the Iranian revolution prevented them from following suit in Sadat's policy of recognising Israel, thereby compelling them to go along with the Iraqi policy of isolating Egypt in a bid to acquire the leading position in the Arab world. During the Iran–Iraq War, the Gulf Arabs realised that they badly needed Egypt's military weight. It was out of fear of Iran that Saudi Arabia paved the way for Egypt's return into the Arab state system, as a prelude to their complete return to the fold. The Kuwait crisis and the second Gulf War of 1990–91 ultimately helped to restore the Saudi–Egyptian axis and the full return of Egypt to its Arab leadership role.

THE OCTOBER WAR AND EMPLOYMENT OF THE ARAB
OIL WEAPON

In the context of the discussion following a lecture on OPEC given by this
author in Lagos at the Nigerian Institute for International Affairs (see note
8), a colleague raised against my line of argument (which revolved primarily around the political process) the fact that oil is a 'commodity',
subject like all others to market laws. My referral to the economist Morris
Adelman, author of an opus magnum on the oil problematique, by way of
a reply to this objection was not made simply out of a desire to seek refuge
with an internationally recognised authority. Adelman stresses that 'the
world oil problem is political before it is economic.'[8] The way the price of
the oil 'commodity' grew during the October War supports this assertion
all too clearly: the price quadrupled within only a few months. The reasons
for this sharp rise were primarily political, and only secondarily economic.

Representatives of the oil-consuming countries (oil companies) and the
oil-producing countries alike themselves deal with the oil 'commodity'
politically. During the 1950s the 'Big Seven' oil companies succeeded,
through price policy measures, in artificially reducing the proportion of coal
on the energy market, thereby creating a market in Europe for their own
product.[9] Their political manipulation of prices affected not only European industrial countries (forcing coal out of the market by means of low
oil prices), but also the oil-producing countries, which were adversely
affected by the artificially low price of oil. It was this state of affairs that
formed the background to the founding of OPEC as a 'functional organisation'.[10] As one minister in an oil-producing country, the author Otaiba,
stresses,[11] OPEC initially pursued the sole aim of securing the oil revenues
of its member states through the political stabilisation of oil prices. OPEC
came into existence in September 1960 and was dominated from the outset
by an Arab majority, whose objectives encompassed more than the market
economy. However, the employment of oil as a 'weapon' played only a
minor role in the Arab–Israeli conflict prior to the October War.[12] Employment of the oil weapon took place in the context of measures taken by
OAPEC, the Arab faction within OPEC, during the October War itself, and
had a dramatic effect on the international energy market.

There was considerable turbulence between the two Middle East wars.
The 1969–70 period saw the War of Attrition between Egypt and Israel (up
to August 1970), and in September 1970 civil war broke out between
Palestinians and King Hussein's troops in Jordan. At the height of the
crisis, Syria was on the verge of occupying the Kingdom of Jordan with its
armed forces.[13] In these unsettled times at the beginning of the 1970s, the

possibility of employing oil as a political weapon was already being discussed in the Arab press. In one widely discussed article published in *al-Ahram*, the journalist Heikal, well known in the West as an author, argued that the Arabs should utilise their oil resources in the struggle.[14] Even oil-producing monarchies generally regarded as 'moderate and conservative', at least on the verbal level, were prepared to exact these requirements in order to underpin their own legitimacy. The 'Palestinian question' is widely recognised as the core issue for all regimes in Arab politics when it comes to legitimacy.[15] At that time, the Kuwaiti National Assembly was still well disposed towards the Palestinians, and in a resolution of 6 January 1973 it recommended the employment of the oil weapon against Israel. Even the Saudi King Faisal had taken various opportunities in May 1973 to point out to the USA that they imported their oil from the Arab states and not from Israel, calling on them to practise a foreign policy that reflected this. Terzian asserts that talks were held with Sadat on this topic in May 1973 during a visit by Faisal to Cairo.[16] The pro-Saddam attitude of the Palestinians during the Gulf War of 1990–91 has rendered this positive Gulf Arab disposition towards the Palestinians a thing of the past. The Palestinians, once central to the economy and politics of Kuwait,[17] are now *personae non gratae*.

War broke out on 6 October, shortly before the 8 October date set long before that for the 36th OPEC Conference in Vienna. The call for a price rise was renewed, while OAPEC Arab members of OPEC were under Arab pressure to put their verbal support for employing the oil weapon into action. Parallel with a deterioration in the military position of the Arab states in the October War and the setting up of an intensive US American airlift to renew Israeli arms supplies, an OAPEC conference was set for 16 October in Kuwait. That same day, the Saudi foreign minister, Saqqaf, flew under Faisal's instructions to Washington for prearranged talks with President Nixon. As an indirect ally of the USA, Saudi Arabia still hoped to be able to act as a moderating influence on the USA with regard to the latter's military support for Israel. Nixon, however, made the mistake of postponing the agreed talks with Saqqaf until 17 October. Anyone familiar with bedouin cultural norms will be aware that King Faisal would be bound to take this as an affront.[18] Nothing now stood in the way of employing the oil weapon as a foreign policy instrument, especially against the USA. On 17 October, the Arab oil ministers in Kuwait adopted a resolution from which the salient passages read as follows:

> The Oil Ministers of the member States of the Organisation of Arab Petroleum Exporting Countries (OAPEC) held a meeting in the city of

Kuwait . . . to consider employing oil in the battle currently raging between the Arabs and Israel. Following a thorough discussion of this question the Oil Ministers . . . *decided* that each Arab oil exporting country immediately cut its oil production by a recurrent monthly rate of no less than 5 per cent to be initially counted on the virtual production of September, thenceforth on the last production figure until such a time as the international community compels Israel to relinquish our occupied territories . . . Nevertheless, the countries that support the Arabs actively and effectively or that take important measures against Israel to compel its withdrawal shall not be prejudiced by this production cut . . . The participants also recommend the countries party to this resolution that the United States be subjected to the most severe cut . . . The participants also recommend that this progressive reduction lead to the total halt of oil supplies to the United States from every individual country party to the resolution.[19]

The following day, Saudi Arabia, Algeria and Qatar reduced their production by 10 per cent instead of the 5 per cent as stated in the resolution. On 4–5 November 1973, the Arab oil ministers met again in Kuwait, where they agreed to a further 25 per cent cut in production in addition to the progressive monthly reduction of 5 per cent.[20] These resolutions adopted by oil ministers were confirmed at the sixth summit meeting of Arab heads of state and monarchs taking place from 26 to 28 November in Algiers.[21] Egypt and Saudi Arabia had already reached agreement on their plan of action during Sadat's visit to Saudi Arabia, prior to the second meeting of Arab oil ministers in Kuwait and the Arab summit in Algiers. Commenting on the Kuwait resolutions, the oil expert Maull states that it was 'Saudi Arabia that dominated the conference . . . clearly in close coordination with Egypt'.[22]

This is not the right place to examine the dramatic rise in the price of oil that occurred in this context.[23] Suffice it to say that the price quadrupled during the winter of 1973/74. The oil embargo was lifted parallel with the success of Henry Kissinger's shuttle diplomacy (see Chapter 6), which aimed at preventing Israel from continuing the October War to the detriment of Egypt. Meeting in Vienna on 17–18 March, Arab oil ministers decided to reward the American achievement in reaching a troop disengagement agreement between Egypt and Israel by lifting the oil embargo. Their original condition, that the embargo would only be lifted after Israeli withdrawal from the occupied Arab territories held since the June 1967 War, was dropped.[24]

Seen from the economic viewpoint, Arab employment of the oil weapon might not necessarily have had the dramatic impact that it did on prices had the oil companies not seized on it as the right moment to pursue their own political strategy of shifting energy resources. The essence of this strategy was to raise the price of oil in order to cover the expenses of technological (such as shale-oil and tar-sand processing), as well as geographical diversification of energy sources (expensive oil from Alaska and the North Sea, etc.). It was for this reason that the oil companies refrained from exhausting their potential for neutralising the price policy effects incurred by employment of the oil weapon.[25]

It is clear today that the oil embargo in fact had a minimal impact on energy supplies. The American-dominated oil companies were able to set oil prices at a level to suit themselves since they had all the necessary organisational means available (vertical integration). Arab oil was thus shipped to 'friendly' countries, that is those not affected by the embargo, while non-Arab oil exports were shipped to those countries that were affected by the Arab embargo (chiefly the USA and Holland).[26] Moreover, the proportion of oil imported by the United States was not so high in that 1973–74 period as it is today. One of the chief victims of the energy crisis was the West European economy, which lost its competitive advantage over the USA (the cheap energy supply to its industry) with the rise in the price of oil. The oil-importing countries of the Third World, however, were even more adversely affected by this increase.[27] European interest in the Middle East has grown since that time. The Euro-Arab Dialogue[28] emerged from the employment of the oil weapon during the October War. The tensions that arose at that time in the NATO alliance between Western Europe and the USA stemmed from their disparate energy policy interests.[29] France had already grasped this predicament during the 1967 June War, as we saw in Chapter 4, where we also cited the appraisal of the American energy expert Robert Lieber, that accommodation of the energy situation is beyond the scope of European potential.[30]

In short then, the impact of employing the oil weapon was to raise the profit margins of American oil companies and Arab oil monarchies in equal measure.[31] There are, of course, OAPEC states such as Algeria, Iraq and Libya who are not among the oil monarchies. Taking into account the difference within OAPEC between *high absorber* states (i.e. those who completely utilise their oil revenues) and *low absorber* states (i.e. those who retain a substantial proportion of their oil revenues in the form of surplus) helps to clarify the essence of the term *petro-dollar power*. Arab oil monarchies, with vast petro-dollar reserves from these surpluses which they invest predominantly in Europe and the USA,[32] have effectively constituted a petro-dollar power since 1973. These countries nevertheless remain underdeveloped bedouin societies lacking – apart from petro-dollars – all the prerequisites for establishing themselves and acting as regional powers. The military vulnerability of the oil-rich Gulf states is the greatest obstacle to their playing a leading role. This fact became all too clear during the Kuwait crisis. Without external support, chiefly from the USA, as well as Egypt and Syria, Saudi Arabia would have been unable to defend itself against Saddam Hussein. During the crisis, Tony Walker pointed out: 'Wealth alone does not guarantee security. In spite of many billions spent on weapons, Saudi Arabia could not deter Iraqi aggression against Kuwait nor guarantee its own security.'[33] This fact helps to shed light on the huge importance of the Arab country with the most developed infrastructure: Egypt. The essence of the *Saudi–Egyptian axis*, which came into existence in 1973 and lasted until the separate peace between Egypt and Israel, is closely related to this regional context. Egypt's subsequent expulsion from the Arab community at the instigation of Iraq (Baghdad summit of 19 November 1978) did not last long. With the aid of Saudi Arabia, now that the second Gulf War has ended, Egypt has regained its leading role within the Arab state system. The loser has been Iraq, which used the Camp David accords to expel Egypt from the Arab community in a bid to take over the leadership. Now the tables are turned and Iraq is the expelled member of the Arab community.

THE EGYPTIAN–SAUDI AXIS AND COMPETITION FOR A POSITION OF POWER SINCE THE OCTOBER WAR

At an all-Arab conference on strategy held in Amman (September 1987),[34] a paper prepared at the al-Ahram Center for Political and Strategic Studies was discussed, which put forward the thesis that the years from 1967 to 1975 had been the best for the 'contemporary Arab regional order' in terms of Arab reconciliation and cooperation. The author of this paper, Usama al-Ghazali,[35] justified this to me in a communication at the al-Ahram Center. He argued that during this period, the Arab states gave up their ideology-laden inter-Arab rivalries and concentrated instead on overcoming jointly the consequences of their defeat in the Six Day War. After 1967, Arab politics became more pragmatic. It is true that the 'Arab Cold War' of the Nasser period came to an end then. It is true that a number of Arab states, heartened by the weakening of Egypt's position, began to lay claim to regional leadership – foremost among these at the time was Iraq, although Syria, Libya and Algeria made similar claims.[36] However, it is not possible to view these ideological claims to leadership separately from processes taking place at that time within the Middle East-subsystem or its environment. Pawelka has noted that an increasing involvement of the Arab states in the system of international economic relations led 'decisively by the elites of the oil-producing countries'.[37] In the course of his analysis Pawelka arrives at a systematic classification of the Egyptian–Saudi axis in its regional–international context: 'Dominated by the oil-producing countries, a remarkable institutionalisation of inter- and transnational relations took place in the seventies . . . By this time Egypt had made friends with the conservative states again.'[38] Structural changes in the regional economy during this period were characterised by intensified structural interconnectedness. This translateral process of integration was brought about by a flow of capital from the petro-dollar states into the poorer but structurally more developed Arab societies, first and foremost Egypt, as well as by a migration of labour from the latter to the rich Gulf states.[39]

The foundations for the first Egyptian–Saudi axis of the 1970s had been laid even before the October War. Saudi Arabia and Egypt had been moving towards closer relations since 1967, but as long as Nasser was still alive they remained cool. After Sadat came to power these relations were intensified to the point of including foreign policy coordination.[40] In February 1971, the Egyptian foreign minister visited Riyadh, where he confirmed a 'complete consonance of views'.[41] The following March the Saudi foreign minister, Saqqaf, returned this visit in Cairo, speaking of a bond of 'friendship and warmth that will become deeper still'.[42] In June of the same year the Saudi King Faisal himself made a trip to Cairo, and the following year Sadat made a visit to Saudi Arabia and Kuwait.

After the October War King Faisal paid another visit to Cairo 'to meet the heroes of the Canal crossing'.[43] This time he made a gift of a thousand million dollars to Egypt, also granting them a facility of interest-free credit up to 500 million dollars. *Al-Ahram* described the encounter between Sadat and Faisal as the 'beginning of a process of unfolding'. The foundations of this cooperation naturally also included access to the religio-political services of the Azhar University as part of a cultural agreement.[44] The office of Rector of Azhar (Sheikh al-Azhar) constitutes the highest authority in Sunni Islam for the issuing of religious legal judgement (*fetwa*). It is worth noting here that it was of central importance to the Saudis during the Gulf War that Sheikh al-Azhar Jadulhaq legitimated the *deployment* of American troops in Saudi Arabia, in August 1990, by means of a *fetwa* to that effect.[45] After Sadat's visit to Jerusalem in November 1977, also incidentally legitimated by an Azhar *fetwa*, the Saudis grew very concerned. The then Crown Prince Fahd visited Cairo in August 1978, where Sadat assured him that there would be no separate peace between Egypt and Israel.[46]

The Saudis therefore felt betrayed by Sadat when a peace agreement was concluded after the Camp David talks. They were now under pressure to join the radical Anti-Sadat Front led by Iraq.[47] The leading Egyptian newspaper *al-Ahram* reacted to the breaking-off of Saudi–Egyptian relations by Saudi Arabia in April 1979 with the following supercilious commentary:

> The Saudi position is based on the following: 1. fear of threats from the Ba'th Party and the Palestinians to bring the conflict into Saudi bedrooms, 2. protest against the USA, who let go the demise of the Shah of Iran and could do the same with the Saudis, and 3. the Saudi claim to Arab leadership – a burden to which they are not even remotely equal. The breaking-off of relations will break neither the position nor the power of Egypt.[48]

With the hindsight of the Gulf War the above-quoted *al-Ahram* text reads prophetically with its hints about the Iraqi Ba'th and the Palestinians. In the light of political developments in the Middle East during the 1980s, and above all during the Kuwaiti crisis of 1990, *al-Ahram* was right. The PLO-backed Iraqi invasion of Kuwait openly – and without manoeuvre – forced the Gulf Arabs to commit themselves openly to their security concerns.

Sadat was fully aware of the regional and international importance of Egypt. He was not going to be misled by the Baghdad boycott, and made his foreign policy decisions accordingly.[49] He knew that the USA would make up for the loss of Saudi financial aid, and that Egypt's isolation from the Arab states would be without major repercussions. Following the Camp David accords Egypt became the second largest recipient of US aid after Israel.[50] What Sadat could not have known was that he would pay for these decisions with his life. He was assassinated in October 1981 by fanatical Islamic fundamentalists.[51] The deeds of religious fanatics are not as easy to predict as foreign policy decisions. It gives cause for concern, therefore, that many Western foreign policy experts have no notion of political Islam and fail to take into account the security policy problems associated with it.[52]

The first Gulf War between Iraq and Iran, which lasted for eight years, broke out in Sadat's lifetime. However, inasmuch as the Iran–Iraq War spilled over beyond the interstate level, that is affecting both Egypt and Saudi Arabia, it is also of interest to us here. As the Gulf War intensified, and with it the Iranian threat to Saudi Arabia,[53] the Islamic monarchy made every effort to bring Egypt back into the Arab community of states. Even radical Iraq, whose Ba'th leaders had once put the Saudis under pressure to join the Anti-Sadat Front, now spoke of 'Iraqi–Egyptian friendship'. Without Egyptian military aid to Iraq,[54] the cost of which was met by the Saudis, Iraq could never have withstood eight years of war. Saddam Hussein forgot about this aid when he invaded Kuwait on 2 August 1990 and adopted a hostile position towards Egypt. Iraq, which had emerged strengthened from the first Gulf War, was seeking to take over the hegemonic leadership of the Arab world that Egypt had formerly enjoyed under Nasser. After the first Gulf War (1980–88) was over the two former belligerent parties, Iraq and Iran, began to flood the international market with their oil exports. Both countries were dependent on their respective revenues to cover the cost of war damage. The highest ever oil price was, of course, recorded during the Iran–Iraq War itself in December 1980: US$40 a barrel. This extremely high price was reached again during the Gulf crisis in October 1990.[55] In neither the first nor the second Gulf War could this trend be sustained, however. During the Iran–Iraq War the supply of oil exceeded demand by an average of 7 per cent, hence the subsequent drop in price as a result of the 'oil glut' phenomenon described in the introduction. At the OPEC conference of July–August 1986, a maximum output level and a quota system were agreed on for all OPEC members except Iraq, which enabled them to halt the drop in price at US$7 a barrel in April 1986. This price then rose again to stabilise at US$18 a barrel.

The end of the Iran–Iraq War dramatically upset this quota system: OPEC members began to cheat one another by exceeding their allotted production quotas. The 'war with oil' waged indirectly by OPEC in 1973 against five leading Western industrial countries, parallel with employment of the Arab oil weapon, was now from 1988 to 1990, before the second Gulf War, waged within OPEC itself. First, Saudi Arabia no longer adhered to its allotted production quota of 4.3 million barrels a day. At that time, the monarchy was producing an average of 6.7 million barrels daily, and threatened to step up its oil production to 10 million barrels a day. In October 1988, this could have resulted in a price drop from US$10–12 per barrel to US$5.[56] Despite this threat which, had it been put into effect, would have resulted in a number of oil-producing countries stopping production altogether since it would no longer have been viable for them to produce (production costs being higher than the market price), OPEC failed to achieve control of the market through the practice of a binding regulation for all thirteen members.[57] A formal resolution adopted by OPEC oil ministers at the 84th regular conference in Vienna on 28 November 1988 – that their states would agree on a maximum production level of 18.5 million barrels daily as part of a quota system (i.e. 4 million barrels less than was actually being produced) – was received sceptically by experts even at the time.[58]

To sum up, it may be concluded that the 'war with oil' that strengthened the petro-dollar monarchies parallel with the 1973 October War, was then waged within their own ranks from 1980 to 1990, particularly after the first Gulf War was over in 1988. The Kuwaiti crisis, ushered in by Saddam Hussein's speech of 17 July 1990, was closely related to this situation, as we shall be seeing in more detail in Part Four. Saddam's aim was to force the Gulf states to produce less oil so that the price would rise, and Iraq's oil revenues with it.[59] This crisis led to another war, and this in turn to disaster for Iraq, devastating its economy. Having wanted to take over Egypt's place as leader of the Arab world, it found itself emerging from the war utterly destroyed and politically isolated. With Saudi help, Egypt since the Gulf War has regained its position as the leading Arab regional power, following a complete restitution of the Egyptian–Saudi axis. Even before the destruction of the Iraqi war machine began on 17 January, economics experts were making predictions about the post-war era that have since come true. Michael Field wrote in the *Financial Times*, on 12 December 1990: 'Egypt will emerge as a leading Saudi and Gulf business partner.'[60] In the same issue of the *FT*, Tony Walker continues this analysis on political grounds by stating: 'Strengthening the links with Egypt . . . and the Saudi willingness to cast aside the holy grail of regional affairs, namely the barren search for consensus, may well have established the ground rules of a new Arab order'.[61] In the light of the lessons learned from the second Gulf War, the Saudis are seeking to shelve their former brand of 'cheque diplomacy of the purse strings', which consisted of 'buying off potentially troublesome neighbours' such as the PLO. With Egypt's help, they are seeking instead to replace this defensive policy with a more offensive stance of which there have been many signs recently, not least with reference to Saudi oil policy.

This tough new approach started at the OPEC meeting in March 1991, in Geneva, where they abandoned their former reticence and willingness to compromise, staking a resolute claim to a future dominant position in OPEC.[62] The Saudis refused, for example, to give up their present production level of 8.5 million barrels a day and to return to their pre-Gulf War 1990–91 level of 5.4 million barrels a day.

The Saudis are planning to use their increased revenues to cover not only the costs of the Gulf War itself, but also the burden of dealing with its consequences. According to statements issued by Abdullah Bishara, Secretary-General of the Saudi-led Gulf Cooperation Council, the organisation is planning to make available an initial sum of US$5 billion, to be increased to a possible 15 billion, to work together with Egypt and Syria towards the 'emergence of a new Arab social and economic order'.[63] This vision of the future heralds the emergence of new patterns of leadership in the Middle East regional subsystem, aimed at building a new order there on the ruins of the Gulf War through the medium of a new Egyptian–Saudi axis.[64]

Part Four

The Gulf War, its Linkages and Background: Regional Dynamic and the Fragmentation of the Middle East in the Post-Cold War Era

Introduction

In 1990, Europeans were celebrating peace in the aftermath of the break-down of communism in Eastern Europe and the end of the Cold War that had accompanied it. They were interrupted and taken unawares in their celebrations by the Gulf crisis, which resulted in an international war led by the United States and carried out by armed forces provided by twenty-eight nations. Three Arab nations, Egypt, Syria and Morocco, provided military divisions to participate in that war against an Arab state led by an oriental despot aiming to restore Arab imperial glory, although he lacked the capabilities to do so successfully.

Prior to the Iraqi invasion of Kuwait on 2 August, which might to all intents and purposes be considered as an act of war, as well as the beginning of the Gulf War itself, students of the Middle East regarded the Six Day War as the most decisive event in the post-Second World War history of the region. The recent war initiated by Saddam Hussein's Iraq, however, has surpassed in both its impact and implications all previous political events in the region since the First World War. In the aftermath of the Arab Revolt of 1916 and the following dissolution of the Ottoman Empire, the Arab state that had been promised did not come about. The formerly Arab part of the Ottoman Empire was divided up among the colonial powers, and colonial boundaries were drawn. It is precisely this historical background to which the initial outbreak of the Gulf crisis refers and which the repercussions of the war affect. It is for this reason that the recent Gulf War – in terms of its constraints and repercussions – is so significant. It has utterly shattered the Arab order.

Part Four accommodates three additional chapters which were not included in the original German edition. The first of these (Chapter 8) provides an analysis of the pre-Gulf War Middle East as shaped by the earlier October War, as well as by the 1980–88 Iran–Iraq War. Chapter 9 deals with the development of the Gulf crisis into a war, pointing out that although hostilities started on 2 August 1990 it was not yet an international war until after 17 January 1991. Finally, in Chapter 10 we shall be dealing with the prospects for security and peace in the region in the aftermath of the war, while attempting to place the Gulf War in the overall framework of conflict and peace in the Middle East.

8 The Middle East between the 1973 October War and the 1990–91 Gulf War: An Epidemically Militarised Region of Conflict?

As we saw in the Introduction, modern European history before 1945 was a history of wars.[1] Classic works by Norbert Elias and Reinhard Bendix[2] deal with the important function of wars in European history as midwives of social change and order creation. Recent research has led to the conclusion that nowadays wars take place predominantly in Third World countries. Gerald Braun speaks of these countries utilising war as an instrument for the pursuit of political ends in the Clausewitzian sense, 'up to the point where industrial societies enter the post-Clausewitzian age'.[3] The war of June 1967, for example, was planned and carried out by Israel with the express strategic intention of destroying Nasser's development model. In the October War of 1973, Egypt was pursuing the strategic aim of improving its negotiating position *vis-à-vis* Israel. The Camp David peace accord was the outcome of this improvement. In this regard, therefore, both wars may be classified as strategic wars. The question nevertheless suggests itself whether the state of affairs left in the wake of the two major regional wars – the minor ongoing wars that occurred between 1973 and 1990 – might better be described as 'epidemic' in the sense meant by Rapoport.[4] If the wars of 1967 and 1973 were, in the Clausewitzian sense, carried out to achieve strategic aims, and were short-lived, the interminable subsequent wars (including the 1980–88 Iran–Iraq War and the Lebanon War among others) might be assessed in the sense meant by Tolstoy as 'cataclysmic', that is destructive and futile. These latter wars are not strategically thought-out acts based on a political concept.

Since 1973 wars in the Middle East have acquired the dynamic of epidemics. The distinguished Swiss journalist Arnold Hottinger thus asks: are we facing 'The Thirty Years War of the Arabs?'[5] In the Introduction to this book, we saw how that protracted European war resulted in 1648 in the Westphalian Peace, that is a European order that in its day was the starting point for a European states system. Analysts can find few signs of a new order developing out of today's wars in the Middle East, however. The only consequences seem to be destruction and fragmentation, giving the Middle East regional subsystem the character of a 'disordered system'.[6] Since the Gulf War, President Bush cherishes hopes of a new order for the Middle East as part of a sought-after New World Order. Nevertheless, future prospects promise disorder rather than order, both regionally and globally.[7]

The 1967 June War upset the regional position of the Soviet superpower's two allies, Egypt and Syria. Although both superpowers avoided direct intervention during the war (see Chapter 3), the conviction persists to this day among Arabs that Israel could not have won the war without American backing.[8] The brusque rejection by the Arabs of the USA, whose image in the Middle East grows ever more negative, needs to be seen in this context.[9] The Gulf War has contributed to a strengthening of anti-American feeling in the Middle East. Earlier the USA did substantially improve its position in the region by turning the Arab defeat in the 1967 June War and the crisis associated with it into a starting point for renewed penetration of the region.[10] By the time the October War was at its height the USA was able to pursue two aims simultaneously: the prevention of a second Arab defeat, and avoidance of a confrontation with the other superpower (see Chapter 6). The effect of this strategy was to win Egypt as an ally for the USA. Since that time Egypt has been, next to Israel, the most important US ally in the Middle East.[11] Sadat's shift to a pro-American policy for his country was linked with an outlook described as 'political Sadatism' by left-wing Egyptian authors.[12] The separate Camp David Peace was the logical result of this outlook.[13] No one would doubt the moral integrity of the strongly ethically minded US President Carter, who had a laudable vision of laying at Camp David the foundation stone for a 'comprehensive peace solution'. He himself writes in his recent book: 'Since the Israeli–Egyptian Peace treaty was signed, much blood has been shed unnecessarily and hopes for a negotiated peace have faded.'[14] The separate peace with Israel concluded by Sadat cannot seriously be explained using terms such as 'betrayal of the Arab cause', as Arab conspiracy-ridden discussion asserted at the time. Sadiq Jalal al-'Azm, a critical author quoted a number of times in Part One, while declaring his rejection of Sadatism, discusses analytically the underlying regional and international conditions in which this political action occurred.[15]

Egypt's economic crisis compelled a search for new sources of aid. Even Arab petro-dollar donations were not enough to tide them over the crisis. Sadat's idea was that opening up his country to the West would be more likely to improve rather than worsen its relations with Saudi Arabia, itself an indirect American ally. The Soviet Union was unable to provide Egypt with the help it needed: the key instrument of Soviet foreign policy was 'to organise its military aid in such a way that promised the most enduring possible potential for political influence'.[16] Until its dissolution the Soviet Union was a military superpower, but never an economic one, and for a variety of reasons was – with some justice – portrayed as an 'incomplete superpower'.[17] The decay of the USSR's influence supports this view. After the October War, Egypt needed economic aid, especially foodstuffs (American grain), not arms, in the first instance. The Soviet Union was not able to meet these needs – a fact that offers one of the principal explanations for the post-1973 shift in Egyptian foreign policy, through its opening up to the West and its break with the Soviet Union.[18] Although both superpowers were stepping up their penetration of the region at the time, neither had any consistent concept for a feasible comprehensive solution to the conflict.[19] Since the 1990–91 Gulf War the USA has been the only acting superpower in the region, but American foreign policy clearly reveals the lack of a consistent strategic concept for dealing properly with the Middle East.

Egypt's opting-out of the Arab front in the Arab–Israeli conflict began in 1975 with the Sinai II Accord,[20] followed two years later in November 1977 by Sadat's unexpected visit to Jerusalem as a diplomacy of surprise. The Camp David negotiations in September 1978 and the signing of the separate Israeli–Egyptian treaty of March 1979 were the next steps. A resolution to use sanctions against Egypt was adopted at the Baghdad Summit Conference of November 1978, and confirmed at the Arab Summit in Tunis in 1979. First, Egypt was isolated from its Arab environment.[21] One clear consequence of this is that *major regional wars* between Israel and its Arab neighbours can no longer take place, because they are not feasible without Egyptian military potential. However, this does not mean peace by any means. The variety of regional wars of the 1980s and the recent international Gulf War provide evidence to support this assessment. One major lesson to be learned from the latest war is that the Arab–Israeli conflict is not the exclusive source of armed conflicts in the Middle East.

The shattering of Egypt's hegemonical position in June 1967 was followed by an initial period of chaos: the Middle East subsystem was diffuse from 1967 to 1970. After Nasser's death the Egyptian–Saudi axis described in Chapter 7 began to unfold, taking on perceptible contours after October 1973, only to come to an end in 1977. In the wake of Nasser's death, claims raised to take the place of Egypt and hence achieve regional hegemony have contributed to the increasingly polycentric form of the subsystem since that time. Wars in the Middle East took on a corresponding character during the

1980s: they were fragmented, had indeterminate fronts, were confined to the subregional level, and yet were utterly epidemic. Those in power do not treat war as a politically calculated instrument, but as a long-term situation that enables them to retain power. In the article already cited, Hottinger observes how the present-day power structures of Middle Eastern societies 'are themselves formed by war and tailored to suit the needs of war'. In this region, he continues, wars 'increasingly constitute the foundation of life for the peoples'. Where war is not really being waged the aim is 'to constantly prepare for war without actually causing it to break out'.[22] Hottinger even speaks in this context of a 'Middle Eastern Thirty Years War'. Although comparisons of this kind lack any historical basis, they do nevertheless indicate to what extent the region is militarised and disordered.

One element in this ongoing war situation is the political rise of the Palestinians discussed in Chapter 4. After June 1967, the Palestinians freed themselves from their Arab custodians and by the time of the second Gulf War had raised themselves to the status of a conflict factor in their own right. Since 1967 the PLO's role in international politics has been that of a quasi-state.[23] First, the Palestinians set up a 'state within a state' on Jordanian territory, although they were driven out of it during the crisis of September 1970.[24] Lebanon served as a substitute for this lost military base from then until the Israeli invasion of June 1982.[25] It should be stressed that the civil war that broke out in Lebanon in 1975[26] was not the work of the Palestinians. Strictly speaking, the role of the Palestinians should be reduced to one of the parties to the conflict. The cause of the civil war lay in the disrupted confessional make-up of Lebanon itself, not in the presence of the Palestinians in Lebanon. The consequences of the two major regional wars of 1967 and 1973 exacerbated this confessional conflict in Lebanon: the Palestinians merely triggered it off.[27]

At one time, secular Arab nationalism was able to unite Christians and Muslims of all confessions. The post-1967 crisis of the at first diffuse and then fragmented Middle East subsystem brought about the 'end of Pan-Arabism' (Ajami). Pan-Arab nationalism was replaced by ethnic and religious ideologies, both of which were equally divisive. The repoliticisation of Islam and the revival of ethnic identities can be traced back to this process. The crisis has helped to strengthen political Islam, whose adherents are about to fill the vacuum left by delegitimisation. Egypt was a setting for the political resurgence of Islam long before that of Iran.[28]

Even the victors of 1967 were affected by system-changing consequences of war consisting – as the internationally renowned Israeli sociologist Shmuel Eisenstadt informs us – 'of a process of decline and decay setting into the institutional model'.[29] Eisenstadt is referring here to the model of a secular modern state based on democracy. He points to the 'growth of diverse religious movements and of ethnic consciousness and ethnic militancy',[30] and questions the primacy of the political over the military institution in Israel.[31] If this development were to persist, Israel would forfeit, apart from the ethno-religious exclusivity pointed out by the Israeli political scientist Dan Diner,[32] its advantage over its neighbours, namely the fact that it is a democratic state based on civil society. This would push the prospects for peace even further into the unforeseeable future. Fundamentalists and ethnic militants, who are currently winning the upper hand on both the Israeli and the Arab sides, are unable to communicate:[33] a peaceful solution could never be negotiated through them. Looking at the Middle East region as a whole it is possible to observe, side by side with the perceptible polycentric character of the subsystem, a return to the diffuse symptoms that manifested after June 1967. Until the Gulf War a number of Arab candidates were competing to succeed Egypt as regional power in the Arab part of the subsystem. It was clear from the outset that Iraq under Saddam Hussein was the leading contender among them. The others were Syria, Libya and Algeria. Syria and Iraq are ruled by military regimes dominated by the pan-Arab Ba'th party,[34] which has a secular ideology but recruits its cadres on a sectarian basis (Alawite Shiites in Syria and Sunnis in Iraq).[35] Before developing its potential in the Iran–Iraq War, Iraq was not in a position to carry through its claim to take over pan-Arab leadership,[36] let alone pursue its ambitions in the Gulf region, where Iran under the Shah was the undisputed power in the Gulf subregional order. Iraq emerged strengthened from the first Gulf War, and began to voice its claims to leadership openly. It was these claims that led to the second Gulf War and ultimately to Iraq's destruction.

Compared to Egypt and Iraq (with populations of 54 and 18 million respectively), Syria is a relatively small country, with a population of 12 million and neither sizeable oil fields nor other important resources at its disposal. This non-communist country did nevertheless rise in October 1973 to become the most important regional client state of the Soviet Union. The Soviet superpower was trying at that time to build up a new base as a substitute for Egypt.[37] This is the sole explanation for how in the 1978–82 period Syria, according to data in the SIPRI Yearbook (1983), climbed to first place in the table of the twenty leading arms importers in the Third World as a whole (9.4 per cent of total Third World arms imports).[38] In the 1980–82 period, Syria was listed in these statistics of the SIPRI Yearbook (1985) as in second place with 10.5 per cent of total Third World arms imports, behind Egypt with 10.6 per cent.[39]

Syria is in a position to threaten Jordan militarily, and has repeatedly used this leverage to bring pressure to bear on Jordan's allies, Saudi Arabia and Kuwait, into making petro-dollar payments. Even before Assad's take-over in November 1970, Syria had intervened in Jordan on 19 and 20 September. During the crisis of September 1970 Syria posed an even greater threat to the Jordanian monarch[40] than the armed troops of the PLO which were at that time still active in his country. Since 1976, Syria has had a decisive military presence in Lebanon.[41] Compared to Israel, however, Syria is weak. Despite the inevitable war rhetoric during the Israeli invasion of Lebanon, Syria did everything in its power to avoid a military confrontation with Israel. Although it lacks the prerequisites for such status, Syria is one of the countries in the subsystem making serious claims to regional leadership.

Until the subsiding of Soviet military aid under Gorbachev, Syria pursued a policy linked to the strategic concept of achieving military parity with Israel. On this basis, Assad tried to set himself up as Nasser's successor to Arab leadership.[42] Based on Syrian claims, as well as on its armament, strategic commentators such as Goodman and Carus wrongly predicted that the future battlefield would be between Syria and Israel.[43] In fact, that battlefield was in the Gulf, for Syria could never wage a war against Israel on its own. Hafiz al-Assad is not as adventurous as Saddam Hussein. Given this, since Camp David there could never be an overall Arab–Israeli war like the previous ones between 1948 and 1973. It is clear that the economic weakness of Syria has prevented it from carrying through its ideological claims to leadership. Another factor working against Syria is its lack of the foreign policy capabilities appropriate to the weight that a regional power would need to have. Syria made successful use of the second Gulf War to stabilise its military and political position in Lebanon by disposing of its opponents (General Aoun among others). Like Egypt after the 1973 October War, Syrian policy shifted towards the West during the 1990–91 Gulf War. As early as August 1990, Syria joined the US-led anti-Iraq front and consented to send troops to Saudi Arabia[44] in return for a cash payment of a billion US$.

The two remaining contenders for the leadership, Algeria and Libya, both lie outside the centre of the subsystem and are not directly involved in the central zone of the Arab–Israeli conflict – a factor that places constraints on their respective foreign policies. Both are oil-producing countries and OPEC members, and therefore better off than Syria in terms of resources. Since gaining sovereignty in 1962, Algeria has supported Egypt as an expression of gratitude for Egyptian arms supplies during their struggle for independence. Not least, the Algerians have not forgotten that France fought Egypt during the Suez War in an attempt to cut off this source of support for the Algerian independence movement, the FLN. Algerian troops were symbolically involved in the 1967 June War. Even prior to Nasser's death, however, Algerian relations with Egypt were growing cooler, since Algeria disapproved of Egypt's spirit of compromise.[45] Still feeding on the memory that it was once a liberation movement, the FLN, which after 1962 moved on to become the sole ruling party,[46] has focused support on the Palestinian Liberation Organisation (PLO).[47] Since the death of Boumedienne and the rise of Chadhli Benjedid (deposed 1992), Algeria's foreign policy has been very moderate and taken on the character of 'mediator'[48] (e.g. in the Lebanon conflict and the first Gulf War) rather than that of combatant. The dissolution of the FLN mid January 1992 and the rise of the 'State Committee' (Comitée d'Etat) marked the turn of Algeria to focus on domestic policy.

A different case is Libya, which has declared itself a model for all Arab lands on the strength of its *jamahirriyya* [49] (a new Arabic word with the approximate meaning 'revolutionary people's councils republic').[50] Although this sparsely populated desert country (population 4 million) has vast oil resources, which it uses as an instrument of its foreign policy, it is structurally one of the most backward Arab states. Leaving aside the strident statements of its leader Qadhafi, Libya lacks in its foreign policy the needed capabilities vital for a regional great power to sustain and exercise its position. An additional factor working against Libya is that Qadhafi has completely exhausted the potential of his country in his war against Chad and other equally disastrous military adventures in black Africa.[51] Libya's claim to regional leadership in the Middle East is viewed with equal scepticism and amusement by experts and experienced politicians. This shift of attention towards Africa may serve as a compensation for the fact that under Qadhafi Libya was unable to attain pan-Arab leadership.[52]

Given the isolation imposed on Egypt by its Arab neighbours between Camp David and the Arab Summit of Amman in November 1987, the only other candidate for political leadership of the region up to that time – apart from the Iraqi, Syrian, Algerian and Libyan actors outlined above – was Saudi Arabia. In the course of this book (see Chapter 4), I have had cause to modify the thesis I developed in my 1984 article, 'From Centre of Revolution (Egypt) to Centre of the Petro-Dollar (Saudi Arabia)', on the basis of my recent research. While in one sense Saudi Arabia has undoubtedly taken on more and more the role of leading regional power since the defeat of Egypt in the 1967 Six Day War, and particularly since the October War, this has nevertheless occurred without Saudi politicians ever making overt claims to leadership of the kind asserted by Assad in Syria or Qadhafi in Libya. Its style of leadership is less a matter of laying claim to hegemonical power as 'in preventing the hegemony of any single Arab state in the region',[53] as Quandt has aptly put it. In the cited book, Quandt points out in detail how 'the Saudis have shown in recent years an awareness of the limits of their power . . . It was primarily foreigners, not the Saudis themselves, who viewed the kingdom as an emerging superpower.'[54] The recent Gulf War has clearly demonstrated these limits. Saudi Arabia could never have protected itself with its own means against the real threats of Saddam Hussein's Iraq. It needed external support.

Until the Gulf War, the Saudi regional leadership pursued a policy of upholding its security interests using petro-dollar diplomacy as a means of neutralising any impending threats to destabilise the monarchy arising from the regional environment. This always formed the basis of cooperation between the Islamic oil monarchies and their neighbours. John Duke Anthony has pertinently described this form of cooperation as follows: 'The other Arab states desire a close relationship with Saudi Arabia for a multitude of reasons – money, oil, and political support. The Saudis, for their part, acknowledge that cordial relations with the rest of the Arab world are a key to their own security. They feel threatened, they need good regional relations and they can pay for them.'[55] Since the Gulf War the Saudis seem to have abandoned this purse strings diplomacy, because it failed. Currently, in the aftermath of the Gulf War, they are keen to establish an Arab order under their leadership, with Syria and Egypt as its pillars, and are willing to provide US$15 billion to fund it.[56]

The Egyptian–Saudi axis of the 1970s offered a good basis for such a model of regional relations. At that time, the Saudis were aware that in the absence of serious military potential they could not achieve their goal of regional peace, in line with their security policy, by means of petro-dollar cheque-book diplomacy alone. The Iranian Revolution, coupled with the Camp David Peace, compelled the Saudis to end the axis with Egypt abruptly but reluctantly. The eight-year Iran–Iraq Gulf War altered this situation. It was waged simultaneously with a number of other wars in the same region (in the Western Sahara, Lebanon, southern Sudan and by Libya in Chad), contributing both to a fragmentation and a destabilisation of the Middle East subsystem. Syria and Libya, for a time even Israel, supplied arms to Iran, while Jordan, the Gulf states and Egypt supported Iraq. This predicament forced Saudi Arabia and some of the other Arab states to rethink their positions. The Iran–Iraq War paved the way for the return of Egypt to Arab politics in the role of protector,[57] but not as a leading political power with a legitimating development model such as Nasserism.

This claim was now being made by Iraq.[58] By now, Egypt wielded military potential supplied by the USA, and would have been capable in the 1980s of protecting Iraq and the Gulf Arabs against Iran. The threat from Iran that accompanied the Iran–Iraq War was the impetus behind this return of Egypt to the Arab fold under President Mubarak.[59]

The Iran–Iraq War started on 22 September 1980 when Iraqi troops invaded Iranian territory, triggering the first Gulf War, which dragged on for eight years and may be termed an epidemic war. This military operation was named the 'Battle of Qadisiyya' by Iraqi leaders.[60] Iraqi conduct of the war was based from the outset on a false assessment of Iranian military potential, and on a misreading of the strategic and political situations.[61] The Iraqi leadership under Saddam Hussein based their calculations on the initially correct information that the Iranian armed forces (prior to the deposition of the Shah Iran had the second most powerful military potential in the region after Israel) were in disarray. Working on the additional assumption that the Sunni Arab population living in the Iranian border province of Khuzestan (the Iraqis call it 'Arabistan' to support their territorial claim) would back Iraqi troops marching into it, Saddam Hussein was convinced that success in a blitzkrieg would force Khomeini to sign a new border treaty in favour of Iraq. This would nullify an earlier treaty concluded by Iraq in Algiers, in 1975, and respect what in the Iraqi view was the correctly drawn boundary, along the Shat-al-Arab waterway (the confluence of the Tigris and Euphrates to its estuary in the Gulf). The formal *casus belli* was that this waterway, which has a mere fifty-mile-long access to the Gulf, constituted a lifeline threatened by Iran.

In fact the real causes of this war extended far beyond a simple border dispute. They embraced a multitude of historical (enmity between the Arabs and Persians since the seventh century), religio-political (tension between Arab Sunna and Iranian Shia), economic and political (the struggle between Iraq and Iran for hegemony in the Gulf), and even territorial issues (Khomeini's claims on Shiite shrines located in Iraq and an Iraqi claim on the Iranian province of Khuzestan). All this makes it impossible to reduce the causes of the war[62] to any single issue, although the claim of Iraq to be a regional power in the Gulf might with hindsight be considered the most important single aspect.

Iraqi recourse to the name al-Qadisiyya in itself reveals the ideological substance behind the military offensive. However, Saddam Hussein underestimated the unifying political force of the potent socio-psychological synthesis in Iran between Shia Islam and Persian nationalism, which is based on a deeply rooted hostile ideological image of Arab Sunnis, who persecuted Persian Shiites for centuries.[63] Saddam Hussein similarly underestimated the force of Khomeini as a charismatic leader symbolising all these ideas.[64] During the early stages of the eight-year war the Iraqis were able to win Iranian territory with success. Only a year after the outbreak of war, however, in September 1981, the Iranians successfully broke through the siege of the Iranian town of Abadan, which lies on the Shat al-Arab (where there are huge oil refineries). From November 1981 onwards the Iraqis lost the offensive, as Iranian troops, who had been in disarray at the time war broke out, were increasingly united by religio-nationalist fervour and launched a counter-attack. This first Gulf War could not be won on the battlefield. The Iraqi leadership realised its strategic error and was prepared to put an end to the war on the basis of Resolution 598 passed by the UN Security Council on 20 July 1987. Iran at that time had two conditions to be met: the deposition of Saddam Hussein's regime and the payment of reparations by Iraq to Iran. Since neither of these conditions could be met, the war raged on until the summer of 1988. During the final phase, the military position of Iraq improved as a consequence of deploying chemical weapons. The Iraqi air force, which was able to retain air superiority, deployed these weapons, as well as concentrating bomb attacks on economic targets in Iran, including non-Iranian oil tankers loaded with Iranian oil. It became more and more difficult for Iran to export its oil.

Iran's unconditional acceptance in August 1988 of UN Security Council Resolution 598 was preceded by a stepping-up of Iraqi military operations that improved their bargaining position and not only severely affected the Iranian economy, but also threatened the safety of the civilian population as a result of the deployment of chemical weapons. The first months of 1988, moreover, saw the resort by both sides to a city war, which included surface-to-surface missiles directed against major cities and whose victims were exclusively the civilian population. Iranian intransigence in the face of the unanimously passed UN Resolution 598 led to its isolation. The Iranian leadership responded to the destruction of its economic centres by the superior and still intact Iraqi air force with death commando missions by Iranian 'gunboats' against oil tankers. Apart from sporadic exceptions the Iranian air force was effectively out of action. A lone sortie by a single Iranian combat aircraft that fired missiles on 2 February 1988, for example, was the first of its kind in two years. This, as well as the mining of the Gulf by Iran and the consequent danger to oil shipments, resulted in the USA stepping up its military presence there with naval task forces.

Following the successful Saudi–Jordanian initiative at the Arab summit in Amman to bring Egypt back into the Arab world, Egypt despatched military personnel to the Gulf states with the aim of improving their defences against Iran. Saudi Arabia imposed an economic embargo on Iran.

The international community was willing, at least verbally, to impose an arms embargo on intransigent Iran. At that time, Saddam Hussein's Iraq enjoyed the support of the international community while it was pursuing its military build-up. Under these circumstances the Iranian leadership acquiesced. Even Khomeini publicly declared his willingness to swallow UN Security Council Resolution 598 – in his words 'worse than poison'. There was a de facto ceasefire on 3 August which officially came into force on 20 August under the supervision of UN military observers. Five days later peace negotiations between Iran and Iraq began in Geneva, mediated by the UN Secretary-General, although on an entirely open basis that did not rule out a resumption of hostilities. Paragraph 4 of Resolution 598 envisaged a comprehensive peace solution without loss of face for either of the belligerent parties.

From the formal point of view, the Shat al-Arab issue (the drawing of the boundary either as stipulated by Iran along the Thalweg, or in line with Iraqi demands along the Iranian east bank of the waterway) forms the core issue of the Iraqi–Iranian dispute. The ceasefire of August 1988 *did not* include a settlement of the Shat al-Arab boundary conflict. The settlement of this dispute was reached, however, during the 1990–91 Gulf War – some weeks after the hostilities begun with the invasion of Kuwait – on 15 September 1990, when Iraq offered Iran peace fully on Iranian terms. Iraq's aim was thereby to neutralise the Iranian front after Iraq had been encircled by international armed forces. Saddam Hussein, who with his call to Muslims to wage a Holy War became a sudden convert to Islamic fundamentalism, was also hoping to build an Islamic front against the USA and its Arab allies. Like other illusions of Saddam Hussein this one, too, remained pure fantasy. There was overall Islamic support for Saddam. However, an Islamic upheaval against the West did not come about.

The impact of the eight-year Iran–Iraq War on the overall situation in the Gulf region is of more interest to us here than details of the war itself. In Chapter 2 we saw how together with the Mashrek and Maghreb the Gulf region forms one of the three subregions in the Middle East regional subsystem. Another question, of related interest, is whether this interstate conflict between Iran and Iraq, having widened into a war through militarisation, became an issue concerning the region as a whole. This would give it an overall political and military regional dimension comparable with the Arab–Israeli conflict. Some observers speak exaggeratedly of a 'shift of focus' arising out of the Iran–Iraq War, inferring that the first Gulf War has swung the focus from the Arab–Israeli conflict to the Gulf as the hub of subsystem-related conflict formation in the Middle East. Pursuing the perception elaborated and formulated on the basis of a study of history in the Introduction, our concern here is to examine the overall consequences of wars. The 1967 and 1973 wars are the central theme of the preceding Parts Two and Three of this book. Our primary concern in this chapter is to examine 'the Middle East in the shadow of the 1967 and 1973 wars', which includes the consequences of the Iran–Iraq War, not in the first instance the war itself. Suffice it to say at this point that the Islamic Revolution in Iran had repercussions on the entire region. The first Gulf War should be seen in this context; through this war the Iranian Islamic Revolution acquired an even more complex form. It helped, among other things, to renew the Saudi–Egyptian axis of the 1970s. Viewed from the perspective of that time, the legitimacy of the Saudi king's role as defender of the holy shrines of Islam in Mecca and Medina would have been seriously compromised if the Saudi monarch were to continue an alliance with a country that had concluded peace with Israel. Moreover, since the Six Day War Israel had held the Old Quarter of Jerusalem with the Aqsa Mosque, one of the great holy places of Islam, the third after Mecca and Medina.

During the Iran–Iraq War, however, the Iranian Islamic Revolution had the opposite effect: Saudi Arabia felt threatened, and therefore sought out Egypt as a protector. During the time of the annual Pilgrimage in August 1987, Iranian Pasdaran, the revolutionary guards caused massive turmoil at one of the most revered Islamic shrines, the *al-Ka'aba* (the Black Stone) of Mecca. The title of the Saudi king is *khadim al-haramayn al-sharifayn* ('custodian of the two holy shrines', i.e. *al-Ka'aba* in Mecca and the Tomb of the Prophet in Medina). It was in this precise capacity that the Saudi king was being challenged by Khomeini and his revolutionary guard. Saudi Arabia is unable to defend itself militarily. Prior to the second Gulf War, the Saudi monarchy, legitimating itself through Islam, had pursued a policy of allowing no US troops on its soil. At that time, the Saudis still refused to step across the boundary of 'non-military cooperation' (oil, trade and diplomacy).[65] Before 2 August 1990 all attempts on the part of American strategists to set up a military logistics base in Saudi Arabia and other Gulf states were thwarted by this Saudi refusal.[66] Even during the Iran–Iraq War the Gulf Cooperation Council (GCC) passed a resolution at its 25–26 February 1981 meeting reaffirming 'that the region's security and stability are the responsibility of its peoples and countries . . . they call for keeping the entire region free of international conflicts, particularly the presence of military fleets and foreign bases'.[67] It has been the unintended achievement of Saddam Hussein to reverse this stance shared by all Arab Gulf states. Prior to the Iraqi invasion of Kuwait these states had absolute preference for Arab–Muslim aid, particularly from Egypt, to support their security interests. It is only by bearing this framework in mind that the revived importance of Egypt as an Arab Islamic country becomes comprehensible. The 1990–91 Gulf War has radically altered this Gulf security framework. By threatening Saudi Arabia, Saddam Hussein inadvertently supported the US Gulf strategy to gain direct access to the Gulf area[68] with a view to establishing a ground logistic for naval military bases in that region.

Many social scientific studies in the discipline of International Relations are overtaken by events only a matter of years after publication, if not sooner. This is inevitable given the rapid change inherent in the subject matter of this scholarly discipline. Nevertheless, painstaking structural analysis that manages to penetrate its fabric is not marred by this temporal failing. This calibre of scholarly study includes a paper written by Paul Jabber in 1980, although it was not published until 1982, the themes of which encompass that of the Saudi–Egyptian axis. Although writing only a year after the Egyptian–Israeli peace treaty, Jabber points out that Egyptian military potential continues to remain for Saudi Arabia 'the most attractive option open to Riyadh for external assistance in meeting its principal security requirements'.[69] He argues further that only the existence of Egyptian military potential, even under the conditions of non-existent Egyptian–Saudi relations, can offer the Saudis security.[70] Bearing in mind that the American rearmament of Egypt after the October War helped to create a military potential with external military deployment capability,[71] even in 1980 Jabber could not exclude the possibility of the Egyptian–Saudi axis being revived, despite the peace treaty with Israel.[72] Jabber's 1980 scenario of future prospects still sounds relevant today: 'The Cairo–Riyadh axis will, despite temporary setbacks and unfavorable frictions, probably reemerge in the 1980s as a balance wheel of the inner-Arab regional system.'[73] Political events did indeed develop in precisely this direction in the second half of the 1980s. Even after the Gulf War this trend will continue to shape the 1990s decisively.

Any expert on Egypt or the Middle East interested in the rearmament of the Egyptian armed forces using Western weapons systems, predominantly from the USA, will have reached the same conclusion as Jabber about the future scenario. Since 1975 the Egyptian armed forces have not been equipped with war material for 'high intensity' wars such as those of June 1967 and October 1973. Instead of replacing its tank capacity destroyed in the October War, for example, Egypt has acquired anti-tank weapons, and substantially increased its combat helicopter capacity as part of an overall shift towards 'low intensity' warfare. Newly acquired aircraft (e.g. American F-16s) excel in their capacity to attack remote targets from the air. This overall rearmament process bears out what Lewis Snider calls the 'redirection of Egyptian military priorities since 1975'.[74] Since that time, Egypt has built up a military potential that has given its armed forces the capacity for highly mobile intervention. They are now trained and appropriately armed for 'low intensity' combat with a view to possible intervention in Saudi Arabia, the Gulf region, Libya, Ethiopia or South Yemen, rather than for renewed combat with Israel. Even before the first Gulf War, it had become clear that only this military capability gained since 1975 makes it possible for Egypt to enact its political role 'as a regional power in Africa or the Arab Middle East'.[75] The Iran–Iraq War demonstrated that the more Gulf Arab fear of Iran intensifies, the louder the call will be for Egypt to return to the 'Arab world'. Iraq also wanted to protect the Gulf Arabs, and even to become a member of the Gulf Cooperation Council, but even before 2 August 1990, the Gulf Arabs' fear of Iraq was no less than their fear of Iran.[76]

Following the acts perpetrated during the Pilgrimage in Mecca, in 1987, and in a situation of regional economic crisis, Saudi and Kuwaiti petrodollar cheques helped to underpin and bring to fruition the diplomatic efforts of the Jordanian King Hussein, then still a close ally. In September and October of 1987 diplomatic efforts were aimed at convening an Arab summit to focus on the security threat of Iran to the Arab Gulf states – not as at all previous Arab summits on the Arab–Israeli conflict. King Hussein had huge obstacles to overcome. The reader should bear in mind that two Arab countries, Syria and Libya, sided with Iran against Iraq, and that Algeria, non-partisan in the first Gulf War as in other conflicts, was unwilling to relinquish its above-mentioned mediating function (Algeria had acted as mediator between Iran and the USA during the 1980 hostage crisis). An Arab summit with this envisaged function took place from 8 to 11 November 1987 in Amman, where a definitive resolution was successfully adopted concerning future development in the region. In his opening speech, King Hussein enumerated from the Arab perspective the sources of threat to national security in the following order: 'in the Gulf, in Palestine and in Lebanon'. He added: 'This Iraqi–Iranian War . . . today threatens more than Iraq alone: nowadays it equally concerns the fraternal states of Kuwait and Saudi Arabia . . . and poses a threat to the security of the entire region.'[77] This speech by King Hussein of Jordan reveals that he managed to become a spokesman for Iraq even before its invasion of Kuwait in 1990.

The lengthy resolution adopted in Amman accommodates a range of subresolutions relating to the fourteen points on the agenda, headed by the Iran–Iraq War. On this point the resolution declares its 'condemnation of Iranian occupation of Arab territory . . . Complete solidarity with Iraq and support of its defence policy'.[78] The second point concerned UN Security

Council Resolution 598 on the Iran–Iraq War (adopted on 20 July 1987), with which Iran still refused to comply. Arab heads of state declared this resolution to be the basis for further negotiations. The third point on the agenda concerned Iranian attacks on Arab Gulf states; these are summarily condemned in the Arab resolution. No less than six subresolutions pertain to this one point, among them the imposing of boycott measures against countries supplying arms to Iran. The expressed willingness of the People's Republic of China on 8 March 1988 to support the arms embargo against Iran by halting its supply of Silkworm missiles may be viewed from this perspective. Point four concerned the disruptive action of Iranian revolutionary guards in Mecca. Here Arab heads of state declared their 'complete solidarity with Saudi Arabia . . . and support Saudi measures aimed at securing appropriate conditions for carrying out the duty of pilgrimage and preventing violation of Islamic holy places'. The Arab–Israeli conflict does not appear until point five on the agenda. A verbal assurance that 'Palestine remains the core Arab issue' is deemed sufficient. Arab heads of state refer here to resolutions adopted at the Fez summit (1982) in which they plead for a 'comprehensive and just peace solution', including the handing over of the occupied territories and the 'solution of the Palestine question'.

Point eight of the Amman resolution concerned what since Camp David and the Arab Baghdad summits of 1978 and 1979 (resolutions to isolate Egypt) had been the taboo issue of 'relations with Egypt'. The relevant passage in the new resolution reads: the Arab heads of state have resolved 'that diplomatic relations of members of the Arab League with Egypt are a matter affecting the sovereignty of every member state, but not the Arab League itself, whose area of competence does not include discussion of this question'. Couched in more straightforward terms, this resolution means that the Arab summit of Amman released Arab states from their obligation to the boycott strategy against Egypt adopted in Baghdad.[79] This enabled the Arab Gulf states among others to resume their previously broken off formal, i.e. diplomatic, relations with Egypt. In January 1988, President Mubarak visited all six Arab Gulf states, as well as Iraq, also resuming diplomatic relations with them at the same time. The remaining Arab states followed suit, with the exception of Syria, Libya, Algeria and Lebanon. Abdulmajid, the Egyptian Foreign Minister at that time, who was in Washington shortly before the Amman summit, had stressed in a lecture to the Brookings Institution that Egypt would welcome the resumption of diplomatic relations, but attached little weight to a formal return to the Arab League. Arguing from a superior position, he reasoned that the Arab League was no more than an empty shell without Egypt. The way had already been paved for the return of the Arab League to Cairo in September 1990.

Recalling the opening passage to this chapter in which the Middle East was described as a disordered regional system,[80] it should be stressed here that the Amman resolutions, which made it possible for Egypt to rejoin the Arab League, had little tangible impact on real events. In an ordered regional subsystem such as the European Community, there is usually a general consensus among member states as to fundamental policy. In a 'disordered system' such as the Middle East since the Six Day War, on the other hand, there is no general consensus among states themselves, nor do they have at their disposal the structures of a 'capability-based hierarchy'. Disorder, therefore, is their hallmark, and political fragmentation is the result. In International Relations terminology, the notion of 'capabilities' refers to the military or economic potential of a state actor. These include instruments of foreign policy (including economic and military potential) that may be employed in order to achieve an aim. As a regional actor, a state can only achieve the position of regional power when it has the prerequisite capabilities at its disposal. Saudi Arabia is a financial power but not an economic one, since it is unable to impose sanctions on its opponents. Petro-dollar reserves, that is vast sums kept in accounts in European and American banks – as well as oil in the ground– are proof of wealth, but do not constitute a basis for economic power to be reckoned with in the regional and international spheres. Unlike Saudi Arabia, Egypt, although poor, does have significant military potential, which makes it the only serious Arab military power, and second only to Israel in importance. This helps to explain why Gulf Arabs are seeking so earnestly to reintegrate Egypt, which can protect them both from Iraq and Iran. Nowadays, however, Egypt is an indebted and overpopulated country with anything but rosy prospects for the future. Egyptian engagement in the Gulf War helped the country to receive billions of Saudi petro-dollars, as well as to enjoy the cancelling of debts to the USA amounting to billions of dollars. This aside, the Middle East as a whole is a disordered region without a hope in sight.

The question as to whether or not the Gulf conflict has replaced Arab–Israeli hostilities in terms of the addressed shift of focus apparent since the Iran–Iraq War and intensified by the recent Gulf War is wrongly formulated. This question overlooks the linkages that exist between the two conflicts.[81] The 1980–88 Iran–Iraq War, unlike the Arab–Israeli wars of 1967 and 1973, involved the direct participation of only two states, and in this sense did not constitute a regional war in subsystems terms *per se*. Nevertheless, its epidemic forms did have an impact on the region as a whole. Shortly after the ceasefire between Iran and Iraq in August 1988, the Iraqi military potential in the form of its C-weapon- and gas-deploying air force was being directed against the 4 million Kurds of the country who would not submit to Saddam Hussein's regime. There was no respite in the proliferation of arms, and the concomitant militarisation of the Middle East continued to escalate until the invasion of Kuwait by Iraq on 2 August. Even since the end of the Gulf War and the destruction of the Iraqi war machine, the epidemic militarisation of the Middle East subsystem has continued unabated. The hope that the two superpowers will 'dictate a peace' is a vain one. The international system, until recently characterised by a bipolar structure, was sustained by the two superpowers in a state of continuous competition for hegemony. Formerly, the two superpowers sought regional allies as client states in the respective regional subsystems, with whose help they could further their own interests. Superpower competition[82] had never been the cause of conflicts in these regions, however. Subsystems have rivalries and conflicts of their own into which the superpowers tend to be drawn through their patron–client relationships. The 1990–91 Gulf War has clearly shown that regional conflicts in the Middle East persist regardless of the end to rivalry between the two superpowers. Increasing penetration of the Middle East region by the superpowers since the Six Day War has allowed the militarisation process to reach the extremes that led to the 1990–91 Gulf War. The Middle East continues to be at war, even since the defeat of Iraq. The external war has persisted internally against Kurds in the north and Shiites in the south. The nominal nation-states of the Middle East are falling apart. The Gulf War has thrown into question not only the fragile state system, but also the imposed nation-state itself.[83]

The Camp David Peace put an end to the phase of Arab–Israeli wars[84] by neutralising Egypt, the most powerful military pole in the Arab–Israeli conflict. This did not bring about peace, however – not even in the Arab–Israeli conflict, which is only one of many conflicts in the region. American and Soviet 'Middle East Peace Plans'[85] have proved equally fruitless. The only remaining superpower now, the USA, never did have a consistent Middle East concept: its Middle East policy was and still is, as one expert has expressed it, a 'Politics of Indecision' that has done nothing to further the 'Search for Mideast Peace'.[86] The degree of entrenchment evident in conflicts in the Gulf reached its height in the 1990–91 Gulf War, which will form the subject of the following chapter.

9 From the Iraq–Kuwait Conflict to the Gulf War

Although the effects of the Gulf War following the Iraqi invasion of Kuwait are proving to be far fewer than predicted,[1] the statement that this war has been *the* major event in the Middle East since the First World War and the concomitant dissolution of the Ottoman Empire still holds good. It is true that none of the political regimes of the Middle East – not even that established by Saddam Hussein – has fallen. It is also true that no changes have occurred in the boundaries of existing nominal nation-states in the region, as many pundits claiming to be Middle East experts predicted in the mass media. The list of predictions that have not come true could be continued. However, the fact that existing boundaries and regimes have not altered, either during the war itself or in its aftermath, should not be taken to mean that the former status quo is simply continuing. Some experts argue that we have returned to pre-war conditions, in as much as the *status quo ante* has in legal terms been re-established. The tribe of the al-Sabbah dynasty has returned to power in Kuwait,[2] the Saudis[3] are still in possession of the monarchy, while the artificial nation-state of Iraq[4] has survived not only the war, but even the ethno-religious revolts of Shiites in the south and Kurds in the north.

Yet the Middle East since the Gulf War is not the same region it was previously. With the onset of the crisis, its development into a regional war when Iraq invaded Kuwait, and later escalation into an international war[5] on 17 January 1991, the Middle East sustained a massive fragmenting blow[6] that shattered its political order. This latest Gulf War on the one hand continued a process of regional development that had started with the Iran–Iraq War (also known as the first Gulf War), and on the other hand has related these regional developments to ongoing global developments taking place in the international system in the post-bipolar, post-Cold War era. The focus in this chapter will be on the local and regional constraints that led to this war, while also making an attempt to place these developments in the global context.

After failure to reach a peaceful settlement of the Iraqi–Kuwaiti July crisis (17 July to 1 August 1990), the Iraqi army invaded the state of Kuwait on 2 August 1990.[7] In keeping with his totalitarian pan-Arab Ba'th Party ideology,[8] the Iraqi dictator Saddam Hussein, having built up a 'Republic of Fear'[9] in his own country, issued a decree incorporating Kuwait as the nineteenth province of Iraq. In addition to criticism of the drawing of colonial boundaries whereby 'the united Arab territory, once ruled from Baghdad, the capital of all Arabs, was split into separate territories',[10] the decree also puts forward the argument that Kuwait is a *fir'* (branch) belonging to the *al-Kul wa al-asl* ('the entirety and the origin'),[11] and hence to Iraq. This ostensible unification of Iraq and Kuwait according to pan-Arab ideology took place in flagrant violation of international law, and flouted the generally accepted norms of the world order.

As outlined in the Introduction to this book, the modern nation-state based world order[12] first evolved in Europe, from where later in the course of history it was imposed on the Middle East as part of an overall process of globalisation. Mutual respect for the sovereignty of participating states and the norms and values related to it are part and parcel of this world order. The cited Iraqi document on *al-wihda al-indimajiyya* (the pan-Arab unification of Iraq and Kuwait) infers that the West was responsible for splitting the Arab homeland, and purports to undo this process. It is with reference to the emergence of the nation-state based Arab political system as part of the wider international order that the Gulf War and its associated challenge to existing boundaries have shattered the Arab order. Saddam Hussein counted on popular disavowal of these boundaries and obtained it. The mass pro-Saddam Hussein demonstrations that took place throughout the Arab world also support the idea put forward in the Introduction that the world order is in a state of crisis as a result of a lack of shared norms and values in the present international community, which is divided into industrial states and the Third World.

The Cold War was just drawing to a close as the international violation that was the invasion of Kuwait took place. Bipolarity has been presented in this book as the dominant structural order in the international system at the time of the 1967 and 1973 Middle East wars. This had not quite disappeared by the beginning of 1990. Saddam Hussein invaded Kuwait with the misgiving that in this new war – in the aftermath of the Cold War and the superpower rivalry that had accompanied it – he would no longer be able to manipulate this bipolar structure in his own favour as he had done before. It had proved useful to his policies during the Iran–Iraq War.[13] As the final stages of the Cold War[14] were being eased in equal measure by German reunification and by the Gulf crisis caused by the Iraqi invasion of Kuwait, the bipolar structure of the international system also appeared to be coming to an end. For Saddam Hussein, and many other Third World politicians who had been able to make use of the East–West conflict for their regional conflicts (see the analysis of 'patron–client' relations in Chapter 1), the

(Bush–Gorbachev) superpower summit of Helsinki on 9 September 1990 came as a massive shock. The Helsinki communiqué[15] contains a declaration by both superpowers of their unanimous opposition to the Iraqi invasion of Kuwait. Both also called on Iraq to withdraw peacefully from Kuwaiti territory. The UN likewise took on a new role in international politics during the Gulf crisis up to the implementation of UN Security Council Resolution 678. For the first time in UN history, the UN Security Council was able, beginning with Resolution 660, to adopt no less than twelve resolutions without having one vetoed. Two more resolutions of enormous significance followed after hostilities came to an end.[16] Before the international phase of the armed conflict began on 17 January 1991, UN Secretary-General Perez de Cuellar made a trip to Baghdad in an eleventh-hour unsuccessful attempt to avert war.[17]

The question that suggests itself here is why the end of the Cold War and of bipolarity – an event already enshrined in a resolution on a new peaceful order in Europe, adopted in 1990 in Paris at the Conference on Security and Cooperation in Europe – has proved unable to exert a positive effect on regional conflicts in the Third World. This book on *Conflict and War in the Middle East* hopes to provide an answer with its central thesis of the 'regional dynamic of Third World conflicts'. All parts of the book argue against globalism, which wrongly seeks to interpret regional conflicts – in the Middle East in particular and in the rest of the Third World in general – as a function of the East–West conflict. When hostilities broke out on 17 January 1991, the peace movement laudably and justifiably protested against the use of violence as a means of resolving conflicts. What they failed to perceive, however, was that war had not broken out on 17 January 1991, but on 2 August 1990. The persistent recourse to the globalist scheme of the North–South conflict by numerous left-wing German journalists also strikes this author as a fruitless attempt to explain the present situation in the Gulf, since it fails, through lack of expert data, to take into account the regional dynamic of the Gulf conflict. This chapter represents an attempt to explain the regional dynamic of this conflict and the conditions that shape it.

As already mentioned above, the Iraqi invasion of Kuwait on 2 August 1990 was preceded by the July crisis, which had nothing whatsoever to do either with the superpowers or with any North–South conflict. It had to do solely with the Gulf region itself. The Gulf region is here defined as a subregion within the Middle East subsystem, encompassing the core states of Iraq, Iran, Saudi Arabia and Kuwait. The rest of the Gulf states are peripheral to the subregion. In its own perception, Iraq had emerged as the victor from the Iran–Iraq War,[18] although from the military standpoint the end of the war had been inconclusive. Iraq had made substantial military expenditures during the war years, and these were stepped up in the period 1988–90, indebting Iraq to the tune of US$70 000 million despite its not inconsiderable oil revenues.[19] This situation forms the background to the July crisis, ushered in with a speech by Saddam Hussein,[20] which was triggered by Iraq's economic need to obtain additional revenues, either through direct payments by Kuwait or an increase in hard currency revenues from oil exports. The escalation of the conflict was thus closely related to the financial need of the autocratic ruler in Iraq,[21] who nurtured ambitions to build up his country into a regional superpower and therefore needed to make substantial military expenditures. Iraqi territorial claims arising out of its need for access to the Gulf waters were likewise reactivated. Iraq's access to the Gulf consists of a restricted coastal strip only fifty miles in length which is unsuitable for the construction of a deep water harbour. As a quasi-interior country, therefore, it sought to overcome its landlocked state.[22]

• In an explanatory paper given to the Arab League, Iraqi Foreign Minister Tareq Aziz argued that overproduction of oil by the Gulf states had led to a fall in the price of crude oil. Iraqi estimates place their losses as a result of this oversupply of oil at US$90 000 million for the 1981–90 period. The same paper contains an unmistakable hint by the Iraqi government that it be released from war debts to the other Gulf states incurred during the Iran–Iraq War. The justification for this was that Saddam Hussein had defended the Arab states against the Iranian enemy, an act for which, so Iraq argued, payments should be made. Three causes lay at the root of Iraqi conduct during the crisis:

1. A renewed claim to the Rumaila oil field[23] was intended to serve the purpose of setting aside border disputes in favour of Iraq, while at the same time compelling Kuwait to pay compensation for supplies from this oil field during the Iran–Iraq War.
2. The Iraqi threat of violence against Kuwait was an attempt to force both Kuwait and the United Arab Emirates to release Iraq from its war debts.
3. The threat against Kuwait may be described as oil policy using military means. Iraq's aim here was to push the Arab Gulf states into drastically cutting back their oil output, which would benefit Iraq and thereby implement a 'policy of expensive oil', increasing Iraqi oil revenues.

However, the economic objectives pursued by Iraq during the July crisis cannot be analysed separately from the long-term political and geostrategic aims of Saddam Hussein. As we have seen, apart from a very restricted fifty-mile Gulf coastline, Iraq is virtually an interior country. The Iraqi claim on Kuwait, or at least on the Kuwaiti islands of Warba and Bubiyan, is thus also a geopolitical claim for access to the Gulf. As an interior country, Iraq is not only constrained in terms of its ambitions to become a regional superpower, but in view of the lack of an Iraqi deep water harbour is, moreover, largely dependent on the good will of its neighbours to be able to export its oil. Tensions between Iraq and Syria, for example, led to the closure in April 1982 of the Iraqi pipeline running across Syrian territory to the Mediterranean.[24] Most Iraqi oil then had to be diverted by expanding the pipelines running through Turkey to the Mediterranean. It was under these circumstances that new pipelines running across Saudi Arabia to the Red Sea were developed. Before then Iraqi oil had to be shipped by land through Jordan in oil tanker trucks. Clearly, Iraq could not hope to enhance its regional power basis while remaining dependent upon its neighbours to export its oil.[25] Aside, therefore, from the need to gain access to the Gulf waters to export its oil, Iraq under Saddam also built up its war machine in order to deter neighbouring countries from disrupting Iraqi oil exports. While Turkey is a powerful member of NATO, Saudi Arabia is a weak state: although wealthy, like Kuwait it is unable to defend itself. The invasion of Kuwait was thus also intended as a lesson to Saudi Arabia. Without the presence of the American troops whose help they sought, the Saudis would never have been able to close the Iraqi pipeline on Saudi territory[26] and defend itself against possible Iraqi attack.

The causes behind the Iraqi invasion of Kuwait cannot be fully understood without alluding to Saddam Hussein's claim to be the Arab leader of the 1990s. This claim was justified in terms of the alleged victory of Iraq over Iran, and based on the ideology of the pan-Arab Ba'th Party. Central to this issue is the intellectual and political influence on the Ba'th Party of the spiritual father of pan-Arabism, Sati al-Husri.[27] In his book on Saddam Hussein's 'Republic of Fear', the exiled Iraqi author Samir al-Khalil argues that Sati al-Husri's thought has influenced Saddam Hussein himself.[28] As this author showed in another study, al-Husri cherished the pan-Arab dream that one day an 'Arab Bismarck' would through war bring about 'an Arab 1871' after the German model, just as Bismarck once united the Germans during the Franco-Prussian war of 1871.[29] Nasser proved unable to take on the role of an Arab Bismarck: he failed as a pan-Arabist. His pan-Arab project, the United Arab Republic with Syria (1958–61) was short-lived, while other plans involving military means would have been equally difficult to implement, apart from the military engagement of Egypt in Yemen after the fall of the monarchy in 1961. The invasion of Kuwait by Saddam Hussein and the resulting annexation of Kuwaiti territory as an Iraqi province[30] is now presented in Iraqi propaganda as a pan-Arab act aimed at rectifying the 'colonial map of Arab fragmentation', against both 'imperialists and Zionists' and their Arab 'agents'. The latter are referred to by Saddam pejoratively in his speeches as 'oil emirs'.

To sum up, the Iraqi invasion of Kuwait was the result of a variety of both short-term and long-term economic, political and ideological factors. In taking this step, Iraq was aiming not only to shore up its ailing economy and increase its oil revenues, but also to gain access to the Gulf shores so as to reduce its geographical dependence on its neighbours – and ultimately to raise its status to that of pan-Arab power in the Gulf with its sights set on the rest of the Arab world.

Our remarks so far have largely been confined to the local Iraqi–Kuwaiti context of the crisis. A more comprehensive and complete understanding will entail elaborating these ideas to include an analysis of the wider context, comprising not only the whole of the Gulf region, but also the Middle East as a regional subsystem. This will involve a deeper exploration of the above mentioned Iraqi claim to pan-Arab leadership. In this context the two relevant key events for any analysis of the background to the present situation are the peace treaty between Egypt and Israel in 1979, known as the Camp David Accords, and the end of the Iran–Iraq War in 1988. In 1979, Egypt was expelled from the Arab League after its separate peace with Israel following the Camp David negotiations. This forced expulsion of Egypt from the Arab political scene meant that Iraq under Saddam Hussein could now replace Egypt as the leading regional power, claiming pan-Arab leadership for itself alone. It was no coincidence that the 1978 Arab summit responsible for Egypt's expulsion took place in Baghdad.

With the benefit of hindsight, the observer can now perceive in Iraqi policy at that time more of a claim to Arab leadership than an act directed against recognition of Israel. Although the setting up of the Arab Cooperation Council (ACC) involving Egypt and Iraq in February 1989 marked Egypt's return to Arab politics, this does not contradict the above interpretation. Iraq was hoping to reintegrate Egypt into Arab politics under its own leadership. In the eighties Iraq was in need of Egyptian aid during its war with Iran. During the first Gulf War of 1980–88 close military cooperation developed between Egypt and Iraq, since Iraq was dependent not only on Egyptian military aid but also on Egyptian migrant labour (1.7 million). Although Egypt made a full return to Arab politics by becoming a member of the Arab Cooperation Council, it did so without laying claim to a leading role. This was claimed by Iraq alone. Since 2 August 1990, Egypt has availed itself of the present situation to retrieve its former role as leader of the Arab world. In September 1990, the Arab League returned to Cairo,[31] albeit with the entire Arab world in a totally fragmented state. Nevertheless, the declaration by Iraq on 7 August 1990 of a Holy War against the West, a call repeated on 5 September 1990 and further intensified after the outbreak of the internationalised phase of the war on 17 January 1991, gave Iraq sole legitimacy in the eyes of the majority of Arab Muslims, now generally turning towards radical fundamentalism. Political Islam directed against the West in the service of Saddam Hussein has today shown itself to wield far more influence with the masses than any form of Arabism. Saddam Hussein has succeeded in devising a synthesis of Arabism and Islamism for the 'Arab–Islamic street'.[32]

The second key event for understanding the present situation is the end of the 1980–88 Iran–Iraq War, the first Gulf War. Our prime concern here focuses around which of its demands Iraq was able to cull from this event. Saddam Hussein felt that he had at last earned the right to be officially regarded as Defender of the Gulf,[33] as he had styled himself at the start of the war, although at that stage it was no more than a claim. In the eyes of Saddam Hussein this claim had become reality by 1988. It is open to question, however, whether the Gulf Arabs at that time really wanted to be defended by Saddam. It is true that at the start of the Islamic Revolution and throughout the entire Khomeini era Iran was perceived as a threat by the Gulf states in terms of the possible 'export of the Islamic Revolution'. However, the Gulf states never sought protection from Iraq either during the Iranian Revolution or afterwards. Although concerned about Iran, they had hardly less reason to fear Iraq itself. Indeed, after the outbreak of the Iran–Iraq War the Gulf states, led by the Saudis, closed ranks to inaugurate the Gulf Cooperation Council (GCC) that had first been proclaimed in January 1981 in Kuwait.[34] Had the GCC been no more than an association of Arab Gulf states against Iran, then obviously Iraq, as a Gulf state, could also have become a member. As the Swiss Gulf expert Graz correctly perceives, however: 'The Gulf-states obviously did not want Iraq as a member of the Gulf Cooperation Council.'[35] Although the GCC states provided Iraq with annual financial aid amounting to US$15 000 million during its eight-year war against Iran, it was clear from the very outset that this aid was neither whole-hearted nor comprehensive.

With the end of the Iran–Iraq War in August 1988, and even in the first months after the ceasefire on the Iraqi–Iranian border, the Gulf Arabs began to grow nervous. Iraq wanted to be accepted as the seventh member of the Gulf Cooperation Council. The Iraqi leadership under Saddam Hussein chose not to see that the setting up of the GCC had been a reaction to the war, or more precisely to the ambitions of both their neighbour states, Iraq and the Islamic Republic of Iran. After 1988, Saudi Arabia and Kuwait made concerted efforts to build up an institutional network of cooperation between the GCC and its neighbouring countries, including Iran, aimed at neutralizing Iraq. The GCC states were pleased in February 1989 to see the establishment of the Arab Cooperation Council (ACC) between Iraq, Egypt and Jordan: it meant that Iraq could now definitely be kept out of the GCC. Only weeks after the establishment of the ACC in February 1989 the Saudi King Fahd flew to Baghdad to draw up a non-aggression treaty between his country and Iraq. The significance of this visit lies not only in its contribution to the abatement of Saudi fears of Iraq, but also in the fact that it ensured that Iraq would remain outside the GCC. Even before the Iraqi invasion of Kuwait on 2 August, regional experts such as Fred Halliday[36] recognised and pointed out the threat of Iraq to political security in the region.

After the ceasefire of August 1988, Iran no longer posed a threat to Iraq. Iraq also had friendly relations with Turkey. Not only did Turkey permit Iraq to export its oil to the Mediterranean through Iraqi pipelines on Turkish territory, but Iraq also gave Turkey the right to pursue Kurdish rebels[37] on to Iraqi territory. In other words, with the end of the first Gulf War all the dangers to political security that might have compelled Iraq to enhance its military build-up had been removed. And yet its military expenditure failed to drop: on the contrary, after 1988, Iraq continued its armament efforts and built up an immense arms industry. The message was now loud and clear: putting the armaments industry in first priority enabled Iraq to amass a wide range of weaponry[38] and to transform some of it, such as the Hussein and Abbas missiles developed from the Scud system. Of particular cause for concern was the arsenal of chemical and biological weapons systems acquired by Iraq[39] which had already been deployed in the Iran–Iraq War, and after 1988 in Kurdish areas in Iraq itself. A particularly grave aspect of this was how in so doing Iraq 'showed the whole world, and particularly the Third World how easy it was for a country with average technological capabilities to make them without too many risks. The raw material can be fairly simple and the whole operation easily disguised as a fertilizer factory.'[40] With its chemical weapons, Iraq is a vivid demonstration of what experts have termed 'the nuclear bomb of the poor countries'. By 2 August 1990 when Iraqi troops marched into Kuwait, thereby triggering the war that continued on 17 January, Iraq had one of the most powerful armies in the world.[41]

Bearing in mind the preceding remarks, it is reasonable to assume that without the massive and successful international reaction to the annexation of Kuwait, Saddam Hussein would certainly have set his sights on a second victim in the Gulf to help further install his imperial might in the region. Despite their fears the Gulf states in general would not entertain the idea of any foreign military assistance at all, let alone American assistance, before 2 August. They persistently refused all external military aid whenever it was offered. On 26 February 1981, the Gulf Cooperation Council, founded in Kuwait, officially declared that the GCC 'reaffirms that the region's security and stability are the responsibility of its peoples and countries . . . They call for keeping the entire region free of . . . the presence of military fleets and foreign bases.'[42] The Gulf states wanted to defend themselves, and the GCC was hence primarily an association for ensuring political security. As such it failed, not only because of the structural weaknesses of its members, but also because of the bedouin mentality of its leaders. All GCC states are bedouin states, and no bedouin trusts another tribe like his own.

The local Iraqi–Kuwaiti war, combined with the even greater Iraqi threat to Saudi Arabia, forced the Gulf Arabs to accept the stationing of American-led multinational troops in the Gulf. On 17 January, the war that had started on 2 August was taken to a new stage by these American-led allied armed forces, using the very latest in consummate military technology. During the Gulf War the USA pursued only vague political objectives, lacking any kind of overall strategy in the Clausewitzian sense. This interpretation,[43] put forward by this author in the *Frankfurter Allgemeine Zeitung* in December 1990, has been fully vindicated since the end of the war, as the USA has been taken unawares by events such as the Shiite uprising in the south and the Kurds in the north. US decision-makers had no strategy for dealing with this post-war situation, any more than they had had during the war itself. It is most regrettable, as the prominent American historian Arthur Schlesinger wrote in an influential article, that the USA not only 'doesn't know what it's doing in the Gulf', but even 'doesn't know that it doesn't know'.[44]

The second Gulf War was tough, however much shorter than the first one. It lasted only forty-two days. Contrary to the predictions of most military experts, the air phase was the longer and the ground war the shorter part of the war. The air war lasted thirty-eight days and the ground combats only four days. The war ended with a shattering defeat for Saddam Hussein, the ejection of Iraqi troops from Kuwait and the occupation of southern Iraq.[45] Lacking a consistent strategy the US 'Commanders' were not unanimous in their views, but subject to the will of President Bush.[46]

Saddam Hussein had counted on a war like the Suez War – one in which he might fail militarily, but win politically. He had no idea how punishing the air war was going to be. The tyrant was obviously never fully informed by his fearful aides as to the full extent of damage occurring. The war started on 17 January with a 'Relentless Assault',[47] as the *International Herald Tribune* reported. Some 1300 sorties were flown in the first twenty hours. In the course of the war the number of sorties flown over Iraq and Kuwait increased to 2500 daily, reaching 54 000 sorties in the first twenty-three days.[48] Before starting the ground war President Bush set Iraq an ultimatum to withdraw from Kuwait[49] by Saturday 23 February. Technically, however, this deadline was impossible to meet, given that most of the Iraqis in Kuwait were dug into the ground. The ground war started on Sunday 24 March, resulting in a massive thrust against the Iraqis,[50] who fled rather than fought, although their president had promised the world an *um al-ma'arik* ('Mother of all Battles'). The result was a mother of all defeats. Most of the Iraqi forces were destroyed in fierce battle.[51] President Bush prematurely ordered his forces to stop fighting, thus helping Saddam to salvage a remnant of his forces, who later helped him crack down on the Shiite uprising in the south and the Kurds in the north in March. American critics accused President Bush of 'moral crisis'.[52] General Schwarzkopf acknowledged in one interview that he was ordered to stop fighting prematurely.[53] Saddam Hussein survived the war and acceded to all ceasefire demands. There has been no capitulation such as the one Germany had to submit to after the Second World War. The Sabbah tribe returned to Kuwait[54] and forgot all about promises of democratisation. The Saudis wanted to undo the rules of history, which teaches us that wars are the midwives of change.[55] This has proved to be the outcome of the second Gulf War.

The end of bipolarity has led people who love peace and want to live in peace to believe in the possibility of a better world without destructive weapons systems. They seem to have overlooked the fact that many countries in the Third World are armed to the teeth. The dissolution of this bipolar structure, which had at the same time ensured a balance of power and a degree of control, has released the constraints on these states and allowed armed conflicts to hatch. This fear was already expressed in the Introduction. Iraq is not an isolated case, but a case in point. The only thing that prevents Pakistan, for example, from attacking India with the ostensible aim of 'liberating Kashmir' is the fact that India is as well-armed as Pakistan itself.[56] There is no such force to act as a restraint on Iraq, either in the Gulf or in the Arab subsystem as a whole.

Bipolarity has now been consigned to the history books. In a speech to the American Congress, on 11 September 1990, after his return from the Helsinki summit meeting with Gorbachev, President Bush proclaimed a 'New World Order'. In his own words, this should be one promising 'an era in which the nations of the world, East and West, North and South, can prosper and live in harmony'.[57] Even the very beginnings of this pledge are proving to be a chimera. The USA seems to have been solely responsible for UN Resolution 678, which made war absolutely necessary, however much approved by all UN Security Council members. The USA put its full weight behind pushing this resolution through, thereby placing not only itself but also its unconsulted European and Arab allies in the cleft stick of the 15 January 'deadline'. In his significant article on the 'New World Order' proclaimed by President Bush, Edward Mortimer[58] criticises the USA's apparent unwillingness to accept 'power sharing' with its allies, and the way it presents them with ready-made decisions and *faits accomplis*. In another article, Mortimer asks whether this promised 'New World Order' is not likely to turn out to be a 'World Disorder'.[59]

Despite a formal–legal return to the *status quo ante*, the Gulf War did shatter the Middle East and has brought no fruits worth mentioning. Saddam is still in power and has been allowed to kill thousands of Shiites and Kurds while restoring his 'Republic of Fear'. The war has, moreover, not brought democratisation either to Saudi Arabia or to Kuwait. It has only deepened still further the chasm that already existed between the Islamic world and the West. None the less, the Islamic world is doing itself a serious disservice by portraying itself as the world of oriental despotism, as it did during the recent war by identifying itself with the horrendous phenomenon that is Saddam Hussein. The Islamic world has known better 'days of light' in its annals, such as those when Avicenna and Averroës were developing the ideas of Islamic rationalism. Muslims would do better to hold up as an example the model state, the *al-madina al-fadilah*,[60] of the Islamic philosopher al-Farabi than the 'Republic of Fear' of the Iraqi despot Hussein. In the ideal state of the Islamic philosopher al-Farabi, who lived and worked in the golden age of his Islam, the head of state is a philosopher whose authority is based on reason (*al-aql*). In the 'Republic of Fear' of Saddam Hussein the dictator rules as an 'oriental despot'[61] through the apparatus of his intelligence services (*mukhabarat*). The choice that now lies before the Arab Muslims of today in the *Middle Eastern conflict region* is a crucial one between two forms of government and two mutually exclusive visions of civilisation. This choice is the *crisis of modern Islam*,[62] which Arab Muslims in the Middle East are now having to accommodate. Which choice they make in this historical era of crisis depends on them alone. The future of the *Middle East as a conflict region* and the judgement of the civilised world on the inhabitants of that region also rests with them.

10 The Historical Context of Conflict and War in the Middle East in the Light of the Gulf War

Since the defeat of 1967 the people of the Middle East have been living under desperate conditions. They are suffering not only from the misery of economic hardship related to ill-developments in the region, but also from a lack of freedom and a vision of the future. Stephen Howe draws the attention of the world to the present situation in the Middle East, in which 'the whole region [is] a cultural desert with its creative minds driven into exile, sycophancy or silence'.[1] A complex combination of legitimacy crisis, deadlock in political, economic and even more so in cultural development has contributed to the mobilising of a generation of frustrated Arabs; it has allowed them to run behind a new oriental despot, who claimed to liberate them, but never thought more than to establish and bolster his 'Republic of Fear' as a modern variety of oriental despotism. He promised his subjects to lead all Arabs and Muslims to success over the 'Crusaders' in the 'Mother of all Battles' (*um al ma'arik*),[2] but in fact delivered the opposite.

Despite the self-satisfied announcement on Baghdad Radio that Iraq, 'united behind President Saddam Hussein, put an end to the war, having taught the world a lesson in steadfastness', the world, apart from Saddam supporters with their selective grasp of truth, knows that the 'Mother of all Battles' ended in a 'Mother of all Defeats'. The 1980–88 Iran–Iraq War (the first Gulf War) had witnessed a similar 'Waterloo' for Saddam in the form of the Battle of Qadisiyya (Qadisiyya is the Arabic name for a battle that took place in AD 637 when the Arabs conquered Sassanid Iran). Saddam was unable to achieve any of his political or military objectives in either of these Gulf wars. He does nevertheless seem, unwittingly, to have drawn the attention of world public opinion to the importance of the Middle East, the most war- and conflict-ridden region in the world, and the need to find solutions to Middle East conflicts. A speech given by President Bush to both houses of Congress on 6 March 1991 would seem to affirm this statement. Not that the USA had only just discovered the importance of the region, but rather that it had realised the importance and urgency of conflict solution as a prerequisite for a peaceful order in the Middle East. The fact remains, however, that US decision-makers are still lacking a concept to this end. For purely propaganda reasons, Saddam insisted on a 'linkage' between all Middle Eastern conflicts and the Kuwait conflict.[3] Aside from opportunistic Iraqi propaganda, however, a degree of interconnectedness between these regional conflicts cannot be denied. President Bush raised this point in his forty minutes speech to Senators and Representatives, enumerating a solution to the Arab–Israeli conflict as third in his list of priorities for the post-war order in the Middle East. Numerous missions by US Secretary of State Baker to the Middle East, covering a total distance of thousands of kilometres, produced no results. While there is an awareness of the need for conflict solution, there is still no formula in sight that would be acceptable to all the actors involved. Given this state of deadlock it is necessary to bear in mind that the search for possible means of resolving Middle Eastern conflicts within the sought after, peaceful post-war order entails allocating the latest conflict its rightful place in the overall structural history of Middle East conflict formations. This is the aim of this final chapter on 'Conflict and War in the Middle East'.

When Saddam Hussein gave the order for his troops to march into Kuwait on the night of 1–2 August 1990, there was undoubtedly no notion in his mind of a 'linkage' between all Middle Eastern conflicts. His mind is far more likely to have been preoccupied with the huge burden of Iraqi debts, amounting to between US\$70 and 90 billion. These debts stood in the way of Iraq enhancing its regional basis as a Middle East superpower. Appropriating the wealth of Kuwait would have removed that obstacle. In those first days of August 1990 there was no talk of 'Holy War' by Muslims 'against the Infidel', or of a simultaneous link between a solution to the Kuwait crisis and all other Middle Eastern conflicts, such as was later heard in the subsequent calls of Saddam to *Jihad* (Holy War). Saddam only began these subterfuges after the isolation of Iraq instigated by Arab states (the emergence of an anti-Iraqi majority faction in the Arab League) and the groundswell of world public opinion against the piracy of Iraq was activated, following the resolutely expressed position adopted by the UN. On August 7, he declared a *Jihad*[4] with the aim of rallying Islamic fundamentalists to his side. On August 12, he made his ideologically inspired initiative (*al-mubadara*) declaring a 'linkage' between the Kuwait issue and all other Middle Eastern conflicts. In both these Arabic texts Saddam Hussein addresses the Palestinian question and the drawing of colonial boundaries in the Arab region after the First World War and the dissolution of the Ottoman Empire. Up to the First World War all Arab territories with the exception of Morocco were provinces of the Ottoman Empire, be it only formally (*de facto* all North African Arab territories came under European control in the course of the nineteenth century) or in fact (the *Mashrek*). Leaving aside the propaganda aims of Saddam Hussein, the Gulf War has given rise to a questioning of the existing Arab state order and the boundaries related to it as they were drawn after the First World War.[5]

There can be no doubt that Saddam Hussein initially pursued economic objectives related to the idea of an imperial Iraq.[6] His plan was to extort as many petro-dollars as possible from the Gulf Arabs, first and foremost the Saudis, through military intimidation. Had the Kuwaitis been willing to pay up and suspend the war debts Iraq owed them, the invasion of Kuwait might not have taken place. Whatever alternative scenarios there may have been, Iraq did invade Kuwait, but never counted with such a strong response from the regional and international environment.

The resort by Saddam Hussein during the conflict to the stratagem of political Islam, on the one hand, and the linkage tactic, on the other, – that is linking the solution of the Kuwait issue to other questions – is an indication not of honourable intentions, but of using Islam, the Palestinian question and other conflicts (e.g. Lebanon) to serve the power-political ambitions   of an oriental despot. The fact remains, however, that the Gulf conflict and the war that was waged in that context is part and parcel of the overall regional structure of conflicts in the Middle East, a structure that corresponds to the emergence of Middle Eastern boundaries and the order associated with it since the First World War. The fact that Iraq abandoned its linkage tactic after the defeat of its troops, submitting to all the demands of the UN resolutions, does not eliminate the necessity of viewing the Gulf conflict in the wider context of Middle Eastern conflicts.

The link between the armed conflict in the Gulf and the other Middle Eastern conflicts begins with the fact that all Middle Eastern boundaries were drawn along colonial lines. Border disputes consequently occupy first place among conflicts in the region. The present Gulf crisis clearly derives from the territorial conflict over boundaries between Iraq and Kuwait which can be traced back to 1922.[7] It was in that year that the British colonial officer Major-General Sir Percy Cox, in his tent in the Gulf village of Uqair, arbitrarily drew the future boundaries between Kuwait, Iraq and the then Najd Sultanate (now part of Saudi Arabia). The remaining boundaries in the Middle East were similarly drawn, i.e. in colonial fashion. As was pointed out in the introductory section, until the First World War all Arab territories with the exception of Morocco were part of the Islamic confessional empire – the Ottoman Turkish Empire. Islam, which was both the state religion and determined the culture of the Empire, recognised no internal boundaries and made no distinction between ethnic and national groups. These ethnic and national differentiations aroused conflicts after the dissolution of the Ottoman Empire.[8] The notion of the state *(dawla)* is not central to Islam, but the concept of *umma* (the community of all Muslims) is. The dissolution of the Ottoman Empire, which had pursued the Islamic separation of the *dar al-Islam* (the House of Islam) from the *dar al-harb* (the House of War) up to its decisive military defeats (Vienna 1683, Carlowitz 1699, Passarowitz 1718), resulted in a fragmentation of former imperial territory. The British and French colonial powers divided up the Islamic empire of the *dar al-Islam* between themselves.

Even before the dissolution of the Ottoman Islamic Empire the European idea of the nation, alien to Islam, was already beginning to penetrate the Islamic Middle East.[9] European-educated Muslims came to identify themselves less and less with Islam and more in terms of 'national' identity, whether real or imagined. Arab Muslims thus began to distinguish themselves as Arabs, as distinct from other Persian and Turkish Muslims, who were now perceived as foreigners. However, this process, whereby the idea of the nation began to spread throughout the Middle East, was not simply a matter of importing a Western notion into the region, or as some observers have called it, the 'Western imported virus of nationalism'.[10] This kind of perspective, which ignores the manifest institutional structures of the nation-state and the international system based on its globalisation, is flawed. The modern world as a whole has been organised in nation-states since the globalisation of the European nation-state order. The 'nation', therefore, is more than a mere notion: it is the global structure of an international system that persists to this day.[11] The Arabs, colonised by the French and British after the dissolution of the Ottoman Empire, could only free themselves from the colonial yoke by claiming the status of nation-states. The problem was that since the dissolution of the Ottoman Empire there had been no unified, discrete Arab territory: the Arab map was still divided up along colonial boundaries. It was out of this colonial division that the later 'imposed nation-states'[12] emerged. Some states, such as Iraq for example, were put together artificially, cobbled together from former Ottoman provinces – in the case of Iraq out of three: Kurdish Mosul, Sunni Baghdad and Shiite Basra.[13] Throughout centuries of Ottoman rule there had been no 'Iraq', merely three Ottoman provinces relatively independent of one another. It follows from this, contrary to state propaganda, that there is no unified Iraqi national identity. The identity of most Iraqis (such as that of Saddam, from Takrit) is essentially ethnic or confessional, or a mixture of the two. Under Saddam Hussein there has been an attempt, in addition to recourse to Islam and Arabism, to construct an Iraqi ideological identity around the Mesopotamian and Babylonian traditions.[14]

It follows that an understanding of the above mentioned historical context since the First World War is vital for comprehending the diverse conflicts that have plagued the Middle East since the Second World War. With the founding of the Arab League on 22 March 1945, the post-Second World War Middle East witnessed the emergence of an Arab state system based on the independent states of that time. Contained within that state system was the conflict structure that has persisted to this day. The five founder states – Egypt, Transjordan, Saudi Arabia, Iraq and Yemen – were all monarchies. Only two, Syria and Lebanon, were republics.[15] Under Ottoman rule the two latter countries had formed the northern part of the province of Syria. Later, under French colonial rule, they had been divided into two separate territories, from which the independent nation-states of Syria and Lebanon then emerged.[16] It is necessary to bear in mind this entity of 'Greater Syria' in order to understand international tolerance of the Syrian occupation of Lebanon.[17] Some modern Arab states, including Egypt and Iraq, were sovereign states before the Second World War, and in conflict with each other for leadership in the region from the 1930s onwards.[18]

The early history of the Arab League was characterised by a struggle among the three central Arab monarchies – Egypt (independent since 1922), Iraq (since 1932) and Saudi Arabia (not a colony, but founded only in 1932 as a Wahhabite monarchy). This conflict for regional hegemony was waged in the name of the struggle for Arab unity, a notion for which the 'Arab nation' formula was elaborated. With the founding of the Arab League after the Second World War this inter-Arab conflict was conducted in the form of a struggle for influence in Syria. The British journalist Patrick Seale reconstructs this central conflict in his classic work *The Struggle for Syria: A Study in Post-War Arab Politics 1945–1958*.[19] After the founding of the state of Israel in 1948 the focus shifted. The first Arab–Israeli War was followed by the Arab–Israeli state conflict, which continues to this day as the central conflict in the region. Since that time, Arab states have always used the Palestinian issue as a central aspect of their legitimacy.[20] The Iran–Iraq War, the 1980–88 conflict between the Arab state of Iraq and the Muslim but non-Arab state of Iran, shifted the focus away from the Arab–Israeli conflict to the Gulf conflict for the first time.[21] The Arab summit in Amman in November 1987 was the first of its kind to adopt a communiqué dealing in first place with a conflict (the Iran–Iraq War) other than the Arab–Israeli conflict.[22]

The Palestinian uprising, the *intifada*,[23] would seem at first sight to have shifted the action back to Palestine. However, the Iraqi invasion of Kuwait on 2 August 1990 brought the Gulf back into full focus. Saddam Hussein sought to reverse this by claiming a linkage between the two conflict-ridden subregions. Since the end of the Gulf War on 28 February 1991 world public opinion seems to have accepted the idea that 'Middle East conflicts' are linked with one another. Inasmuch as Middle Eastern *conflicts* since the Second World War all have their roots in the same structure of the Arab state system and its colonially drawn state boundaries, it is true that they are *mutually inseparable*. However, the argument put forward by the Iraqi dictator Saddam Hussein in his 12 August initiative is predominantly of a propaganda nature. He argued that the Iraqi occupation of Kuwait and the Israeli occupation of the West Bank and Gaza Strip could be dealt with and solved together as a single 'package' of interlinked conflicts. Saddam Hussein was fully aware that Israel would never voluntarily relinquish the occupied territories, and constructed his plan to incorporate Kuwait as the nineteenth province of Iraq on this very fact. Ironic though it may seem, it is nevertheless true that Israel, through its action against Palestinians in East Jerusalem on Temple Mount, on 8 October 1990, actually helped Saddam Hussein to consolidate his proposed 'linkage' between Kuwait and Palestine. Arnold Hottinger wrote in the *Neue Zürcher Zeitung* of a 'present for Saddam Hussein from Israel'.[24] It is equally true that no one has damaged the Palestinian cause to the same extent as Saddam Hussein and the PLO leadership under Arafat. Urgent as the need is to find a solution to this conflict, the prospect seems remote.

The Middle East region consists of sovereign nation-states, that is political entities constituted along the lines of modern European states. They are nevertheless only nominal nation-states, since they lack one of the major hallmarks of the European state: popular sovereignty.[25] This state form has never really been able to establish stable internal foundations in the Middle East, with the result that there are frequent examples of greater or lesser political disorder. Excluding the monarchy in Morocco, which has endured since the seventeenth century (1666), and Egypt, which has a centuries-old state tradition based on a hydraulic culture, Middle Eastern states are fragile, artificial entities. In this region, the state is manifestly of a violent and oppressive character, able to procure the loyalty of its subjects only through harsh ruthlessness. There is no democracy in the Arab Middle East. The primary source of conflicts thus lies in these structurally unstable political orders. Iraq is a good example of how the stability of Middle Eastern states is based on oppression of their populations. If this oppression is relaxed, the regime collapses. This latent or manifest instability exerts a corresponding effect on the regional order, as well as on the regional conduct of the Middle Eastern states. They have adopted governmental technology using the model of the modern democratic nation-state, but not the logic of modern polity that we know as the sovereign nation-state.[26] Political power tends to be monopolised by particularist groups (e.g. the Takrit clientele in Iraq, the Alawites in Syria, etc.) and, in the absence of a polity representative of all citizens, tends not to be organised into democratic structures based on participation and representation.

The absence of political legitimation accepted by the population[27] and the sectarian character of incessant power struggles, along with the instability associated with them, are typical features of how political struggles are conducted by these states. Their conduct is made more complex by this situation, and the search for solutions to conflicts is thereby considerably impeded. Bearing all this in mind, one cannot fail to recognise how unrealistic it is to envisage forcing a peaceful order on the region from outside.

Three forms of conflict may be discerned in the Middle East region. Since the actors of the regional subsystem are nation-states wielding no more than nominal internal and external sovereignty, the interstate, that is *local level of conflict*, is the first of these forms. To illustrate this argument, two extreme examples may be given: Lebanon and Sudan. Both these states are currently grappling with violent conflicts arising out of the nominal character of their national statehood. Both states lack the substance of the nation-state in their polity.[28] Conflicts of this kind do not remain confined to the local level, however, but can have regional spillover effects which cause them to widen into interstate hostilities. While *interstate conflicts in the subregional context* form the second type of Middle Eastern disputes, *overall regional conflicts* constitute the third form. An example of subregional unrest would be the Iran–Iraq conflict, which took the form of a war between 1980 and 1988. The conflicts in the Western Sahara (Morocco–Polisario) and others between the Maghreb states up to the founding of the Union du Maghreb Arabe in February 1989 are also of a subregional character. The struggle in Lebanon is also subregional, although it has widened considerably since 1975. However, from the formation of the Middle Eastern state system after the Second World War *up until 2 August 1990*, only the Arab–Israeli dispute and Palestinian dissension could be classified as overall regional conflicts. Even during the 1980–88 Iran–Iraq War the Gulf problem was always subregional. The Iraqi invasion of Kuwait shifted the Gulf conflict not only into an overall regional dimension, but went even further and internationalised it. None of what have so far been symbolic Arab–Israeli wars shattered the Middle Eastern region to the same extent as the Gulf War that started on 2 August 1990.

As regards the Arab–Israeli and Palestine conflicts, it would be appropriate at this point to explain the reasons for dividing into two subunits what was generally regarded as one single unit. The Arab–Israeli problem as such is between the state of Israel and all Arab states that treat the Palestine issue as the 'foremost all-Arab core concern'[29] in terms of their foreign policy and internal political legitimacy, although clearly the latter is often purely a matter of rhetoric. *This makes the Arab–Israeli issue primarily a state conflict.* In contrast to this state problem is the additional Palestine conflict, which concerns the claim of Palestinians to a territory of their own, although this takes various forms.[30] A solution to the Arab–Israeli dispute as a state matter would *not automatically* lead to a solution to the Palestine conflict. Conversely, however, a solution to the Palestine issue, by conferring the right to a Palestinian state in the occupied territories, would render the Arab–Israeli conflict superfluous. Both varieties of the same conflict have local, regional and international dimensions.

During the period between the creation of the state of Israel and 1967 there were three Arab–Israeli wars. At that time, Israel was regarded as the enemy of all Arabs, so that the policy of all Arab states towards Israel was formulated in pan-Arab terms. The distinction between the Arab–Israeli and the Palestine conflicts was already discernible at that stage, but much less developed. In those days Arab states used the Palestinian issue by resorting to the motto of the 'liberation of Palestine' as a well-tried means of constructing an image of an external enemy. This proved very useful for camouflaging their own internal instability through an artificial but effective rousing of the masses. The Palestinians were politically weak and did not yet have their own leadership, independent from the Arab states. Even the PLO itself was effectively founded by Nasser in 1964, not by the Palestinians themselves. In its early years, therefore, the PLO was a policy instrument of the Arab states. After the Six Day War in 1967 the Palestinians took their cause into their own hands. Since that time there is reference to a 'Palestinianization of the Arab–Israeli conflict'.[31] The recent alliance between the PLO and the Iraqi dictator Saddam Hussein has again exposed the Palestinians to being ruled by the would-be leader of the Arabs, thus setting them back ten years. In the aftermath of the Gulf War, the PLO needs to recover from this setback, and will have to work hard to re-establish its legitimacy.

A further factor impeding the search for a solution to the Palestinian issue is that another dangerous formula appears to have surfaced: the 'Islamicisation' of the Arab–Israeli and Palestinian conflicts.[32] This formula testifies to the rise of Islamic fundamentalism as a central source of conflict in the Middle East region. There is not a single conflict in the Middle East today that does not involve Islamic fundamentalism. An Arab peace with Israel would have to be preceded by compromises on both sides, and Islamic and Jewish fundamentalists alike are equally unwilling to agree to this. Religious radicalism, whether Jewish or Islamic, is an obstacle to peace.[33] The impact of this problem has been clearly discernible in the conflict-constellation that has intensified since the Iraqi invasion of Kuwait. Saddam Hussein has used existing fundamentalist formulas as instruments for his own ends, thereby prolonging an already persistent lack of peace. His declaration of *Jihad*, Holy War, and his appeal to the anti-Western tendencies of Islamic fundamentalists fell on particularly fertile soil, even though such a Holy War never took place and never will. The very propagation of *Jihad*[34] as a political idea and the process of raising it to the status of a mass ideology is a major obstacle to finding a peaceful solution to the dispute.

Since 2 August 1990 conflicts in the Middle East can be subdivided, on the one hand, into those between Arab states (Arab interstate conflicts) and, on the other, into those between some Arab states and their own populations (Arab intrastate conflicts). First, during the Gulf War the Arab League was pared down to a truncated body of only twelve members (a hard core of states focused around Egypt, Saudi Arabia, the remaining Gulf states and Syria), who together constituted the anti-Saddam Hussein front. Until the eventual defeat of Iraq there then appeared a quasi-pro-Saddam Hussein front, organised around Jordan, Sudan, the PLO, Mauritania and Yemen. The five Maghreb states apart from Mauritania were against the Iraqi annexation of Kuwait, but equally adamantly against the stationing of American troops in Saudi Arabia and the Riyadh–Cairo–Washington axis. Essentially, the five Maghreb states united in the Union du Maghreb Arabe retain to this day five different positions.

In addition to these interstate conflicts there are also intrastate conflicts, such as that between the Syrian government and its local population.[35] Syria's abrupt shift in foreign policy in favour of the Cairo–Riyadh–Washington axis exacerbated this conflict. There were massive pro-Iraqi demonstrations against the Assad regime in Syria which were brutally suppressed, ending in bloodshed. The Syrian leadership managed to make use of the Gulf War to mobilise new sources of revenue in the form of Saudi petro-dollars, and to put an end to the isolation that had hitherto been demanded by Iraq.[36]

In the post-Second World War period in the Middle East, as the Arab League was being founded, the idea of Arab unity was widely propagated. Most Arab states paid no more than lip service to pan-Arabism. Contrasting with the unifying ideology of pan-Arabism, however, real events in the Middle East since 1945 testify only to fragmentation. This process accelerated on a massive scale after the 1967 June War, and has reached its highest point so far as a result of the Iraqi invasion of Kuwait and the circumstances either of the war itself or the conflicts that have been triggered by it.[37] Consequently, all Arabs will continue in the light of their respective political cultures to hold fast to the rhetoric of pan-Arab unity. In the *Realpolitik* of the states involved, the idea of pan-Arabism will continue to be linked with expansionism as a result of the Saddam Hussein experience, and will therefore still to be perceived as a threat by the weak but wealthy Arab Gulf states. The real 'End of Pan-Arabism'[38] occurred after the 1990–91 Gulf War rather than the 1967 Six Day War.

To sum up, it may be discerned that the Middle Eastern context of conflict and war since the Second World War has local, regional and international determinants that are interwoven with one another through *linkage* structures. In speaking of the regional dynamic of conflict, this book is by no means suggesting through the emphasis of endogenous factors that conflict in the Middle East has an independent existence of its own. On the contrary, no conflict in the Middle East today can be adequately interpreted without taking the international environment into account. The Gulf War is proof of this. Consideration of the international factor, however, is not the same thing as supporting the conspiracy-driven political thought to which Arabs mostly subscribe. Arabs perceive themselves collectively, and are prone to see conspiracies involving 'Western crusading imperialists and Zionists'[39] as the main source of their conflicts. This often leads them to overlook the local and regional factors that shape the dynamic of conflict in the Middle East.

A solution to this multitude of conflicts must begin in the first instance with the Arabs themselves, that is with endogenous factors. Nevertheless, one should not be misled into imagining that modern Arab states are capable of accomplishing this on their own. In their search for conflict resolution[40] the Arabs, fragmented among themselves to the point of hostility, are in need of third-party mediation for talks both among themselves and with Israel, Iran and Turkey, on the road to resolving existing conflicts. The widespread anti-American feeling that exists in the Middle East precludes the USA from playing such a mediating role successfully. Despite all anti-Western feeling, Europe would be a more acceptable third party in the mediation process. The need for a peaceful order in the Middle East region thus poses a challenge to the political aplomb of the European Community, as well as to the world order that is yet to emerge in the 1990s as a substitute for the now dissolved bipolar world order. The Gulf War will prove to be a major determining factor in the future development of the post-Cold War international system, as well as in the unfolding of the much-needed regional order in the Middle East itself.

Notes and References

Introduction: Middle Eastern Wars from the World Historical and International Systemic Perspectives

1. One such peace researcher is Ekkehard Krippendorff, *Staat und Krieg*, Frankfurt am Main, 1985.
2. Martin van Creveld, *Technology and War: From 2000 BC to the Present*, New York 1989, Part II 'The Age of Machines', pp. 81ff. This age begins around 1500. The historian Geoffrey Parker, *The Military Revolution: Military Innovation and the Rise of the West 1500–1800*, Cambridge, 1989, relates the beginning of this age to the rise of the West.
3. Anthony Giddens, *The Nation-State and Violence*, Berkeley, 1987, chapter 9, pp. 222ff.
4. David B. Ralston, *Importing the European Army: The Introduction of European Military Techniques and Institutions into the Extra-European World 1600–1914*, Chicago, 1990.
5. On both wars see Larry H. Addington, *The Patterns of War since the Eighteenth Century*, Bloomington, 1984, chapters 4 and 6. See also the contributions in Robert I. Rotberg and Theodore K. Rabb (eds), *The Origins and Preventions of Major Wars*, Cambridge, 1989, pp. 225ff. and 281ff.
6. Kalevi J. Holsti, *Peace and War: Armed Conflicts and International Order 1648–1989*, Cambridge, 1991, p. 303.
7. Ibid.
8. On Clausewitz see the authoritative work by Peter Paret, *Clausewitz and the State: The Man, his Theories and his Time*, Princeton, NJ, 1976, and the chapter on Clausewitz in Peter Paret (ed.), *Makers of Modern Strategy*, Princeton, NJ, 1986, pp. 186–213.
9. This position is intelligently presented by Panajotis Kondylis, *Theorie des Krieges. Clausewitz-Marx-Engels-Lenin*, Stuttgart, 1988, pp. 28ff. See the review article on this book by B. Tibi 'Kriegstheorie und Kulturphilosophie', in *Frankfurter Allgemeine Zeitung*, 7 December 1988, p. 10.
10. Holsti (note 6), p. 327. On war in the nuclear age see John Newhouse, *War and Peace in the Nuclear Age*, New York, 1989.
11. Klaus-Jürgen Gantzel, *Die Kriege nach dem Zweiten Weltkrieg bis 1984*, Munich-London, 1986, pp. 27–60.
12. Holsti (note 6), pp. 274–8.
13. See for example Robert Litwak and Samuel Wells (eds), *Superpower Competition and Security in the Third World*, Cambridge, Mass., 1988.
14. See Marshall D. Shulman (ed.), *East–West Tensions in the Third World*, New York, 1986.
15. See Robert Jervis and Seweryn Bialer (eds), *Soviet-American Relations after the Cold War*, Durham, London, 1991.
16. See Dan Tschirgi and Bassam Tibi, *Perspectives on the Gulf Crisis*, Cairo: American University of Cairo Press, 1991.

17. In fact most Middle Eastern nation-states lack substance: see B. Tibi, 'The Simultaneity of the Unsimultaneous: Old Tribes and Imposed Nation-States in the Modern Middle East', in Philip Khoury and Joseph Kostiner (eds), *Tribes and State Formation in the Middle East*, Berkeley, 1990, pp. 127–152.
18. Holsti (note 6), p. 311.
19. Ibid., p. 305.
20. Friedrich V. Kratochwil, *Rules, Norms and Decisions: On the Conditions of Practical and Legal Reasoning in International Relations and Domestic Affairs*, Cambridge, Mass., 1990.
21. Holsti (note 6), p. 334.
22. Hedley Bull, *The Anarchical Society: A Study of Order in Worla Politics*, New York, 1977, p. 261.
23. Ibid., p. 273.
24. On Islamic fundamentalism from a world order perspective see the book by B. Tibi, *Crisis of Modern Islam: A Pre-Industrial Culture in the Scientific-Technological Age*, Salt Lake City: Utah University Press 1988, and B. Tibi, *Islam and the Cultural Accommodation of Social Change*. Boulder, Col.: Westview Press 1990, in particular Part Four.
25. Hedley Bull, 'The Revolt against the West', in Hedley Bull and Adam Watson (eds), *The Expansion of International Society*, Oxford 1988, pp. 217–28, in particular p. 223 on Islamic fundamentalism.
26. Holsti (note 6), p. 328.
27. Ibid., p. 304.
28. Ibid., p. 323.
29. Bull (note 22), p. 267.
30. See the new chapter 'Arab Nationalism Revisited' added to the 2nd edn of B. Tibi, *Arab Nationalism: A Critical Inquiry*, London, New York: Macmillan, 1990.
31. On the Arab-Israeli wars and the Middle Eastern wars see Ritchie Ovendale, *The Arab–Israeli Wars*, London, 1987, and Sydney D. Bailey, *Four Arab–Israeli Wars and the Peace Process*, 3rd edn, London, New York, 1990. On the first Gulf War see the books by Anthony H. Cordesman and Abraham R. Wagner, *The Lessons of Modern War*, vol. II: *The Iran–Iraq War*, Boulder, Col. 1990; Sharam Chubin and Charles Tripp, *Iran and Iraq at War*, Boulder, Col. and Dilip Hiro, *The Longest War: The Iran–Iraq Military Conflict*, New York, 1991.
32. On this see Oye Ogunbadejo, 'Qaddafi and Africa's International Relations', in *Journal of Modern African Studies*, vol. 24, (1986), pp. 33–68, esp. pp. 42ff. on the Chad War. See also René Lemarchand, *The Green and the Black: Qadhafi's Policies in Africa*, Bloomington, 1988, here pp. 106–24.
33. John Damis, 'The Western Sahara Dispute as a Source of Regional Conflict in North Africa', in H. Barakat (ed.), *Contemporary North Africa*, London, Washington, 1985, pp. 138–53; from the perspective of the interests of the middle-range and superpowers: Werner Ruf, 'The Role of World Powers', in Richard Lawless and Laila Momalan (eds), *War and Refugees: The Western Sahara Conflict*, London, 1987.
34. From the Lebanese viewpoint, Wadi D. Haddad, *Lebanon: The Politics of Revolving Doors*, Washington, 1985, and from the Israeli viewpoint, Itamar

Rabinovich, *The War for Lebanon 1970–1985*, 2nd edn, Ithaca, London, 1985.

35. On this see John Spanier and Christopher Shoemaker, *Patron–Client State Relationships: Multilateral Crises in the Nuclear Age*, New York, 1984. This book will be discussed further in Chapter 3 on the October 1973 War.

36. Hedley Bull (ed.), *Intervention in World Politics*, 2nd printing, Oxford, 1985, especially the paper by Windsor.

37. Barry H. Blechmann and Stephen Kaplan *et al.*, *Force without War: US Armed Forces as a Political Instrument*, Washington, DC, 1978 (on the Middle East see the contribution, contained in the case study section of this volume, by William Quandt: 'Lebanon 1958 and Jordan 1970', pp. 222–88).

38. Stephen S. Kaplan, *Diplomacy of Power: Soviet Armed Forces as a Political Instrument*, Washington, DC. 1981; see the case study by P. Jabber and R. Kolkowicz on the 1967 and 1973 Middle East wars, pp. 412–67, as well as that on 'Air Support in the Arab East' by A. Rubinstein, pp. 468–518.

39. Quincy Wright, *A Study of War*, Chicago, 1947, p. 34.

40. On this see W. M. Watt and Alford T. Welch, *Der Islam I*, Stuttgart, 1980, pp. 152f, and B. Tibi, *Islam and the Cultural Accommodation of Social Change* (note 24), p. 33.

41. According to this romantic view, Africa for example was an 'intact world' in precolonial times (Nkruhma's *Communalism*, Senghor's *Négritude*, Nyerere's *Ujamaa*); on this see B. Tibi, 'Politische Ideen in der Dritten Welt während der Dekolonisation', in I. Fetscher and H. Münkler (eds), *Pipers Handbuch der politischen Ideen*, vol. V, Munich, 1987, pp. 361–402, here Part 4, pp. 375ff. With regard to Islam as an ideological source of Third-Worldism, see the contribution by Nikki Keddie in Jean Pierre Digard (ed.), *Le Cuisinier et le philosophe. Hommage à Maxime Rodinson*, Paris, 1982.

42. Quincy Wright (note 39), p. 35.

43. Charles Tilly (ed.), *The Formation of National States in Western Europe*, Princeton, NJ, 1975, Introduction, p. 45.

44. On the meaning of this war for the formative period of the international system, see the chapter by Holsti (note 6), pp. 25–42.

45. See B. Tibi, 'Structural and Ideological Change in the Arab Subsystem Since the Six-Day-War', in Y. Lukacs and A. Battah (eds), *The Arab–Israeli Conflict*, Boulder, Col., 1988, pp. 147–63.

46. Norbert Elias, *The Civilizing Process*, 2 vols., New York, vol. I 1978, vol. II 1982, here particularly vol. II, chapter 2, pp. 91–161.

47. Reinhard Bendix, *Kings or People: Power and the Mandate to Rule*, Berkeley, 1978, p. 331.

48. Ibid., p. 334.

49. Ibid., chapter 10, Tilly (note 43) and Albert Soboul, *Die Grosse Französische Revolution*, 4th edn, Darmstadt, 1983, p. 540ff.

50. The seminal work on this subject is Anthony Giddens (note 3).

51. B. Tibi (note 17). See also the remarkable study of Robert H. Jackson, *Quasi-States: Sovereignty, International Relations and the Third World*, Cambridge 1990.

52. Charles Tilly, *Coercion, Capital and European States*, Cambridge, Mass., Oxford, 1990, p. 76.

53. Ibid., p. 181.
54. Christopher Chase-Dunn, *Global Formation*, Cambridge, Mass., Oxford, 1989, Part II, in particular pp. 151ff.
55. Tilly (note 52), p. 191. Emphasis added.
56. Bull (note 22), p. 8 and pp. 9–20.
57. Tilly (note 52).
58. Helmuth Plessner, *Die verspätete Nation*, Frankfurt am Main, 1974, p. 33.
59. See Theda Skocpol, *States and Social Revolutions*, Cambridge, Mass., 1979, p. 23; see also p. 21, and Theodore H. von Laue, *The World Revolution of Westernization*, New York, 1987.
60. Tilly (note 52), p. 225.
61. Taken from contributions to discussion by Edmund Burke in House of Commons debates, in *The Parliamentary History of England* XXVIII, Sp. 781.
62. Hans-Gerd Schumann, *Edmund Burkes Anschauungen vom Gleichgewicht in Staat und Staatensystem*, Meisenheim, Glan., 1964, p. 113.
63. Bull (note 22), p. 260.
64. Ibid., p. 275.
65. See Keith Nelson and Spencer Olin, *Why War? Ideology, Theory and History*, Berkeley, 1980.
66. On the variety of these regional conflicts see Richard N. Haas, *Conflicts Unending*, New Haven, 1990.
67. Kenneth N. Waltz, 'Toward Nuclear Peace,' in Robert Art and K. N. Waltz (eds), *International Politics and Foreign Policy*, 3rd printing, New York, 1983, pp. 573–601, here p. 597.
68. Robert Gilpin, *War and Change in World Politics*, Cambridge, 1981, p. 238.
69. Edward Mortimer, 'Reality versus Rhetoric in New World Order', in *Financial Times*, 28 September, 1990, p. 8, and E. Mortimer, 'Judgement of History: The New World Order has Become the New World Disorder', in *Financial Times*, 18 January 1991, p. 15.
70. Gerrit W. Gong, *The Standard of Civilization in International Society*, Oxford, 1984, esp. chapters I and II.
71. Gilpin (note 68), p. 236f.
72. Ibid., p. 238.
73. Mary Kaldor, *The Imaginary War: Understanding the East–West Conflict*, Cambridge, Mass., Oxford, 1990, p. 5.
74. See the references in notes 13 and 14 above.
75. Kaldor (note 73), p. 6.
76. See the useful contributions in Adam Roberts and Benedict Kingsbury (eds), *United Nations, Divided World: The UN's Roles in International Relations*, Oxford, 1989.
77. Joseph S. Nye Jr, *Bound to Lead: The Changing Nature of American Power*, New York, 1990, p. 185.
78. Ibid., p. 174.
79. As John Burton, *Conflict: Resolution and Prevention*, London, 1990, pp. 202ff. and 211ff. shows, conflict resolution and conflict solving do relate to culture. Normative differences over rules thus hinder attempts to reach mutually accepted procedures.
80. Jervis in his introduction to *Soviet–American Relations* (note 15), p. 15.
81. Ibid., p. 16.

82. Ibid., p. 305.
83. See Oles M. Smolansky and Bettie M. Smolansky, *The USSR and Iraq: The Soviet Quest for Influence*, Durham, London, 1991.
84. Ethnic turmoil in the former Soviet Union is multifarious, although largely focused around the Soviet Muslim republics of the south. See Rasma Karklins, *Ethnic Relations in the USSR: The Perspectives from Below*, Boston, 1986, and Michael Rywkin, *Moscow's Muslim Challenge: Soviet Central Asia*, revised edn, Armonk, New York, 1990. See also Alexander J. Motyl, *Will the Non-Russians Rebel? State, Ethnicity and Stability in the USSR*, Ithaca, London, 1987, and W. R. Duncan and C. M. Ekedahl, *Moscow and the Third World under Gorbachev*, Boulder, Col., 1990.
85. Stephen White, *Gorbachev in Power*, Cambridge, 1990, p. 179. See also Edward Kolodziej and Roger Kanet (eds), *The Limits of Soviet Power in the Developing World*, London, 1989.
86. White (note 85), p. 182.
87. Paul Dibb, *The Soviet Union: The Incomplete Superpower*, 2nd edn, London, 1988.
88. See the special issues of *Foreign Affairs*: 'The Road to War' and 'After the War', vol. 70, nos. 1 and 2 (1991) respectively.

1 The Science of International Relations: Between Globalism and Regionalism

1. For a useful introduction to International Relations, see the handbook by Margot Light and A. J. R. Groom quoted in note 22 below, and K. J. Holsti quoted in note 2 below.
2. From the copious American literature on International Relations the following may be mentioned: Steve Smith, *International Relations: British and American Perspectives*, London, New York, 1985; T. Taylor (ed.), *Approaches and Theory in International Relations*, London, 1978; L. Jensen, *Explaining Foreign Policy*, Englewood Cliffs, NJ, 1982; W. C. Olson, D. S. McLellan and F. A. Sondermann (eds), *The Theory and Practice of International Politics: A Framework for Analysis*, 4th edn, Englewood Cliffs, NJ, 1967. On the plurality of approaches and the impossibility of achieving a unified analysis in this discipline, see K. J. Holsti, *The Dividing Discipline: Hegemony and Diversity in International Theory*, Boston, London, 1985. See also the textbook quoted in note 22. German handbooks on International Relations are mostly based on translations of Anglo–Saxon contributions and will therefore not be quoted.
3. Morton Kaplan, *System and Process in International Politics*, New York, 1957.
4. W. T. R. Fox, *The Super Powers: The United States, Britain and the Soviet Union – Their Responsibility for Peace*, New York, 1944.
5. Ernst Haas, *The Uniting of Europe*, Stanford, 1958, 2nd edn, 1968.
6. Stanley Hoffmann, 'Discord in Community: The North Atlantic Area as a Partial International System', in *International Organization*, vol. 17 (1963), pp. 521–49.
7. However, this did not always occur as a result of the kind of scientific inquiry

stemming from an obligation to seek the truth. See B. Tibi, *Internationale Politik und Entwicklungsländer-Forschung*, Frankfurt am Main, 1979. The critique made at that time would nevertheless require some revision. See also the work of Irene Gendzier, *Managing Political Change. Social Scientists and the Third World*, Boulder, Col., 1985.

8. Fox (note 4), p. 3.
9. On this phase, see David Horowitz, *From Yalta to Vietnam: American Foreign Policy in the Cold War*, New York, 1967. On the latter period see Fred Halliday, *The Making of the Second Cold War*, 2nd edn, London, 1984.
10. A German example of this Wallerstein approach is Klaus Busch, *Die multinationalen Konzerne. Zur Analyse der Weltmarktbewegung des Kapitals*, Frankfurt am Main, 1974.
11. More on this in Rudolf von Albertini, *Dekolonisation*, Cologne, Opladen, 1966, and by the same author (ed.), *Moderne Kolonialgeschichte*, Cologne, Berlin, 1970 (chapter 4 on Decolonisation, pp. 365ff.). On empires see Michael Doyle, *Empires*, Ithaca, 1985. On the British Empire in the Middle East see Roger Louis, *The British Empire in the Middle East*, Oxford, 1984.
12. On this, see Dieter Schröder, *Die Konferenzen der 'Dritten Welt': Solidarität und Kommunikation zwischen nachkolonialen Staaten*, Hamburg, 1968, pp. 87ff.
13. Leonard Binder, 'The New States in International Affairs', in Robert Goldwin (ed.), *Beyond the Cold War*, Chicago 1965, pp. 195–216.
14. L. Binder, 'The Middle East as a Subordinate International System', in *World Politics*, vol. 10, no. 3 (1958), pp. 408–29, also published in Falk and Mendlovitz (note 15).
15. The two standard works on this subject are Louis J. Cantori and Steven L. Spiegel, *The International Politics of Regions: A Comparative Approach*, Englewood Cliffs, NJ, 1970 and Richard Falk and Saul H. Mendlovitz (eds), *Regional Politics and World Order*, San Francisco, 1973. Since that time, discussion has continued mostly in scholarly journals. These respective approaches are discussed in more detail in the second section of this Chapter 1. For a new contribution on this subject see the book by Thornton quoted in note 51 below.
16. For a discussion of 'order' in the international system as a crucial issue within the discipline of international relations, see the seminal work by Hedley Bull, *The Anarchical Society: A Study of Order in World Politics*, New York, 1977, esp. pp. 3–98 and pp. 257ff., esp. p. 260. For an overview on the world order debate see R. D. McKinlay and R. Little, *Global Problems and World Order*, Madison, Wisconsin, 1986.
17. Jorge I. Dominguez, 'Mice that Do Not Roar: Some Aspects of International Politics in the World's Peripheries', in *International Organization*, vol. 25 (1971), pp. 175–208.
18. Ibid., p. 176.
19. Ibid.
20. On this complex of questions, the reader might care to compare the influential journals *Foreign Affairs* and *Foreign Policy*.
21. *Die Zeit*, 4 March, 1986. Theo Sommer is not alone in his biased view; on this, see B. Tibi, 'Das Orient-Bild der deutschsprachigen Publizistik', in *Neue Politische Literatur*, vol. 16 (1971), pp. 547–64. At the root of this notion lies

the traditional European conception of 'homo islamicus': see B. Tibi, 'Die Deutschen und die Welt des Islams', in *Deutschland. Portrait einer Nation*, 10 vols., here vol. 10, Gütersloh, revised 2nd edn. 1991, pp. 264–75, esp. the section entitled 'Selbst- und Fremdbilder'.

22. Michael Banks, 'The Inter-Paradigm Debate', in Margot Light and A. J. R. Groom (eds), *International Relations: A Handbook of Current Theory*, London, 1985, pp. 7–26, here p. 7.
23. Thomas S. Kuhn, *The Structure of Scientific Revolutions*, Chicago, 1962, p. 15.
24. Ibid., p. X.
25. Kuhn in a postscript to the new German edition of the cited work (1978), p. 194. See also Kuhn's article 'Neue Überlegungen zum Begriff des Paradigmas', in T. S. Kuhn, *Die Entstehung des Neuen*, Frankfurt am Main, 1977, pp. 389ff.
26. Banks (note 22), pp. 8f.
27. Ibid., p. 9.
28. Karl-Heinz Haag, *Philosophischer Idealismus: Untersuchungen zur Hegelschen Dialektik mit Beispielen aus der Wissenschaft der Logik*, Frankfurt am Main, 1967, p. 5.
29. On this, see the collective standard work: Hedley Bull and Adam Watson (eds), *The Expansion of International Society*, Oxford, 1984, and Charles Tilly (ed.), *The Formation of National States in Western Europe*, Princeton, NJ, 1975.
30. Hans-Gerd Schumann, *Edmund Burkes Anschauungen vom Gleichgewicht in Staat und Staatensystem*, Meisenheim, Glan., 1964.
31. Morton Kaplan, 'Variants on Six Models of the International System', in James N. Rosenau (ed.), *International Politics and Foreign Policy: A Reader in Research and Theory*, New York, 1969, pp. 291–303, here p. 296.
32. Alexis de Tocqueville, *On Democracy, Revolution and Society*, ed. by John Stone and Stephen Mennell – selected writings, Chicago, 1980, p. 350.
33. On this, see the title chapter 'Nonalignment, positiver Neutralismus und Blockfreiheit', in B. Tibi, *Militär und Sozialismus in der Dritten Welt*, Frankfurt am Main, 1973, pp. 265ff.
34. See Volker Matthies, *Die Blockfreien: Ursprünge, Entwicklung, Konzeption*, Opladen, 1985.
35. See the account of this by Peter Blackburn, 'Chad a Disaster for Gaddafi', in *Financial Times*, 27 March 1987, p. 1, cont. p. 18. See also René Lemarchand (note 65 to Chapter 2).
36. See Binder (note 14).
37. For more details on this see Leonard Binder (ed.), *The Study of the Middle East*, New York, 1976.
38. It was the American expert Rosenau who introduced the concept of 'linkage': 'Hence we will use a linkage as our basic unit of analysis, defining it as any recurrent sequence of behaviour that originates in one system and is reacted to in another. In order to distinguish between the initial and the terminal stages, we shall refer to the former as an output and to the latter as an input. Each of these in turn will be classified in terms of whether they occur in a polity or its external environment (i.e., the international system).' See the new edition of James Rosenau, *The Scientific Study of Foreign Policy: Essays*

on the Analysis of World Politics, 2nd edn, London, New York, 1980, esp. the section on the linkage model, pp. 370–401, here p. 381.
39. Binder (note 14), p. 414.
40. See Roland Yalem, *Regionalism and World Order*, Washington, DC, 1965, excerpts of which may be found under the heading 'Theories of Regionalism' in Falk and Mendlovitz (note 15 above), pp. 218–31.
41. Binder (note 14).
42. George Modelski, 'International Relations and Area Studies: The Case of South-East Asia', in *International Relations*, vol. 2 (1961), pp. 143–55; Yalem (note 40 above); Oran Young, 'Political Discontinuities in the International System', in Falk and Mendlovitz (note 15), pp. 34–49, and William R. Thompson, 'The Regional Subsystem: A Conceptual Explication and a Propositional Inventory', in *International Studies Quarterly*, vol. 17 (1973), pp. 87–117.
43. Michael Brecher, 'International Relations and Asian Studies: the Subordinate State System of Southern Asia', in *World Politics*, vol. 15 (1963), pp. 213–35, and William Zartman, 'Africa as a Subordinate State System in International Relations', in *International Organization*, vol. 21, no. 3 (1967), pp. 545–64.
44. Stanley Hoffmann (note 6).
45. Dominguez (note 17).
46. Cantori and Spiegel (note 15).
47. L. Binder (note 13), p. 202. The subsequent article published by Binder on this subject in 1972, is purely descriptive: L. Binder, 'Transformation in the Middle Eastern Subordinate System after 1967', in M. Confino and S. Shamir (eds), *USSR and the Middle East*, Jerusalem 1972, pp. 251–71.
48. Thompson (note 42), p. 93; see also his more recent article 'Delineating Regional Subsystems: Visit Networks and the Middle Eastern Case', in *International Journal of Middle East Studies*, vol. 13 (1981), pp. 213–35.
49. On the OAU see the articles by Patricia B. Wild in Paul A. Tharp Jr, *Regional International Organizations: Structures and Functions*, New York, 1971, on this pp. 36ff and pp. 182ff; on the significance of regional organisations for regional subsystems see Lynn H. Miller, 'Regional Organizations and Subordinate Systems', in Cantori and Spiegel (note 15), pp. 357–80.
50. Thomas Hodgkin, 'The New West African State System', in *University of Toronto Quarterly*, vol. 31 (1961), pp. 74–82. With reference to Africa, the region/subsystem debate was taken up again later by S. A. Gitelson, 'The Transformation of the Southern African Subordinate State System', in *Journal of Modern African Studies*, vol. 4 (1977–8), pp. 367–91.
51. Thomas P. Thornton, *The Challenge to US Policy in the Third World: Global Responsibilities and Regional Devolution*, Boulder, Col., 1986, pp. 97–8.
52. Bruce M. Russett, *International Regions and the International System*, Chicago, 1967. See esp. pp. 10ff and pp. 191ff.
53. Robert O. Keohane, *After Hegemony: Cooperation and Discord in the World Political Economy*, Princeton, NJ, 1984.
54. See note 38 above for a full reference.
55. Erich Gysling, *Zerreissprobe in Nahost*, Zürich, Cologne, 1986; Gysling is chief director at Swiss DRS television; Arnold Hottinger is Near East corre-

spondent of the *Neuer Zürcher Zeitung* and author of several books. Wolfgang Günter Lerch is the Middle East expert of the *Frankfurter Allgemeine Zeitung* and author of the book: *Kein Friede für Allah's Völker*, Frankfurt/M. 1991.

56. Edward Mortimer, *Faith and Power: The Politics of Islam*, New York, 1982. Mortimer is a *Financial Times* correspondent. Tony Walker is Middle East correspondent of the *Financial Times*.

57. Lacouture and Rouleau write for *Le Monde*. Rouleau has since left journalism and entered the diplomatic service as an ambassador. Both are authors of numerous books published in French.

58. Christopher S. Shoemaker and John Spanier, *Patron–Client State Relationships: Multilateral Crises in the Nuclear Age*, New York, 1984; see esp. pp. 132ff.

59. Johan Galtung, *Strukturelle Gewalt*, Reinbek, Hamburg, 1975, p. 120.

60. The hierarchy of the international system, however, is examined more precisely by Steven L. Spiegel, in *Dominance and Diversity: The International Hierarchy*, Boston, 1972; see esp. chapter 3, pp. 93ff.

61. Galtung (note 59), p. 120.

62. This is particularly the case with the German IR scholar Dieter Senghaas. In fairness to him, however, it must be added that his work, inspired by Galtung and Amin, did have a positive function in the 1970s, by shifting the then strongly romantic Third World debate on to a more scholarly footing.

63. William R. Thompson, 'The Arab Sub-System and the Feudal Pattern of Interaction: 1965', in *Journal of Peace Research*, vol. 7 (1970), pp. 151–67.

64. In addition to the above-mentioned negative effect of Galtung, the work of Immanuel Wallerstein should also be mentioned: in contrast to conservative globalists, his starting point is a leftist one, on the basis of which he devises a global 'world system' with no regional differentiation at all. See James Lee Ray, 'The "World-System" and the Global Political System: A Crucial Relationship?' in Pat McGowan and Charles W. Kegley Jr (eds), *Foreign Policy and the Modern World System*, Beverly Hills, London, 1983, pp. 13–34.

65. John Waterbury, 'The Middle East and the New World Economic Order', in John Waterbury and R. el-Mallakh, *The Middle East in the Coming Decade*, New York, 1978, pp. 21ff., esp. pp. 27ff.

66. One example of such superpower arrogance with regard to voting majorities: when American intervention in Grenada met with UN condemnation, with Third World countries in the majority, Reagan commented on American TV: 'It did not upset my breakfast.'

67. See B. Tibi, 'Die afro-arabischen Beziehungen seit der Dekolonisation unter besonderer Berücksichtigung der Erdöldimension', in *Africa Spectrum*, vol. 21, no. 3 (1986), pp. 315–35.

68. An example of globalism of this kind is given by the authors Robert G. Darius, John W. Amos and Ralph H. Magnus (eds), *Gulf Security into the 1980s*, Stanford, 1984. See my review of this in *International Journal of Middle East Studies*, vol. 18 (1986), pp. 393–94. See the chapter on foreign policy in *The Reagan Presidency*, ed. Dilys Mill and Raymond Moore, London 1990, pp. 179–98.

2 The Middle East: Its Location and Delimitation

1. See B. Tibi, 'Orient und Okzident. Feindschaft oder interkulturelle Kommunikation?', in *Neue Politische Literatur*, vol. 29 (1984), pp. 267–86.
2. UN report of the 'Ad Hoc Committee of the Middle East' (UN Economic and Social Council/Official Records E1360 and E/AC 26/16).
3. L. Carl Brown, *International Politics and the Middle East: Old Rules, Dangerous Games*, Princeton, NJ, 1984, p. 5.
4. Ibid., p. 7.
5. See B. Tibi, *Vom Gottesreich zum Nationalstaat: Islam und panarabischer Nationalismus*, 2nd edn, Frankfurt am Main, 1991, esp. chapter II. English translation: Bassam Tibi, *Arab Nationalism: A Critical Enquiry*, 2nd edn., London, New York: Macmillan, 1990. On empires see the historical overview by Michael Doyle, *Empires*, Ithaca, 1986.
6. See Nohlen and Nuschler (eds), *Handbuch der Dritten Welt*, vol. 6: Nord-Afrika und Naher Osten, Hamburg, 1983.
7. Roderic H. Davison, 'Where is the Middle East?', in Richard Nolte (ed.), *The Modern Middle East*, New York, 1963, pp. 13–29, here p. 20. On Mahan, see P. A. Crowl, 'Mahan: The Naval Historian', in Peter Paret (ed.), *Makers of Modern Strategy*, Princeton, 1986, pp. 444–77.
8. See E.-S. Samland, *Die regionale Konfiguration weltgesellschaftlicher Konfliktformationen – am Beispiel des arabisch-persischen Golfes*, Frankfurt, Bern, 1985, pp. 165ff, esp. 176 (originally a dissertation, Göttingen 1982). See my review of this book in *Middle East Journal*, vol. 40, no. 3 (1986) pp. 506–7.
9. Davison, op. cit. (note 7), p. 23.
10. Ibid., p. 27. This view is also put forward by Nikki R. Keddie, 'Is there a Middle East?', in *International Journal of Middle East Studies*, vol. 4 (1973), pp. 255–71, on this p. 267. In this article, Keddie focuses on the question of the extent to which Iran belongs to the 'Middle East'.
11. Jamil Matar and Ali Eddin Hillal, *al-nizam al-iqlimi al-'arabi. Dirasah fi al-'alaqat al sisyasiyya al-'arabiyya* (The Arab Regional System: An Examination of Inter-Arab Political Relations), 3rd extended edn, Beirut, 1983.
12. Saad Eddin Ibrahim, *The New Arab Social Order: A Study of the Social Impact of Oil Wealth*, Boulder, Col., 1982. Both Ibrahim and Hillal cooperated as authors in a research project of the al-Ahram Center in Cairo and UCLA, the results of which were published in M. H. Kerr and El-Sayed Yassin (eds), *Rich and Poor States in the Middle East. Egypt and the New Arab Order*, Boulder, Col., 1982. The Cairo political scientist Ali Hillal Dessouki publishes in Arabic under the name Ali Hillal.
13. Matar and Hillal Dessouki (note 11), pp. 25f. and 30f.
14. Ibid., p. 31.
15. Ibid., p. 32.
16. Frederic Pearson, 'Interaction in an International Political Subsystem: The Middle East 1963–64', in *Peace Research Society* (International Papers), vol. 15 (1970), pp. 73–99, here p. 78.
17. Ibid.
18. William R. Thompson, 'Delineating Regional Subsystems: Visit Networks and the Middle Eastern Case', in *International Journal of Middle East*

Studies, vol. 13, (1981), pp. 213–5, and A. Diskin and S. Mishal, 'Spatial Models and Centrality of International Communities: Meetings between Arab Leaders 1966–1978', in *Journal of Conflict Resolution*, vol. 25 (1981), pp. 655–76.

19. Michael C. Hudson, 'The Middle East', in James Rosenau *et al.* (eds), *World Politics*, New York, 1976, pp. 466–500, here p. 474.
20. Louis J. Cantori and Steven L. Spiegel, *The International Politics of Regions: A Comparative Approach*, Englewood Cliffs, NJ, 1970, p. 8.
21. Ibid., p. 6.
22. For documentation of this, see John L. Esposito (ed.), *Voices of Resurgent Islam*, New York, Oxford 1983; for an interpretation, see B. Tibi, *Islam and the Cultural Accommodation of Social Change*, Boulder, Col: Westview Press 1990, pp. 122–34.
23. On the diversity of segmentation (ethnic, confessional, etc.), see Michael Hudson, *Arab Politics: The Search for Legitimacy*, 2nd edn, New Haven, 1979, pp. 56–81. Milton J. Esman and Itamar Rabinovich (eds), *Ethnicity, Pluralism and the State in the Middle East*, Ithaca, London, 1988, is also an informative book.
24. F. Ajami, 'The End of Pan-Arabism', in *Foreign Affairs*, vol. 57 (1978–9), pp. 355–73. See also Carl Leiden, 'Arab Nationalism Today', in *Middle East Review*, vol. 11 (1978–9), pp. 45–51. See also the new chapter 'Arab Nationalism Revisited', in B. Tibi (note 5 above).
25. B. Tibi, 'The Iranian Revolution and the Arabs: The Quest for Islamic Identity and the Search for an Islamic System of Government', in *Arab Studies Quarterly*, vol. 8, no. 1 (1986), pp. 29–44.
26. See Charles Issawi, 'The Bases of Arab Unity', in Issawi (ed.), *The Arab World's Legacy*, Princeton, NJ, 1981, and Elie Chalala, 'Arab Nationalism: A Bibliographical Essay', in T. E. Farah (ed.), *Pan-Arabism and Arab Nationalism*, Boulder, Col., 1987, pp. 18–56 and B. Tibi (note 5 above).
27. The great cultural diversity within Islam has been taken into account by C. Geertz in *Islam Observed*, New Haven, 1968.
28. See B. Tibi, 'Die Deutschen und die "Welt des Islams"', in *Deutschland: Portrait einer Nation*, 10 vols., here vol. 10, Gütersloh, 1986, pp. 262–71, 2nd rev. edn., 1991.
29. For more on this, see B. Tibi, *The Crisis of Modern Islam*, Salt Lake City: Utah University Press 1988, and B. Tibi (note 22 above).
30. The authoritative work on this is still Robert W. Macdonald, *The League of Arab States: A Study in the Dynamics of a Regional Organization*, Princeton, NJ, 1965.
31. Andrew Axline, 'Underdevelopment, Dependence, and Integration: The Politics of Regionalism in the Third World', in *International Organization*, vol. 31, no. 1 (1977), pp. 83–105.
32. Matar and Hillal Dessouki (note 11), pp. 173ff, pp. 179ff.
33. H. Askari and John T. Cummings, 'The Future of Economic Integration within the Arab World', in *International Journal of Middle East Studies*, vol. 8 (1977), pp. 289–315, here pp. 308f.
34. For a detailed account, see S. E. Ibrahim, op. cit. (note 12).
35. Matar and Hillal Dessouki (note 11), pp. 168ff.
36. See Askari and Cummings (note 33), p. 314.

37.   For a detailed account of this problematique, see Charles Issawi, 'Growth and Structural Change in the Middle East', in *The Middle East Journal*, vol. 25 (1971), pp. 309–24, and also the more recent Robin Barlow, 'Economic Growth in the Middle East 1950–1972', in *International Journal of Middle East Studies*, vol. 14 (1982), pp. 129–57.

38.   Michael Brecher, 'The Middle East Subordinate System and its Impact on Israel's Foreign Policy', in *International Studies Quarterly*, vol. 13 (1969), pp. 117–39, here p. 119.

39.   Cantori and Spiegel (note 20), p. 9.

40.   Hudson (note 19), p. 483.

41.   Ibid.

42.   On the GCC see Eric R. Peterson, *The Gulf Cooperation Council*, Boulder, Col., 1988.

43.   B. Tibi, 'Die Golf-Region im globalen Kräftefeld', in Fred Scholz (ed.), *Die Golf-Staaten*, Braunschweig, 1985, pp. 17–35. See also Liesl Graz, *The Turbulent Gulf*, London, 1990, in particular pp. 1–18.

44.   Mohammed Abed Jabri, 'The Evolution of the Maghrib Concept', in Halim Barakat (ed.), *Contemporary North Africa: Issues of Development and Integration*, Washington, London, 1985, pp. 63–86.

45.   See Hudson (note 19).

46.   See B. Tibi, 'Die irakische Kuwait-Invasion und die Golf-Krise', in *Beiträge zur Konfliktforschung*, vol. 20, no. 4 (1990), pp. 5–34.

47.   John Waterbury, 'The Middle East and the New World Economic Order', in J. Waterbury, Ragaei el-Mallakh, *The Middle East in the Coming Decade*, New York, 1978, pp. 21ff, here pp. 27ff.

48.   S. E. Ibrahim (note 12), pp. 132ff., 148ff.

49.   Ibid., pp. 139ff.

50.   On this, see Daniel Dishon, 'Inter-Arab Relations', in Colin Legum and Halm Shaked (eds), *Arab Relations in the Middle East: The Road to Realignment*, London, 1979, pp. 1–32, as well as the chapter 'Stateness and Inter-Arab Relations', in Gabriel Ben-Dor, *State and Conflict in the Middle East: Emergence of the Post-Colonial State*, New York, 1983, pp. 138–84. More recently Bassam Tibi, The Gulf Crisis and the Fragmentation of the Middle East, in: *Cairo Papers in Social Science* (The American University of Cairo), vol. 14, 1 (Spring 1991), pp. 71–107.

51.   See Robert Jervis, *Perception and Misperception in International Politics*, Princeton, NJ, 1976.

52.   Yair Evron, *The Middle East: Nations, Superpowers and Wars*, New York, Washington, 1975, pp. 164f.

53.   On this conflict see the insightful contribution by Everett Mendelsohn, *A Compassionate Peace: A Future for Israel, Palestine and the Middle East*, 2nd edn, New York, 1989.

54.   See Eberhard Kienle, *Ba'th versus Ba'th: The Conflict Between Syria and Iraq 1968–1989*, London, 1990.

55.   Malcom Kerr, murdered by Islamic fundamentalists in Beirut in January 1984, wrote a masterpiece on this: *The Arab Cold War: Abd al-Nasir and his Rivals*, New York, 1974.

56.   See John Damis, *Conflicts in Northwest Africa: The Sahara Dispute*, Stanford, 1984. The recent reconciliation between Algeria and Morocco seems to have

somewhat defused this conflict. See A. Gowers, 'UN-Peace Plans Accepted for the Sahara', in *Financial Times*, 31 August 1988.

57. See the chapter on the Soviet Union in Seth Tillman, *The United States in the Middle East: Interests and Obstacles*, Bloomington, 1982, pp. 230–74. Christian Hacke, *Amerikanische Nahost-Politik*, Munich, 1985, is also worth reading. Most interesting is Dan Tschirgi, *The American Search for Mideast Peace*, New York, 1989.

58. See Robert O. Freedman, *Soviet Policy toward the Middle East since 1970*, 2nd edn, New York, 1978.

59. Itamar Rabinovich, *The War for Lebanon 1970–1985*, Ithaca, 1985, on this pp. 121ff.

60. See S. Chubin and C. Tripp, *Iran and Iraq at War*, Boulder, Col., 1988, and more recently Anthony Cordesman and Abraham Wagner, *The Iran–Iraq War*, vol. II of *The Lessons of War*, Boulder, Col., 1990.

61. For chronological information on this, see Wadi D. Haddad, *Lebanon: The Politics of Revolving Doors*, Washington, 1985, for analysis see Samir Khalaf, *Lebanon's Predicament*, New York, 1987.

62. A. M. Farid (ed.), *The Red Sea: Prospect for Stability*, New York, 1984, and Roberto Aliboni, *The Red Sea Region*, Syracuse, New York, 1985.

63. On Ethiopia's relations with the superpowers, see David Korn, *Ethiopia, the United States and the Soviet Union*, London 1986.

64. See Damis (note 56).

65. On Afro-Arab interregional relations, see B. Tibi, 'Die afro-arabischen Beziehungen seit der Dekolonisation unter besonderer Berücksichtigung der Erdöl-Dimension', in *Afrika Spectrum*, vol. 21, no. 3 (1986), pp. 315–35. For a specific account of Libya's Africa policy, see René Lemarchand (ed.), *The Green and the Black: Qadhafi's Policies in Africa*, Bloomington, 1988.

66. A comprehensive political geography of the entire region, making use of social scientific concepts such as regional integration, identity, conflict, cultural cohesion and state formation, has been compiled by Alasdair Drysdale and Gerald H. Blake, *The Middle East and North Africa: A Political Geography*, Oxford, New York, 1985. An introduction written under the impact of the Cold War is provided by Peter Duignan and L. H. Gann, *The Middle East and North Africa: The Challenge to Western Security*, Stanford, 1981, as the title suggests, takes an American view of the region from the point of view of the politics of security.

3 The Six Day War of 1967: The Background and Multifaceted Character of an Escalated Regional Conflict

1. Edgar O'Ballance, *The Third Arab–Israeli War*, London, 1972, p. 268. There is an informative overview of all the Arab–Israeli wars in Ritchie Ovendale, *The Origins of Arab–Israeli Wars*, 5th edn, London, 1987, and Sydney D. Bailey, *Four Arab–Israeli Wars and the Peace Process*, 3rd edn, London, New York, 1990.

2. L. Carl Brown, *International Politics and the Middle East: Old Rules, Dangerous Games*, Princeton, NJ, 1984, pp. 87ff, 107ff. For an overview of the

economic incorporation of the Middle East into the world economy see Roger Owen, *The Middle East in the World Economy*, London, 1981.

3. See B. Tibi, 'Die Golf-Region im globalen Kräftefeld', in Fred Scholz (ed.), *Die Golf-Staaten*, Brunswick, 1985, pp. 17–35, here pp. 18ff.

4. See Edgar O'Ballance, *The Sinai Campaign, 1956*, London, 1959, and also Roger Owen and Louis W. Roger (eds), *Suez 1956: The Crisis and its Consequences*, Washington, 1987.

5. David Gordon, *The Passing of French Algeria*, London, Oxford, 1966, p. 59, and Hartmut Elsenhans, *Frankreichs Algerien-Krieg 1954–1962*, Munich, 1974, pp. 21ff.

6. For a full account of this, see my chapter 'Der Dekolonisationsprozess Algeriens', in Gerhard Grohs and Bassam Tibi (eds), *Soziologie der Dekolonisation in Afrika*, Frankfurt am Main, 1973, pp. 13–79.

7. See E.-S. Samland, *Die regionale Konfiguration weltgesellschaftlicher Konfliktformationen am Beispiel der arabisch-persischen Golfes*, Frankfurt am Main, 1985, pp. 165ff.

8. In addition to the works by Binder quoted in Part One, see also the chapter entitled 'The Middle East as a Subordinate International System', in Leonard Binder, *The Ideological Revolution in the Middle East*, New York, 1964, pp. 254ff (identical with his 1958 article in *World Politics*).

9. On Nasserism, see the extensive chapter III in B. Tibi, *Militär und Sozialismus in der Dritten Welt*, Frankfurt am Main, 1973; see also Nissim Rejwan, *Nasserist Ideology: Its Exponents and Critics*, New York, 1971. See also chapter 7 in Binder (note 8 above), pp. 198ff.

10. For a detailed account of this, see Hans Henle, *Der Neue Nahe Osten*, Hamburg, 1966, pp. 74ff.

11. See Edgar O'Ballance, *The War in the Yemen*, London, 1971, and Manfred W. Wenner, *Modern Yemen 1961–1966*, Baltimore, 1967; on this pp. 193ff.

12. A typology of Arab political systems has been devised by B. Tibi, 'A Typology of Arab Political Systems', in Samih Farsoun (ed.), *Arab Society*, London 1985, pp. 48–64, as well as in B. Tibi, 'Die Verschiedenheit der politischen Systeme in der arabischen Region', in K. Kaiser and U. Steinbach (eds), *Deutsch-Arabische Beziehungen*, Munich, 1981, pp. 13–26.

13. Kamel Abu-Jaber, *The Arab Ba'th Socialist Party: History, Ideology and Organization*, Syracuse, NY, 1966 remains a standard work on the Ba'th Party. See also John Devlin, *The Ba'th Party*, Stanford, 1976.

14. See L. Carl Brown (note 2), pp. 199ff. See also R. Immerman, *John Foster Dulles and the Diplomacy of the Cold War*, Princeton, NJ, 1990.

15. O'Ballance (note 1), p. 45. On the reparations problematique, see Amnon Neustadt, *Die Deutsch-Israelischen Beziehungen im Schatten der EG-Nahostpolitik*, Frankfurt am Main, 1983, pp. 28ff.

16. Malcom Kerr, *The Arab Cold War: Abd-al-Nasir and his Rivals 1958–1970*, 3rd edn, New York, 1974.

17. Quoted from the German translation of Eric Rouleau, J. F. Held and Jean Lacouture, *Die Dritte Schlacht: Israel und die Araber*, Frankfurt am Main 1967; on Rouleau, see Chapter 1, note 57 in this book.

18. O'Ballance (note 1), p. 68.

19. Rouleau (note 17), German translation, p. 101.

20. H. M. Azzam, *Der Islam*, Stuttgart, 1981, p. 52. On this problematique, see

the chapter on language in B. Tibi, *Islam and the Cultural Accommodation of Social Change*, Boulder, Col.: Westview Press, 1990.

21. Rouleau was very quick to grasp this (note 17), German translation p. 91.
22. Sadiq Jalal al-'Azm, 'al-'Ilm al-hadith wa al-naksa al-akhira' ('Modern Science and the Recent Defeat'), in *Dirasat 'Arabiyya* (Beirut), vol. 3, no. 10 (1967), pp. 34–53, here p. 39.
23. On the following, see O'Ballance (note 1), pp. 49ff., 56ff, and Donald Neff, *Warriors for Jerusalem: The Six Days that Changed the Middle East*, New York, 1984, esp. pp. 201ff.
24. Rouleau (note 17), pp. 63ff, 65ff. For an interpretation, see S. N. Antabawi, 'The United Nations and the Middle East Conflict of 1967', in I. Abu-Lughod (ed.), *The Arab–Israeli Confrontation of June 1967: An Arab Perspective*, Evanston, Ill., 1970, pp. 122–37.
25. Rouleau (note 17) interprets Nasser's plans as consisting of a three-phase strategy: 1. to bluff as a deterrent, 2. escalation, and 3. 'to avert war and thus achieve a great political victory, the sovereignty of the Madiq Tiran straits in return for certain concessions to Israel'. Hisham Sharabi, 'Prelude to War: the Crisis of May–June 1967', in Abu-Lughod (note 24), pp. 49–65, on this p. 53 puts forward a similar interpretation. Walter Laqueur, *Nahost – Vor dem Sturm: Die Vorgeschichte des Sechs-Tage-Krieges*, Frankfurt am Main, 1968, pp. 81ff, offers a different viewpoint.
26. Michael Hudson, *Arab Politics: The Search for Legitimacy*, 2nd edn, New Haven, 1979, p. 5.
27. John Waterbury, *The Egypt of Nasser and Sadat: The Political Economy of Two Regimes*, Princeton, NJ, 1983, pp. 83ff, esp. p. 100. Waterbury (p. 93) points out how failure was attributed to external causes rather than to their own mistakes.
28. See Robert Jervis, *Perception and Misperception in International Politics*, Princeton, NJ, 1976, and in this context the work of John W. Amos II, *Arab–Israeli Military/Political Relations: Arab Perceptions and the Politics of Escalation*, New York, 1979; on the Six Day War, see pp. 28ff, 63ff.
29. Syria is put forward here only as an example. On this problematique, see B. Tibi (note 9), on this pp. 78ff.
30. On Egypt under Nasser's military, see A. Abdel-Malek, *Egypte, Société Militaire*, Paris, 1962.
31. See King Hussein of Jordan, *My War with Israel*, New York, 1969.
32. The core of the Jordanian army consists of bedouins, and developed out of the 'Arab Legion' set up by the British General Glubb. For a detailed account, see P. J. Vatikiotis, *Politics and the Military in Jordan: A Study of the Arab Legion 1921–1957*, London 1967, pp. 57ff, 75ff.
33. A detailed description of the air battle can be found in O'Ballance (note 1), pp. 62ff; see also Rouleau, Held and Lacouture (note 17), pp. 96ff, and D. Neff (note 23), pp. 203ff.
34. King Hussein (note 31). See also the book by the chief press officer at the court of Hussein: Samir A. Mutawi, *Jordan in the 1967 War*, Cambridge, 1987, esp. pp. 122f.
35. O'Ballance (note 1), p. 167, also pp. 154 and 165; see also the new two-volume Egyptian book on the Six Day War by A. Ramadan cited in note 61 to Chapter 6.

4   The Regional and International Repercussions of the Six Day War: the End of Nasserism and the Beginning of a New Historical Epoch

1. On the emergence of the state of Israel and the conflict potential connected with it, see the habilitation thesis of Dan Diner, *Israel in Palästina, Über Tausch und Gewalt im Vorderen Orient*, Königstein, TS, 1980, and Alasdair Drysdale and Gerald H. Blake, *The Middle East and North Africa: A Political Geography*, Oxford, 1985, pp. 263–312 (with useful cartographic material).
2. Cheryl A. Rubenberg deals with the view that Israel is a strategic asset in her book, *Israel and the American National Interest: A Critical Examination*, Urbana, Chicago, 1986, pp. 1–22.
3. Abdallah Laroui, *The Crisis of the Arab Intellectual: Traditionalism or Historicism?*, Berkeley, 1976, pp. VII–IX.
4. See the relevant articles in Tareq Y. Ismael *et al.*, *Government and Politics of the Contemporary Middle East*, Homewood, Ill., 1970.
5. B. Tibi, 'Von der Selbstverherrlichung zur Selbstkritik. Zur Kritik des politischen Schrifttums der zeitgenössischen arabischen Intelligenz', in *Die Dritte Welt*, vol. 1 (1972), pp. 158–84. This German article is based on an earlier one in Arabic in the then newly founded Arab periodical *Mawaqif*: 'Fi al fikr al-'Arabi al-Mu'asir', *Mawaqif*, no. 3 (1969), pp. 93–117 (Fouad Ajami evaluates this periodical, established by Adonis, in his book (cited in note 10), both in the introduction and in chapter 1; see also pp. 28–29); a new version was given in the form of a paper ten years later in Tunis at the Centre d'Etudes et de Recherches Economiques et Sociales (CERES) of the University of Tunis at a conference on 'al-'arab amam masirahum/Les Arabes face à leur destin'; the critique formulated in it still applies; this paper appeared in Tunis: CERES (ed.), *al-'Arab amam masirahum/Les Arabes face à leur destin*, Tunis, 1982, pp. 177–215.
6. Sadiq Jalal al-'Azm, *al-naqd al-dhati ba'd al-hazima* (Self-criticism after the Defeat), Beirut, 1968. See Ajami's appreciation of this book (note 10), pp. 30–7.
7. al-'Azm, op. cit., p. 87; see also pp. 29ff.
8. Ibid., p. 69. The Arab cultural notion of *mu'amarah* – conspiracy of non-Arabs against the Arabs – was and still is the prevailing pattern. See B. Tibi, 'Das arabische Kollektiv und seine Feinde', in *Frankfurter Allgemeine Zeitung*, 9 February 1991, reprinted in *Tagesanzeiger* (Zurich), 28 February 1991, and *Kurier* (Vienna), 14 February 1991.
9. Laroui (note 3), p. VIII.
10. Fouad Ajami, *The Arab Predicament: Arab Political Thought and Practice since 1967*, Cambridge, 1981, p. 25 (now in its sixth reprint).
11. B. Tibi, 'Madha ta'allamna mina al-naksa al-akhira?' (What Have We Learned from the Recent Defeat?), in *Dirasat 'Arabiyya*, vol. 4, no. 6 (1968), pp. 28–50; see also note 5. My articles in Arabic at that time (1968–1970) were published in *Mawaqif, Dirasat 'Arabiyya, al-Adab, al-'Ulum, al-Hurriya*, and *al-Tali'a*. The hopes that created the drive to write these Arabic articles were fading by the early 1970s.
12. General Salih M. 'Ammash, al-Wihda 'Askariyyan, *al-Madmun al-'askari li'l-*

widha al-'Arabiyya, (Unity from the Military Viewpoint: The Military Dimension of Pan-Arabism), 2nd edn, Beirut, 1970, and Haitham Kaylani, *al-Janib al-'askari fi al-nidal fi ajl al-wihda al-'arabiyya*, (The Military Dimension of the Struggle for Pan-Arabism), Beirut, 1973.

13. Ajami (note 10), pp. 26f.
14. An illustration of this manner may be found in the influential work by Lutfi al-Khuli, *5 Junio. Al-Haqiqa wa al-mustaqbel* (June 5th, the Truth and the Future), Cairo, 1968, pp. 120ff, 135ff; al-Khuli's thought is utterly conspiracy-driven.
15. Giovanni Donini, 'Saudi Arabia's Hegemonic Policy and Economic Development in the Yemen Arab Republic', in *Arab Studies Quarterly*, vol. 4, no. 4 (1979), pp. 299–308, on this p. 305.
16. Tawfiq Y. Hasou, *The Struggle for the Arab World: Egypt's Nasser and the Arab League*, London, Boston, 1985, pp. 17ff, 136ff, 162ff.
17. On the founding of the Arab League, see A. M. Gomaa, *The Foundation of the League of Arab States*, London, 1977, as well as the main chapter on this in Y. Porath, *In Search of Arab Unity*, London, 1986 (chapter 5), pp. 257–311, with an extensive prehistory account. The authoritative work on this, however, is still the book by Macdonald quoted in Part One, Chapter 2, note 30.
18. Wahid al-Dali, 'Jami'at al-duwal al-'Arabiyya wa al-alaqat al-duwaliyya' (The Arab League and International Politics), in *al-Siyasa al-Duwaliyya* (Cairo), vol. 4, no. 13 (1968), pp. 536–43.
19. Butrus Ghali, 'al-'Amal al-'Arabi al-mushtarak fi itar al-jami'a al-'Arabiyya' (Arab Cooperation in the Context of the League), in *al-Siyasa al-Duwaliyya*, vol. 6, no. 20 (1970), pp. 266–91. Three years later, Ghali took a step further, calling the Arab League as outmoded as the Arab states themselves (p. 303) in his article: 'al-Diplomasiya al'Arabiyya fi muwajahat al-munaza'at al-iqlimiyya' (Arab Diplomacy in the Light of Regional Conflict), in *al-Siyasa al-Duwaliyya*, vol. 9, no. 32 (1973), pp. 278–303.
20. Muhammad Aziz Shukri, 'Al-Takamul al-wadhifi fi al-'alam al-'Arabi' (Functional Integration in the Arab Region), in *al-Siyasa al-Duwaliyya*, vol. 8, no. 28 (1972), pp. 318–65.
21. Hassan Abu-Talib, 'Mu'tamarat al-qumma wa tahadiyat al-'amal al-'arabi al-mushtarak' (Arab Summit Conferences, and the Call for Arab Cooperation), in *al-Siyasa al-Duwaliyya*, no. 80 (1985), pp. 296–311.
22. On this, see Paul C. Noble, 'The Arab System: Opportunities, Constraints, and Pressures', in: B. Korany and A. E. Hillal Dessouki (eds), *The Foreign Policies of Arab States*, Boulder, Col., 1984, pp. 41–77, on this pp. 52ff.
23. Ajami (note 10), pp. 77ff.
24. See Lilian Craig Harris, *Libya, Qadhafi's Revolution and the Modern State*, Boulder, Col., 1986, pp. 64f.
25. Tareq Y. Ismael, *International Relations of the Contemporary Middle East*, Syracuse, 1986, pp. 64f.
26. Robert Springborg, 'On the Rise and Fall of Arab Isms', in *Australian Outlook*, vol. 31 (1977), pp. 92–109, here p. 98.
27. Hassan Abu-Talib, 'Azmat siyasat al-tadamun al-'Arabi' (The Policy Crisis in Arab Solidarity), in *al-Siyasa al-Duwaliyya*, no. 68 (1982), pp. 359–61, on this p. 359.

28. Bahgat Korany, 'Political Petrolism and Contemporary Arab Politics, 1967–1983', in *Journal of Asian and African Studies*, vol. 21, no. 1/2 (1986), pp. 66–80, on this pp. 69f.
29. B. Tibi, 'Vom Zentrum der Revolution zum Zentrum des Petro-Dollars. Ägypten und Saudi-Arabien in der Neuen Arabischen Sozialordnung', in *Beiträge zur Konfliktforschung*, vol. 14, no. 2 (1984), pp. 101–28.
30. El-Sayed Yassin, editorial to *al-Siyasa al-Duwaliyya*, no. 62 (1980), p. 928.
31. L. Turner and J. Bedore, 'Saudi Arabia: The Power of Purse-Strings', in *International Affairs*, vol. 54 (1978), pp. 405–20.
32. Ibrahim Shahata, 'al-Instithmarat al-'Arabiyya fi al-watan al-'Arabi' (Arab Investment in the Arab Region), in *al-Siyasa al-Duwaliyya*, vol. 4 no. 12 (1968), pp. 352–65.
33. For a detailed account of this, see chapter III on Egypt in B. Tibi, *Militär und Sozialismus in der Dritten Welt*, Frankfurt am Main, 1973, and D. Hopwood, *Egypt, Politics and Society*, London, 1982, pp. 130ff.
34. John Waterbury, *The Egypt of Nasser and Sadat: The Political Economy of Two Regimes*, Princeton, NJ, p. 100.
35. Daniel Crecelius, 'Saudi–Egyptian Relations', in *International Studies*, vol. 14 (1975), pp. 563–85, here pp. 578f.
36. On the ASU see Rainer Büren, *Die Arabische Sozialistische Union*, Opladen, 1970.
37. On the abolition of the ASU in an analysis of Egyptian party history drawing on Huntington's theory of institutionalisation, see B. Tibi, 'Schwache Institutionalisierung als politische Dimension der Unterentwicklung. Der Fall Ägypten', in *Verfassung und Recht in Übersee*, vol. 13, no. 1 (1980), pp. 3–26, here pp. 20ff.
38. *al-Tali'a* (Cairo), January/March, 1985, pp. 14–18. *al-Tali'a* was published from 1965 (for twelve years); since May 1984 it has been published again as an occasional periodical, whereas it was previously a monthly.
39. al-Tali'a, ibid., pp. 16–28.
40. On these two models (Muhammad Ali and the Wahhabites), see the appropriate chapter in B. Tibi, *Arab Nationalism: A Critical Enquiry*, 2nd extended edn, London, 1990, pp. 75ff.
41. Fouad Ajami, 'The End of Pan-Arabism', in *Foreign Affairs*, vol. 57, no. 2 (1978–9), pp. 355–73, here p. 357; reprinted in T. E. Farah, *Pan-Arabism and Arab Nationalism*, Boulder, Col., 1987, pp. 96–114.
42. Jean Lacouture, 'The Changing Balance of Forces in the Middle East', in *Journal of Palestine Studies*, vol. 2, no. 4 (1972–3), pp. 25–32, here pp. 25f.
43. Ibid., p. 26.
44. Ralf Hoppe, 'Saudi-Arabiens Aussenpolitik als Versuch einer eigenständigen kriseneindämmenden Regionalpolitik im Nahen Osten', in *Orient*, vol. 26 (1985), pp. 205–27.
45. Naji 'Allush, *al-Thaurah al-Filastiniyya. Ab'aduha wa qadayaha* (The Palestinian Revolution, its Range and Problems), Beirut, 1970; *Nayif Hawatimah, Harakat al-muqawamah al-filastiniyya* (The Palestinian Resistance Movement), 2nd edn, Beirut, 1970; and Munir Shafiq, *Haul al-tanaqud wa al-mumurasa fi al-thaura al-filastiniyya* (On Contradiction and Practice in the Palestinian Revolution), Beirut, 1971.
46. See the monograph by Helena Cobban, *The Palestinian Liberation Organisa-*

tion: People, Power and Politics, Cambridge, 1984. Prior to June 1967 the Arab states were the custodians of the Palestinians; see Barry Rubin, *The Arab States and the Palestine Conflict*, Syracuse, 1981 (1948–1956).

47. Naji 'Allush (ed.), *Munaqashat haul al-thaura al-filastiniyya* (Discussions on the Palestinian Revolution), Beirut, 1970 (contains major documentation on all groups involved in the PLO).

48. Daniel Heradstveit, *Nahost-Guerillas: Eine politologische Studie*, Berlin, 1973, p. 14 (originally Oslo 1971); see also a study from the military science standpoint by Bard O'Neill, *Armed Struggle in Palestine: A Political–Military Analysis*, Boulder, Col., 1978.

49. On the Jordanian civil war of September 1970 (Black September), see John Bulloch, *The Making of a War: The Middle East from 1967 to 1973*, London, 1974, pp. 49ff.

50. Derek Hopwood, *Egypt, Politics and Society 1945–1981*, London, 1982, p. 81.

51. Geoffrey Furlonge, 'Nasser and After: A Symposium', in *Asian Affairs*, vol. 58 (1971), pp. 12–23, here p. 15.

52. Anis Sayigh (ed.), 'Abdul Nasser wa ma ba'd', Beirut, 1980 (special issue of *Qadaya 'Arabiyya*).

53. The text of the speech may be found in volume 3 of *Nasser's Speeches* (in Arabic) (Feb. 1960–Jan. 1962), Cairo Information Office 1962, pp. 228ff.

54. See the pioneering book by Robert Jervis, *Perception and Misperception in International Politics*, Princeton, NJ 1976.

55. For a full account of this, see Roy Fullick and Geoffrey Powell, *Suez: The Double War*, London, 1979, and Robert Bowie, *International Crisis and the Role of Law. Suez 1956*, Oxford, 1974. On the war itself, see O'Ballance, *The Sinai Campaign 1956*, London, 1959. See also Roger Owen and Louis W. Roger (eds), *Suez 1956: The Crisis and its Consequences*, Washington, 1987.

56. Anthony Verrier, *Through the Looking Glass: British Foreign Policy in an Age of Illusions*, London, 1983, p. 125.

57. On the USA's policy towards Egypt before the Suez War, and the importance of the Aswan Dam, see the new book by Geoffrey Aronson, *From Sideshow to Center Stage: US Policy toward Egypt 1946–1956*, Boulder, Col., 1986, on Soviet arms supplies from 1955 see pp. 125ff, on the Aswan Dam, pp. 154ff.

. ` Donald MacLean, *British Foreign Policy since Suez 1956–1968*, London, 1970, p. 174.

59. Ibid., p. 173.

60. Ibid., p. 177.

61. Anthony Verrier (note 56), p. 119.

62. Ibid., p. 156.

63. Hartmut Elsenhans, 'Die französische Erdölpolitik. Zwischen Kooperation mit der Dritten Welt und Integration in der Front der angelsächsischen Majors', in: Elsenhans (ed.), *Erdöl für Europa*, Hamburg 1974, pp. 202ff., here p. 203.

64. Edward A. Kolodziej, *French International Policy under de Gaulle and Pompidou*, Ithaca, London, 1974, pp. 489ff.

65. The text of Resolution 242 can be found in Everett Mendelsohn, *A Compassionate Peace*, New York, 1989, pp. 279ff.

66. Kolodziej (note 64), p. 515.

67. On the Rogers Plan (including text), see John Bulloch (note 49), pp. 172ff., and Bernard Reich, *Quest for Peace: United States–Israel Relations and the Arab–Israeli Conflict*, New Brunswick, NJ, 1977, pp. 109ff.

68. Kolodziej (note 64), p. 507.

69. Ibid., pp. 123ff., especially 130f., and Amos Yoder, *The Conduct of American Foreign Policy since World War II*, New York, 1986, pp. 98f.

70. Ernest Mandel, *Die EWG und die Konkurrenz Europa–Amerika*, Frankfurt am Main, 1968, 3rd edn, 1969. The number of reprints is an indication of the popularity of the thesis.

71. See the documentation on the Hamburg proceedings of this dialogue: Derek Hopwood (ed.), *Euro-Arab Dialogue: The Relations between two Cultures*, London, 1985. For the Arab view, see S. al-Mani and S. al-Shaikhly, *The Euro-Arab Dialogue: A Study in Associative Diplomacy*, New York, 1983.

72. On this, see Wolfgang Hager, 'Western Europe: The Politics of Muddling Through', in J. C. Hurewitz (ed.), *Oil, the Arab–Israeli Dispute and the Industrial World*, Boulder, Col., 1976, pp. 34–51.

73. R. J. Lieber, 'Europe and America in the World Energy Crisis', in *International Affairs*, vol. 55 (1979), pp. 531–45, here p. 534.

74. A well-documented discussion of this problematique can be found in Philip Windsor, 'Superpower Intervention', in Hedley Bull (ed.), *Intervention in World Politics*, 2nd edn, Oxford, 1985, pp. 45ff.

75. See Salah ad-Din al-Hadidi, 'Military Dependence: The Egyptian Case', in T. Asad and Roger Owen (eds), *The Middle East*, London, 1983, pp. 65ff.

76. Hedley Bull, 'Intervention in the Third World', in H. Bull (note 74), pp. 135–56, here p. 152.

77. On this highly sensitive problematique, see Seth P. Tillman, *The United States in the Middle East: Interests and Obstacles*, Bloomington, 1982, pp. 62–7, and James L. Ray, *The Future of American–Israeli Relations*, Lexington, Kentucky, 1985, pp. 25–30. See also the recent book by A. F. K. Organski, *The $36 Billion Bargain: Strategy and Politics in US Assistance to Israel*, New York, 1990.

78. Comprehensive data on this can be found in SIPRI (Stockholm International Peace Research Institute), *The Arms Trade with the Third World*, Stockholm, New York, 1971, pp. 505ff, see also *SIPRI Yearbook 1982*, London, 1982, diagrams 6.1, 6.2; *SIPRI Yearbook 1983*, London 1983, pp. 270–2; and *SIPRI Yearbook 1985*, London, 1985, pp. 254f. and 347–50.

79. Fred M. Gottheil, 'An Economic Assessment of the Military Burden in the Middle East. 1960–1980', in *Journal of Conflict Resolution*, vol. 18, no. 3 (1974), pp. 502–13, on this pp. 502f.

80. Ibid., p. 512. On this problematique, see the comprehensive analysis on arms trade structures (suppliers and receivers) by Andrew J. Pierre, *The Global Politics of Arms Sales*, Princeton, NJ 1982, pp. 129–209 for the Middle East.

81. Quoted from Steven L. Spiegel, *The Other Arab–Israeli Conflict: Making America's Middle East Policy, from Truman to Reagan*, Chicago, 1985, p. 151.

82. See Arthur Hall, *The United Nations and the Middle East Crisis 1967*, New York, 1968, pp. 11ff; on UNEF see Abdel-Latif M. Zeidan, *The United Nations Emergency Force 1956–1967*, Stockholm, 1976; on Egyptian calls for the withdrawal of the UNEF, see pp. 141ff; see also the literature quoted in Chapter 3, note 24.

83. Ray (note 77), p. 14.
84. Quoted after Reich (note 67), p. 47.
85. Spiegel (note 81), p. 152.
86. Ibid., p. 120.
87. Ibid., p. 153.
88. On the history of the US Gulf strategy see Amitav Acharya, *US Military Strategy in the Gulf*, London, 1989.
89. Spiegel (note 81), pp. 158ff. See the book by Dan Tschirgi, *The American Search for Mideast Peace*, New York, 1989.
89. Spiegel (note 81), p. 127 and p. 159.
90. Ibid., p. 164.
91. For a detailed account of Johnson's Five Point Plan, see Reich (note 67), pp. 83ff.
92. Rubenberg (note 2), p. 126.
93. Reich (note 67), pp. 116f.
94. See Michael Kidron, *Rüstung und wirtschaftliches Wachstum*, Frankfurt am Main, 1971.
95. See the *SIPRI Yearbooks* quoted in note 78.
96. Klaus von Beyme, *Die Sowjetunion in der Weltpolitik*, Munich, 1983, p. 152.
97. J. M. Mackintosh, *Strategy and Tactics of Soviet Foreign Policy*, Oxford, 1962, p. 126.
98. This is illustrated using Egypt as an example in a dissertation by G. Shanneik, *Die Entwicklung des ägyptischen Militärregimes unter besonderer Berücksichtigung der ägyptisch-sowjetischen Beziehungen 1952–1970*, Göttingen, 1978, pp. 175ff.
99. Hans Henle, *Der Neue Nahe Osten*, Hamburg, 1966, pp. 314f.
100. German translation: *Klassen und Klassenkampf in Entwicklungsländern*, 3 vols., vol. I: *Die Klassenstruktur*, East Berlin, 1969; vol. II *Probleme der ökonomischen Unabhängigkeit*, East Berlin, 1970; vol. III *Die Wahl des Weges*, East Berlin, 1970.
101. For more details, see B. Tibi, 'Zur Kritik der sowjetmarxistischen Entwicklungstheorie', in B. Tibi and Volkhard Brandes (eds), *Unterentwicklung*. Politische Ökonomie, Handbook 2, Frankfurt am Main, Cologne, 1975, pp. 64–86.
102. von Beyme (note 96), p. 162. See also A. Pierre (note 80), pp. 73ff, and R. Menon, *Soviet Power and the Third World*. New Haven, 1988, pp. 167ff.
103. Herbert Marcuse, *Soviet Marxism: A Critical Analysis*, New York, 1958 remains the seminal theoretical critique of Soviet Marxism.
104. Mackintosh (note 97), p. 244.
105. Robin Edmonds, *Soviet Foreign Policy 1962–1973: The Paradox of Superpower, 1962–1973*, London, Oxford, 1975, pp. 56f.
106. Ibid., p. 102. On Soviet Middle East policy during the 1970s, see Robert O. Freedman, *Soviet Policy toward the Middle East since 1970*, 2nd edn, New York, 1978, here chapter III, pp. 47ff; on arms policy Jon Glassman, *Arms for the Arabs: The Soviet Union and the War in the Middle East*, 2nd edn, Baltimore, 1977. See also the recent work by Galia Golan, *Soviet Policies in the Middle East from World War II to Gorbachev*, Cambridge, 1990.
107. See the Section entitled 'Die Armee, die Staatspartei und der politische Aufstieg Sadats', in B. Tibi, *Militär und Sozialismus* (note 33), pp. 319ff.
108. For a detailed account, see M. Heikal, *The Sphinx and the Commissar*, New York, 1978, pp. 241–6, and Tibi (note 33), pp. 337ff.

109. On the Lebanon War of 1982 see Itamar Rabinovich, *The War for Lebanon*, revised edn, Ithaca, London, 1986.
110. See Part Four of this book.

5 The Yom Kippur, Ramadan or October War? Historical Continuity from the Six Day War to the Nineteen Day War

1. Peter Pawelka, *Herrschaft und Entwicklung im Nahen Osten: Ägypten*, Heidelberg, 1985, p. 268. See my review in *International Journal of Middle East Studies/IJMES*, vol. 22, no. 3 (1990) pp. 346–50.
2. On the political structure of the West Jordan area, see Avi Plascov, *The Palestinian Refugees in Jordan 1948–1957*, London, 1981, and Arthur R. Day, *East Bank/West Bank: Jordan and the Prospects for Peace*, New York, 1986, especially pp. 21ff. On the *intifada*, see the standard work by David McDowall, *Palestine and Israel: The Uprising and Beyond*, Berkeley, 1989.
3. John Bulloch, *The Making of a War: The Middle East from 1967 to 1973*, London, 1974, p. 170.
4. On the outcome of Kissinger's diplomacy, see Gil Carl AlRoy, *The Kissinger Experience: American Policy in the Middle East*, New York, 1975, and Edward Sheehan, *The Arabs, Israelis and Kissinger*, New York, 1976; see also Chapter 6 of this book.
5. Hassan Badri, Taha Majdub and Dia'uddin Zahdi, *Harb Ramadan. Al-Jawla al-'arabiyya al-Israeliyya al-rab'ia* (The Ramadan War. The Fourth Arab–Israeli Battle), Cairo, 1974.
6. A recording of this telephone conversation, taped by the Israeli secret service, is contained in ZDF documentation on the 20th anniversary of the Six Day War by G. Knopp and H. Schott, 'Blitzkrieg im Heiligen Land' (ZDF 7 June 1987, 10.00 p.m.). ZDF (Zweites Deutsches Fernsehen) is one of the two public German TV channels.
7. Frank Aker, *October 1973, The Arab–Israeli War*, Hamden, Conn., 1985, pp. 66ff.
8. Ibid., p. 31.
9. See Dan Diner, *Israel in Palästina. Über Tausch und Gewalt im Vorderen Orient*, Königstein, Ts., 1980, pp. 246ff. See also the excellent article by Diner in volume 21 of the book series *Friedensanalysen:Kriegsursachen*, Frankfurt am Main, 1987, pp. 308–33.
10. Aker (note 7), p. 84.
11. Ibid., p. 5.
12. Galia Golan, *Yom Kippur and After: The Soviet Union and the Middle East Crisis*, Cambridge, London, 1977, pp. 74ff. See also the most recent book by Golan, *Soviet Policies in the Middle East*, Cambridge 1990.
13. Sharon quoted after Aker (note 7), p. 130.
14. Aker, p. 7; see also Alan Dowty, *Middle East Crisis*, Berkeley, 1984, p. 112.
15. Jon D. Glassman, *Arms for the Arabs: The Soviet Union and War in the Middle East*, 2nd edn, Baltimore, London, 1977, pp. 65ff.
16. On this see the section 'Die ägyptische Armee und die Ausweisung der sowjetischen Militärberater 1972', in B. Tibi, *Militär und Sozialismus in der Dritten Welt*, Frankfurt am Main, 1973, pp. 337ff.
17. In addition to the following remarks on the events of the war, see the works

by Aker (note 7), Peter Allen, *The Yom Kippur War*, New York, 1982, as well as the quasi-official Egyptian account by Generals Badri, Majdub and Zahdi (note 5).

18. Taufiq al-Hakim, quoted after Badri *et al.* (note 5), p. 97.
19. Badri *et al.* (note 5), p. 108.
20. Ibid., pp. 57ff.
21. Allen (note 17), p. 131.
22. Aker (note 7), p. 21.
23. Glassman (note 15), p. 141.
24. See chapters II and III in Aker (note 7), and p. 83, as well as the work of the Allen (note 17), and Glassman (note 15), especially pp. 139f.
25. Aker (note 7), p. 36.
26. Glassman (note 15), pp. 127f. A quarter of total Israeli plane losses were incurred on the first day of the war.
27. Dayan, quoted after Glassman (note 15), p. 131.
28. Aker (note 7), p. 53.
29. For a detailed account of this, see Nikolaos van Dam, *The Struggle for Power in Syria: Sectarianism, Regionalism and Tribalism in Politics 1961–1978*, London, 1979, especially pp. 31–50. On minorities in the Syrian army, pp. 83ff; on the Alawi sect of the president, pp. 98ff. On Syria under the Alawite Assad see M. Ma'oz and A. Yaniv (eds), *Syria under Assad*, New York, 1986.
30. Nikolaos van Dam, 'Minorities and Political Elites in Iraq and Syria', in T. Asad and R. Owen (eds), *The Middle East*, London, 1983, pp. 127ff., on this p. 136f.
31. Badri *et al.* (note 5), pp. 145ff, Glassman (note 15), pp. 134f.
32. Aker (note 7), pp. 94ff, especially pp. 105 and 108f.; even the Egyptian generals conceded the success of this infiltration: see Badri *et al.* (note 5), p. 158.
33. Texts of UN Resolutions 242 and 338 are included in the appendices to Everett Mendelsohn, *A Compassionate Peace*, New York, 1989, pp. 279–84.
34. On the Battle of Badr, see W. M. Watt and A. T. Welch, *Der Islam I*, Stuttgart, 1980, p. 151.

6 The Superpowers and the October War

1. Frank Aker, *October 1973, The Arab–Israeli War*, Hamden, Conn., 1985, p. 31.
2. Jon D. Glassman, *Arms for the Arabs: The Soviet Union and War in the Middle East*, Baltimore, London, 1977, p. 138.
3. Aker (note 1), p. 127.
4. Ibid., p. 31.
5. Galia Golan, *Yom Kippur and After: The Soviet Union and the Middle East Crisis*, Cambridge, 1977, pp. 118ff.
6. Quoted after C. Shoemaker and J. Spanier, *Patron–Client Relationships: Multilateral Crises in the Nuclear Age*, New York, 1984, p. 169; see also J. Glassman (note 2), p. 158 and Alan Dowty, *Middle East Crisis*, Berkeley, 1984, pp. 242ff.
7. Shoemaker and Spanier (note 6), pp. 158 and 166.

8. Richard Woyke, *NATO in den siebziger Jahren*, Hannover, 1976, p. 63, asserts: 'the pressures on the Atlantic Alliance during the fourth Middle East War (in October 1973) threatened to destroy the Alliance'.

9. William Quandt, *Decade of Decisions: American Foreign Policy toward the Arab–Israeli Conflict 1967–1976*, Berkeley, 1977, p. 197; see also Shoemaker and Spanier (note 6), p. 171.

10. Stephen T. Hosmer and Thomas W. Wolfe, *Soviet Policy and Practice toward Third World Conflicts*, Lexington, Mass., 1983, pp. 50–2.

11. Quandt (note 9), p. 197.

12. Richard Nixon, *The Memoirs of Richard Nixon*, New York, 1978, p. 938.

13. Martin J. Slominski, 'The Soviet Military Press and the October War', in *Military Review*, vol. 54, May issue (1974), pp. 39–47.

14. On this see Glassman (note 2), p. 137.

15. Shoemaker and Spanier (note 6), p. 171.

16. On this see especially Dan Diner, *Israel in Palästina*, Königstein, Ts., 1980, pp. 246ff. On the special relationship between Israel and the USA see the appropriate chapter in Seth P. Tillmann. *The United States in the Middle East*, Bloomington, 1982, pp. 123–71. On the October War, see Bernard Reich, *The United States and Israel: Influence in the Special Relationship*, New York, 1984, pp.19ff, 29ff, and James Ray, *The Future of American–Israeli Relations*, Lexington, Kentucky, 1985.

17. Anwar el-Sadat, *In Search of Identity*; German translation: *Unterwegs zur Gerechtigkeit, Auf der Suche nach Identität. Die Geschichte meines Lebens*, Vienna, Zurich, 1978, pp. 275ff., especially pp. 280ff. and 269ff.

18. Quandt (note 9), p. 179.

19. Golan (note 5), pp. 84ff., and W. Quandt, 'Soviet Policy in the October Middle East War' in *International Affairs*, vol. 53, nos. 3 and 4 (1977), pp. 377–89 and 587–603, as well as Alvin Rubinstein, *Red Star on the Nile: The Soviet–Egyptian Influence Relationship since the June War*, Princeton, NJ 1977, here chapter 8, pp. 248–87.

20. Quandt (note 9), pp. 183ff.

21. Shoemaker and Spanier (note 6), p. 161.

22. Stanley Hoffmann, *Primacy or World Order: American Foreign Policy since the Cold War*, New York, 1978, p. 295.

23. Gabriel Sheffer, 'Independence in Dependence of Regional Powers: the Uncomfortable Alliances in the Middle East before and after the October War 1973', in *Orbis*, vol. 19, no. 4 (1976), pp. 1519–38. This deals with the problem of domesticating the foreign policy of the Third World states within a bipolar international order. See Christopher Clapham (ed.), *Foreign Policy Making in Developing States: A Comparative Approach*, 2nd edn, Westmead, Hunts., 1979. Specifically on the countries on this particular region, see B. Korany and A. Hillal Dessouki (eds), *The Foreign Policies of Arab States*, Boulder, Col., 1984. Prior to this book, Korany outlined his theoretical ideas in a case study of Egypt (chapter VII): Bahgat Korany, *Social Change, Charisma and International Behaviour: Toward a Theory of Foreign Policy-Making in the Third World*, Leiden, Geneva, 1976; on the subsystem debate, see pp. 140ff, on Egypt see pp. 267ff.

24. Gabriel Sheffer, 'Superpowers and Client States: Middle East Relationships since 1973', in *Wiener Library Bulletin* (GB), vol. 27 (1974), pp. 48–53, here p. 52.

25. Paul Jabber and Roman Kolkowicz, 'The Arab–Israeli Wars of 1967 and 1973', in S. Kaplan (ed.), *Diplomacy of Power: Soviet Armed Forces as a Political Instrument*, Washington, 1982, pp. 412–67, here p. 467.

26. See *SIPRI* (Stockholm International Peace Research Institute) *Yearbook 1983*, London, New York, 1983, p. 270. The twenty major arms-importing states of the Third World also include, in order of import volume, the following Middle East countries: Libya, Saudi Arabia, Egypt, Iraq and Israel. On Syria and the Soviet Union, see Efraim Karsh, *The Soviet Union and Syria*, London, 1988.

27. Quoted after Quandt (note 9), pp. 199f.

28. On Kissinger's 'shuttle diplomacy', see among others Gil Carl AlRoy, *The Kissinger Experience: American Policy in the Middle East*, New York, 1975, and Sheehan (note 32 below). This view is not shared by Stanley Hoffmann in his book quoted in note 22 above.

29. Rubinstein (note 19), pp. 289f.

30. Quandt (note 9), p. 221.

31. Henry Kissinger, *Years of Upheaval*, London, 1982, pp. 646ff.

32. Edward Sheehan, *The Arabs, Israelis and Kissinger: A Secret History of American Diplomacy in the Middle East*, New York, 1976, pp. 48f.

33. Sadat (note 17), p. 338.

34. Kissinger (note 31), p. 799.

35. Lawrence L. Whetten, *The Canal War: Four-Power Conflict in the Middle East*, Cambridge, Mass., 1974, p. 295.

36. Kissinger (note 31), pp. 792ff., see also Quandt (note 9), pp. 223f.

37. Rubinstein (note 19), p. 305.

38. Quandt (note 9), p. 236.

39. Sadat (note 17), p. 336.

40. Ibid., p. 340.

41. Israeli decisions during this period have been analysed by Michael Brecher in a decision-making theory context in *Decisions in Crisis: Israel 1967 and 1973*, Berkeley, Los Angeles, 1980, here pp. 286ff. A similar decision-making theory study on the Six Day War may be found in Janice Gross-Stein and Raymond Tanter, *Rational Decision-Making: Israel's Security Choices, 1967*, Columbus, Ohio, 1980. Unfortunately, no comparable study of Egypt or Syria has yet been completed, probably because of lack of access to the needed material.

42. Chaim Herzog, *The War of Atonement*, London, 1975, p. 270.

43. Ibid., p. 279.

44. Ibid., p. 291.

45. After the October War Kissinger travelled to the Middle East on 5 November, met Sadat on 7 November and also visited other countries in the region. In the strict sense, the term 'shuttle diplomacy' applies only to his two major trips, in January–February, and his summer trip (see note 49). On these two trips, see Kissinger (note 31), pp. 799ff, 935ff, and also Quandt (note 9), p. 232.

46. Whetten (note 35), p. 298.

47. Rubinstein (note 19), p. 293.

48. This heading, used by Kissinger in his memoirs, denotes his Boeing 707: see pp. 818ff. From this plane he could reach any institution in the world either by telephone or wireless.

49. The 'Syrian Shuttle' – from a heading in Kissinger's memoirs, pp. 1032ff,

was the most prolonged, lasting for twenty-seven days without interruption; see also Quandt (note 9), pp. 238ff.

50. Rubinstein (note 19), p. 297; see also Robin Edmonds, *Soviet Foreign Policy 1962–1973: The Paradox of Superpower*, London, 1975, pp. 144ff.
51. See note 49 on the Syrian Shuttle and Syrian foreign policy; for an account of Syrian foreign policy, especially in that period, see R. Hinnebusch, 'Revisionist Dreams, Realist Strategies: The Foreign Policy of Syria', in Korany and Hillal Dessouki (note 23), pp. 283–322, especially pp. 305ff.
52. Stanley Hoffmann (note 22), pp. 72ff, 78ff.
53. Kissinger (note 31), pp. 72ff (on the effects of Watergate on foreign policy); see also Quandt (note 9), pp. 207ff, and Chr. Hacke, *Amerikanische Nahost-Politik*, Munich, 1985, pp. 28–37.
54. Quandt (note 9), pp. 251f.
55. Whetten (note 35), p. 299, and Kissinger (note 31), pp. 707ff.
56. Shoemaker and Spanier (note 6), p. 158.
57. On this, see the monograph by Edward Kolodziej, *French International Policy under de Gaulle and Pompidou: The Politics of Grandeur*, Ithaca, London, 1974, as well as the discussion of this issue in Chapter 4 of this book.
58. See Joseph Nye, *Bound to Lead: The Changing Nature of American Power*, New York, 1990.
59. For more details see Alan Dowty, *Middle East Crisis: US Decision-Making in 1958, 1970 and 1973*, Berkeley, Los Angeles, 1984, on this Part III, especially pp. 241ff. On the theoretical discussion about international crises, see Richard N. Lebow, *Between Peace and War: The Nature of International Crisis*, Baltimore, London 1981, and Charles F. Hermann (ed.), *International Crisis*, New York, 1972.
60. Glenn H. Snyder and Paul Diesing, *Conflict Among Nations*, Princeton, NJ 1977, p. 6.
61. According to a comprehensive two-volume account of the periods before and after June 1967 compiled by the Egyptian historian 'Abdulazim Ramadan, the crisis before June 1967 comprises only a brief period from May–June – see vol. 1, pp. 35–88; in his view, however, the War of Attrition of 1969–70 and the Jordanian–Syrian crisis of 1970 were a component in the crisis leading up to the October War of 1973 (he devotes the entire second volume to this period): 'Abdulazim Ramadan, *Tahtim al-Aliha: Dissat harb Junio 1967* (The Destruction of the Gods: The History of the 1967 June War), 2 volumes, Cairo, 1985, 1986. The term 'destruction of the gods' refers to the loss of legitimacy after June 1967.
62. Snyder and Diesing (note 60), p. 450.
63. See Chapter 9 on the 1990–1 Gulf War in this book.

7 October 1973: The War with Arms and the War with Oil: Petro-dollar Power and the 1973–77 Saudi–Egyptian Axis; its Revival during the Iran–Iraq War and its Aftermath

1. G. M. Brown, 'The Consequences of Yom Kippur', in *Australian Outlook*, vol. 28, August (1974), pp. 196–204, here p. 202.

2. B. Tibi, 'Der Ölpreissturz und seine Opfer', in *Anno 86*, Bertelsmann-Jahrbuch, Gütersloh, 1986, pp. 91–5 (with statistics). The London-based monthly *Petroleum Economist* is the most reliable publication on this subject.
3. Wolfgang Hager (ed.), *Erdöl und internationale Politik*, Munich, 1975, and Mason Wilrich, *Energy and World Politics*, New York, 1975, esp. pp. 180ff.
4. On this see Michael I. Handel, *Diplomacy of Surprise: Hitler, Nixon, Sadat*, Cambridge, Mass., 1981; on Sadat see pp. 241–97.
5. On the challenge of the Iranian revolution, see B. Tibi, 'The Iranian Revolution and the Arabs', in *Arab Studies Quarterly*, vol. 8, no. 1 (1986), pp. 29–44. See also the recent volume John Esposito (ed.), *The Iranian Revolution: Its Global Impact*, Miami, 1990, in particular Part Two, pp. 83ff. On the revolution itself see Said A. Arjomand, *The Turban for the Crown: The Islamic Revolution in Iran*, Oxford, New York, 1988.
6. On Camp David see the seminal book by William Quandt, *Camp David: Peace-Making and Politics*, Washington, 1986, and *The Middle East: Ten Years After*, ed. William Quandt, Washington, 1988. For the relevant documents see Paul Jureidini and R. D. McLaurin, *Beyond Camp David*, Syracuse, 1981. For a conceptually based interpretation see Shibley Telhami, *Power and Leadership in International Bargaining: The Path to the Camp David Accords*, New York, 1990.
7. On the consequences of Camp David for Egypt see Joseph Lorenz, *Egypt and the Arabs; Foreign Policy and the Search for National Identity*, Boulder, Col., 1990, chapter 9, pp. 92–101. See also B. Tibi, 'Ägypten und seine arabische Umwelt', in *Beiträge zur Konfliktforschung*, vol. 12, no. 4 (1982), pp. 33–60.
8. This assertion by Adelman forms the motto heading a lengthy monograph-like treatment resulting from that lecture: B. Tibi, 'OPEC-25-Jahrfeier in einer Doppelkrise. Entstehung, Entwicklung und Desintegration eines Rohstoff-Kartells', in *Beiträge zur Konfliktforschung*, vol. 15, no. 4 (1985), pp. 73–103 (with a comprehensive bibliography). This paper was based on the above-mentioned high table lecture given at the Nigerian Institute for International Affairs. Adelman's *magnum opus* is *The World Petroleum Market*, 2nd edn, Baltimore, 1973.
9. This line of argument is followed using numerous tables in B. Tibi, 'Die Rohstoffe der Peripherie-Länder und der Reproduktionsprozess der Metropolen: Das Beispiel Erdöl', in V. Brandes (ed.), *Perspektiven des Kapitalismus*, Frankfurt am Main, Cologne, 1974, pp. 105–47.
10. John Evans, *Opec, Its Member States and the World Energy Market*, London, 1986 (680pp.) is a reliable handbook on this subject. In another important handbook, A. LeRoy Bennett, *International Organizations, Principles and Issues*, Englewood Cliffs NJ, 1984, pp. 377–8 classifies OPEC under the heading of 'functional regional organisations'.
11. Mana S. al-Otaiba, *OPEC and the Petroleum Industry*, 2nd edn, London, 1976, pp. 1 and 50. Otaiba is oil minister of the United Arab Emirates.
12. See Hanns Maull, *Ölmacht*, Frankfurt am Main 1975, pp. 11–16 and 51ff for the period after October 1973. During the 1967 Six Day War there was an effort to employ the oil weapon, although it proved futile.
13. For a comprehensive account see the book by Alan Dowty, *Middle East Crisis*, Berkeley, 1984, pp. 111–96. Judging from the PLO's recent alliance

with King Hussein, the Palestinian victims of the civil war in Jordan in September 1970 were entirely forgotten by the PLO by the time of the 1990–91 Gulf crisis.

14. *Al-Ahram*, 21 July 1972.
15. Michael C. Hudson, *Arab Politics: The Search for Legitimacy*, 2nd edn, New Haven, 1979, pp. 5, 28 and passim.
16. Pierre Terzian, *OPEC: the Inside Story*, London, 1985, p. 165.
17. See the chapter on Kuwait in Laurie A. Brand, *Palestinians in the Arab World*, New York, 1988, pp. 107–48.
18. Cf. Terzian (note 16), OPEC.
19. Quoted after the comprehensive documentation, which covers all documents of the 1973–74 energy crisis, of Jordan Paust and Albert Blaustein (eds), *The Arab Oil Weapon*, Dobbs Ferry, NY, 1977, here pp. 44ff.
20. Ibid., pp. 46–9 (full text of the document).
21. Ibid., pp. 54–62 (Communiqué of the sixth Arab summit meeting in Algiers) and pp. 63–4 for the oil resolution adopted there.
22. Maull (note 12), p. 64.
23. This is undertaken in my monograph, quoted in note 8, where a full table showing oil price developments from 1935 to 1985 is given on pp. 84f.
24. For an analytical assessment of the impact of the oil embargo see Roy Licklider, *Political Power and the Arab Oil Weapon: The Experience of Five Nations*, Berkeley, 1988.
25. This argument is developed systematically in my article quoted in note 9.
26. Maull (note 12), pp. 64 and 69.
27. M. Tietzel and J. Melcher, *Erdöl und Dritte Welt*, Bonn, 1975. A more recent work with numerous statistics is P. Hallwood and S. Sinclair, *Oil, Debt and Development: OPEC in the Third World*, London, 1981, pp. 74ff; Shireen Hunter, *OPEC and the Third World*, Bloomington, 1984; Parts 1, 4 and 5, in particular are concerned with the OPEC contribution to alleviating these effects through Third World aid.
28. See the documentation on the mammoth proceedings of this dialogue, held in the Hotel Atlantik in Hamburg: Derek Hopwood (ed.), *Euro-Arab Dialogue: the Relations between the two Cultures*, Acts of the Hamburg Symposium, London, 1985; and from the Saudi standpoint S. al-Mani and S. al-Shaikhly, *The Euro-Arab Dialogue*, New York, 1983.
29. See J. C. Hurewitz (ed.), *Oil, the Arab–Israeli Dispute, and the Industrial World*, Boulder, Col., 1976, esp. the contributions by Hager on pp. 34ff., and by Karl Kaiser in the volume by Hager (quoted in note 3 above), pp. 73ff.
30. See Lieber, quoted in note 73 to Chapter 4.
31. Seminal contributions on the problematique of Middle East oil have been compiled by J. E. Peterson (ed.), *The Politics of Middle Eastern Oil*, Washington, 1983, see esp. pp. 65ff., pp. 103ff. and Part III, pp. 303ff.
32. For a full account of this see Richard P. Mattione, *OPEC's Investments and the International Financial System*, Washington, DC, 1985 (chapter 5 on Saudi Arabia and chapter 6 on Kuwait), esp. chapter 10, pp. 185ff.
33. Tony Walker, 'Riches Do Not Buy Security', in *Financial Times*, 12 December 1990, section III: Financial Times Survey Saudi Arabia.
34. On this see the reports in the *al-Ahram*, 28 September 1987 and *al-Muntada* (monthly bulletin of the *Arab Thought Club*) (Amman) October, 1987, pp. 4ff

and November, 1987, pp. 4ff. See the published proceedings referenced in note 35 below.

35. Al-Ghazali's paper has since been published in the Acts of this conference: al-Ahram Center for Political and Strategic Studies (ed.), *al-nizam al-iqlimi al-Arabi. A'mal al-mu'tamar al-istrtiji al-'Arabi al-awwal*, (Amman, September 15–17, 1987), Cairo 1989, pp. 235–80.

36. On the foreign policies of these states see the case studies in B. Korany and Ali H. Dessouki (eds), *The Foreign Policy of Arab States*, Boulder, Col., 1984; Hinnebusch on Syria, pp. 283ff; Ahmad on Iraq, pp. 147ff; Zartmann and Kluge on Libya pp. 175ff; and Korany on Algeria, pp. 79ff.

37. Peter Pawelka, *Herrschaft und Entwicklung im Nahen Osten: Ägypten*, Heidelberg, 1985, p. 285.

38. Ibid., pp. 376f.

39. Malcom Kerr and Sayed Yassin (eds), *Rich and Poor States in the Middle East*, Boulder, Col., 1982, esp. part II, pp. 99f. See also G. Luciani and G. Salamé (eds), *The Politics of Arab Integration*, London, 1988.

40. Daniel Crecelius, 'Sa'udi-Egyptian Relations', in *International Studies* (India), vol. 14, no. 4 (1975), pp. 563–85, on this esp. pp. 581ff.

41. *al-Ahram*, 2 February 1971.

42. *al-Ahram*, 3 March 1971.

43. *al-Ahram,* 3 August 1974.

44. *al-Ahram*, 7 August 1974.

45. The Arabic text of the *fetwa* issued by al-Azhar Sheik Jadulhaq Ali Jadulhaq, as well as the *fetwa* of Sayyid Tantawi, Grand Mufti of Egypt, is printed in *al-Wafd* (Cairo), 22 August 1990, p. 5. On both *fetwas* see the article by B. Tibi, 'Dürfen sich Muslime von Ungläubigen verteidigen lassen? Über zwei Fetwas aus Ägypten', in *Frankfurter Allgemeine Zeitung*, 10 October 1990, p. 8.

46. *al-Ahram,* 31 July and 9 August 1978.

47. On the Arab anti-Sadat front, see Sabri Jiryis, 'The Arab World at the Crossroads: An Analysis of the Arab Opposition to the Sadat Initiative', in *Journal of Palestine Studies*, vol. 7 (1978), pp. 26–61.

48. *al-Ahram*, 2 May 1979.

49. On Sadat's foreign policy decisions, see Jamal Ali Zahran, *al-siyasa al-kharijiyya li Misr 1970–1981* (Egyptian Foreign Policy 1970–1981), Cairo, 1987; see especially pp. 105ff for Sadat's assessment of the balance of power in the Middle East subsystem.

50. More details about this in William Quandt, *The United States and Egypt*, Washington, DC, 1990, in particular pp. 40ff.

51. See Johannes J. G. Jansen, *The Neglected Duty: The Creed of Sadat's Assassins and Islam Resurgence in the Middle East*, New York, London, 1986, esp. chapter 1. The term 'Neglected Duty' refers to the title of a pamphlet by Sadat's assassins.

52. On this see B. Tibi, *The Crisis of Modern Islam*, Salt Lake City: Utah University Press 1988, and B. Tibi, *Islam and the Cultural Accommodation of Social Change*, Boulder, Col.: Westview Press 1990, in particular the section on political Islam in Egypt in chapter 9.

53. Quandt, a Middle East expert and former adviser to President Carter who now works in the Brookings Institution, clearly and precisely shows the mechan-

isms in Saudi Arabian foreign policy for fending off threats: William Quandt, *Saudi Arabia in the 1980s: Foreign Policy, Security and Oil*, Washington, DC, 1981, pp. 76ff.

54. Iraq's rapprochement with Egypt as part of this military aid, which according to Helms's estimation reached US$ 2.7 billion in 1984, began under Sadat and was continued intensively under Mubarak: C. M. Helms, *Iraq: Eastern Flank of the Arab World*, Washington, DC, 1984, pp. 185ff.

55. Steven Butler, 'Oil Hits $40 a Barrel on Threat of War', in: *Financial Times*, 10 October 1990. Shortly after this the price fell to US$36.

56. See James Tanner, 'Saudis Plan to Produce Petroleum All Out if OPEC Can't Agree', in *Wall Street Journal*, 17 November 1988, p. 1 and A 10.

57. J. Tanner and A. Sullivan, 'OPEC Ministers Open Talks Amid Fear That Output Conflict Won't be Solved', in *Wall Street Journal*, 18 November 1988, p. A 10, and Steven Butler, 'OPEC Deadlocked as Iran Rejects Quota Proposal', in: *Financial Times*, 21 November 1988.

58. The United Arab Emirates, for example, rejected the quota system. Saudi Arabia favoured a floating price (between US$15 and 18) over a fixed price of US$18. See reports in the Business section: 'OPEC-Kompromiss wackelt trotz Zustimmung Irans', in *Neue Zürcher Zeitung* (NZZ), 29 November 1988, p. 11, and 'Abschluss der Wiener OPEC-Konferenz' and 'Kräftiger Ölpreis-Schub in New York', both in: *NZZ*, 30 November 1988, FA, p. 13. The price of oil rose after the OPEC conference to US$15 on the spot and futures markets, although it remained below the price fixed by OPEC.

59. See the report 'Militärisch untermalte Erdöl-Politik', in *Neue Zürcher Zeitung*, 27 July 1990.

60. Michael Field in the *Financial Times Survey*: Saudi Arabia (12 December 1990); full reference in note 33 above.

61. Tony Walker in the *Financial Times Survey* (as in note 33 above).

62. Deborah Hargreaves, 'Saudi Plan to Reassert Dominant Role in OPEC', in *Financial Times*, 12 March 1991.

63. David Ottoway, 'Gulf States Will Court Egypt and Syria', in *International Herald Tribune*, 6–7 April 1991.

64. For more details on this see the survey article by Bassam Tibi, Politik und Geld am Golf, in the business section of *Frankfurter Allgemeine Zeitung*, July 1991, p. 11.

8 The Middle East between the 1973 October War and the 1990–91 Gulf War: An Epidemically Militarised Region of Conflict?

1. For an overview see Larry H. Addington, *The Patterns of War since the Eighteenth Century*, Bloomington, 1984.

2. These works are Norbert Elias, *The Civilizing Process*, two volumes, vol. 1, New York 1978, vol. 2, New York 1982, and Reinhard Bendix, *Kings or People*, Berkeley, 1978.

3. Gerald Braun, 'Kriege und Konflikte in der Dritten Welt', in D. Oberndörfer and Th. Hanf (eds), *Entwicklungspolitik*, Stuttgart, 1986, pp. 46ff., here p. 57.

4. Anatol Rapoport, 'Tolstoi und Clausewitz', in E. E. Krippendorff (ed.), *Friedensforschung*, Cologne, Berlin, 1968, pp. 87–105.

5. Arnold Hottinger, 'Dreissigjähriger Krieg der Araber?', in *Neue Zürcher Zeitung*, 24 November 1987, FA 272, p. 3.
6. On 'disordered' as opposed to 'ordered systems': James H. Lebovic, 'The Middle East: The Region as a System', in *International Interaction*, vol. 12, no. 3 (1986), pp. 267–89.
7. See Edward Mortimer, 'The Judgement of History: The New World Order has Become the New World Disorder', in *Financial Times*, 18 January 1991. See also the recent contributions by Ted G. Carpenter The New World Disorder, in: *Foreign Policy*, no. 84 (Fall 1991), pp. 24–39 and Richard K. Herrmann, The Middle East and the New World Order, in: *International Security*, 16, 2 (Fall 1991), pp. 42–75.
8. Mahmud Riad, *Amerika wa al-'Arab* (America and the Arabs), vol. 3 of the Riad Memoirs, Cairo, 1986, esp. pp. 36ff. Riad was for many years (1964–71) Egyptian Foreign Minister, and from 1972 Secretary-General of the Arab League.
9. See Michael C. Hudson, 'US Decline in the Middle East', in *Orbis*, vol. 26 (1982), pp. 19–25.
10. See Peter Pawelka, *Herrschaft und Entwicklung im Nahen Osten: Ägypten*, Heidelberg, 1985, pp. 268ff.
11. See William Quandt, *The United States and Egypt*, Washington, DC, 1990, pp. 32–9.
12. Lutfi al-Khuli, *Madrasat al-Sadat al-siyasiyya* (Political Sadatism), 2nd edn, Cairo, 1986; on the USA pp. 45ff., on the Arab environment pp. 67ff.
13. The most comprehensive account of this so far has been written by one of the participants of the Camp David process: William B. Quandt, *Camp David Peace Making and Politics*, Washington, DC, 1986.
14. Jimmy Carter, *The Blood of Abraham: Insights into the Middle East*, Boston, 1985, p. 195.
15. Sadiq Jalal al-'Azm, *Ziyarat al-Sadat wa bu's al-salam al-'adil* (Sadat's Visit and the Poverty of the Just Peace), Beirut, 1978, pp. 7ff, pp. 47ff, pp. 95ff.
16. J. Krause, 'Sowjetmacht und Dritte Welt. Machtprojekt und Militärhilfe', in H. Adomeit *et al.* (eds), *Die Sowjetunion als Militärmacht*, Stuttgart, 1987, pp. 252ff, here p. 256.
17. See Paul Dibb, *The Soviet Union: The Incomplete Superpower*, 2nd edn, Urbana, Chicago, 1988.
18. Karen Dawisha, *Soviet Foreign Policy Toward Egypt*, New York, 1979, pp. 72ff. See also the other volume by Karen and Adeed Dawisha (eds), *The Soviet Union in the Middle East*, London, 1982.
19. See the chapter 'Supermächte in Nahost', in Erich Gysling, *Zerreissprobe in Nahost*, Zurich, 1986, pp. 239ff.
20. William B. Quandt, *Decade of Decisions: American Policy towards the Arab–Israeli Conflict 1967–1976*, Berkeley, 1977, pp. 271ff.
21. Joseph Lawrenz, *Egypt and the Arabs*, Boulder, Col., 1990, pp. 92–101; see also B. Tibi, 'Ägypten und seine arabische Umwelt: Eine historische Retrospektive über Ägyptens Abkopplung nach Sadat's Friedensinitiative', in *Beiträge zur Konfliktforschung*, vol. 12, no. 4 (1982), pp. 33–60.
22. Hottinger (note 5).
23. See Kemal Kirişçi, *The PLO and World Politics: A Study of the Mobilization Support for the Palestinian Cause*, London, 1986, esp. the summary on

pp. 152ff. See also the volume edited by Augustus Richard Norton and Martin Greenberg, *International Relations of the PLO*, Carbondale etc., 1989.

24.   Alan Dowty, *The Middle East Crisis*, Berkeley, 1984, here pp. 111–96.

25.   Itamar Rabinovich, *The War for Lebanon 1970–1985*, 3rd edn, Ithaca, London, 1986, here pp. 121ff.

26.   Helena Cobban, *The Making of Modern Lebanon*, London, 1985, pp. 125ff.

27.   On Lebanon see Samir Khalaf, *Lebanon's Predicament*, New York, 1987. See also the most comprehensive interpretation by Theodor Hanf, *Koexistenz im Krieg.Staatszerfall und Entstehen einer Nation im Libanon*, Baden-Baden 1990.

28.   For more details see the case studies in Part 4 of B. Tibi, *Islam and the Cultural Accommodation of Social Change*, Boulder, Col.: Westview Press 1990, in particular the chapter on Egypt, pp. 135–46.

29.   S. N. Eisenstadt, *Die Transformation der israelischen Gesellschaft*, Frankfurt am Main, 1987, p. 585.

30.   Ibid., p. 583.

31.   On the consequences for Israeli society of the 1967 and 1973 wars see Ibid., pp. 502ff and 563ff, as well as my Eisenstadt review article 'Zwischen Traum und Realität', in *Frankfurter Allgemeine Zeitung*, 8 December 1987.

32.   Dan Diner, *Israel in Palästina*, Königstein, Ts., 1980, esp. ch. 1.

33.   See the contributions in Emmanuel Sivan and Menachem Friedman (eds), *Religious Radicalism and Politics in the Middle East*, Albany, NY, 1990.

34.   Nikolaos van Dam, 'Minorities and Political Elites in Iraq and Syria', in T. Assad and R. Owen (eds), *Sociology of Developing Societies: The Middle East*, London, 1983, pp. 127–44. See also Eberhard Kienle, *Ba'th v Ba'th: The Conflict between Syria and Iraq 1968–1989*, New York, 1990.

35.   On this see the articles by Hanna Batatu, 'Some Observations on the Social Roots of Syria's Ruling Military Group' and 'Iraq's Underground Shi'a Movements', both in *The Middle East Journal*, vol. 35, no. 3 (1981), pp. 331–44 and no. 4, pp. 578–94.

36.   Elfatih Abdullahi-Abdelsalam, *Panarabism and Charismatic Leadership: A Study of Iraq's Foreign Policy Behavior towards the Arab Region 1967–1982*, unpublished Ph.D. thesis, Northwestern University, Evanston, Ill., 1984.

37.   For more details see Pedro Ramet, *The Soviet–Syrian Relationship since 1955*, Boulder, Col., 1990, in particular chapter 5 and also chapter 6. See also Efraim Karsh, *The Soviet Union and Syria: The Assad Years*, London, 1988.

38.   *SIPRI Yearbook 1983*, London 1983, pp. 270f.

39.   *SIPRI Yearbook 1985*, London 1985, p. 351.

40.   Dowty (note 24), pp. 152ff.

41.   Naomi Joy Weinberger, *Syrian Intervention in Lebanon*, New York, Oxford, 1986, pp. 209ff; on the regional and international context pp. 241ff, 291ff.

42.   Moshe Ma'oz, *Assad: The Sphinx of Damascus*, New York, 1988, pp. 83ff; see also the contribution in Moshe Ma'oz and Avner Yaniv (eds), *Syria under Assad*, New York, 1986.

43.   Hirsch Goodman and W. Seth Carus, *The Future Battlefield and the Arab–Israeli Conflict*, New Brunswick, 1990.

44.   See my chapter in Dan Tschirgi and Bassam Tibi, *Perspectives on the Gulf*

Crisis, American University of Cairo, Cairo 1991, in particular the section on Syria, pp. 82–6.

45. Rudolf J. Lauff, *Die Aussenpolitik Algeriens 1962–1978*, Munich, 1981, pp. 104ff.
46. Henry F. Jackson, *The FLN of Algeria*, Westport, Conn., 1977.
47. Lauff (note 45).
48. Thomas Ross, 'Ehrlicher Makler im Maghreb: Algerien ist der angesenhenste Vermittler in der arabischen Welt', in *Frankfurter Allgemeine Zeitung*, 25 November 1987.
49. Hanspeter Mattes, *Die Volksrevolution in der Sozialistischen Libyschen Arabischen Volksgamahiriyya*, Heidelberg, 1982.
50. On Qadhafi's foreign policy see Lillian C. Harris, *Libya: Qadhafi's Revolution and the Modern State*, Boulder, Col., 1986, chapter 5, pp. 83ff.
51. On this see René Otayek, 'La Libye revolutionaire au sud du Sahara', in *Maghreb/Machrek* (1981), no. 94, pp. 5–35, and Oye Ogunbadejo, 'Qadhafi and Africa's International Relations', in *Journal of Modern African Studies*, vol. 24, no. 1 (1986), pp. 33–68.
52. See the contributions in René Lemarchand (ed.), *The Green and the Black: Qadhafi's Politics in Africa*, Bloomington, 1988.
53. William B. Quandt, *Saudi Arabia in the 1980s*, Washington, DC, 1981, p. 34.
54. Ibid., p. 135.
55. John D. Anthony, 'Foreign Policy: The View from Riyadh', in *Wilson Quarterly*, vol. 3, no. 3 (1979), pp. 73–82, here p. 82.
56. See the reports by David Ottoway, 'Gulf States will Court Egypt and Syria', in *International Herald Tribune*, 6–7 April 1991. 'What is strikingly new is that the Gulf states are now providing their new billions of dollars to *dictate* the terms for building a *new Arab order* based largely on their economic and political values. It illustrates how the Gulf crisis has brought about a radical shift in the focus of power in the Arab world.'
57. Charles Tripp and Shahram Chubin, *Iran and Iraq at War*, Boulder, Col., 1988, pp. 146–7.
58. For more details on this see the chapter on Iraq in Liesl Graz, *The Turbulent Gulf*, London, 1990, pp. 19–51, in particular pp. 30–2.
59. See the contributions in Roger Owen and Charles Tripp (eds), *Egypt under Mubarak*, London, 1989.
60. The Battle of Qadisiyya took place in AD 637 when the Arabs conquered and converted to Islam the then Sassanid Iran.
61. For a military analysis of the first Gulf War see Anthony H. Cordesman and Abraham Wagner, *The Iran–Iraq War*, vol. III of *The Lessons of Modern War*, Boulder, Col., 1990; see also the contributions in Efraim Karsh (ed.), *The Iran–Iraq War: Impact and Implications*, New York, 1989, and also the vol. by Tripp and Chubin quoted in note 57 above.
62. J. Levy and M. Froelich, 'Causes of the Iran–Iraq War', in J. Brown and W. Snyder (eds), *The Regionalization of Warfare*, New York, 1985, pp. 127–43, and John Amos, 'The Iran–Iraq War', in Robert Darius et al. (eds), *Gulf Security into the 1980s*, Stanford, 1984, pp. 49–81.
63. A. C. Turner, 'Nationalism and Religion: Iran and Iraq at War', in Brown and Snyder (note 62), pp. 144–63.

64. R. G. Darius, 'Khomeini's Policy toward Mideast', in Darius *et al.* (note 62), pp. 31–48.
65. Fred Halliday, 'A Curious and Close Liaison: Saudi Arabia's Relations with the United States', in Tim Niblock (ed.), *State, Society and Economy in Saudi Arabia*, New York, 1982, pp. 125–47.
66. For more details see Amitav Acharya, *US Military Strategy in the Gulf*, London 1989, in particular chapter five.
67. Quoted by Acharya, op. cit., p. 110.
68. See B. Tibi, 'Saddam Hussein öffnet den USA das Tor zu militärischer Golf-Präsenz', in *Basler Zeitung*, 16 March 1991, p. 7.
69. Paul Jabber, 'Oil, Arms and Regional Diplomacy: Strategic Dimensions of the Saudi–Egyptian Relationship', in M. Kerr and S. Yassin (eds), *Rich and Poor States in the Middle East*, Boulder, Col., 1982, pp. 415–47, here p. 434.
70. Ibid., p. 438.
71. Ibid., p. 439.
72. Ibid., p. 434.
73. Ibid., p. 445.
74. Lewis Snider, 'Egyptian Foreign Policymaking', in R. D. McLaurin *et al.* (eds), *Middle East Foreign Policy*, New York, 1982, pp. 31–71, here pp. 64f.
75. Ibid., p. 66.
76. The Swiss Gulf expert Liesl Graz (note 58), pp. 227 states: 'The establishment of the GCC was much more a response to . . . the ambitions of the two powerful neighbours, Iraq and the brand new Islamic Republic of Iran.' Graz also shows that 'the Gulf states obviously did not want Iraq as a member of the GCC', p. 258.
77. The complete Arabic text is published in *al-Muntada*, vol. 2, no. 27 (1987), pp. 4–5, from which this extract has been cited.
78. The text of the Amman resolution of the Arab head of states is published in the issue of *al-Muntada* cited in note 77, pp. 11–15, from which this and following quotations are cited.
79. See the NZZ (*Neue Zürcher Zeitung*) articles 'Ägyptens Isolation formell beendet', 12 November 1987, and 'Breite Wendung der Golf-Staaten zum Nil', 19 November 1987.
80. See note 6 above.
81. See the contributions in the now somewhat elderly volume: Rashid Khalidi and Camille Mansour, Institute of Palestine Studies (eds), *Palestine and the Gulf*, Beirut, 1982.
82. Robert Litwak and Samuel Wells (eds), *Superpower Competition and Security in the Third World*, Cambridge, Mass., 1988.
83. See B. Tibi, 'The Simultaneity of the Unsimultaneous: Old Tribes and Imposed Nation-States in the Modern Middle East', in Philip S. Khoury and Joseph Kostiner (eds), *Tribes and State Formation in the Middle East*, Berkeley, 1990, pp. 127–52.
84. Sydney D. Baily, *Four Arab–Israeli Wars and the Peace Process*, New York, 1990.
85. See the American and Soviet contributions in Willard A. Beling (ed.), *Middle East Peace Plans*, New York, 1986.
86. This conclusion is also among the findings in the books of Dan Tschirgi, *The Politics of Indecision*, New York, 1983, and *The American Search for Mideast Peace*, New York 1989.

9 From the Iraq–Kuwait Conflict to the Gulf War

1. See for instance the scenarios of Bruno Etienne, 'From the Gulf Crisis a New Power Balance Will Emerge', in *International Herald Tribune*, 3 September 1990, p. 2.
2. On Kuwait see among others Jacqueline S. Ismael, *Kuwait: Social Change in Historical Perspectives*, Syracuse, 1982.
3. Sandra Mackey, *The Saudis: Inside the Desert Kingdom*, New York, 1990.
4. On the modern history of Iraq see the two authoritative works by Phebe Marr, *The Modern History of Iraq*, Boulder, Col., 1985, and Peter and Marion Sluglett, *Iraq since 1958: From Revolution to Dictatorship*, London, 1990.
5. For a full account see the references in note 45 below.
6. B. Tibi, 'The Gulf Crisis and the Fragmentation of the Arab World,' in Dan Tschirgi and Bassam Tibi, *Perspectives on the Gulf Crisis*, Cairo: American University of Cairo Press 1991, pp. 71–107.
7. For details see B. Tibi, 'Die irakische Kuwait-Invasion und die Golf-Krise', in *Beiträge zur Konfliktforschung*, vol. 20, no. 4 (1990), pp. 5–34.
8. On the history of the Ba'th Party, see J. F. Devlin, *The Ba'th Party: A History from its Origins to 1966*, Stanford, 1976. On the pan-Arab ideology of the Ba'th and its origins see B. Tibi, *Arab Nationalism: A Critical Inquiry*, 2nd edn, London, New York: Macmillan, 1990. On the split between the Ba'th parties currently ruling in Syria and Iraq see Eberhard Kienle, *Ba'th versus Ba'th: The Conflict between Syria and Iraq 1968–1989*, London, New York, 1990.
9. Samir al-Khalil, *Republic of Fear: The Politics of Modern Iraq*, Berkeley, 1989, and B. Tibi, 'Saddam Hussein und seine Republik der Angst', in *Frankfurter Allgemeine Zeitung*, 29 August 1990.
10. The Arabic text of the decree may be found in Gulf documentation of the bulletin *al-Muntada* (Amman), vol. 5, no. 60 (September 1990), pp. 19–20.
11. Ibid.
12. On the world order problematique see the standard work by Hedley Bull, *The Anarchical Society: A Study of World Order*, New York, 1977, the literature cited in the Introduction to this book, and Ian Clark, *The Hierarchy of States: Reform and Resistance in the International Order*, Cambridge, Mass., 1989.
13. On Iraq and the superpowers during the first Gulf War see Sharam Chubin and Charles Tripp, *Iran and Iraq at War*, Boulder, Col., 1988, chapter 11. The indicated misgiving of Saddam Hussein is referred to by James Ridgeway (ed.), *March to War*, New York, 1991, pp. 25ff, and by Efraim Karsh and Inari Rautsi, *Saddam Hussein: A Political Biography*, New York, 1991, p. 214. To a certain extent, Iraq was a client state of the Soviet Union: see Oles and Bettie Smolansky, *The USSR and Iraq*, Durham, 1991, chapter 7 on the first Gulf war.
14. Bogdan Denitch, *The End of the Cold War*, Minneapolis, 1990.
15. See Quentin Peel, 'Superpowers Condemn Iraq', in *Financial Times*, 10 September 1990. The text of the communiqué can be found in *International Herald Tribune*, 10 September 1990, p. 6.
16. On these resolutions, their numbers and contents, see Adel Darwish and Gregory Alexander, *Unholy Babylon: The Secret History of Saddam's War*, New York, 1991, pp. 308–10.

222 *Notes and References*

17. Robert Mauthner *et al.*, 'UN Eleventh-Hour Attempt to Avert War', in *Financial Times*, 16 January 1991.
18. See Chapter 8 and also Efraim Karsh (ed.), *The Iran–Iraq War: Impact and Implications*, New York, 1989, and vol. 2 of the trilogy by Anthony Cordesman and Abraham Wagner, *The Lessons of Modern War*, Boulder, Col., 1990. The whole of the 647-page volume is devoted to the Iran–Iraq War.
19. Anthony McDermott, 'Iraq Economy Struggling since Gulf War', in *Financial Times*, 4–5 August 1990, p. 2, and chapter 7 in Kamran Mofid, *Economic Consequences of the Gulf War*, London, New York, 1990, pp. 82–90. Phebe Marr indicates a figure of about US$90 billion in August 1990: see Phebe Marr, 'Iraq's Uncertain Future', in *Current History*, vol. 90 no. 552 (1991), pp. 1–4, 39–42, here p. 2.
20. On Saddam's July speech, see Arnold Hottinger, 'Irakische Drohungen gegen Kuwait und VAE', in *Neuer Zürcher Zeitung*, 20 July, 1990, p. 3.
21. See the biography of Saddam Hussein by Efraim Karsh and Inari Rautsi quoted in note 13 above.
22. See Christine M. Helms, *Iraq: Eastern Flank of the Arab World*, Washington, DC, 1984, pp. 46–9 (although the figure of *15 km* for the Iraqi coastline is incorrect: the Iraqi coastal strip is 50 miles long).
23. On this see the informative report by Thomas Hayes, 'Oil Field is Heart of the Feud', in *International Herald Tribune*, 4 September, 1990, p. 7. See also the chapter entitled 'Iraq–Kuwait', in Alan Day (ed.), *Border and Territorial Disputes*, 2nd edn, London, 1987, pp. 244–7.
24. For more details on this Iraqi–Syrian dispute, see Kienle (note 8), pp. 112–14, and p. 165.
25. See the section entitled 'Protecting Oil Exports', in Helms (note 22), pp. 49–54.
26. Steven Butler, 'Saudis Ponder Whether to Throw in Their Lots with US and Cut Iraqi Pipeline', in *Financial Times*, 6 August 1990, p. 2, and James Rupert, 'Saudi Move Breaks with Traditional Caution', in *Washington Post*, 8 August 1990, p. A–14.
27. More information on Sati al-Husri can be found in the chapter on this subject in Tibi (note 8), Parts Three and Four.
28. On al-Husri's influence on the Ba'th Party and on Saddam Hussein see al-Khalil (note 9), pp. 152–60. Samir al-Khalil is the pseudonym for the Iraqi Kan'an Makiyya who revealed his real identity in a public meeting with this author at Harvard's Center for International Affairs.
29. Tibi (note 8), p. 127.
30. On the traditional Iraqi claim to sovereignty over Kuwait, aside from pan-Arab propaganda, see R. V. Pillai and M. Kumar, 'The Political and Legal Status of Kuwait', in *International and Comparative Law Quarterly*, vol. 11 (1962), pp. 108–30, and also the chapter 'Iraqi Claim to Sovereignty over Kuwait', in Husain M. al-Baharna, *The Legal Status of Arabian Gulf States*, Manchester, 1968, pp. 250–7.
31. 'Jami' at al-duwal al-Arabiyya 'adat ila Misr' (The Arab League Returns to Egypt), in *al-Musawwar* (Cairo), 14 September 1990, p. 4.
32. See the new chapter to the 2nd edn of B. Tibi (note 8), entitled 'Arab Nationalism Revisited', pp. 1–26, notes on pp. 208–19. See also: *Islamic Fundamentalism and the Gulf Crisis* ed. James Piscatori, Chicago 1991 (with case studies).

33. See the chapter on Iraq in Liesl Graz, *The Turbulent Gulf*, London 1990, pp. 19–51. See also the most comprehensive standard work to date on Iraq by Phebe Marr (note 4); on the Ba'th-Saddam era, see chapters 8–10, pp. 211–311.

34. For a detailed account see Erik R. Peterson, *The Gulf Cooperation Council: Search for Unity in a Dynamic Region*, Boulder, Col., 1988.

35. Graz (note 33), p. 258.

36. Fred Halliday, 'Iraq and its Neighbours: The Cycles of Insecurity', in *The World Today*, vol. 46, no. 6 (1990), pp. 104–6.

37. On the Iraqi Ba'th and the Kurds see Edmund Ghareeb, *The Kurdish Question in Iraq*, Syracuse, NY, 1981, pp. 71ff. On the Kurdish opposition see Peter Sluglett, 'The Kurds', in Committee Against Repression and For Democratic Rights in Iraq (ed.), *Saddam's Iraq*, 2nd rev. edn, 1990, pp. 177–202.

38. Data on this in Shlomo Gazit *et al.* (eds), *The Middle East Military Balance 1988–1989*, Boulder, Col., 1989, pp. 174–84.

39. See Viktor Utgoff, *The Challenge of Chemical Weapons*, London, 1990, on Iraq pp. 80–7.

40. Graz (note 33), p. 42.

41. See note 38 and Darwish and Alexander (note 16), pp. 85–193.

42. Quoted by Amitav Acharya, *US Military Strategy in the Gulf*, London, 1990, p. 110.

43. B. Tibi, 'Kriegsdrohung und Friktionen: Ein Szenarium zur Golf-Krise nach Clausewitz', in *Frankfurter Allgemeine Zeitung*, 7 December 1990, p. 10.

44. Arthur Schlesinger Jr, 'America Doesn't Know What it's Doing in the Gulf', in *International Herald Tribune*, 17 December 1990.

45. For a full account see the useful books edited by Ridgeway (note 13) and Micah L. Sifry and Christopher Cerf (eds), *The Gulf War Reader: History, Documents, Opinions*, New York, 1991.

46. See the interesting revelations by Bob Woodward, *The Commanders*, New York, 1991.

47. See the first-page report 'Relentless Assault: Allied Aircraft Smash Hundreds of Iraqi Targets', in *International Herald Tribune*, 18 January 1991.

48. *International Herald Tribune*, 9–10 February 1990, p. 1.

49. 'Ultimatum, Bush Sets Saturday Deadline for Iraq to Begin Withdrawal', in *International Herald Tribune*, 23–24 February 1991.

50. 'Allied Assault, Massive Thrust North Against the Iraqis', in *International Herald Tribune*, 25 February 1991.

51. 'US Tanks Trap Iraqis in Fierce Battle', in *International Herald Tribune*, 28 February 1991, and the report 'In Full Retreat. Iraqi Troops Routed', in *International Herald Tribune*, 27 March, 1991.

52. William Safire, 'Bush's Moral Crisis', in *New York Times*, 1 April 1991, p. A17.

53. Excerpts of this interview were printed in the *Washington Post*, 28 March 1991, p. A35.

54. 'Emir Flies Home to Kuwait 2 Weeks after War's End', in *International Herald Tribune*, 15 March 1991.

55. Steve Coll, 'Saudis Uneasy with Victory and Changes War Brought', in *International Herald Tribune*, 13 March 1991, p. 1, continued p. 3. A review of the Gulf War in civilisational terms while employing the theory of Norbert

Elias is provided in the essay by Bassam Tibi, Der Löwe sammelt seine Kräfte. Ein Jahr nach dem Einmarsch in Kuwait (*Süddeutsche Zeitung* 27/28. July 1991), re-written with footnoting and published as an appendix to Bassam Tibi, *Islamischer Fundamentalismus, moderne Wissenschaft und Technologie*, Frankfurt/M. 1992, pp. 170–84 under the new title "*Krieg und zivilisatorische Krisen*".

56. For details on this see the contributions in Stephen P. Cohen (ed.), *The Security of South Asia*, Urbana, Chicago, 1987.

57. Bush quoted by Edward Mortimer, 'Reality versus Rhetoric in New World Order', in *Financial Times*, 28 December 1990, p. 8; see also note 6.

58. Ibid.

59. Edward Mortimer, 'Judgement of History: The New World Order has become World Disorder', in *Financial Times*, 18 January 1991.

60. There is an English translation with the original Arabic text of al-Farabi's work, which dates from happier days in Islamic history, by Richard Walzer, *al-Farabi on the Perfect State/Ara'ahl al-madina al-fadilah*, Oxford, 1985.

61. Karl Wittfogel, *Die orientalische Despotie*, Cologne, Berlin, 1962, p. 188: 'The despot has unlimited control over the army, police and intelligence services. He has prison guards, torturers, executioners and all necessary means to arrest, torment and kill suspects' (translated from the German).

62. B. Tibi, *Crisis of Modern Islam*, Salt Lake City: Utah University Press 1988.

10 The Historical Context of Conflict and War in the Middle East in the Light of the Gulf War

1. Stephen Howe, 'Sands of Time', in *New Statesman and Society*, 22 February 1991, p. 36: 'There are . . . many ruthlessly self-scrutinizing . . . Arab responses to such questions from writers like Fouad Ajami, Samir al-Khalil, Bassam Tibi and Sadiq al-Azm . . .'

2. See Saddam Hussein's speech reprinted in an English translation in M. L. Sifry and C. Cerf (eds), *The Gulf War Reader*, New York, 1991, pp. 315–6.

3. The relevant text of Saddam's 'Mubadarat Insihabat Mutabadala and Shamila' is printed in *al-Muntada* (Amman/Bulletin of al-Muntada al-fikr al-Arabi), vol. 5, no. 60 (September 1990), pp. 25–6.

4. Saddam's call to *Jihad* of 7 August 1990 is printed in Arabic in the *al-Muntada* issue quoted in note 3, pp. 21–2. Regarding the second call to *Jihad* on 6 September see the report 'Iraqi Chief renews Jihad call', in *International Herald Tribune*, 6 September 1991, p. 3.

5. For more details on the overall context of this issue, see L. Carl Brown, *International Politics in the Middle East*, Princeton, NJ, 1984. See also David Fromkin, *A Peace to End all Peace. The Fall of the Ottoman Empire and the Creation of the Modern Middle East*, New York, 1989.

6. See Adel Darwish and Gregory Alexander, *Unholy Babylon: The Secret History of Saddam's War*, New York, 1991.

7. See the chapter on Iraq–Kuwait in Alan Day (ed.), *Border and Territorial Disputes*, London, 1987, pp. 244–7.

8. Kemal Karpat, 'The Ottoman Ethnic and Confessional Legacy in the Middle East', in Milton Esman and Itamar Rabinovich (eds), *Ethnicity, Pluralism*

and the State in the Middle East, Ithaca, London, 1988, pp. 35–53, here p. 44f.

9. For more details see B. Tibi, *Arab Nationalism: A Critical Inquiry*, 2nd edn, London, New York: Macmillan, 1990 (paperback edn 1991).

10. L. Carl Brown, 'The June War 1967: A Turning Point?', in Y. Lukacs and A. Battah (eds), *The Arab–Israeli Conflict: Two Decades of Change*, Boulder, Col., 1988; see also my critique of Carl Brown in the subsequent chapter of the same book, and my book on *Arab Nationalism* (note 9).

11. See Anthony Giddens, *The Nation-State and Violence*, Berkeley, 1987, chapter 10, and B. Tibi, 'Arab Nationalism Revisited', the new chapter in *Arab Nationalism*, 2nd edn (note 9).

12. B. Tibi, 'The Simultaneity of the Unsimultaneous: Old Tribes and Imposed Nation States in the Modern Middle East', in Philip Khoury and Joseph Kostiner (eds), *Tribes and State Formation in the Middle East*, Berkeley, 1990, pp. 127–52.

13. For more details, see Phebe Marr, *The Modern History of Iraq*, Boulder, Col., 1985, chapter 1.

14. Amatzia Baram, *Culture, History and Ideology in the Formation of the Ba'thist Iraq, 1968–89*, New York, 1991, in particular chapters 9 and 10.

15. Robert W. MacDonald, *The League of Arab States*, Princeton, NJ, 1965.

16. For more details, see Philip Khoury, *Syria and the French Mandate*, Princeton, NJ, 1987.

17. See Daniel Pipes, *Greater Syria: The History of an Ambition,* New York 1990, in particular pp. 189ff.

18. For more details, see Yehoshua Porath, *In Search of Arab Unity 1930–1945*, London, 1986.

19. Patrick Seale, *The Struggle for Syria: A Study of Post-War Arab Politics 1945–1958*, new edn, London, 1986.

20. Barry Rubin, *The Arab States and the Palestine Conflict*, Syracuse, 1981.

21. R. K. Ramazani, *Revolutionary Iran: Challenge and Response in the Middle East*, Baltimore, London, 1986, in particular Part Two.

22. The Arabic text of the Amman summit Resolution adopted by Arab heads of state in November 1987 is printed in *al-Muntada* (Bulletin of the Muntada al-fikr al-Arabi, Amman), vol. 2, no. 27 (1987), pp. 11–15. The Gulf conflict is ranked ahead of Palestine in the resolution.

23. For an overview, see David McDowall, *Palestine and Israel: The Uprising and Beyond*, Berkeley, 1989.

24. Arnold Hottinger, 'Ein Geschenk Israels für Saddam Hussein', in *Neue Zürcher Zeitung*, 12 October 1990, p. 3.

25. See the reference in note 12.

26. See Gabriel Ben-Dor, 'Ethnopolitics and the Middle Eastern State', in Esman and Rabinovich (note 8), pp. 71–92.

27. Michael C. Hudson, *Arab Politics: The Search for Legitimacy*, New Haven, 1979, pp. 1–30.

28. On Lebanon see Theodor Hanf, *Koexistenz im Krieg. Staatsverfall und Entstehen einer Nation im Lebanon*, Baden-Baden, 1990, and Samir Khalaf, *Lebanon's Predicament*, New York, 1987; on Sudan see Tim Niblock, *Class and Power in Sudan*, Albany, New York, 1987.

29. Hudson (note 27), p. 5.

30. Walter Reich, *A Stranger in my Land: Jews and Arabs*, New York, 1984.
31. Herbert Kelman, 'The Palestinianization of the Arab–Israeli Conflict', in Lukacs and Battah (note 10), pp. 332–43.
32. See among others Ahmad Izuldin, *Harakat al-muqawamah al-Islamiyya Hamas fi Falastin*, Cairo, 1989, and Rif'at Sayid Ahmad, *al-Islam wa Qadaya al-sira'. Dirasat fi al-Islam wa qadaya al-sira' al arabi al-Israeli*, Cairo, 1989.
33. On both varieties see the articles in E. Sivan and M. Friedman (eds), *Religious Radicalism and Politics in the Middle East*, Albany, New York, 1990.
34. See Muhammad Shadid, *al-Jihad fi al-Islam*, Cairo, 1989.
35. This conflict in Syria is essentially of a political character, although disguised in a religious form as one between Sunni Muslims and the ruling Alawites. See Umar F. Abd-allah, *The Islamic Struggle in Syria*, Berkeley, 1983.
36. See the section on Syria in Bassam Tibi, 'The Gulf Crisis and the Fragmentation of the Middle East', in Dan Tschirgi and Bassam Tibi, *Perspectives on the Gulf Crisis*, Cairo, 1991, pp. 71–107, here pp. 82–6.
37. Ibid.
38. See the contribution by Fouad Ajami in Tawfic Farah (ed.), *Pan-Arabism and Arab Nationalism: The Continuing Debate*, Boulder, Col., 1987, pp. 96–114.
39. This view of the world is put forward in various contemporary Arab writings, for example in Ali Muhammad Jarisha and Muhammad Sharif Zaibaq, *Asalib al-ghazu al-fikri li al-alam al-Islami*, 2nd edn, Cairo, 1978. On this issue see the essay by Bassam Tibi, Das arabische Kollektiv und seine Feinde, in: *Frankfurter Allgemeine Zeitung*, February 9, 1991 extended and footnoted version: Bassam Tibi, 'Kreuzzug oder Dialog. Der Westen und die arabo-islamische Welt nach dem Golf-Krieg', in Volker Matthies (ed.), *Kreuzzug oder Dialog. Die Zukunft der Nord-Süd-Beziehungen*, Bonn, 1992, pp. 107–20.
40. On conflict resolution see the recent contribution by John Burton, *Conflict: Resolution and Prevention*, London, 1990.

Bibliography

1. Regional Subsystems and International Relations Theory, Including Studies Approaching the Middle East as a Regional Subsystem

Axline, Andrew, 'Underdevelopment, Dependence and Integration: The Politics of Regionalism in the Third World', in *International Organization*, vol. 31, no. 1 (1977), pp. 83–105.

Bendix, Reinhard, *Kings or People: Power and the Mandate to Rule* (Berkeley, Cal.: University of California Press, 1978).

Ben-Dor, Gabriel, *State and Conflict in the Middle East: Emergence of the Post-Colonial State* (New York: Praeger, 1983).

Binder, Leonard, 'The Middle East as a Subordinate International System', in *World Politics*, vol. 10, no. 3 (1958), pp. 408–29.

Binder, Leonard, 'The New States in International Affairs', in Robert A. Goldwin (ed.), *Beyond the Cold War*, 2nd edn (Chicago: Rand McNally, 1965), pp. 195–216.

Binder, Leonard, 'Transformation in the Middle Eastern Subordinate System after 1967', in M. Confino and Sh. Shamir (eds), *USSR and the Middle East* (Jerusalem: Israel University Press, 1972), pp. 251–71.

Boulding, Kenneth E., *The World as a Total System* (Beverly Hills; London: Sage Publications, 1985).

Brecher, Michael, 'International Relations and Asian Studies: The Subordinate State System of Southern Asia', in *World Politics*, vol. 15, no. 2 (1963), pp. 213–35; see also R. A. Falk and S. H. Mendlovitz (eds), *Regional Politics and World Order*, (San Francisco: W. H. Freeman, 1973), pp. 369–82.

Brecher, Michael, 'The Middle East Subordinate System and its Impact on Israel's Foreign Policy', in *International Studies Quarterly*, vol. 13, no. 2 (1969), pp. 117–39.

Brecher, Michael, *The New States of Asia: A Political Analysis* (Oxford; London: Oxford University Press, 1963).

Bull, Hedley, *The Anarchical Society: A Study of Order in World Politics* (New York: Macmillan, 1977).

Bull, Hedley (ed.), *Intervention in World Politics*, 2nd edn (Oxford: Clarendon Press, 1985).

Bull, Hedley, 'The Revolt against the West', in Hedley Bull and Adam Watson (eds), *The Expansion of International Society*, 3rd edn (Oxford: Clarendon Press, 1988), pp. 217–28.

Bull, Hedley and Watson, Adam (eds), *The Expansion of International Society*, 3rd edn (Oxford: Clarendon Press, 1988).

Cantori, Louis J. and Spiegel, Steven L. (eds), *The International Politics of Regions: A Comparative Approach* (Englewood Cliffs, NJ: Prentice-Hall, 1970).

Cantori, Louis J. and Spiegel, Steven L., 'International Regions: A Comparative Approach to Five Subordinate Systems', in *International Studies Quarterly*, vol. 13, no. 4 (1969), pp. 361–80.

Chase-Dunn, Christopher, *Global Formation* (Cambridge, Mass.; Oxford: Basil Blackwell, 1989).

Clapham, Christopher (ed.), *Foreign Policy Making in Developing States: A Comparative Approach*, 2nd edn (Westmead: Saxon House, 1979).

Clark, Ian, *The Hierarchy of States: Reform and Resistance in the International Order* (Cambridge, Mass.: Cambridge University Press 1989).

Diskin, A. and Mishal, S., 'Spatial Models and Centrality of International Communities: Meetings between Arab Leaders 1966–1978', in *Journal of Conflict Resolution*, vol. 25, no. 4 (1981), pp. 655–76.

Dominguez, Jorge I., 'Mice that Do Not Roar: Some Aspects of International Politics in the World's Peripheries', in *International Organization*, vol. 25, no. 1 (1971), pp. 175–208.

Dyer, Hugh and Mangasarian, Leon (eds), *The Study of International Relations: The State of the Art* (Basingstoke: Macmillan, 1989).

Elias, Norbert, *The Civilizing Process*, 2 vols.; vol. I (New York: Urizen Books, 1978), vol. II (New York: Urizen Books, 1982).

Evron, Yair, *The Middle East: Nations, Superpowers and Wars* (New York; Washington: Praeger, 1975).

Falk, Richard A. and Mendlovitz, Saul H. (eds), *Regional Politics and World Order* (San Francisco: W. H. Freeman, 1973).

Fox, W. T. R., *The Superpowers: The United States, Britain and the Soviet Union – Their Responsibility for Peace* (New York: Harcourt, Brace, 1944).

Frankel, Joseph, *International Relations in a Changing World* (Oxford: Oxford University Press 1988).

Giddens, Anthony, *The Nation-State and Violence* (Berkeley, Cal.: University of California Press, 1987).

Gitelson, Susan Aurelia, 'The Transformation of the Southern African Subordinate State System', in *Journal of Modern African Studies*, vol. 4, no. 4 (1977–8), pp. 367–91.

Haas, Ernst B., *The Uniting of Europe*, 2nd edn (Stanford: Stanford University Press, 1968).

Hodgkin, Thomas, 'The New West African State System', in *University of Toronto Quarterly*, vol. 31 (1961), pp. 74–82.

Hoffmann, Stanley (ed.) *Contemporary Theory in International Relations*, 2nd edn (Westport, Conn.: Greenwood Press, 1977).

Hoffmann, Stanley, 'Discord in Community: The North Atlantic Area as a Partial International System', in *International Organization*, vol. 17 (1963), pp. 521–49.

Hoffmann, Stanley, *Janus and Minerva. Essays in the Theory and Practice of International Politics* (Boulder, Col.: Westview Press, 1987).

Holsti, K. J., *The Dividing Discipline: Hegemony and Diversity in International Theory* (London; Boston: Allen & Unwin, 1985).

Holsti, K. J., *International Politics: A Framework for Analysis*, 4th edn (Englewood Cliffs, NJ: Prentice-Hall, 1967).

Hudson, Michael C., 'The Middle East', in James Rosenau (ed.), *World Politics* (New York: The Free Press 1976), pp. 466–500.

Ismael, Tareq Y., *International Relations of the Contemporary Middle East: A Study in World Politics* (Syracuse, NY: Syracuse University Press, 1986).

Jervis, Robert, *Perception and Misperception in International Politics* (Princeton, NJ: Princeton University Press 1976).

Kaplan, Morton A., *System and Process in International Politics* (New York: John Wiley, 1957).

Keohane, Robert O., *After Hegemony: Cooperation and Discord in the World Political Economy* (Princeton, NJ: Princeton University Press, 1984).

Kratochwil, Friedrich V., *Rules, Norms and Decisions: On the Conditions of Practical and Legal Reasoning in International Relations and Domestic Affairs* (Cambridge, Mass.: Cambridge University Press, 1990).

Lang, Winfried, *Der internationale Regionalismus: Integration und Desintegration von Staatenbeziehungen in weltweiter Verflechtung* (Vienna; New York: Springer, 1982).

Laue, Theodore H. von, *The World Revolution of Westernization* (New York: Oxford University Press, 1987).

Lebovic, James H., 'The Middle East: The Region as a System', in *International Interaction*, vol. 12, no. 3 (1986), pp. 267–89.

Light, Margot, *The Soviet Theory of International Relations* (New York: St Martin's Press, 1988).

Light, Margot and Groom, A. J. R. (eds), *International Relations: A Handbook of Current Theory* (London: Pinter, 1985).

McGowan, Pat and Kegley, Ch. W., Jr (eds), *Foreign Policy and the Modern World System* (Beverly Hills; London: Sage Publications, 1983).

Miller, Lynn H., 'Regional Organizations and Subordinate Systems', in L. J. Cantori and S. L. Spiegel (eds), *The International Politics of Regions* (Englewood Cliffs, NJ: Prentice-Hall, 1970), pp. 357–80 and R. A. Falk and S. H. Mendlovitz (eds), *Regional Politics and World Order* (San Francisco: W. H. Freeman, 1973), pp. 412–31.

Modelski, George, 'International Relations and Area Studies: The Case of South-East Asia', in *International Relations*, vol. 2 (1961), pp. 143–55.

Northrop, Filmer S. C., *The Taming of the Nations: A Study of the Cultural Bases of International Policy* (Woodbridge, Conn.: Ox Bow Press, 1987).

Pearson, Frederic, 'Interaction in an International Political Subsystem: The Middle East 1963–1964', in *Peace Research Society* (International Papers), vol. 15 (1970), pp. 73–99.

Rays, James Lee, 'The "World-System" and the Global Political System: A Crucial Relationship?', in P. McGowan and Ch. W. Kegley, Jr (eds), *Foreign Policy and the Modern World System* (Beverly Hills; London: Sage Publications 1983), pp. 13–34.

Rosenau, James, *The Scientific Study of Foreign Policy*, rev. (London; New York: Pinter, 1980).

Russett, Bruce M., *International Regions and the International System* (Chicago: Rand McNally, 1967).

Schröder, Dieter, *Die Konferenzen der 'Dritten Welt', Solidarität und Kommunikation zwischen nachkolonialen Staaten* (Hamburg: Hamburger Gesellschaft für Völkerrecht und Auswärtige Politik, 1968).

Sheffer, Gabriel, 'Independence in Dependence of Regional Powers: The Uncomfortable Alliances in the Middle East before and after the October War 1973', in *Orbis*, vol. 14, no. 4 (1976), pp. 1519–38.

Sheffer, Gabriel, 'Superpowers and Client States: Middle East Relationship since 1973', in *Wiener Library Bulletin*, vol. 27 (1974), pp. 48–53.

Shoemaker, Christopher and Spanier, John, *Patron–Client State Relationships – Multilateral Crisis in the Nuclear Age* (New York: Praeger, 1984).

Skocpol, Theda, *States and Social Relations* (Cambridge, Mass.: Cambridge University Press 1979).

Smith, Steve, *International Relations: British and American Perspectives* (London; New York: Basil Blackwell, 1985).

Spiegel, Steven L., *Dominance and Diversity: The International Hierarchy* (Boston: Little, Brown, 1972).

Taylor, T. (ed.), *Approaches and Theory in International Relations* (London: Longman, 1978).

Tharp, Paul A., Jr (ed.), *Regional International Organizations – Structures and Functions* (New York: St Martin's Press, 1971).

Thompson, William R., 'The Arab Sub-System and the Feudal Pattern of Interaction: 1965', in *Journal of Peace Research*, vol. 7 (1970), pp. 151–67.

Thompson, William R., 'Delineating Regional Subsystems: Visit Networks and the Middle Eastern Case', in *International Journal of Middle East Studies*, vol. 13 (1981), pp. 213–35.

Thompson, William R., 'The Regional Subsystem: A Conceptual Explication and a Propositional Inventory', in *International Studies Quarterly*, vol. 17 (1973), pp. 87–117.

Tibi, Bassam, 'Die afro-arabischen Beziehungen seit der Dekolonisation: Unter besonderer Berücksichtigung der Erdöl-Dimension', in *Afrika-Spectrum*, vol. 21, no. 3 (1986), pp. 315–35.

Tibi, Bassam, 'Der amerikanische Area-Studies-Approach in den "International Studies"', in *Orient*, vol. 24 (1983), pp. 260–84.

Tibi, Bassam, *Internationale Politik und Entwicklungsländer-Forschung* (Frankfurt/M.: Suhrkamp, 1979).

Tibi, Bassam, *Militär und Sozialismus in der Dritten Welt: Allgemeine Theorien und Regionalstudien über arabische Länder* (Frankfurt/M.: Suhrkamp, 1973).

Tilly, Charles, *Coercion, Capital and European States* (Cambridge, Mass.; Oxford: Basil Blackwell,1990).

Tilly, Charles (ed.), *The Formation of National States in Western Europe* (Princeton, NJ: Princeton University Press, 1975).

Walzer, Richard, *Al-Farabi on the Perfect State/Ara' ahl al-madina al-fadilah* (Oxford: Clarendon Press, 1985).

Waterbury, John, 'The Middle East in the New World Economic Order', in J. Waterbury and R. el-Mallakh, *The Middle East in the Coming Decade* (New York: McGraw-Hill, 1978), pp. 21–145.

Yalem, Ronald J., *Regionalism and World Order* (Washington, DC: Public Affairs Press, 1965).

Yalem, Ronald J., 'Theories of Regionalism', in R. A. Falk and S. H. Mendlovitz (eds), *Regional Politics and World Order* (San Francisco: W. H. Freeman, 1973), pp. 218–31.

Young, Oran R., 'Political Discontinuities in the International System', in *World Politics*, vol. 20, no. 3 (1968), pp. 369–92; see also R. A. Falk and S. H. Mendlovitz (eds), *Regional Politics and World Order* (San Francisco: W. H. Freeman, 1973), pp. 34–49.

Zartman, William, 'Africa as a Subordinate State System in International Relations', in *International Organization*, vol. 21, no. 3 (1967), pp. 545–64; see also R. A. Falk and S. H. Mendlovitz (eds), *Regional Politics and World Order* (San Francisco: W. H. Freeman, 1973), pp. 384–98.

2 The Middle East: Regional Actors and Structures

Abdullahi-Abdelsalam, Elfatih, *Panarabism and Charismatic Leadership: A Study of Iraq's Foreign Policy Behavior towards the Arab Region 1967–1982*, unpublished Ph.D. thesis (Northwestern University, Evaston, Ill., 1984).

Ajami, Fouad, *The Arab Predicament: Arab Political Thought and Practice since 1967* (Cambridge, Mass.: Cambridge University Press, 1981).

Ajami, Fouad, 'The End of Pan-Arabism', in *Foreign Affairs*, vol. 57 (1978–9), pp. 355–73.

Ajami, Fouad, 'Stress in Arab Triangle', in *Foreign Policy*, vol. 29 (1977–8), pp. 90–108.

Anthony, John Duke, 'Foreign Policy: The View from Riyadh', in *Wilson Quarterly*, vol. 3, no. 1 (1979), pp. 73–82.

Arjomand, Said A., *The Turban for the Crown: The Islamic Revolution in Iran* (New York: Oxford University Press, 1989).

Aronson, Geoffrey, *Israel, Palestinians and the Intifada: Creating Facts on the West Bank*, (London: Kegan Paul, 1988).

Askari, H. and Cummings, J. T., 'The Future of Economic Integration within the Arab World', in *International Journal of Middle East Studies*, vol. 8 (1977), pp. 289–315.

Assiri, Abdul-Reda, *Kuwait's Foreign Policy: City-State in World Politics* (Boulder, Col.: Westview Press, 1990).

al-'Azm, Sadiq Jalal, *al-Naqd al-dhati ba'd al-hazima* (Self-criticism After the Defeat) (Beirut, 1968).

Al-Baharna, Husain M., *The Legal Status of Arabian Gulf States* (Manchester: Manchester University Press, 1968).

Barlow, Robin, 'Economic Growth in the Middle East, 1950–1972', in *International Journal of Middle East Studies*, vol. 14 (1982), pp. 129–57.

Bar-Siman-Tov, Yaacov, *Linkage Politics in the Middle East: Syria between Domestic and External Conflict* (Boulder, Col.: Westview Press, 1983).

Batatu, Hanna, *The Egyptian, Syrian and Iraqi Revolutions* (Washington, DC: Georgetown University Press 1984).

Binder, Leonard, *The Ideological Revolution in the Middle East* (New York; London: John Wiley, 1964).

Borthwick, Bruce M., *Comparative Politics of the Middle East: An Introduction* (Englewood Cliffs, NJ: Prentice-Hall, 1980).

Brynen, Rex, *Sanctuary and Survival: The PLO in Lebanon* (Boulder, Col.: Westview Press, 1990).

Cobban, Helena, *The Making of Modern Lebanon* (London: Hutchinson, 1985).

Cobban, Helena, *The Palestinian Liberation Organization* (Cambridge, Mass.: Cambridge University Press, 1984).

Crecelius, Daniel, 'Sa'udi-Egyptian Relations', in *International Studies*, vol. 14, no. 4 (1975), pp. 563–85.

Dam, Nikolaos van, *The Struggle for Power in Syria: Sectarianism, Regionalism and Tribalism in Politics 1961–1978* (London: Croom Helm, 1979).

Davison, Roderic H., 'Where is the Middle East?', in Richard H. Nolte (ed.), *The Modern Middle East* (New York: Atherton Press 1963), pp. 13–29.

Dawisha, Adeed (ed.), *Islam in Foreign Policy* (Cambridge, Mass.: Cambridge University Press, 1983).

Day, Arthur R., *East Bank/West Bank: Jordan and the Prospects for Peace* (New York: Council on Foreign Relations, 1986).

Devlin, John F., *The Ba'th Party: A History from its Origins to 1966* (Stanford: Hoover Institution Press, 1976).

Devlin, John F., *Syria: Modern State in Ancient Land* (Boulder, Col.: Westview Press, 1983).

Dishon, Daniel, 'Inter-Arab Relations', in Colin Legum and Haim Shaked (eds), *Arab Relations in the Middle East: The Road to Realignment* (London: Holmes & Meier, 1979), pp. 1–32.

Donini, Giovanni, 'Saudi Arabia's Hegemonic Policy and Economic Development in the Yemen Arab Republic', in *Arab Studies Quarterly*, vol. 1, no. 4 (1979), pp. 299–308.

Drysdale, Alasdair and Blake, Gerald, *The Middle East and North Africa: A Political Geography* (New York; Oxford: Oxford University Press, 1985).

Duignan, Peter and Gann, L. H., *The Middle East and North Africa: The Challenge to Western Security* (Stanford: Hoover Institution Press, 1981).

Esman, Milton J. and Rabinovich, Itamar (eds), *Ethnicity, Pluralism, and the State in the Middle East* (Ithaca: Cornell University Press, 1988).

Esposito, John L. (ed.), *Voices of Resurgent Islam* (New York; Oxford: Oxford University Press, 1983).

Evron, Yair, *War and Intervention in Lebanon: The Israeli–Syrian Deterrence Dialogue* (London: Croom Helm, 1987).

Farah, Tawfic E. (ed.), *Pan-Arabism and Arab Nationalism: The Continuing Debate* (Boulder, Col.: Westview Press 1987).

Feoktistov, A., 'Saudi Arabia and the Arab World', in *International Affairs* (Moscow), July 1977, pp. 101–7.

Ghareeb, Edmund, *The Kurdish Question in Iraq* (Syracuse: Syracuse University Press, 1981).

Gomaa, Ahmed M., *The Foundation of the League of Arab States: Wartime Diplomacy and Inter-Arab Politics 1941 to 1945* (London: Longman, 1977).

Gottheil, Fred M., 'An Economic Assessment of the Military Burden in the Middle East 1960–1980', in *Journal of Conflict Resolution*, vol. 18, no. 3 (1974), pp. 502–13.

Haddad, Wadi D., *Lebanon: The Politics of Revolving Doors* (Washington, DC: Praeger, 1985).

Hameed, Mazher A., *Saudi Arabia, the West, and the Security of the Gulf* (London: Croom Helm, 1986).

Harris, Lillian C., *Egypt: International Challenges and Regional Stability* (London: Routledge & Kegan Paul, 1988).

Harris, Lillian C., *Libya: Qadhafi's Revolution and the Modern State* (Boulder, Col.: Westview Press, 1986).

Hasou, Tawfig, *The Struggle for the Arab World: Egypt's Nasser and the Arab League* (London; Boston: KPI Press, 1985).

Heikal, Mohammed H., 'Egyptian Foreign Policy', in *Foreign Affairs*, vol. 56, no. 4 (1978), pp. 714–27.

Helms, Christine Moss, *Iraq: Eastern Flank of the Arab World* (Washington, DC: Brookings Institution, 1984).

Hinnebusch, Raymond A., *Authoritarian Power and State Formation in Ba'thist Syria: Army, Party and Peasant* (Boulder, Col.: Westview Press, 1990).

Hiro, Dilip, *Holy Wars: The Rise of Islamic Fundamentalism* (New York: Routledge, 1989).

Hopwood, Derek, *Egypt: Politics and Society 1945–1981* (London: Allen & Unwin, 1982).

Hudson, Michael C., *Arab Politics: The Search for Legitimacy*, 2nd edn (New Haven: Yale University Press 1979).

Ibrahim, Ibrahim (ed.), *Arab Resources: The Transformation of a Society* (Washington, DC; London: Croom Helm, 1983).

Ibrahim, Saad Eddin, *The New Arab Social Order: A Study of the Social Impact of Oil Wealth* (Boulder, Col.: Westview Press, 1982).

Ismael, Jaqueline S., *Kuwait: Social Change in Historical Perspectives* (Syracuse, NY: Syracuse University Press, 1982).

Issawi, Charles, 'The Bases of Arab Unity', in Charles Issawi (ed.), *The Arab World's Legacy*, (Princeton, NJ: Darwin Press, 1981), pp. 179–97.

Issawi, Charles, 'Growth and Structural Change in the Middle East', in *The Middle East Journal*, vol. 25 (1971), pp. 309–24.

Jabri, Mohammed Abed, 'Evolution of the Maghrib Concept', in H. Barakat (ed.), *Contemporary North Africa* (Washington, DC; London: Croom Helm, 1985), pp. 63–86.

Karsh, Efraim and Rautsi, Inari, *Saddam Hussein: A Political Biography* (New York: Free Press, 1991).

Keddie, Nikki, 'Is there a Middle East?', in *International Journal of Middle East Studies*, vol. 4 (1973), pp. 255–71.

Keddie, Nikki and Gasiorowski, Mark J. (eds), *Neither East nor West: Iran, the Soviet Union and the United States* (New Haven: Yale University Press, 1990).

Kerr, Malcolm H., *The Arab Cold War* (New York: Oxford University Press, 1974).

Kerr, Malcolm H. and Yassin, El-Sayyid (eds), *Rich and Poor States in the Middle East* (Boulder, Col.: Westview Press, 1982).

Khalaf, Samir, *Lebanon's Predicament* (New York: Columbia University Press, 1987).

al-Khalil, Samir, *Republic of Fear: The Politics of Modern Iraq* (Berkeley, Cal.: University of California Press, 1989).

Kirişçi, Kemal, *The PLO in World Politics: A Study of the Mobilization of Support for the Palestinian Cause* (London: Pinter, 1986).

Korany, Bahgat, 'Political Petrolism and Contemporary Arab Politics, 1967–1983', in *Journal of Asian and African Studies*, vol. 21, no. 1/2 (1986), pp. 66–80.

Korany, Bahgat, *Social Change, Charisma and International Behaviour: Toward a Theory of Foreign Policy-Making in the Third World* (Leiden; Geneva: Sijthoff, 1976) (chap. 6 and 7 about Egypt pp. 221–315).

Korany, Bahgat and Dessouki, Ali E. H. (eds), *The Foreign Policies of Arab States* (Boulder, Col.: Westview Press, 1984).

Kostiner, Joseph, *South Yemen's Revolutionary Strategy, 1970–1985: From Insurgency to Bloc Politics* (Boulder, Col.: Westview Press, 1990).

Laroui, Abdallah, *The Crisis of the Arab Intellectual: Traditionalism or Historicism?* (Berkeley, Cal.; Los Angeles: University of California Press, 1976) (original in French 1974, Arab edition: Beirut, 1978).

Lemarchand, René, *The Green and the Black: Qadhafi's Policies in Africa* (Bloomington: Indiana University Press, 1988).

Lesch, Ann Mosely and Tessler, Mark A., *Israel, Egypt and the Palestinians: From Camp David to Intifada* (Bloomington: Indiana University Press, 1989).

Lorenz, Joseph P., *Egypt and the Arabs: Foreign Policy and the Search for National Identity* (Boulder, Col.: Westview Press, 1990).

Macdonald, Robert W., *The League of Arab States: A Study in the Dynamics of Regional Organization* (Princeton, NJ: Princeton University Press, 1965).

McDowall, David, *Palestine and Israel: The Uprising and Beyond* (Berkeley, Cal.: University of California Press, 1989).

Mackey, Sandra, *The Saudis: Inside the Desert Kingdom* (New York: Signet Books, 1990).

Marr, Phebe, *The Modern History of Iraq* (Boulder, Col.: Westview Press, 1985).

Martin, Lenore G., *The Unstable Gulf: Threats from Within* (Lexington, Mass.: Lexington Books, 1984).

Matar, Jamil and Hillal, Ali Eddin, *al-Nizam al-iqlimi al-'arabi* (The Arab Regional Order), 3rd edn (Beirut, 1983).

Niblock, Tim (ed.), *State, Society, and Economy in Saudi Arabia* (New York: St Martin's Press, 1982).

Norton, Augustus R. and Greenberg, Martin (eds), *International Relations of the PLO* (Carbondale: Southern Illinois University Press, 1989).

Odeh, B. J., *Lebanon: Dynamics of Conflict. A Modern Political History* (London: Zed Books, 1985).

Owen, Roger and Asad, Talal (eds), *The Middle East* (London: Macmillan, 1983).

Pawelka, Peter, *Herrschaft und Entwicklung im Nahen Osten: Ägypten* (Heidelberg: C. F. Müller Juristischer Verlag, 1985).

Perlmutter, Amos, *Military and Politics in Israel: Nation-Building and Role Expansion* (London: Frank Cass, 1977).

Peterson, Eric R., *The Gulf Cooperation Council: The Search for Unity in a Dynamic Region* (Boulder, Col.: Westview Press, 1988).

Peterson, John E., *The Arab Gulf States: Steps towards Political Participation* (New York: Praeger, 1988).

Pillai, R. V. and Kumar, M., 'The Political and Legal Status of Kuwait', in *International and Comparative Law Quarterly*, vol. 11 (1962), pp. 108–30.

Piscatori, James (ed.), *Islam in the Political Process* (Cambridge, Mass.: Cambridge University Press, 1983).

Piscatori, James, *Islam in a World of Nation-States* (Cambridge, Mass.: Cambridge University Press, 1986).

Porath, Yehoshua, *In Search of Arab Unity, 1930–1945* (London: Frank Cass, 1986).

Quandt, William B., *Saudi Arabia in the 1980s: Foreign Policy, Security, and Oil* (Washington, DC: Brookings Institution, 1981).

Ramazani, Rouhollah K., *Revolutionary Iran: Challenge and Response in the Middle East* (Baltimore: Johns Hopkins University Press, 1987).

Roy, Oliver, *Islam and Resistance in Afghanistan* (Cambridge, Mass.: Cambridge University Press, 1986).

Safran, Nadav, *Saudi Arabia: The Ceaseless Quest for Security* (Ithaca: Cornell University Press, 1988).

Saint-John, Ronald B., *Qaddafi's World Design: Libyan Foreign Policy, 1969–1987* (London: Saqi Books, 1987).

Sandwick, John A. (ed.), *The Gulf Cooperation Council: Moderation and Stability in an Interdependent World* (Washington, DC: Westview, 1987).

Schiff, Ze'ev, Ya'ari, Ehud and Friedman, Ina (eds), *Intifada: the Palestinian Uprising: Israel's Third Front* (New York: Simon & Schuster, 1990).

Scholz, Fred (ed.), *Die Golf-Staaten* (Brunswick: Westermann, 1985).

Seale, Patrick, *Assad of Syria: The Struggle for the Middle East* (Berkeley, Cal.: University of California Press, 1988).

Sivan, Emmanuel and Friedman, Menachem (eds), *Religious Radicalism and Politics in the Middle East* (Albany, NY: State University of New York Press, 1990).

Sluglett, Peter and Sluglett, Marion, *Iraq since 1958* (London: KPI Press, 1990).

Tarabischi, George, *al-Daula al-qutriyya wa al-nazariyya al-quamiyya* (The Nation-State and the Theory of Nationalism), Beirut, 1982 (on the conflict between nation-state and pan-Arabism).

Taylor, Alan R., *The Arab Balance of Power* (Syracuse, NY: Syracuse University Press, 1982).

Tibi, Bassam, *Arab Nationalism: A Critical Inquiry* (London: Macmillan; New York: St Martin's Press, 1990).

Tibi, Bassam, *The Crisis of Modern Islam: A Pre-Industrial Culture in the Scientific-Technological Age* (Salt Lake City: University of Utah Press, 1988).

Tibi, Bassam, 'Islam and Arab Nationalism', in Barbara Freyer Stowasser (ed.), *The Islamic Impulse* (London; Washington, DC: Croom Helm, 1987), pp. 59–74.

Tibi, Bassam, *Islam and the Cultural Accommodation of Social Change* (Boulder, Col.: Westview Press, 1990).

Tibi, Bassam, 'The Simultaneity of the Unsimultaneous: Old Tribes and Imposed Nation-States in the Modern Middle East', in Philip Khoury and Joseph Kostiner (eds), *Tribes and State Formation in the Middle East* (Berkeley, Cal.: California University Press, 1990), pp. 127–52.

Tibi, Bassam, 'A Typology of Arab Political Systems', in S. Farsoun (ed.), *Arab Society – Continuity and Change* (London: Croom Helm, 1985), pp. 48–64.

Vatikiotis, P. J., *Politics and the Military in Jordan: A Study of the Arab Legion, 1921–1957* (London: Frank Cass, 1967).

Waterbury, John, *The Egypt of Nasser and Sadat: The Political Economy of Two Regimes* (Princeton, NJ: Princeton University Press, 1983).

Wenner, Manfred W., *Modern Yemen, 1918–1966* (Baltimore: Johns Hopkins University Press, 1967).

3 Conflicts and Wars in the Middle Eastern Subsystem, 1956–1991

Abdulghani, J. M., *Iraq and Iran: The Years of Crisis* (London: Croom Helm,1984).

Abu-Lughod, Ibrahim (ed.), *The Arab–Israeli Confrontation of June 1967: An Arab Perspective* (Evanston, Ill.; Northwestern University Press, 1970).

Aker, Frank, *October 1973: The Arab–Israeli War* (Hamden, Conn.: Archon Books, 1985).

Allen, Peter, *The Yom Kippur War* (New York: Charles Scribner's Sons, 1982).

AlRoy, Gil Carl, *The Kissinger Experience: American Policy in the Middle East* (New York: Horizon Press, 1975).

Amos, John W., *Arab–Israeli Military/Political Relations: Arab Perceptions and the Politics of Escalation* (New York: Pergamon Press, 1979).

Ansari, Hamied, *Egypt: The Stalled Society* (Albany, NY : State University of New York Press, 1986).

Ashkar, Riad, 'The Syrian and Egyptian Campaigns', in *Journal of Palestine Studies*, vol. 3, no. 2 (1974), pp. 15–33.

Azar, Edward and Burton, John W., *International Conflicts Resolution: Theory and Practice* (Boulder, Col.: Lynne Rienner, 1986).

Badri, Hassan, Magdub, Taha and Zahdi, Dia'uddin, *Harb Ramadan. Al-Gaula al-'arabiyya al-israeliyya al-rabi'a* (The Ramadan War. The Fourth Arab–Israeli Battle) (Cairo: al-Sharika al-muttahida, 1984).

Bailey, Sydney D., *Four Arab–Israeli Wars and the Peace Process*, 3rd edn (Basingstoke; New York: Macmillan, 1990).

Ball, George W., *Error and Betrayal in Lebanon: An Analysis of Israel's Invasion of Lebanon and the Implications for US–Israeli Relations* (Washington, DC: Foundation for the ME Peace, 1984).

Behbehani, Hashim S. H., *The Soviet Union and Arab Nationalism, 1917–1966* (London: KPI Press, 1986).

Beling, Willard A. (ed.) *Middle East Peace Plans* (London: Croom Helm, 1986).

al-Bitar, Salah al-Din, 'The Implications of the October War for the Arab World', in *Journal of Palestine Studies*, vol. 3, no. 2 (1974), pp. 34–45.

Bowie, Robert R., *International Crisis and the Role of Law: Suez 1956* (Oxford: Oxford University Press, 1974).

Brecher, Michael, *Decisions in Crisis: Israel, 1967 and 1973* (Berkeley, Cal.: University of California Press, 1980).

Breznitz, Shlomo (ed.), *Stress in Israel* (New York: Van Nostrand Reinhold, 1983).

Brown, James and Snyder, Williams P. (eds), *The Regionalization of Warfare: The Falkland/Malvinas Islands, Lebanon, and the Iran–Iraq Conflict* (New Brunswick; Oxford: Transaction Books, 1985) (Israel's invasion in Lebanon chap. II and the Iran–Iraq War chap. III).

Bulloch, John, *The Making of a War: The Middle East from 1967 to 1973* (London: Longman, 1974).

Chubin, Sharam and Tripp, Charles, *Iran and Iraq at War* (Boulder, Col.: Westview Press, 1988).

Cohen, Raymond, *Culture and Conflict in Egyptian–Israeli Relations: A Dialogue of the Deaf* (Bloomington: Indiana University Press, 1990).

Cohen, Stephen Ph., *The Security of South Asia* (Urbana; Chicago: University of Illinois Press, 1987).

Cordesman, Anthony H., *The Arab–Israeli Military Balance and the Art of Operations: An Analysis of Military Lessons and Trends and Implications for Future Conflicts* (Lanham: University Press of America 1987).

Cordesman, Anthony H., *The Gulf and the Search for Strategic Stability: Saudi Arabia, the Military Balance in the Gulf, and Trends in the Arab–Israeli Military Balance* (Boulder, Col.: Westview Press, 1984).

Cordesman, Anthony H. and Wagner, Abraham R., *The Lessons of Modern War* (Boulder, Col.: Westview Press, 1990) (vol. I: The Arab–Israeli Conflicts, 1973–1989; vol. II: The Iran–Iraq War; vol. III: The Afghan and Falkland Conflicts).

Damis, John, *Conflicts in Northwest Africa: The Sahara Dispute* (Stanford: Hoover Institution Press, 1984).

Damis, John, 'The Western Sahara Dispute as a Source of Regional Conflict in North Africa', in H. Barakat (ed.), *Contemporary North Africa* (London; Washington, DC: Croom Helm, 1985), pp. 138–54.

Darius, Robert G. *et al.*, *Gulf Security into the 1980s: Perceptual and Strategic Dimensions* (Stanford: Hoover Institution Press, 1984).

Darwish, Adel and Alexander, Gregory, *Unholy Babylon: The Secret History of Saddam's War* (New York: St Martin's Press, 1991).

Day, Alan (ed.), *Border and Territorial Disputes*, 2nd edn (London: Keesing's, 1987).

Diner, Dan, *Israel in Palästina: Über Tausch und Gewalt im Vorderen Orient* (Königstein, Ts.: Athenäum-Verlag, 1980).

Farid, Abdel M., *The Red Sea: Prospects for Stability* (New York: Croom Helm, 1984).

Feldman, Shai and Rechnitz-Kijner, H., *Deception, Consensus and War: Israel in Lebanon* (Boulder, Col.: Westview Press, 1984).

Foreign Affairs, Special Issue: 'The Road to War', vol. 70, no. 1 (1991).

Foreign Affairs, Special Issue: 'After the War', vol. 70, no. 2 (1991).

Freedman, Robert O., *The Middle East after the Israeli Invasion of Lebanon* (Syracuse, NY: Syracuse University Press, 1986).

Fullick, Roy and Powell, Geoffrey, *Suez: The Double War* (London: Hamish Hamilton, 1979).

Gavron, Daniel, *Israel after Begin: Israel's Options in the Aftermath of the Lebanon War* (Boston: Houghton Mifflin, 1984).

Goodman, Hirsh and Carus, Seth, *The Future Battlefield and the Arab–Israeli Conflict* (New Brunswick: Transaction Publ.,1990).

Graz, Liesl, *The Turbulent Gulf* (London: I. B. Tauris, 1990).

Gross-Stein, Janice and Tanter, Raymond, *Rational Decision-Making: Israel's Security Choices, 1967* (Columbus, Ohio: Ohio State University Press, 1980).

Grummon, Stephen R., *The Iran–Iraq War* (New York: Praeger, 1982).

Heradstveit, Daniel, *The Arab–Israeli Conflict: Psychological Obstacles to Peace* (Oslo; Bergen; New York: Universitetsforlaget, 1981).

Heradstveit, Daniel, *Nahost-Guerillas: Eine politologische Studie* (Berlin: Berlin-Verlag 1973).

Hiro, Dilip, *The Longest War: The Iran–Iraq Military Conflict* (New York: Routledge, 1991).

Jabber, P. and Kolkowicz, R., 'The Arab–Israeli Wars of 1967 and 1973', in Stephen Kaplan *et al.* (eds) *Diplomacy of Power: Soviet Armed Forces as a Political Instrument* (Washington, DC: Brookings Institution, 1981), pp. 412–67.

Jansen, Michael, *The Battle of Beirut* (London: Zed Press, 1982).

Karsh, Efraim (ed.), *The Iran–Iraq War: Impact and Implications* (New York: Macmillan 1989).

Keddie, Nikki R. and Cole, Juan R. (eds), *Shi'ism and Social Protest* (New Haven: Yale University Press, 1986).

Khadduri, Majid, *The Gulf War: The Origins and Implications of the Iraq–Iran Conflict* (New York: Oxford University Press, 1988).

Khalaf, Samir, *Lebanon's Predicament* (New York: Columbia University Press, 1987).

Kienle, Eberhard, *Ba'th versus Ba'th: The Conflict between Syria and Iraq, 1968–1989* (London: New York: St Martin's Press, 1990).

Mofid, Kamran, *Economic Consequences of the Gulf War* (London; New York: Routledge, 1990).

Momen, Moojan, *An Introduction to Shi'i Islam: The History and Doctrines of Twelver Shi'ism* (New Haven: Yale University Press, 1985).

Neff, Donald, *Warriors for Jerusalem: The Six Days that Changed the Middle East* (New York: Linden Press, 1984).

Niblock, Tim, *The Dynamics of Sudanese Politics, 1898–1985* (London: Macmillan, 1987).

Nonneman, Gerd, *Iraq, the Gulf-States and the War: A Changing Relationship, 1980–1986 and Beyond* (London: Ithaca Press, 1986).

O'Ballance, Edgar, *The Sinai Campaign 1956* (London: Faber & Faber, 1959).

O'Ballance, Edgar, *The Third Arab–Israeli War* (London: Faber & Faber, 1972).

Ovendale, Ritchie, *The Origins of the Arab–Israeli Wars* (London: Longman,1987).

Owen, Roger and Roger, Louis W. (eds), *Suez 1956: The Crisis and Its Consequences* (Oxford: Clarendon Press, 1989).

Quandt, Willim B., 'Lebanon 1958, Jordan 1970', in B. M. Blechman and St S. Kaplan (eds), *Force without War* (Washington, DC: Brookings Institution, 1978), pp. 222–88.

Rabinovich, Itamar, *The War for Lebanon, 1970–1985*, rev. edn (Ithaca; London: Cornell University Press, 1985).

Randal, Jonathan, *The Tragedy of Lebanon* (London: Chatto & Windus; The Hogarth Press, 1983).

al-Razzaz, Munif, 'After the October War: New Historical Realities', in *Arab Studies Quarterly*, vol. 1, no. 2 (1979), pp. 83–95.

Ridgeway, James (ed.), *The March to War* (New York: Four Walls Eight Windows, 1991).

Rodinson, Maxime, *Peuple Juif ou Problème Juif?* (Paris: F. Maspero, 1981).

Rubin, Barry, *The Arab States and the Palestine Conflict* (Syracuse, NY: Syracuse University Press, 1981).

Rubinstein, Alvin Z., 'Air Support in the Arab East', in Stephen S. Kaplan (ed.), *Diplomacy of Power: Soviet Armed Forces as a Political Instrument* (Washington, DC: Brookings Institution, 1981), pp. 468–518.

Schenker, Hillel (ed.), *After Lebanon: The Israeli–Palestinian Connection* (New York: Pilgrim Press, 1983).

Schiff, Ze'ev and Ya'ari, Ehud, *Israel's Lebanon War* (London: Allen & Unwin, 1985).

Sifry, Micah L. and Cerf, Christopher (eds), *The Gulf War Reader: History, Documents, Opinions* (New York: Random House, 1991).

Tibi, Bassam, 'Die irakische Kuwait-Invasion und die Golf-Krise' in *Beiträge zur Konfliktforschung*, vol. 20, no. 4 (1990), pp. 5–34.

Tibi, Bassam, 'The Iranian Revolution and the Arabs: The Quest for Islamic Identity and the Search for an Islamic System of Government', in *Arab Studies Quarterly*, vol. 8, no. 1 (1986), pp. 29–44.

Tibi, Bassam, 'Structural and Ideological Change in the Arab Subsystem since the Six-Day War', in A. Battah and Y. Lukacs (eds), *The Arab–Israeli Conflict: Two Decades of Change* (Boulder, Col.: Westview Press, 1988), pp. 147–63.

Tschirgi, Dan and Tibi, Bassam, *Perspectives on the Gulf Crisis* (Cairo: American University of Cairo Press, 1991).

Udovitch, Abraham L. (ed.), *The Middle East: Oil, Conflict and Hope* (Lexington, Mass.: Lexington Books, 1976).

Utgoff, Viktor, *The Challenge of Chemical Weapons* (London: Macmillan, 1990).

Wagner, Heinz, *Der arabisch–israelische Konflikt im Völkerrecht* (Berlin: Düncker & Humblot, 1971).

Weinberger, Naomi Joy, *Syrian Intervention in Lebanon: The 1975–76 Civil War* (Oxford; New York: Oxford University Press, 1986).

Whetten, Lawrence L., *The Canal War: Four-Power Conflict in the Middle East* (Cambridge, Mass.: MIT Press, 1974).

Woodward, Bob, *The Commanders* (New York, 1991).

Yaniv, Avner, *Deterrence Without the Bomb: The Politics of Israeli Strategy* (Lexington, Mass.: Heath, 1987).

Yaniv, Avner, *Dilemmas of Security: Politics, Strategy and the Israeli Experience in Lebanon* (New York: Oxford University Press, 1987).

4 Great- and Superpower Involvement in the Middle East

Acharya, Amitav, *US Military Strategy in the Gulf* (London: Routledge, 1989).

Allison, Graham T. and Ury, William L. (eds), *Windows of Opportunity: From Cold War to Peaceful Competition in US–Soviet Relations* (Cambridge, Mass.: Ballinger, 1989).

Aronson, Geoffrey, *From Sideshow to Center Stage: US Policy toward Egypt, 1946–1956* (Boulder, Col.: Lynne Rienner, 1986).

Azar, Edward E. and Burton, John W. (eds), *International Conflict Resolution: Theory and Practice* (Brighton: Wheatsheaf, 1986).

Beling, Willard (ed.), *Middle East Peace Plans* (London: Croom Helm, 1986) (chap. 'American Proposals' and: chap. 'Soviet Peace Plans').

Bhatia, Shyam, *Nuclear Rivals in the Middle East* (London: Routledge, 1988).

Blechman, Barry M. and Kaplan, Stephen (eds), *Force without War: US Armed Forces as a Political Instrument* (Washington, DC: Brookings Institution, 1978).

Braun, Aurel, *The Middle East in Global Strategy* (Boulder, Col.: Westview Press, 1987).

Brown, L. Carl, *International Politics and the Middle East: Old Rules, Dangerous Games* (Princeton, NJ: Princeton University Press, 1984).

Brun, Ellen and Hersh, Jaques, *Soviet–Third World Relations in a Capitalist World: The Political Economy of Broken Promises* (Basingstoke: Macmillan, 1990).

Carter, Jimmy, *The Blood of Abraham: Insights into the Middle East* (Boston: Houghton Mifflin, 1985).

Cottam, Richard W., *Iran and the United States: A Cold War Case Study* (Pittsburgh: University of Pittsburgh Press, 1988).

Curtiss, Richard H., *A Changing Image: American Perceptions of the Arab Israeli Dispute* (Washington, DC: American Educational Trust, 1982).

Dawisha, Karen, *Soviet Foreign Policy Toward Egypt* (New York: St Martin's Press, 1979).

Dawisha, Adeed and Dawisha, Karen (eds), *The Soviet Union in the Middle East: Policies and Perspectives* (London: Heinemann, 1982).

Denitch, Bogdan, *The End of the Cold War* (Minneapolis: University of Minnesota Press, 1990).

Dibb, Paul, *The Soviet Union: The Incomplete Superpower*, 2nd edn (Urbana: University of Illinois Press, 1988).

Dowty, Alan, *Middle East Crisis: US Decision-Making in 1958, 1970 and 1973* (Berkeley, Cal.; Los Angeles: University of California Press, 1984).

Duncan, W. R. and Ekedahl, C. M., *Moscow and the Third World under Gorbachev* (Boulder, Col.: Westview Press, 1990).

Edmonds, Robin, *Soviet Foreign Policy 1962–1973: The Paradox of Superpower* (Oxford; London: Oxford University Press, 1975).

Fahmy, Ismail, *Negotiating for Peace in the Middle East* (London: Croom Helm, 1983).

Freedman, Robert O., (ed.), *The Middle East since Camp David* (Boulder, Col.: Westview Press, 1984).

Freedman, Robert O., *Soviet Policy toward the Middle East since 1970*, 2nd edn (New York: Praeger, 1978).

Glassman, Jon D., *Arms for the Arabs: The Soviet Union and War in the Middle East*, 2nd edn (Baltimore; London: Johns Hopkins University Press, 1977).

Golan, Galia, *Yom Kippur and After: The Soviet Union and the Middle East Crisis* (Cambridge, Mass.; London: Cambridge University Press, 1977).

Gold, Doré, *America, the Gulf and Israel: CENTCOM (Central Command) and Emerging US Regional Security Policies in the Mideast* (Boulder, Col.: Westview Press, 1988).

Hacke, Christian, *Amerikanische Nahost-Politik: Kontinuität und Wandel von Nixon bis Reagan* (Munich: Oldenbourg-Verlag, 1985).

Halliday, Fred, *Cold War, Third World: An Essay on Soviet–US Relations* (London: Hutchinson Radius, 1989).

Halliday, Fred, 'A Curious and Close Liaison: Saudi Arabia's Relations with the United States', in Tim Niblock (ed.), *State, Society, and Economy in Saudi Arabia* (New York: St Martin's Press, 1982), pp. 125–47.

Hasegawa, Tsuyoshi and Pravda, Alex (eds), *Perestroika: Soviet Domestic and Foreign Policies* (London: Sage Publications, 1990).

Heikal, Mohamed, *The Sphinx and the Commissar: The Rise and Fall of Soviet Influence in the Middle East* (New York: Harper & Row, 1978).

Hoffmann, Stanley, *Primacy or World Order: American Foreign Policy since the Cold War* (New York: McGraw-Hill, 1978).

Hopwood, Derek (ed.), *Euro-Arab Dialogue: The Relations between the two Cultures* (London: Croom Helm, 1985).

Hosking, Geoffrey A., *The Awakening of the Soviet Union* (Cambridge, Mass.: Harvard University Press, 1990).

Hosmer, Stephen T., *Constraints on US Strategy in Third World Conflicts* (New York: Crane Russak, 1987).

Hosmer, Stephen T. and Wolfe, Th. W., *Soviet Policy and Practice toward Third World Conflicts* (Lexington, Mass.: Heath, 1983).

el-Hussini, Mohrez M., *Soviet–Egyptian Relations, 1945–1985* (New York: St Martin's Press, 1987).

Immerman, Richard H., *John Foster Dulles and the Diplomacy of the Cold War* (Princeton, NJ: Princeton University Press, 1990).

Jervis, Robert and Bialer, Severyn (eds), *Soviet–American Relations after the Cold War* (Durham; London: Duke University Press, 1991).

Kaldor, Mary, *Imaginary War: Understanding the East–West Conflict* (Cambridge, Mass.; Oxford: Basil Blackwell, 1990).

Kaplan, Stephen, *Diplomacy of Power: Soviet Armed Forces as a Political Instrument* (Washington, DC: Brookings Institution, 1981).

Karklins, Rasma, *Ethnic Relations in the USSR: The Perspective from Below* (Boston: Unwin Hyman, 1990).

Karsh, Efraim, *The Soviet Union and Syria: The Assad Years* (London: Routledge, 1988).

Katz, Mark N., *Russia and Arabia: Soviet Foreign Policy toward the Arabian Peninsula* (Baltimore: Johns Hopkins University Press 1986).

Kirisci, Kemal, *The PLO and World Politics: A Study of the Mobilization of Support for the Palestinian Cause* (London: Pinter, 1986) (chap.: 'PLO/Eastern and Western Europe').

Kissinger, Henry, *Years of Upheaval* (London: Weidenfeld & Nicolson, 1982) (on the October War chap. 11, 12 and 13, shuttle diplomacy chap. 18, 21).

Kolodziej, Edward A., *French International Policy under de Gaulle and Pompidou: The Politics of Grandeur* (Ithaca; London: Cornell University Press, 1974).

Kolodziej, Edward A. and Kanet, Roger (eds), *The Limits of Soviet Power in the Developing World* (Basingstoke: Macmillan, 1989).

Lenczowski, George, *American Presidents and the Middle East* (Durham: Duke University Press, 1990).

Litwak, Robert S. and Wells, Samuel F. (eds), *Superpower Competition and Security in the Third World* (Cambridge, Mass.: Ballinger, 1988).

Long, David E., *The United States and Saudi Arabia: Ambivalent Allies* (Boulder, Col.: Westview Press, 1985).

McKinlay, R. D. and Mughan, A., *Aid and Arms to the Thrid World: An Analysis of the Distribution and Impact of US Official Transfers* (London: Pinter, 1984).

Mackintosh, J. M., *Strategy and Tactics of Soviet Foreign Policy* (London; Oxford: Oxford University Press, 1962).

Maclean, Donald, *British Foreign Policy since Suez, 1956–1968* (London: Hodder & Stoughton, 1970).

Maghroori, Ray and Gorman, Stephen, *The Yom Kippur War: A Case Study in Crisis Decision-Making in American Foreign Policy* (Washington, DC: University Press of America 1981).

Mangold, Peter, *Superpower Intervention in the Middle East* (London: Croom Helm, 1978).

Marantz, Paul and Steinberg, Blema S. (eds), *Superpower Involvement in the Middle East: Dynamics of Foreign Policy* (Boulder, Col.: Westview Press, 1985).

Marshall, Jonathan, *The Iran–Contra-Connection: Secret Teams and Covert Operations in the Reagan Era* (Boston: South End, 1987).

Mitchell, R. Judson, *Ideology of a Superpower: Contemporary Soviet Doctrine on International Relations* (Stanford: Hoover, 1982).

Motyl, Alexander, J., *Will the Non-Russians Rebel? State, Ethnicity and Stability in the USSR* (Ithaca; London: Cornell University Press, 1987).

Nixon, Richard, *The Memoirs of Richard Nixon* (New York; London: Sidgwick & Jackson, 1978) (on the October War/USA chap.: The Presidency 1973, section, October 1973, pp. 920–43).

Nye, Joseph S., Jr, *Bound to Lead: The Changing Nature of American Power* (New York: Basic Books, 1990).

Quandt, William B., *Camp David: Peace Making and Politics* (Washington, DC: Brookings Institution, 1986).

Quandt, William B., *Decade of Decisions: American Foreign Policy toward the Arab–Israeli Conflict, 1967–1976* (Berkeley, Cal.; Los Angeles: University of California Press, 1977).

Quandt, William B., 'Soviet Policy in the Middle East', Part I and II in *International Affairs*, vol. 53 (1977), pp. 377–89 and pp. 587–603.

Quandt, William B., *The United States and Egypt* (Washington, DC: Brookings Institution, 1990).

Ramet, Pedro, *The Soviet–Syrian Relationship since 1955: A Troubled Alliance* (Boulder, Col.: Westview Press, 1990).

Ray, James Lee, *The Future of American–Israeli Relations: A Parting of the Ways?* (Lexington; Kentucky: Kentucky University Press, 1985).

Reich, Bernard, *Quest for Peace: United States–Israel Relations and the Arab–Israeli Conflict* (New Brunswick: Transaction Books, 1977).

Reich, Bernard, *The United States and Israel: Influence in the Special Relationship* (New York: Praeger, 1984).

Riad, Mahmud, *Amerika wa al-'Arab* (America and the Arabs), vol. 3 of the memoirs of M. Riad, (Cairo, 1986).

Roberts, Adam and Kingsbury, Benedict (eds), *United Nations, Divided World: The UN's Roles in International Relations* (Oxford: Oxford University Press, 1989).

Rostow, Eugene v. (ed.), *The Middle East: Critical Choices for the United States* (Boulder, Col.: Westview Press, 1976).

Rubenberg, Cheryl A., *Israel and the American National Interest: A Critical Examination* (Urbana, Chicago: University of Illinois Press, 1986).

Rubinstein, Alvin Z., *Red Star on the Nile: The Soviet–Egyptian Influence Relationship since the June War* (Princeton, NJ: Princeton University Press, 1977).

Ruf, Werner, 'The Role of World Powers', in Richard Lawless and Laila Monahan (eds), *War and Refugees: The Western Sahara Conflict* (London: Pinter, 1987), pp. 65–97.

Rywkin, Michael, *Moscow's Muslim Challenge: Soviet Central Asia*, rev. edn (Armonk, NY: Sharpe, 1990).

Sheehan, Edward R. F., *The Arabs, Israelis, and Kissinger: A Secret History of American Diplomacy in the Middle East* (New York: Thomas Y. Crowell, 1976).

Sheffer, Gabriel, *Dynamics of Dependence: US–Israeli Relations* (Boulder, Col.: Westview Press, 1987).

Shulman, Marshall D. (ed.), *East–West Tensions in the Third World* (New York: Norton, 1986).

Slominski, Martin J., 'The Soviet Military Press and the October War', in *Military Review*, vol. 54, May, (1974), pp. 39–47.

Smolansky, Oles M. and Smolansky, Bettie M., *The USSR and Iraq: The Soviet Quest for Influence* (Durham; London: Duke University Press, 1991).

Snyder, Jed C., *Defending the Fringe: NATO, the Mediterranean and the Persian Gulf* (Boulder, Col.: Westview Press, 1987).

Spiegel, Steven L., *The Other Arab–Israeli Conflict: Making America's Middle Eastern Policy, From Truman to Reagan* (Chicago: University of Chicago Press, 1985).

Tillman, Seth P., *The United States in the Middle East: Interests and Obstacles* (Bloomington: Indiana University Press, 1982).

Treverton, Gregory (ed.), *Crisis Management and the Super-Powers in the Middle East* (Aldershot: Gower, 1983).

Tschirgi, Dan, *The American Search for Mideast Peace* (New York: Praeger, 1989).

Verrier, Anthony, *Through the Looking Glass: British Foreign Policy in an Age of Illusion* (London: Jonathan Cape, 1983).

Wells, Samuel F., Jr and Bruzonsky, Mark A. (eds), *Security in the Middle East: Regional Change and Great Power Strategies* (Boulder, Col.: Westview Press, 1987).

White, Stephen, *Gorbachev in Power* (Cambridge, Mass.: Cambridge University Press, 1990).

Yoder, Amos, *The Conduct of American Foreign Policy since World War II* (New York: Pergamon Press, 1986).

5   Studies on Conflict and War

Addington, Larry H., *The Patterns of War since the Eighteenth Century* (Bloomington: Indiana University Press, 1984).

Art, Robert J. and Waltz, Kenneth (eds), *The Use of Force: International Politics and Foreign Policy*, 2nd edn (Lanham: University Press of America, 1983).

Blainey, Geoffrey, *The Causes of War* (New York: Free Press, 1973).

Burton, John, *Conflict: Resolution and Prevention* (Basingstoke: Macmillan, 1990).

Burton, John and Dukes, Frank (eds), *Conflict: Readings in Management and Resolution* (London: Macmillan, 1990).

Creveld, Martin van, *Technology and War* (New York: Free Press, 1989).

Gantzel, Klaus Jürgen *et al.*, *Die Kriege nach dem Zweiten Weltkrieg bis 1984. Daten und erste Analysen* (Munich: Weltforum Verlag, 1986).

Gilpin, Robert, *War and Change in World Politics* (Cambridge, Mass.: Cambridge University Press, 1981).

Haas, Richard N., *Conflicts Unending* (New Haven: Yale University Press, 1990).

Hermann, Charles F. (ed.), *International Crisis: Insights from Behavioral Research* (New York: Free Press, 1972).

Holsti, Kalevi J., *Peace and War: Armed Conflicts and International Order, 1648–1989* (Cambridge, Mass.: Cambridge University Press 1991).

Howard, Michael, *The Causes of Wars and Other Essays*, 2nd edn (Cambridge, Mass.: Harvard University Press, 1983).

Jansen, Johannes J. G., *The Neglected Duty: The Creed of Sadat's Assassins and Islamic Resurgence in the Middle East* (New York; London: Macmillan, 1986).

Kondylis, Panajotis, *Theorie des Krieges: Clausewitz – Marx – Engels – Lenin* (Stuttgart: Klett-Cotta, 1988).

Lall, Arthur, *The UN and the Middle East Crisis, 1967* (New York: Columbia University Press, 1968).

Lebow, Richard Ned, *Between Peace and War: The Nature of International Crisis* (Baltimore; London: Johns Hopkins University Press, 1981).

Luard, Evan, *War in International Society: A Study in International Sociology* (New Haven: Yale University Press, 1987).

Midlarski, Manus I. (ed.), *Handbook of War Studies* (Boston: Unwin Hyman, 1989).

Nelson, Keith and Olin, Spencer, *Why War? Ideology, Theory and History* (Berkeley, Cal.: University of California Press, 1980).

Newhouse, John, *War and Peace in the Nuclear Age* (New York: Random House, 1989).

North, Robert C., *War, Peace, Survival: Global Politics and Conceptual Synthesis* (Boulder, Col.: Westview Press, 1990).

Paret, Peter, *Clausewitz and the State: The Man, his Theories and his Time* (Princeton, NJ: Princeton University Press, 1986).

Paret, Peter (ed.), *Makers of Modern Strategy: From Machiavelli to the Nuclear Age* (Princeton, NJ: Princeton University Press, 1986).

Parker, Geoffrey, *The Military Revolution: Military Innovation and the Rise of the West, 1500–1800* (Cambridge, Mass.: Cambridge University Press, 1989).

Pelcovits, Nathan A., *Peacekeeping on Arab Israeli Fronts: Lessons from the Sinai and Lebanon* (Boulder, Col.: Westview Press, 1984).

Ralston, David B., *Importing the European Army: The Introduction of European*

Military Techniques and Institutions into the Extra-European World, 1600–1914 (Chicago: University of Chicago Press, 1990).

Ramadan, 'Abdulazim, *Tahtim al-Aliha: Qissat Harb Junio 1967* (The Destruction of the Gods: The History of the June-1967 War), 2 vols (Cairo, 1985, 1986).

Rapoport, Anatol, 'Tolstoi und Clausewitz', in E. Krippendorff (ed.), *Friedensforschung* (Cologne; Berlin: Kiepenheuer & Witsch, 1968), pp. 87–105.

Ruloff, D., *Wie Kriege beginnen*, 2nd edn (Munich: Beck, 1987).

Schumann, Hans-Gerd, *Edmund Burkes Anschauungen vom Gleichgewicht in Staat und Staatensystem* (Meisenheim/Glan: Verlag Anton Hain, 1964).

Snyder Glenn H. and Diesing, Paul, *Conflict among Nations: Bargaining, Decision Making and System Structure in International Crises* (Princeton, NJ: Princeton University Press, 1977).

Stoessinger, John G., *Why Nations go to War*, 4th edn (New York: St Martin's Press, 1985).

Treverton, Gregory (ed.), *Crisis Management and the Superpowers in the Middle East*, Adelphi Library 5, 2nd edn (Aldershot: Gower, 1983).

Tripp, Charles (ed.), *Regional Security in the Middle East*, Adelphi Library 8, (Aldershot: Gower 1984).

Waltz, Kenneth and Art, Robert (ed.), *The Use of Force: International Politics and Foreign Policy*, 3rd edn (New York: University Press of America, 1983).

Wright, Quincy, *A Study of War*, 4th edn (Chicago: University of Chicago Press, 1947).

Zeidan, Abdel-Latif, *The United Nations Emergency Force, 1956–1967* (Stockholm: Almqvist & Wiksell, 1976).

Name Index

Subject Index